D0991186

C. DELORT

C. Delort inv.　　　　　　　　　　　　　L. Boisson sc.

MEMOIRS OF
THE COURT OF CHARLES II

BY COUNT DE GRAMONT

*With a Special Introduction
and Illustrations*

VIGILANS ET AUDAX

NEW YORK
P F COLLIER & SON
PUBLISHERS

Copyright 1910
By P. F. Collier & Son

942.066
G747m
160795

INTRODUCTION

RATHER curiously, these "Memoirs" of a French-man were written by an Englishman in the French language, their largest portion being devoted to the gay doings of English courtiers in England during the reign of Charles II.

Philibert, the Chevalier de Gramont, born in 1621, was the younger son of the French duke of that name. Like most European younger sons, he had to depend chiefly upon his natural gifts for advancement. Destined for the Church, he early revolted against that and devoted himself to the careers of the army and the Court—in brief, to a life of gallantry, in all the senses of that word.

Notably handsome, of high birth, brilliantly witty, gay under all circumstances, fertile in story, sport, or genial talk, keen and merrily unscrupulous in gaming, attractive to and attracted by women of high and low degree, and indomitably courageous, his early army service under the great Generals Condé and Turenne opened to him a career of adventure. He was admired as a soldier, prized as a comrade, popular everywhere; so that when he returned from camp to Court he was an instant favourite. From King Louis XIV. down to the lackeys, every one sought to please him and forward his fortunes. These dazzling successes seem to have turned his head somewhat, since he was venturesome enough to make love to one of the King's own favourites, and early in 1662 was banished.

Before this, De Gramont had visited the English

Court during Cromwell's Protectorate, and had found
it exceedingly dull. But Charles II. was now in power,
and the liveliness, festivities, and social laxities of the
Court of the Restoration offered him a congenial refuge, and he betook himself thither.

Of course, so blithe and attractive a cavalier found
welcome in court circles, and De Gramont was promptly
installed in favour. Here he pursued his customary
courses—gambled with the men, gave and received
splendid hospitalities (for he seems to have been usually well supplied with money, and when that failed
was even more lavish in his hospitalities until the
gaming-table replenished his purse), found time to
galantiser variously among the frail beauties of the
Court, and had a dashing career during the few
years of his sojourn. It is with this period that the
"Memoirs" are chiefly concerned. They are certainly
startling reminiscences of that profligate Court, giving
witty and graphic details of the lives of many indi-
viduals of note, men and women, with their ambitions,
intrigues, loves and hatreds, entertainments and cruel-
ties, practical jokes, doings and undoings.

Among the most winsome of the ladies was Miss
Eliza Hamilton, daughter of Anthony, Count Hamilton, niece of the Duke of Ormonde. With her, De
Gramont seems to have genuinely fallen in love. Amid
his other feminine pursuits he held more constantly to
her than to any other, persistently seeking her in marriage. She evidently favoured him, although to what
extent is uncertain, since in mid-December, 1663, De
Gramont received what he thought to be a recall to
the French Court, authorised by the King, and started
for France. The story goes—although not chronicled
in the "Memoirs"—that on his way to the coast he was
overtaken by George and Anthony, Miss Hamilton's
brothers, who asked him whether he had not forgotten

something in London. "Yes," he replied, "I forgot
to marry your sister." Forthwith he returned, performed that pleasant duty on December 22, and according to his lights—which were variable—made the new
countess a fairly steady husband.

Here the "Memoirs" end. But in 1664 De Gramont
returned to France with his wife, being graciously re-
ceived by the King, and served in the army in the Low
Countries, while his Countess was accepted among the
attendants upon Maria Theresa, Queen Consort of
Louis XIV. Of his two daughters, one married Henry
Howard, Marquis of Stratford, and the other became
Abbess of Poussay, in Lorraine.

Into De Gramont's life now came again his brother-
in-law, Anthony. The Hamilton family having taken
refuge in France after the execution of Charles I.,
Anthony had spent his youth in that country, and became almost a Frenchman. After various experiences
in English Court and army life under the Restoration
and the reign of James II., ending with the disastrous
battle of the Boyne, July 1, 1690, he returned to France.
Here he published divers romantic tales, which had
considerable vogue. He also sought De Gramont, for
whom he evidently had a great admiration, and who
was at that time eighty years of age, but as un-
conquerably gay and adventurous as in earlier years.
Either at the Count's dictation (as he claimed) or
with his cooperative revision, Hamilton wrote these
vivid "Memoirs." Probably he was himself the chief
author, since De Gramont, with all his wit, had no
literary skill, while his wife's brother was a graceful
writer as well as an intimate of the English court,
familiar with all the persons and events described.
The "Memoirs" were published in the original French
in 1713, about five years after De Gramont's death,
and appeared the following year in an English trans-

lation. The essential value of this *chronique scanda-leuse* is that it is true, and presents a genuine depiction of a phase of English Court life during the reign of the second Charles, in contrast to the severities of Puritanism before it and the general course of English royal history thereafter.

De Gramont died in 1707, at the age of eighty-six. Except during a brief interval where a serious illness caused his formal reconciliation with the Church (which on his recovery soon slipped his mind), he was festive and debonair to the last. Niñon de l'Enclos, the famous Parisian, is reported to have said of him: "He was the only man who could affect the follies of youth without being ridiculous." While his utter freedom from the restraints of principle would have wrecked most men over and again, De Gramont's extraordinary gifts maintained him successfully, and have left him uniquely representative of that wantonness of aristocratic life that practically ended the Stuarts in England and finally whelmed the French monarchy in revolution.

THE COURT OF CHARLES II

MEMOIRS OF THE
COUNT DE GRAMONT

CHAPTER I

AS those who read only for amusement are, in
my opinion, more worthy of attention than
those who open a book merely to find fault, to
the former I address myself, and for their entertainment commit the following pages to press, without
being in the least concerned about the severe criticisms
of the latter. I further declare, that the order of time
and disposition of the facts, which give more trouble
to the writer than pleasure to the reader, shall not much
embarrass me in these *Memoirs*. It being my design
to convey a just idea of my hero, those circumstances
which most tend to illustrate and distinguish his character shall find a place in these fragments just as they
present themselves to my imagination, without paying
any particular attention to their arrangement. For,
after all, what does it signify where the portrait is begun, provided the assemblage of the parts forms a
whole which perfectly expresses the original? The
celebrated Plutarch, who treats his heroes as he does
his readers, commences the life of the one just as he
thinks fit, and diverts the attention of the other with
digressions into antiquity, or agreeable passages of
literature, which frequently have no reference to the
subject; for instance, he tells us that Demetrius Poli-
orcetes was far from being so tall as his father. Antig-

onus; and afterwards, that his reputed father, Antigonus, was only his uncle; but this is not until he has begun his life with a short account of his death, his various exploits, his good and bad qualities; and at last, out of compassion to his failings, brings forward a comparison between him and the unfortunate Mark Antony.

In the life of Numa Pompilius, he begins by a dissertation upon his preceptor Pythagoras; and, as if he thought the reader would be anxious to know whether it was the ancient philosopher, or one of the same name, who, after being victorious at the Olympic games, went full speed into Italy to teach Numa philosophy, and instruct him in the arts of government, he gives himself much trouble to explain this difficulty, and, after all leaves it undetermined.

What I have said upon this subject is not meant to reflect upon this historian, to whom, of all the ancients, we are most obliged; it is only intended to authorise the manner in which I have treated a life far more extraordinary than any of those he has transmitted to us. It is my part to describe a man whose inimitable character casts a veil over those faults which I shall neither palliate nor disguise; a man distinguished by a mixture of virtues and vices so closely linked together as in appearance to form a necessary dependence, glowing with the greatest beauty when united, shining with the brightest lustre when opposed.

It is this indefinable brilliancy, which, in war, in love, in gaming, and in the various stages of a long life, has rendered the Count de Gramont the admiration of his age, and the delight of every country wherein he has displayed his engaging wit, dispensed his generosity and magnificence, or practised his inconstancy: it is owing to this that the sallies of a sprightly imagination have produced those admirable *bon mots* which have been with universal applause transmitted to posterity. It is owing to this that he preserved his judgment free and unembarrassed in the most trying situations, and enjoyed an uncommon presence of mind and facetiousness of temper in the most imminent dangers of war. I shall not attempt to draw his portrait: his person has been described by Bussi and Saint-Evremond,[2] authors more entertaining than faithful. The former has represented the Chevalier Gramont as artful, fickle, and even somewhat treacherous in his amours, and indefatigable and cruel in his jealousies. Saint-Evremond has used other colours to express the genius and describe the general manners of the Count; whilst both in their different pictures, have done greater honour to themselves than justice to their hero.

It is, therefore, to the Count we must listen, in the agreeable relation of the sieges and battles wherein he

[2] Voltaire, in the *Age of Louis XIV*. ch. xxiv., speaking of that monarch, says: "Even at the same time when he began to encourage genius by his liberality, the Count de Bussi was severely punished for the use he made of his; he was sent to the Bastille in 1664. *The Amours of the Gauls* was the pretence of his imprisonment; but the true cause was the song in which the king was treated with too much freedom, and which, upon this occasion, was brought to remembrance to ruin Bussi, the reputed author of it.

> "Que Deodatus est heureux,
> De baiser ce bec amoureux,
> Qui d'une oreille à l'autre va!

> "See Deodatus with his billing dear,
> Whose amorous mouth breathes love from ear to ear!

"His works were not good enough to compensate for the mischief they did him. He spoke his own language with purity: he had some merit, but more conceit: and he made no use of the merit he had, but to make himself enemies." Voltaire adds: "Bussi was released at the end of eighteen months; but he was in disgrace all the rest of his life, in vain protesting a regard for Louis XIV." Bussi died 1693. Of Saint-Evremond, see note, *postea*.

distinguished himself under another hero; and it is on him we must rely for the truth of passages the least glorious of his life, and for the sincerity with which he relates his address, vivacity, frauds, and the various stratagems he practised either in love or gaming. These express his true character, and to himself we owe these *Memoirs,* since I only hold the pen, while he directs it to the most remarkable and secret passages of his life.

CHAPTER II

IN those days affairs were not managed in France as
at present. Louis XIII.[1] then sat upon the throne,
but the Cardinal de Richelieu[2] governed the kingdom; great men commanded little armies, and little
armies did great things: the fortune of great men depended solely upon ministerial favour, and blind devotion to the will of the minister was the only sure
method of advancement. Vast designs were then laying
in the heart of neighbouring states the foundation of
that formidable greatness to which France has now
risen: the police was somewhat neglected; the highways
were impassable by day, and the streets by night; but
robberies were committed elsewhere with greater impunity. Young men, on their first entrance into the

[1] Son and successor of Henry IV. He began to reign 14th
May 1610, and died 14th May 1643.
[2] Of this great minister Hume gives the following character:
"This man had no sooner, by suppleness and intrigue, gotten
possession of the reins of government, than he formed at once
three mighty projects: to subdue the turbulent spirits of the
great; to reduce the rebellious Huguenots; and to curb the en-
croaching power of the house of Austria. Undaunted and implacable, prudent and active, he braved all the opposition of the
French princes and nobles in the prosecution of his vengeance;
he discovered and dissipated all their secret cabals and con-
spiracies. His sovereign himself he held in subjection, while he
exalted the throne. The people, while they lost their liberties,
acquired, by means of his administration, learning, order, discipline, and renown. That confused and inaccurate genius of
government, of which France partook in common with other
European kingdoms, he changed into a simple monarchy, at the
very time when the incapacity of Buckingham encouraged the
free spirit of the commons to establish in England a regular
system of liberty" (*History of England,* vol. iv. p. 232). Cardinal Richelieu died 1642.

world, took what course they thought proper. Whoever would, was a chevalier, and whoever could, an abbé: I mean a beneficed abbé: dress made no distinction between them; and I believe the Chevalier Gramont was both the one and the other at the siege of Trino.[3]

This was his first campaign, and here he displayed those attractive graces which so favourably prepossess, and require neither friends nor recommendations in any company to procure a favourable reception. The siege was already formed when he arrived, which saved him some needless risks; for a volunteer cannot rest at ease until he has stood the first fire; he went therefore to reconnoitre the generals, having no occasion to reconnoitre the place. Prince Thomas[4] commanded the army; and as the post of lieutenant-general was not then known,[5] Du Plessis Pralin[6] and the famous Viscount Turenne[7] were his major-generals. Fortified

[3] Trino was taken 4th May 1639.

[4] Of Savoy, uncle of the reigning duke. He died 1656.

[5] The rank of lieutenant-general was (according to the *Memoirs of Turenne*) given to that general in the year 1638.

[6] Afterwards Maréchal and Duke de Choiseul. He retired from the army in 1672. Monsieur Hénault, in his *History of France,* under that year, says: "Le Maréchal du Plessis ne fit pas cette campagne à cause de son grand âge; il dit au roi qu'il portoit envie à ses enfans, qui avoient l'honneur de servir sa majesté, que pour lui il souhaitoit la mort, puisqu'il n'étoit plus bon à rien: le roi l'embrassa, et lui dit: '*M. le Maréchal, on ne travaille que pour approcher de la réputation que vous avez acquise: il est agréable de se reposer après tants de victoires.*"

[7] This great general was killed, 27th July 1675, by a cannon-shot, near the village of Salzbach, in going to choose a place whereon to erect a battery. "No one," says Voltaire, "is ignorant of the circumstances of his death; but we cannot here refrain from a review of the principal of them, for the same reason that they are still talked of every day. It seems as if one could not too often repeat, that the same bullet which killed him, having shot off the arm of St. Hilaire, lieutenant-general of the artillery, his son came and bewailed his misfortune with many tears; but the father, looking towards Turenne said: 'It is not I, but that great man, who should be lamented.' These

places were treated with some respect, before a power which nothing can withstand had found means to destroy them by dreadful showers of bombs, and by destructive batteries of hundreds of pieces of cannon. Before these furious storms which drive governors under ground and reduce their garrisons to powder, repeated sallies bravely repulsed, and vigorous attacks nobly sustained, signalised both the art of the besiegers and the courage of the besieged; consequently, sieges were of some length, and young men had an opportunity of gaining some knowledge. Many brave actions were performed on each side during the siege of Trino; a great deal of fatigue was endured, and considerable losses sustained; but fatigue was no more considered, hardships were no more felt in the trenches, gravity was at an end with the generals, and the troops were no longer dispirited after the arrival of the Chevalier Gramont. Pleasure was his pursuit, and he made it universal.

Among the officers in the army, as in all other

words may be compared with the most heroic sayings recorded in all history, and are the best eulogy that can be bestowed upon Turenne. It is uncommon, under a despotic government, where people are actuated only by their private interests, for those who have served their country to die regretted by the public. Nevertheless, Turenne was lamented both by the soldiers and people; and Louvois was the only one who rejoiced at his death. The honours which the King ordered to be paid to his memory are known to every one; and that he was interred at St. Denis, in the same manner as the Constable du Guesclin, above whom he was elevated by the voice of the public, as much as the age of Turenne was superior to the age of the Constable."

It appears, from the *Memoirs of St. Hilaire*, where Voltaire found his anecdote, that Count Hamilton was present at the death of Turenne. Monsieur de Boze had twice sent to Turenne, to beg him to come to the place where the battery was to be erected, which Turenne, as if by presentiment, declined. Count Hamilton brought the third anxious request from De Boze; and in riding to the place where he was, Turenne received his death-blow. The horse of Montecuculi, the opposite general, was, in the course of the same day, killed by a cannon-shot.

places, there are men of real merit, or pretenders to it. The latter endeavoured to imitate the Chevalier Gramont in his most shining qualities, but without success; the former admired his talents and courted his friendship. Of this number was Matta.[8] He was agreeable in his person, but still more by the natural turn of his wit; he was plain and simple in his manners, but endued with a quick discernment and refined delicacy, and full of candour and integrity in all his actions. The Chevalier Gramont was not long in discovering his amiable qualities; an acquaintance was soon formed, and was succeeded by the strictest intimacy.

Matta insisted that the Chevalier should take up his quarters with him; to which he only consented on condition of equally contributing to the expense. As they were both liberal and magnificent, at their common cost they gave the best designed and most luxurious entertainments that had ever yet been seen. Play was wonderfully productive at first, and the Chevalier restored by a hundred different ways that which he obtained only by one. The generals, being entertained by turns, admired their magnificence, and were dissatisfied with their own officers for not keeping such good tables and attendance. The Chevalier had the talent of setting off the most indifferent things to advantage; and his wit was so generally acknowledged, that it was a kind of disgrace not to submit to his taste. To him Matta resigned the care of furnishing the table and

[8] The Count de Matta (b. 1614, ob. 1674) was the son of Claude de Bourdeille, Baron de Mastas, d'Aumargné and de Beaulieu. He had served some time in the army when Gramont joined the forces at the siege of Trino. The combination of indolence and talent, of wit and simplicity, of bluntness and irony, with which the Count de Matta is represented, may have been derived from tradition, but could only have been united into the inimitable whole by the pen of Hamilton. He was like Gramont in many respects, particularly in regard to his stories and repartees. Several of his *bon mots* have been preserved; but the spirit evapo-

doing its honours; and, charmed with the general applause, persuaded himself that nothing could be more
honourable than their way of living, and nothing more
easy than to continue it. But he soon perceived that
the greatest prosperity is not the most lasting. Good
living, bad economy, dishonest servants, and ill-luck,
all uniting together to disconcert their housekeeping,
their table was going to be gradually laid aside, when
the Chevalier's genius, fertile in resources, undertook
to support his former credit by the following expedient.

They had never yet conferred about the state of their
finances, although the steward had acquainted each,
separately, that he must either receive money to continue the expenses, or give in his accounts. One day,
when the Chevalier came home sooner than usual, he
found Matta fast asleep in an easy-chair, and, being
unwilling to disturb his rest, he began musing on his
project. Matta awoke without his perceiving it; and
having, for a short time, observed the deep contempla-
tion he seemed involved in, and the profound silence
between two persons who had never held their tongues
for a moment when together before, he broke it by a
sudden fit of laughter, which increased in proportion
as the other stared at him. " A merry way of waking,
and ludicrous enough," said the Chevalier; "what is the

rates in translation. "Where could I get this nose?" said Madame D'Albret, observing a slight tendency to a flush in that
feature. "At the sideboard, Madame," answered Matta. When
the same lady, in despair at her brother's death, refused all nour-
ishment, Matta administered this blunt consolation: "If you are
resolved, Madame, never again to swallow food, you do well; but
if ever you mean to eat upon any future occasion, believe me,
you may as well begin just now." Madame Caylus, in her
Souvenirs, commemorates the simple and natural humour of
Matta as rendering him the most delightful society in the world.
Mademoiselle de Montpensier, in her *Memoirs,* alludes to his
pleasantry in conversation, and turn for deep gaming. For fuller
particulars of the Count, see *Notes and Queries, Series* i. vol. x.
pp. 138 and 157.

matter, and whom do you laugh at?" "Faith, Chevalier," said Matta, "I am laughing at a dream I had just now, which is so natural and diverting, that I must make you laugh at it also. I was dreaming that we had dismissed our maître-d'hôtel, our cook, and our confectioner, having resolved, for the remainder of the campaign, to live upon those as others have lived upon us: this was my dream. Now tell me, Chevalier, on what were you musing?" "Poor fellow!" said the Chevalier, shrugging up his shoulders, "you are knocked down at once, and thrown into the utmost consternation and despair at some silly stories which the maître-d'hôtel has been telling you as well as me. What! after the figure we have made in the face of the nobility and foreigners in the army, shall we give it up, and like fools and beggars sneak off, upon the first failure of our money! Have you no sentiments of honour? Where is the dignity of France?" "And where is the money?" said Matta; "for my men say, the devil may take them, if there be ten crowns in the house; and believe you have not much more, for it is above a week since I have seen you pull out your purse, or count your money, an amusement you were very fond of in prosperity." "I own all this," said the Chevalier, "but yet I will force you to confess, that you are but a mean-spirited fellow upon this occasion. What would have become of you if you had been reduced to the situation I was in at Lyons, four days before I arrived here? I will tell you the story."

CHAPTER III

"THIS," said Matta, "smells strongly of romance, except that it should have been your squire's part to tell your adventures." "True," said the Chevalier; "however, I may acquaint you with my first exploits without offending my modesty; besides, my squire's style borders too much upon the burlesque for an heroic narrative.

"You must know, then, that upon my arrival at Lyons——" "Is it thus you begin?" said Matta. "Pray give us your history a little farther back. The most minute particulars of a life like yours are worthy of relation; but, above all, the manner in which you first paid your respects to Cardinal Richelieu: I have often laughed at it. However, you may pass over the unlucky pranks of your infancy, your genealogy, name and quality of your ancestors, for that is a subject with which you must be utterly unacquainted."

"Pooh!" said the Chevalier; "you think that all the world is as ignorant as yourself;—you think that I am a stranger to the Mendores[1] and the Corisandes. So, perhaps I don't know that it was my father's own fault that he was not the son of Henry IV. The King would by all means have acknowledged him for his son, but the traitor would never consent to it. See what the Gramonts would have been now, but for this cross-grained fellow! They would have had precedence of the Cæsars de Vendôme.[2] You may laugh, if you like,

[1] Menad d'Aure.
[2] Cæsar, Duke de Vendome, was the eldest son of Henry IV., by the celebrated Gabrielle d'Estrées. He died in 1665.

17

yet it is as true as the gospel: but let us come to the point.

"I was sent to the college at Pau,[4] with the intention of being brought up to the Church; but as I had quite different views, I made no manner of improvement: gaming was so much in my head, that both my tutor and the master lost their labour in endeavouring to teach me Latin. Old Brinon, who served me both as valet-de-chambre and governor, in vain threatened to acquaint my mother. I only studied when I pleased, that is to say, seldom or never: however, they treated me as is customary with scholars of my quality; I was raised to all the dignities of the forms, without having merited them, and left college nearly in the same state in which I entered it; nevertheless, I was thought to have more knowledge than was requisite for the abbacy, which my brother had solicited for me. He had just married the niece of a minister,[5] to whom every one cringed: he was desirous to present me to him. I felt but little regret to quit the country, and great impatience to see Paris. My brother having kept me some time with him, in order to polish me, let me loose upon the town to shake off my rustic air, and learn the manners of the world. I so thoroughly gained them, that I could not be persuaded to lay them aside when I was introduced at Court in the character of an Abbé. You know what kind of dress was then the fashion. All that they could obtain of me was to put a cassock over my other clothes, and my brother, ready to die with laughing at my ecclesiastical habit, made others laugh

[4] Pau was the capital of the principality of Bearne, and lies on an eminence on the Gave Béarnois, being indeed small and well built, and formerly the seat of a parliament, a bailiwick, and a chamber of accounts. In the palace here was born Henry IV. Exclusive of an academy of sciences and liberal arts, there was in it a college of Jesuits, with five convents and two hospitals.   [5] Richelieu.

"She suffered me to depart, under the protection of the Lord and the sage Brinon."

—p. 20

From the painting by C. Delort.

too. I had the finest head of hair in the world, well curled and powdered, above my cassock, and below were white buskins and gilt spurs. The Cardinal,[6] who had a quick discernment, could not help laughing. This elevation of sentiment gave him umbrage; and he foresaw what might be expected from a genius that already laughed at the shaven crown and cowl.

"When my brother had taken me home, 'Well, my little parson,' said he, 'you have acted your part to admiration, and your parti-coloured dress of the ecclesiastic and soldier has greatly diverted the Court; but this is not all: you must now choose, my little knight. Consider then, whether, by sticking to the Church, you will possess great revenues, and have nothing to do; or, with a small portion, you will risk the loss of a leg or arm, and be the fructus belli of an insensible court, to arrive in your old age at the dignity of a major-general, with a glass eye and a wooden leg.' 'I know,' said I, 'that there is no comparison between these two situations, with regard to the conveniences of life; but as a man ought to secure his future state in preference to all other considerations, I am resolved to renounce the Church for the salvation of my soul, upon condition, however, that I keep my abbacy.' Neither the remonstrances nor authority of my brother could induce me to change my resolution; and he was forced to agree to this last article in order to keep me at the academy. You know that I am the most adroit man in France, so that I soon learned all that is taught at such places, and, at the same time, I also learnt that which gives the finishing stroke to a young fellow's education, and makes him a gentleman, viz., all sorts of games, both at cards and dice; but the truth is, I thought, at first, that I had more skill in them than I really had, as experience proved. When my mother

[6] *Ibid.*

knew the choice I had made, she was inconsolable;
for she reckoned, that had I been a clergyman I should
have been a saint; but now she was certain that I
should either be a devil in the world, or be killed in the
wars.   And indeed I burned with impatience to be a
soldier; but being yet too young, I was forced to make
a campaign at Bidache[7] before I made one in the army.
When I returned to my mother's house, I had so much
the air of a courtier and a man of the world, that she
began to respect me instead of chiding me for my infatuation towards the army.   I became her favourite,
and finding me inflexible, she only thought of keeping
me with her as long as she could, while my little
equipage was preparing.   The faithful Brinon, who was
to attend me as valet-de-chambre, was likewise to discharge the office of governor and equerry, being, perhaps, the only Gascon who was ever possessed of so
much gravity and ill-temper.   He passed his word for
my good behaviour and morality, and promised my
mother that he would give a good account of my person
in the dangers of the war; but I hope he will keep his
word better as to this last article than he has done as
to the former.

"My equipage was sent away a week before me.
This was so much time gained by my mother to give
me good advice.   At length, after having solemnly
enjoined me to have the fear of God before my eyes,
and to love my neighbour as myself, she suffered me to
depart, under the protection of the Lord and the sage
Brinon.   At the second stage we quarrelled.   He had
received four hundred louis d'or[8] for the expenses of
the campaign: I wished to have the keeping of them

[7] A principality belonging to the family of the Gramonts, in
the province of Gascony.
[8] Here, and elsewhere, should be *pistoles:* the value of about
eight shillings, or two dollars.

myself, which he strenuously opposed. 'Thou old scoundrel,' said I, 'is the money thine, or was it given you for me? You suppose I must have a treasurer, and receive no money without his order.' I know not whether it was from a presentiment of what afterwards happened that he grew melancholy; however, it was with the greatest reluctance and the most poignant anguish, that he found himself obliged to yield. One would have thought that I had wrested his very soul from him. I found myself more light and merry after I had eased him of his trust; he, on the contrary, appeared so overwhelmed with grief, that it seemed as if I had laid four hundred pounds of lead upon his back, instead of taking away these four hundred louis.[9] He went on so heavily, that I was forced to whip his horse myself, and turning to me, now and then, 'Ah! sir,' said he, 'my lady did not think it would be so.' His reflections and sorrows were renewed at every stage; for, instead of giving a shilling[10] to the post-boy, I gave him half-a-crown.[11]

"Having at last reached Lyons, two soldiers stopped us at the gate of the city, to carry us before the governnor. I took one of them to conduct me to the best inn, and delivered Brinon into the hands of the other, to acquaint the commandant with the particulars of my journey, and my future intentions.

"There are as good taverns at Lyons as at Paris; but my soldier, according to custom, carried me to a friend of his own, whose house he extolled as having the best accommodations, and the greatest resort of good company in the whole town. The master of this hotel was as big as a hogshead, his name Cerise; a Swiss by birth, a poisoner by profession, and a thief by custom. He showed me into a tolerably neat room, and desired to know whether I pleased to sup by myself

[9] Pistoles.   [10] Ten sols.   [11] Thirty (Vizetelly's translation).

or at the ordinary. I chose the latter, on account of the beau monde which the soldier had boasted of.

"Brinon, who was quite out of temper at the many questions which the governor had asked him, returned more surly than an old ape; and seeing that I was dressing my hair, in order to go downstairs: 'What are you about now, sir?' said he. 'Are you going to tramp about the town? No, no; have we not had tramping enough ever since the morning? Eat a bit of supper, and go to bed betimes, that you may get on horseback by daybreak.' 'Mr. Comptroller,' said I, 'I shall neither tramp about the town, nor eat alone, nor go to bed early. I intend to sup with the company below.' 'At the ordinary!' cried he; 'I beseech you, sir, do not think of it! Devil take me, if there be not a dozen brawling fellows playing at cards and dice, who make noise enough to drown the loudest thunder!'

"I had grown insolent since I had seized the money; and being desirous to shake off the yoke of a governor, 'Do you know, Mr. Brinon,' said I, 'that I don't like a blockhead to set up for a reasoner? Do you go to supper, if you please; but take care that I have post-horses ready before daybreak.' The moment he mentioned cards and dice, I felt the money burn in my pocket. I was somewhat surprised, however, to find the room where the ordinary was served filled with odd-looking creatures. My host, after presenting me to the company, assured me that there were but eighteen or twenty of those gentlemen who would have the honour to sup with me. I approached one of the tables where they were playing, and thought I should have died with laughing: I expected to have seen good company and deep play; but I only met with two Germans playing at backgammon. Never did two country boobies play like them; but their figures beggared all description. The fellow near whom I stood was short, thick, and fat, and as round as a ball, with a ruff, and a prodigious high-crowned hat. Any one, at a moderate distance, would have taken him for the dome of a church, with the steeple on the top of it. I inquired of the host who he was. 'A merchant from Basle,' said he, 'who comes hither to sell horses; but from the method he pursues, I think he will not dispose of many; for he does nothing but play.' 'Does he play deep?' said I. 'Not now,' said he; 'they are only playing for their reckoning, while supper is getting ready; but he has no objection to play as deep as any one.' 'Has he money?' said I. 'As for that,' replied the treacherous Cerise, 'would to God you had won a thousand pistoles of him, and I went you halves; we should not be long without our money.' I wanted no further encouragement to meditate the ruin of the high-crowned hat. I went nearer to him, in order to take a closer survey; never was such a bungler; he made mistake after mistake; God knows, I began to feel some remorse at winning of such an ignoramus, who knew so little of the game. He lost his reckoning; supper was served up; and I desired him to sit next me. It was a long table, and there were at least five-and-twenty in company, notwithstanding the landlord's promise. The most execrable repast that ever was begun being finished, all the crowd insensibly dispersed, except the little Swiss, who still kept near me, and the landlord, who placed himself on the other side of me. They both smoked like dragoons; and the Swiss was continually saying, in bad French, 'I ask your pardon, sir, for my great freedom,' at the same time blowing such whiffs of tobacco in my face as almost suffocated me. Mr. Cerise, on the other hand, desired he might take the liberty of asking me whether I had ever been in his country? and seemed surprised I had so genteel an air, without having travelled in Switzerland.

"The little chub I had to encounter was full as inquisitive as the other. He desired to know whether I came from the army in Piedmont; and having told him I was going thither, he asked me, whether I had a mind to buy any horses; that he had about two hundred to dispose of, and that he would sell them cheap. I began to be smoked like a gammon of bacon; and being quite wearied out, both with their tobacco and their questions, I asked my companion if he would play for a single pistole at backgammon, while our men were supping; it was not without great ceremony that he consented, at the same time asking my pardon for his great freedom.

"I won the game; I gave him his revenge, and won again. We then played double or quits, and I won that too, and all in the twinkling of an eye; for he grew vexed, and suffered himself to be taken in so that I began to bless my stars for my good fortune. Brinon came in about the end of the third game, to put me to bed; he made a great sign of the cross, but paid no attention to the signs I made him to retire. I was forced to rise to give him that order in private. He began to reprimand me for disgracing myself by keeping company with such a low-bred wretch. It was in vain that I told him he was a great merchant, that he had a great deal of money, and that he played like a child. 'He a merchant!' cried Brinon. 'Do not believe that, sir! May the devil take me, if he is not some conjurer.' 'Hold your tongue, old fool,' said I; 'he is no more a conjurer than you are, and that is decisive; and, to prove it to you, I am resolved to win four or five hundred pistoles of him before I go to bed.' With these words I turned him out, strictly enjoining him not to return, or in any manner to disturb us.

"The game being done, the little Swiss unbuttoned his pockets, to pull out a new four-pistole piece, and presenting it to me, he asked my pardon for his great freedom, and seemed as if he wished to retire. This was not what I wanted. I told him we only played for amusement; that I had no design upon his money; and that, if he pleased, I would play him a single game for his four pistoles. He raised some objections; but consented at last, and won back his money. I was piqued at it. I played another game; fortune changed sides; the dice ran for him, he made no more errors. I lost the game; another game, and double or quits; we doubled the stake, and played double or quits again. I was vexed; he, like a true gamester, took every bet I offered, and won all before him, without my getting more than six points in eight or ten games. I asked him to play a single game for one hundred pistoles; but as he saw I did not stake, he told me it was late; that he must go and look after his horses; and went away, still asking my pardon for his great freedom. The cool manner of his refusal, and the politeness with which he took his leave, provoked me to such a degree, that I could almost have killed him. I was so confounded at losing my money so fast, even to the last pistole, that I did not immediately consider the miserable situation to which I was reduced.

"I durst not go up to my chamber for fear of Brinon. By good luck, however, he was tired with waiting for me, and had gone to bed. This was some consolation, though but of short continuance. As soon as I was laid down, all the fatal consequences of my adventure presented themselves to my imagination. I could not sleep. I saw all the horrors of my misfortune, without being able to find any remedy; in vain did I rack my brain; it supplied me with no expedient. I feared nothing so much as daybreak; however, it did come, and the cruel Brinon along with it. He was booted up to the middle, and cracking a cursed whip, which he held in his hand, 'Up, Monsieur le Chevalier,' cried he, opening the curtains; 'the horses are at the door, and you are still asleep. We ought by this time to have ridden two stages; give me money to pay the reckoning.' 'Brinon,' said I, in a dejected tone, 'draw the curtains.' 'What!' cried he, 'draw the curtains! Do you intend, then, to make your campaign at Lyons? you seem to have taken a liking to the place. And for the great merchant, you have stripped him, I suppose? No, no, Monsieur le Chevalier, this money will never do you any good. This wretch has perhaps a family; and it is his children's bread that he has been playing with, and that you have won. Was this an object to sit up all night for? What would my lady say if she knew what a life you lead?' 'M. Brinon,' said I, 'pray draw the curtains.' But instead of obeying me, one would have thought that the devil had prompted him to use the most pointed and galling terms to a person under such misfortunes. 'And how much have you won?' said he; 'five hundred pistoles? What must the poor man do? Recollect, Monsieur le Chevalier, what I have said, this money will never thrive with you. It is, perhaps, but four hundred? three? two? Well, if it be but one hundred pistoles,' continued he, seeing that I shook my head at every sum which he had named, 'there is no great mischief done; one hundred pistoles will not ruin him, provided you have won them fairly.' 'Friend Brinon,' said I, fetching a deep sigh, 'draw the curtains; I am unworthy to see daylight.' Brinon was much affected at these melancholy words, but I thought he would have fainted, when I told him the whole adventure. He tore his hair, made grievous lamentations, the burden of which still was, 'What will my lady say?' And, after having exhausted his unprofitable complaints, 'What will become of you now, Monsieur le Chevalier?' said he, 'what do you intend to do?' 'Nothing,' said I; 'for I am fit for nothing.' After this, being somewhat eased after making him my confession, I thought upon several projects, to none of which could I gain his approbation. I would have had him post after my equipage, to have sold some of my clothes. I was for proposing to the horse-dealer to buy some horses of him at a high price on credit, to sell again cheap. Brinon laughed at all these schemes, and after having had the cruelty of keeping me upon the rack for a long time, he at last extricated me. Parents are always stingy towards their poor children; my mother intended to have given me five hundred louis d'or,[12] but she had kept back fifty as well for some little repairs in the abbey, as to pay for praying for me. Brinon had the charge of the other fifty, with strict injunctions not to speak of them, unless upon some urgent necessity. And this you see soon happened.

"Thus you have a brief account of my first adventure. Play has hitherto favoured me; for, since my arrival, I have had, at one time, after paying all my expenses, fifteen hundred louis d'or.[13] Fortune is now again become unfavourable, we must mend her. Our cash runs low; we must, therefore, endeavour to recruit."

"Nothing is more easy," said Matta; "it is only to find out such another dupe as the horse-dealer at Lyons; but now I think of it, has not the faithful Brinon some reserve for the last extremity? Faith, the time is now come, and we cannot do better than to make use of it."

"Your raillery would be very seasonable," said the Chevalier, "if you knew how to extricate us out of this difficulty. You must certainly have an overflow of wit, to be throwing it away upon every occasion as at present. What the devil! will you always be banter-

[12] Pistoles.   [13] About £1425.

ing, without considering what a serious situation we are reduced to. Mind what I say, I will go to-morrow to the headquarters, I will dine with the Count de Cameran, and I will invite him to supper." "Where?" said Matta. "Here," said the Chevalier. "You are mad, my poor friend," replied Matta. "This is some such project as you formed at Lyons: you know we have neither money nor credit; and, to re-establish our circumstances, you intend to give a supper."

"Stupid fellow!" said the Chevalier, "is it possible, that, so long as we have been acquainted, you should have learned no more invention. The Count de Cameran plays at quinze, and so do I. We want money. He has more than he knows what to do with. I will bespeak a splendid supper; he shall pay for it. Send your maître-d'hôtel to me, and trouble yourself no further, except in some precautions, which it is necessary to take on such an occasion." "What are they?" said Matta. "I will tell you," said the Chevalier; "for I find one must explain to you things that are as clear as noonday.

"You command the guards that are here, don't you? As soon as night comes on, you shall order fifteen or twenty men, under the command of your sergeant La Place, to be under arms, and to lay themselves flat on the ground, between this place and the headquarters." "What the devil?" cried Matta, "an ambuscade? God forgive me, I believe you intend to rob the poor Savoyard. If that be your intention, I declare I will have nothing to say to it." "Poor devil!" said the Chevalier, "the matter is this; it is very likely that we shall win his money. The Piedmontese, though otherwise good fellows, are apt to be suspicious and distrustful. He commands the horse. You know you cannot hold your tongue, and are very likely to let slip some jest or other that may vex him. Should he take it into his head that he is cheated, and resent it, who knows what the consequences might be? for he is commonly attended by eight or ten horsemen. Therefore, however much as he may be provoked at his loss, it is proper to be in such a situation as not to dread his resentment."

"Embrace me, my dear Chevalier," said Matta, holding his sides and laughing; "embrace me, for thou art not to be matched. What a fool I was to think, when you talked to me of taking precautions, that nothing more was necessary than to prepare a table and cards, or perhaps to provide some false dice! I should never have thought of supporting a man who plays at quinze by a detachment of foot: I must, indeed, confess that you are already a great soldier."

The next day everything happened as the Chevalier Gramont had planned it; the unfortunate Cameran fell into the snare. They supped in the most agreeable manner possible: Matta drank five or six bumpers to drown a few scruples which made him somewhat uneasy. The Chevalier de Gramont shone as usual, and almost made his guest die with laughing, whom he was soon after to make very serious, and the good-natured Cameran ate like a man whose affections were divided between good cheer and a love of play; that is to say, he hurried down his victuals, that he might not lose any of the precious time which he had devoted to quinze.

Supper being done, the Sergeant La Place posted his ambuscade, and the Chevalier de Gramont engaged his man. The perfidy of Cerise, and the high-crowned hat, were still fresh in remembrance, and enabled him to get the better of a few grains of remorse, and conquer some scruples which arose in his mind. Matta, unwilling to be a spectator of violated hospitality, sat down in an easy chair, in order to fall asleep, while the Chevalier was stripping the poor Count of his money.

They only staked three or four pistoles at first, just for amusement; but Cameran having lost three or four times, he staked high, and the game became serious. He still lost, and became outrageous; the cards flew about the room, and the exclamations awoke Matta.

As his head was heavy with sleep, and hot with wine, he began to laugh at the passion of the Piedmontese, instead of consoling him. "Faith, my poor Count," said he, "if I were in your place, I would play no more." "Why so?" said the other. "I don't know," said he, "but my heart tells me that your ill-luck will continue." "I will try that," said Cameran, calling for fresh cards. "Do so," said Matta, and fell asleep again. It was but for a short time. All cards were equally unfortunate for the loser. He held none but tens or court-cards; and if by chance he had quinze, he was sure to be the weaker hand, and therefore lost it. Again he stormed. "Did not I tell you so?" said Matta, starting out of his sleep. "All your storming is in vain; as long as you play you will lose. Believe me, the shortest follies are the best. Leave off, for the devil take me if it is possible for you to win." "Why?" said Cameran, who began to be impatient. "Do you wish to know?" said Matta; "why, faith, it is because we are cheating you."

The Chevalier de Gramont was provoked at so ill-timed a jest, more especially as it carried along with it some appearance of truth. "Mr. Matta," said he, "do you think it can be very agreeable for a man who plays with such ill-luck as the Count, to be pestered with your insipid jests? For my part, I am so weary of the game that I would desist immediately, if he was not so great a loser." Nothing is more dreaded by a losing gamester than such a threat; and the Count, in a softened tone, told the Chevalier that Mr. Matta might say what he pleased, if he did not offend him; that as to himself, it did not give him the smallest uneasiness.

The Chevalier de Gramont gave the Count far better treatment than he himself had experienced from the Swiss at Lyons; for he played upon credit as long as he pleased, which Cameran took so kindly, that he lost fifteen hundred pistoles, and paid them the next morning. As for Matta, he was severely reprimanded for the intemperance of his tongue. All the reason he gave for his conduct was, that he made it a point of conscience not to suffer the poor Savoyard to be cheated without informing him of it. "Besides," said he, "it would have given me pleasure to have seen my infantry engaged with his horse, if he had been inclined to mischief."

This adventure having recruited their finances, fortune favoured them the remainder of the campaign, and the Chevalier de Gramont, to prove that he had only seized upon the Count's money by way of reprisal, and to indemnify himself for the losses he had sustained at Lyons, began from this time to make the same use of his money, that he has been known to do since upon all occasions. He found out the distressed in order to relieve them; officers who had lost their equipages in the war, or their money at play; soldiers who were disabled in the trenches; in short every one felt the influence of his benevolence: but his manner of conferring a favour exceeded even the favour itself.

Every man possessed of such amiable qualities must meet with success in all his undertakings. The soldiers knew his merits and adored him. The generals were sure to meet him in every scene of action, and sought his company at other times. As soon as fortune declared for him, his first care was to make restitution, by desiring Cameran to go halves in all parties where the odds were in his favour.

An inexhaustible fund of vivacity and good-humour gave a certain air of novelty to whatever he either said or did. I know not on what occasion it was that Monsieur de Turenne, towards the end of the siege, commanded a separate body. The Chevalier de Gramont went to visit him at his new quarters, where he found fifteen or twenty officers. M. de Turenne was naturally fond of merriment, and the Chevalier's presence was sure to inspire it. He was much pleased with this visit, and by way of acknowledgment, would have engaged him to play.

The Chevalier de Gramont, in returning him thanks, said that he had learned from his tutor, that when a man went to see his friends, it was neither prudent to leave his own money behind him, nor civil to carry off theirs. "Truly," said Monsieur de Turenne, "you will find neither deep play nor much money among us; but, that it may not be said that we suffered you to depart without playing, let us stake every one a horse."

The Chevalier de Gramont agreed. Fortune, who had followed him to a place where he did not think he should have any need of her, made him win fifteen or sixteen horses, by way of joke; but seeing some countenances disconcerted at the loss, "Gentlemen," said he, "I should be sorry to see you return on foot from your general's quarters; it will be enough for me if you send me your horses to-morrow, except one, which I give for the cards."

The valet-de-chambre thought he was bantering. "I speak seriously," said the Chevalier, "I give you a horse for the cards; and, what is more, take whichever you please, except my own." "Truly," said Monsieur de Turenne, "I am vastly pleased with the novelty of the thing; for I don't believe that a horse was ever before given for the cards."

Trino surrendered at last. The Baron de Batteville,[14] who had defended it valiantly, and for a long time, obtained a capitulation worthy of such a resistance. I do not know whether the Chevalier de Gramont had any share in the capture of this place; but I know very well, that during a more glorious reign, and with armies ever victorious, his intrepidity and address have been the cause of taking others since, even under the eye of his master, as we shall see in the sequel of these *Memoirs*.

[14] Correctly speaking, Watteville from Wattenveil in Thurgovia. This officer appears to have been the same person who was afterwards ambassador from Spain to the Court of Great Britain, where he offended the French Court, by claiming precedence of their ambassador, Count d'Estrades, on the public entry of the Swedish ambassador into London, on 30th September 1661 (*vide* Pepys' *Diary*). On this occasion the Court of France compelled its rival of Spain to submit to the mortifying circumstance of acknowledging the French superiority. To commemorate this important victory, Louis XIV. caused a medal to be struck, representing the Spanish ambassador, the Marquis de Fuente, making the declaration to that king, "No concurrer con los ambassadores des de Francia," with this inscription, "Jus præcedendi assertum," and under it, "Hispaniorum excusatio coram xxx legatis principum, 1662." Evelyn drew up an account of the fray by royal command, which is given at the end of his *Diary*. See also Jusserand's *French Ambassador*. Clarendon, speaking of Baron de Watteville, says he was born in Burgundy, in the Spanish quarters, and bred a soldier, in which profession he was an officer of note, and at that time was governor of St. Sebastian, and of that province. "He seemed a rough man, and to have more of the camp, but, in truth, knew the intrigues of a court better than most Spaniards; and, except when his passion surprised him, was wary and cunning in his negotiation. He lived with less reservation and more jollity than the ministers of that crown used to do, and drew such of the Court to his table and conversation as he observed to be loud talkers, and confident enough in the King's presence" (*Continuation of Clarendon*, p. 84.)

CHAPTER IV

MILITARY glory is at most but one-half of the accomplishments which distinguish heroes. Love must give the finishing stroke, and adorn their character by the difficulties they encounter, the temerity of their enterprises, and finally, by the lustre of success. We have examples of this, not only in romances, but also in the genuine histories of the most famous warriors, and the most celebrated conquerors.

The Chevalier de Gramont and Matta, who did not think much of these examples, were, however, of opinion, that it would be very agreeable to refresh themselves after the fatigues of the siege of Trino, by forming some other sieges, at the expense of the beauties and the husbands of Turin. As the campaign had finished early, they thought they should have time to perform some exploits before the bad weather obliged them to repass the mountains.

They sallied forth, therefore, not unlike Amadis de Gaul or Don Galaor after they had been dubbed knights, eager in their search after adventures in love, war, and enchantments. They were greatly superior to those two brothers, who only knew how to cleave in twain giants, to break lances, and to carry off fair damsels behind them on horseback, without saying a single word to them; whereas our heroes were adepts at cards and dice, of which the others were totally ignorant.

They went to Turin, met with an agreeable reception, and were greatly distinguished at Court.

34

Could it be otherwise? They were young and handsome; they had wit at command, and spent their money
liberally. In what country will not a man succeed,
possessing such advantages? As Turin was at that
time the seat of gallantry and of love, two strangers
of this description, who were always cheerful, brisk,
and lively, could not fail to please the ladies of the
Court.

Though the men of Turin were extremely handsome,
they were not, however, possessed of the art of pleasing. They treated their wives with respect, and were
courteous to strangers. Their wives, still more handsome, were full as courteous to strangers, and less respectful to their husbands.

Madame Royale,[1] a worthy daughter of Henry IV.,
rendered her little court the most agreeable in the
world. She inherited such of her father's virtues as
compose the proper ornament of her sex; and with
regard to what are termed the foibles of great souls,
her Highness had in no wise degenerated.

The Count de Tanes was her prime minister. It
was not difficult to conduct affairs of state during his
administration. No complaints were alleged against
him; and the princess, satisfied with his conduct herself, was, above all, glad to have her choice approved

[1] Christina, second daughter of Henry IV., married to Victor
Amadeus, Prince of Piedmont, afterwards Duke of Savoy. She
seems to have been well entitled to the character here given of
her. Keysler, in his *Travels*, vol. i. p. 239, speaking of a fine
villa, called La Vigne[1] de Madame Royale, near Turin, says:
"During the minority under the regent Christina, both the
house and garden were often the scenes of riot and debauchery.
On this account, in the king's advanced age, when he was, as it
were, inflamed with an external flame of religion, with which
possibly the admonitions of his father-confessor might concur,
this place became so odious to him, that, upon the death of
Madame Royale, he bestowed it on the hospital." She died in
1663.

[1] Probably "La Venerie" mentioned on p. 38.

by her whole Court, where people lived nearly according to the manners and customs of ancient chivalry.

The ladies had each a professed lover, for fashion's sake, besides volunteers, whose numbers were unlimited. The declared admirers wore their mistresses' liveries, their arms, and sometimes even took their names. Their office was, never to quit them in public, and never to approach them in private; to be their squires upon all occasions, and, in jousts and tournaments, to adorn their lances, their housings, and their coats, with the ciphers and the colours of their dulcineas.

Matta was far from being averse to gallantry; but would have liked it more simple than as it was practised at Turin. The ordinary forms would not have troubled him; but he found here a sort of superstition in the ceremonies and worship of love, which he thought very inconsistent: however, as he had submitted his conduct in that matter to the direction of the Chevalier de Gramont, he was obliged to follow his example, and to conform to the customs of the country.

They enlisted themselves at the same time in the service of two beauties, whose former squires gave them up immediately from motives of politeness. The Chevalier de Gramont chose Mademoiselle de Saint-Germain, and told Matta to offer his services to Madame de Senantes. Matta consented, though he liked the other better; but the Chevalier de Gramont persuaded him that Madame de Senantes was more suitable for him. As he had reaped advantage from the Chevalier's talents in the first projects they had formed, he resolved to follow his instructions in love, as he had done his advice in play.

Mademoiselle de Saint-Germain was in the bloom of youth; her eyes were small, but very bright and sparkling, and, like her hair, were black; her com-

plexion was lively and clear, though not fair; she had
an agreeable mouth, two fine rows of teeth, a neck as
handsome as one could wish, and a most delightful
shape; she had a particular elegance in her elbows,
which, however, she did not show to advantage; her
hands were rather large and not very white; her feet,
though not of the smallest, were well shaped. She
trusted to Providence, and used no art to set off those
graces which she had received from nature; but, notwithstanding her negligence in the embellishment of
her charms, there was something so lively in her person, that the Chevalier de Gramont was caught at first
sight. Her wit and humour corresponded with her
other qualities, being quite easy and perfectly charming; she was all mirth, all life, all complaisance, and
politeness, and all was natural, and always the same
without any variation.

The Marchioness de Senantes[2] was esteemed fair,
and she might have enjoyed, if she had pleased, the
reputation of having red hair, had she not rather chosen
to conform to the taste of the age in which she lived
than to follow that of the ancients : she had all the
advantages of red hair without any of the inconveniences; a constant attention to her person served
as a corrective to the natural defects of her complexion.
After all, what does it signify, whether cleanliness be
owing to nature or to art? it argues an invidious temper
to be very inquisitive about it. She had a great deal of
wit, a good memory, more reading, and a still greater
inclination towards tenderness.

She had a husband whom it would have been criminal even in chastity to spare. He piqued himself upon
being a Stoic, and gloried in being slovenly and dis-

[2] Walpole said the family of Senantes still remained in Piedmont in his time, and were represented by the Marquis de
Carailles.

gusting in honour of his profession. In this he succeeded to admiration; for he was very fat, so that he
perspired almost as much in winter as in summer.
Erudition and brutality seemed to be the most conspicuous features of his character, and were displayed
in his conversation, sometimes together, sometimes al-
ternately, but always disagreeably; he was not jealous,
and yet he was troublesome; he was very well pleased
to see attentions paid to his wife, provided more were
paid to him.

As soon as our adventurers had declared themselves,
the Chevalier de Gramont arrayed himself in green
habiliments, and dressed Matta in blue, these being the
favourite colours of their new mistresses. They entered immediately upon duty. The Chevalier learned
and practised all the ceremonies of this species of gallantry, as if he always had been accustomed to them;
but Matta commonly forgot one-half, and was not
over perfect in practising the other. He never could
remember that his office was to promote the glory, and
not the interest, of his mistress.

The Duchess of Savoy gave the very next day an
entertainment at La Venerie,[3] where all the ladies were
invited. The Chevalier was so agreeable and diverting, that he made his mistress almost die with laughing. Matta, in leading his lady to the coach, squeezed
her hand, and at their return from the promenade he

[3] This place is thus described by Keysler, *Travels,* vol. i. p.
235: "The palace most frequented by the royal family is La
Venerie, the court generally continuing there from the spring
to December. It is about a league from Turin: the road that
leads to it is well paved, and the greatest part of it planted with
trees on each side: it is not always in a direct line, but runs a
little winding between fine meadows, fields, and vineyards."
After describing the palace as it then was, he adds: "The
palace garden at present consists only of hedges and walks,
whereas formerly it had fine water-works and grottos, besides
the fountain of Hercules and the temple of Diana, of which a
description may be seen in the 'Nouveau Théâtre de Piedmont'

begged of her to pity his sufferings. This was proceeding rather too precipitately, and although Madame
de Senantes was not destitute of the natural compassion of her sex, she nevertheless was shocked at the
familiarity of this treatment. She thought herself
obliged to show some degree of resentment, and pulling away her hand, which he had pressed with still
greater fervency upon this declaration, she went up
to the royal apartments without even looking at her
new lover. Matta, never thinking that he had offended
her, suffered her to go, and went in search of some
company to sup with him: nothing was more easy for
a man of his disposition; he soon found what he
wanted, sat a long time at table to refresh himself
after the fatigues of love, and went to bed completely
satisfied that he had performed his part to perfection.

During all this time the Chevalier de Gramont acquitted himself towards Mademoiselle de Saint-Germain
with universal applause; and without remitting his
assiduities, he found means to shine, as they went
along, in the relation of a thousand entertaining anecdotes, which he introduced in the general conversation.
Her Royal Highness[4] heard them with pleasure, and
the solitary Senantes likewise attended to them. He
perceived this, and quitted his mistress to inquire what
she had done with Matta.

"I!" said she, "I have done nothing with him; but
I don't know what he would have done with me if I
had been obliging enough to listen to his most humble
solicitations."

(1700). But now nothing of these remains, being gone to ruin,
partly by the ravages of the French, and partly by the king's
order that they should be demolished, to make room for something else; but those vacuities have not yet, and probably will
not very soon be filled up." [La Vigne ("the Vineyard")
mentioned in footnote, p. 35, is evidently the same place.]
    [4] The Duchess of Savoy.

She then told him in what manner his friend had treated her the very second day of their acquaintance.

The Chevalier could not forbear laughing at it; he told her that Matta was rather too unceremonious, but yet she would like him better as their intimacy more improved, and for her consolation he assured her that he would have spoken in the same manner to her Royal Highness herself; however, he would not fail to give him a severe reprimand. He went the next morning into his room for that purpose; but Matta had gone out early in the morning on a shooting party, to which he had been invited by his supper companions on the preceding evening. At his return he took a brace of partridges and went to his mistress. Being asked whether he wished to see the Marquis, he said no; and the Swiss porter telling him his lady was not at home, he left his partridges, and desired him to present them to his mistress from him.

The Marchioness was at her toilet, and was decorating her head with all the grace she could devise to captivate Matta, at the moment he was denied admittance; she knew nothing of the matter; but her husband knew every particular. He had taken it in dudgeon that the first visit was not paid to him, and, as he was resolved that it should not be paid to his wife, the Swiss had received his orders, and had almost been beaten for receiving the present which had been left. The partridges, however, were immediately sent back, and Matta, without examining into the cause, was glad to have them again. He went to Court without ever changing his clothes, or in the least considering he ought not to appear there without his lady's colours. He found her becomingly dressed; her eyes appeared to him more than usually sparkling, and her whole person altogether divine. He began from that day to be much pleased with himself for his complaisance to the Chevalier de Gramont; however, he could not help remarking that she looked but coldly upon him. This appeared to him a very extraordinary return for his services, and, imagining that she was unmindful of her weighty obligations to him, he entered into conversation with her, and severely reprimanded her for having sent back his partridges with so much indifference.

She did not understand what he meant; and highly offended that he did not apologise, after the reprimand which she concluded him to have received, told him that he certainly had met with ladies of very complying dispositions in his travels, as he seemed to give to himself airs that she was by no means accustomed to endure.

Matta desired to know wherein he could be said to have given himself any. "Wherein?" said she: "the second day that you honoured me with your attentions, you treated me as if I had been your humble servant for a thousand years; the first time that I gave you my hand you squeezed it as violently as you were able. After this commencement of your courtship, I got into my coach, and you mounted your horse; but instead of riding by the side of the coach, as any reasonable gallant would have done, no sooner did a hare start from her form, than you immediately galloped full speed after her; having regaled yourself, during the promenade, by taking snuff, without ever deigning to bestow a thought on me. The only proof you gave me, on your return, that you recollected me, was by soliciting me to surrender my reputation in terms polite enough, but very explicit. And now you talk to me of having been shooting partridges, and of some visit or other, which, I suppose, you have been dreaming of, as well as of all the rest."

The Chevalier de Gramont now advanced, to the interruption of this whimsical dialogue.[5] Matta was rebuked for his forwardness, and his friend took abundant pains to convince him that his conduct bordered more upon insolence than familiarity. Matta endeavoured to exculpate himself, but succeeded ill. His mistress took compassion upon him, and consented to admit his excuses for the manner, rather than his repentance for the fact, and declared that it was the intention alone which could either justify or condemn in such cases; that it was very easy to pardon those transgressions which arise from excess of tenderness, but not such as proceeded from too great a presumption of success. Matta swore that he only squeezed her hand from the violence of his passion, and that he had been driven, by necessity, to ask her to relieve it; that he was yet a novice in the arts of solicitation; that he could not possibly think her more worthy of his affection, after a month's service, than at the present moment; and that he entreated her to cast away an occasional thought upon him when her leisure admitted. The Marchioness was not offended; she saw very well that she must require an implicit conformity to the established rule of decorum, when she had to deal with such a character; and the Chevalier de Gramont, after this sort of reconciliation, went to look after his own affair with Mademoiselle de Saint-Germain.

His concern was not the offspring of mere good nature, nay, it was the reverse; for no sooner did he perceive that the Marchioness looked with an eye of favour upon him, than this conquest, appearing to him to be more easy than the other, he thought it was prudent to take advantage of it, for fear of losing the opportunity, and that he might not have spent all his

[5] Arrived at this point of the conversation (Vizetelly's translation).

time to no purpose, in case he should prove unsuccessful with the little Saint-Germain.

In the meantime, in order to maintain that authority which he had usurped over the conduct of his friend, he, that very evening, notwithstanding what had been already said, reprimanded him for presuming to appear at Court in his morning suit, and without his mistress's badge; for not having had the wit or prudence to pay his first visit to the Marquis de Senantes, instead of consuming his time, to no purpose, in inquiries for the lady; and, to conclude, he asked him what the devil he meant by presenting her with a brace of miserable red partridges.

"And why not?" said Matta: "ought they to have been blue, too, to match the cockade and sword-knots you made me wear the other day? Plague not me with your nonsensical whimsies: my life on it, in one fortnight your equal in foppery and folly will not be found throughout the confines of Turin; but to reply to your questions, I did not call upon Monsieur de Senantes, because I had nothing to do with him, and because he is of a species of animals which I dislike, and always shall dislike. As for you, you appear quite charmed with being decked out in green ribands, with writing letters to your mistress, and filling your pockets with citrons, pistachios, and such sort of stuff, with which you are always cramming the poor girl's mouth, against her will. You hope to succeed by chanting ditties composed in the days of Corisande and of Henry IV., which you will swear yourself have made upon her. Happy in practising the ceremonials of gallantry, you have no ambition for the essentials. Very well: every one has a particular way of acting, as well as a particular taste: yours is to trifle in love; and, provided you can make Mademoiselle de Saint-Germain laugh, you are satisfied. As for my part, I am persuaded, that women here are made of the same materials as in other places; and I do not think that they can be mightily offended, if one sometimes leaves off trifling, to come to the point. However, if the Marchioness is not of this way of thinking, she may e'en provide for herself elsewhere, for I can assure her, that I shall not long act the part of her squire."

This was an unnecessary menace; for the Marchioness in reality liked him very well, was nearly of the same way of thinking herself, and wished for nothing more than to put his gallantry to the test. But Matta proceeded upon a wrong plan; he had conceived such an aversion for her husband, that he could not prevail upon himself to make the smallest advance towards his good graces. He was given to understand that he ought to begin by endeavouring to lull the dragon to sleep, before he could gain possession of the treasure; but this was all to no purpose, though, at the same time, he could never see his mistress but in public. This made him impatient, and as he was lamenting his ill-fortune to her one day: "Have the goodness, madame," said he, "to let me know where you live: there is never a day that I do not call upon you, at least, three or four times, without ever being blessed with a sight of you." "I generally sleep at home," replied she, laughing, "but I must tell you, that you will never find me there, if you do not first pay a visit to the Marquis: I am not mistress of the house. I do not tell you," continued she, "that he is a man whose acquaintance any one would very impatiently covet for his conversation: on the contrary, I agree that his humour is fantastical, and his manners not of the pleasing cast; but there is nothing so savage and inhuman which a little care, attention, and complaisance may not tame into docility. I must repeat to you some verses upon the subject: I have got them by heart, because they contain a little advice, which you may accommodate, if you please, to your own case.

RONDEAU

" Keep in mind these maxims rare.
You who hope to win the fair;
Who are, or would esteemèd be,
The quintessence of gallantry.
That fopp'ry, grinning, and grimace,
And fertile store of common-place;
That oaths as false as dicers swear,
And iv'ry teeth, and scented hair;
That trinkets, and the pride of dress,
Can only give your scheme success.
Keep in mind.

" Hast thy charmer e'er an aunt?
Then learn the rules of woman's cant,
And forge a tale, and swear you read it,
Such as, save woman, none would credit:
Win o'er her confidante and pages
By gold, for this a golden age is;
And should it be her wayward fate,
To be encumbered with a mate,
A dull, old dotard should he be,
That dulness claims thy courtesy.
Keep in mind."

"Truly," said Matta, "the song may say what it pleases, but I cannot put it in practice: your husband is far too exquisite a monster for me. Why, what a plaguy odd ceremony do you require of us in this country, if we cannot pay our compliments to the wife without being in love with the husband!"

The Marchioness was much offended at this answer; and as she thought she had done enough in pointing out to him the path which would conduct him to success, if he had deserved it, she did not think it worth while to enter into any further explanation; since he refused to cede, for her sake, so trifling an objection: from this instant she resolved to have done with him.

The Chevalier de Gramont had taken leave of his

mistress nearly at the same time : the ardour of his pursuit was extinguished. It was not that Mademoiselle de Saint-Germain was less worthy than hitherto of his attentions : on the contrary her attractions visibly increased. She retired to her pillow with a thousand charms, and ever rose from it with additional beauty : the phrase of increasing in beauty as she increased in years seemed to have been purposely made for her. The Chevalier could not deny these truths, but yet he could not find his account in them: a little less merit, with a little less discretion, would have been more agreeable. He perceived that she attended to him with pleasure, that she was diverted with his stories as much as he could wish, and that she received his billets and presents without scruple; but then he also discovered that she did not wish to proceed any further. He had exhausted every species of address upon her, and all to no purpose : her attendant was gained : her family, charmed with the music of his conversation and his great attention, were never happy without him. In short, he had reduced to practice the advice contained in the Marchioness's song, and everything conspired to deliver the little Saint-Germain into his hands, if the little Saint-Germain had herself been willing : but, alas! she was not inclined. It was in vain he told her the favour he desired would cost her nothing; and that since these treasures were rarely comprised in the fortune a lady brings with her in marriage, she would never find any person, who, by unremitting tenderness, unwearied attachment, and inviolable secrecy, would prove more worthy of them than himself. He then told her no husband was ever able to convey a proper idea of the sweets of love, and that nothing could be more different than the passionate fondness of a lover, always tender, always affectionate, yet always respectful, and the careless indifference of a husband.

Mademoiselle de Saint-Germain, not wishing to take the matter in a serious light, that she might not be forced to resent it, answered, that since it was generally the custom in her country to marry, she thought it was right to conform to it, without entering into the knowledge of those distinctions, and those marvellous particulars, which she did not very well understand, and of which she did not wish to have any further explanation; that she had submitted to listen to him this one time, but desired he would never speak to her again in the same strain, since such sort of conversation was neither entertaining to her, nor could be serviceable to him. Though no one was ever more facetious than Mademoiselle de Saint-Germain, she yet knew how to assume a very serious air, whenever occasion required it. The Chevalier de Gramont soon saw that she was in earnest; and finding it would cost him a great deal of time to effect a change in her sentiments, he was so far cooled in this pursuit, that he only made use of it to hide the designs he had upon the Marchioness de Senantes.

He found this lady much disgusted at Matta's want of complaisance; and his seeming contempt for her erased every favourable impression which she had once entertained for him. While she was in this humour, the Chevalier told her that her resentment was just; he exaggerated the loss which his friend had sustained; he told her that her charms were a thousand times superior to those of the little Saint-Germain, and requested that favour for himself which his friend did not deserve. He was soon favourably heard upon this topic; and as soon as they were agreed, they consulted upon two measures necessary to be taken, the one to deceive her husband, the other his friend, which was not very difficult: Matta was not at all suspicious: and the stupid Senantes, towards whom the Chevalier had already behaved as Matta had refused to do, could not be easy without him. This was much more than was wanted; for as soon as ever the Chevalier was with the Marchioness, her husband immediately joined them out of politeness; and on no account would have left them alone together, for fear they should grow weary of each other without him.

Matta, who all this time was entirely ignorant that he was disgraced, continued to serve his mistress in his own way. She had agreed with the Chevalier de Gramont, that to all appearance everything should be carried on as before; so that the Court always believed that the Marchioness only thought of Matta, and that the Chevalier was entirely devoted to Mademoiselle de Saint-Germain.

There were very frequently little lotteries for trinkets; and the Chevalier de Gramont always tried his fortune, and was sometimes fortunate; and under pretence of the prizes he had won, he bought a thousand things which he indiscreetly gave to the Marchioness, and which she still more indiscreetly accepted: the little Saint-Germain very seldom received anything. There are meddling whisperers everywhere: remarks were made upon these proceedings; and the same person that made them communicated them likewise to Mademoiselle de Saint-Germain. She pretended to laugh, but in reality was piqued. It is a maxim religiously observed by the fair sex, to envy each other those indulgences which themselves refuse. She took this very ill of the Marchioness. On the other hand, Matta was asked if he was not old enough to make his own presents himself to the Marchioness de Senantes, without sending them by the Chevalier de Gramont. This roused him; for of himself, he would never have perceived it: his suspicions, however, were but slight, and he was willing to have them removed. "I must con-

fess," said he to the Chevalier de Gramont, "that they
make love here quite in a new style; a man serves here
without reward: he addresses himself to the husband
when he is in love with the wife, and makes presents
to another man's mistress, to get into the good graces
of his own. The Marchioness is much obliged to you
for——" "It is you who are obliged," replied the
Chevalier, "since this was done on your account: I
was ashamed to find you had never yet thought of presenting her with any trifling token of your attention:
do you know that the people of this Court have such
extraordinary notions, as to think that it is rather
owing to inadvertency that you never yet have had the
spirit to make your mistress the smallest present? For
shame! how ridiculous it is, that you can never think
for yourself!"

Matta took this rebuke, without making any answer,
being persuaded that he had in some measure deserved
it: besides, he was neither sufficiently jealous, nor sufficiently amorous, to think any more of it; however, as
it was necessary for the Chevalier's affairs that Matta
should be acquainted with the Marquis de Senantes, he
plagued him so much about it, that at last he complied.
His friend introduced him, and his mistress seemed
pleased with this proof of complaisance, though she
was resolved that he should gain nothing by it; and the
husband, being gratified with a piece of civility which
he had long expected, determined, that very evening,
to give them a supper at a little country seat of his,
on the banks of the river, very near the city.

The Chevalier de Gramont answering for them both,
accepted the offer; and as this was the only one Matta
would not have refused from the Marquis, he likewise
consented. The Marquis came to convey them in his
carriage at the hour appointed; but he found only
Matta. The Chevalier had engaged himself to play, on

purpose that they might go without him: Matta was
for waiting for him, so great was his fear of being left
alone with the Marquis; but the Chevalier having sent
to desire them to go on before, and that he would
be with them as soon as he had finished his game, poor
Matta was obliged to set out with the man who, of all
the world, was most offensive to him. It was not the
Chevalier's intention quickly to extricate Matta out of
this embarrassment: he no sooner knew that they were
gone, than he waited on the Marchioness, under pretence of still finding her husband, that they might all
go together to supper.

The plot was in a fair way; and as the Marchioness
was of opinion that Matta's indifference merited no better treatment from her, she made no scruple of acting
her part in it: she therefore waited for the Chevalier de
Gramont with intentions so much the more favourable,
as she had for a long time expected him, and had some
curiosity to receive a visit from him in the absence of
her husband. We may therefore suppose that this first
opportunity would not have been lost if Mademoiselle
de Saint-Germain had not unexpectedly come in, almost
at the same time with the Chevalier.

She was more handsome and more entertaining that
day than she had ever been before; however, she appeared to them very ugly and very tiresome. She soon
perceived that her company was disagreeable, and being
determined that they should not be out of humour with
her for nothing, after having passed above a long half
hour in diverting herself with their uneasiness, and
in playing a thousand monkey tricks, which she plainly
saw could never be more unseasonable, she pulled off
her hood, scarf, and all that part of her dress which
ladies lay aside, when in a familiar manner they intend
to pass the day anywhere. The Chevalier de Gramont
cursed her in his heart, while she continued to torment

him for being in such ill-humour in such good company. At last the Marchioness, who was as much vexed as he was, said rather drily that she was obliged to wait on her Royal Highness. Mademoiselle de Saint-Germain told her that she would have the honour to accompany her, if it would not be disagreeable: she took not the smallest notice of her offer, and the Chevalier, finding that it would be entirely useless to prolong his visit at that time, retired with a good grace.

As soon as he had left the house, he sent one of his scouts to desire the Marquis to sit down to table with his company without waiting for him, because the game might not perhaps be finished as soon as he expected, but that he would be with him before supper was over. Having despatched this messenger, he placed a sentinel at the Marchioness's door, in hopes that the tedious Saint-Germain might go out before her; but this was in vain, for his spy came and told him, after an hour's impatience and suspense, that they were gone out together. He found there was no chance of seeing her again that day, everything falling out contrary to his wishes; he was forced, therefore, to leave the Marchioness, and go in quest of the Marquis.

While these things were going on in the city, Matta was not much diverted in the country: as he was prejudiced against the Marquis, all that he said displeased him. He cursed the Chevalier heartily for the *tête-à-tête* which he had procured him; and he was upon the point of going away, when he found that he was to sit down to supper without any other company.

However, as his host was very choice in his entertainments, and had the best wine and the best cook in all Piedmont, the sight of the first course appeased him; and eating most voraciously, without paying any attention to the Marquis, he flattered himself that the supper would end without any dispute; but he was mistaken.

When the Chevalier de Gramont was at first endeavouring to bring about an intercourse between the Marquis and Matta, he had given a very advantageous character of the latter, to make the former more desirous of his acquaintance; and in the display of a thousand other accomplishments, knowing what an infatuation the Marquis had for the very name of erudition, he assured him that Matta was one of the most learned men in Europe.

The Marquis, therefore, from the moment they sat down to supper, had expected some stroke of learning from Matta, to bring his own into play; but he was much out in his reckoning. No one had read less, no one thought less, and no one had ever spoken so little at an entertainment as he had done. As he did not wish to enter into conversation, he opened his mouth only to eat, or ask for wine.

The other, being offended at a silence which appeared to him affected, and wearied with having uselessly attacked him upon other subjects, thought he might get something out of him by changing the discourse to love and gallantry; and therefore, to begin the subject, he accosted him in this manner:

"Since you are my wife's gallant——" "I!" said Matta, who wished to carry it discreetly: "those who told you so, told a damned lie." "Zounds, sir," said the Marquis, "you speak in a tone which does not at all become you, for I would have you to know, notwithstanding your contemptuous airs, that the Marchioness de Senantes is perhaps as worthy of your attentions as any of your French ladies, and that I have known some greatly your superiors, who have thought it an honour to serve her." "Very well," said Matta, "I think she is very deserving, and since you insist upon it, I am her servant and gallant, to oblige you."

"You think, perhaps," continued the other, "that the same custom prevails in this country as in your own, and that the ladies have lovers, with no other intentions than to grant them favours: undeceive yourself, if you please, and know, likewise, that even if such events were frequent in this Court, I should not be at all uneasy." "Nothing can be more civil," said Matta; "but wherefore would you not?" "I will tell you why," replied he.⁶ "I am well acquainted with the affection my wife entertains for me: I am acquainted with her discretion towards all the world; and, what is more, I am acquainted with my own merit."

"You have a most uncommon acquaintance, then," replied Matta; "I congratulate you upon it; I have the honour to drink it in a bumper." The Marquis pledged him; but seeing that the conversation dropped on their ceasing to drink, after two or three healths, he wished to make a second attempt, and attack Matta on his strong side, that is to say, on his learning.

He desired him, therefore, to tell him, at what time he thought the Allobroges came to settle in Piedmont. Matta, who wished him and his Allobroges at the devil, said, that it must be in the time of the civil wars. "I doubt that," said the other. "Just as you like," said Matta. "Under what consulate?" replied the Marquis. "Under that of the League," said Matta, "when the Guises brought the Lansquenets into France; but what the devil does that signify?"

The Marquis was tolerably warm, and naturally savage, so that God knows how the conversation would have ended, if the Chevalier de Gramont had not unexpectedly come in to appease them. It was some time before he could find out what their debate was; for the one had forgotten the questions, and

⁶ The Marquis.

the other the answers, which had disobliged him, in order to reproach the Chevalier with his eternal passion for play, which made him always uncertain. The Chevalier, who knew that he was still more culpable than they thought, bore it all with patience, and condemned himself more than they desired. This appeased them; and the entertainment ended with greater tranquillity than it had begun. The conversation was again reduced to order; but he could not enliven it as he usually did. He was in very ill humor, and as he pressed them every minute to rise from table, the Marquis was of opinion that he had lost a great deal. Matta said, on the contrary, that he had won; but for want of precautions had made perhaps an unfortunate retreat; and asked him if he had not stood in need of Sergeant La Place, with his ambuscade.

This piece of history was beyond the comprehension of the Marquis, and being afraid that Matta might explain it, the Chevalier changed the discourse, and was for rising from table; but Matta would not consent to it. This effected a reconciliation between him and the Marquis, who thought this was a piece of civility intended for him; however, it was not for him, but for his wine, to which Matta had taken a prodigious liking.

The Duchess,[7] who knew the character of the Marquis, was charmed with the account which the Chevalier de Gramont gave her of the entertainment and conversation. She sent for Matta to know the truth of it from himself. He confessed, that before the Allobroges were mentioned the Marquis was for quarrelling with him, because he was not in love with his wife.

Their acquaintance having begun in this manner,

[7] Madame Royale.

all the esteem which the Marquis had formerly expressed for the Chevalier seemed now directed towards Matta. He went every day to pay Matta a visit, and Matta was every day with his wife. This did not at all suit the Chevalier: he repented of his having chid Matta, whose assiduity now interrupted all his schemes; and the Marchioness was still more embarrassed. Whatever wit a man may have, it will never please where his company is disliked; and she repented that she had been formerly guilty of some trifling advances towards him.

Matta began to find charms in her person, and might have found the same in her conversation, if she had been inclined to display them; but it is impossible to be in good humour with persons who thwart our designs. While his passion increased, the Chevalier de Gramont was solely occupied in endeavouring to find out some method, by which he might accomplish his own intrigue; and this was the stratagem which he put in execution to clear the coast, by removing, at one and the same time, both the lover and the husband.

He told Matta that they ought to invite the Marquis to supper at their lodgings, and he would take upon himself to provide everything proper for the occasion. Matta desired to know if it was to play at quinze, and assured him that he should take care to render abortive any intention he might have to engage in play, and leave him alone with the greatest blockhead in all Europe. The Chevalier de Gramont did not entertain any such thought, being persuaded that it would be impossible to take advantage of any such opportunity, in whatever manner he might take his measures; and that they would seek for him in every corner of the city rather than allow him the least repose. His whole attention was therefore employed in rendering the entertainment agreeable, in finding out means of prolonging it, in order ultimately to kindle some dispute between the Marquis and Matta. For this purpose he put himself in the best humour in the world, and the wine produced the same effect on the rest of the company.

The Chevalier de Gramont expressed his concern that he had not been able to give the Marquis a little concert, as he had intended in the morning; for the musicians had been all pre-engaged. Upon this the Marquis undertook to have them at his country-house the following evening, and invited the same company to sup with him there. Matta asked what the devil they wanted with music, and maintained that it was of no use on such occasions but for women who had something to say to their lovers, while the fiddles prevented them from being overheard, or for fools who had nothing to say when the music ended. They ridiculed all his arguments: the party was fixed for the next day, and the music was voted by the majority of voices. The Marquis, to console Matta, as well as to do honour to the entertainment, toasted a great many healths. Matta was more ready to listen to his arguments on this topic than in a dispute; but the Chevalier, perceiving that a little would irritate them, desired nothing more earnestly than to see them engaged in some new controversy. It was in vain that he had from time to time started some subject of discourse with this intention; but having luckily thought of asking what was his lady's maiden name, Senantes, who was a great genealogist, as all fools are who have good memories, immediately began tracing out her family, by an endless, confused string of lineage. The Chevalier seemed to listen to him with great attention; and perceiving that Matta was almost out of patience, he desired him to attend to what the

Marquis was saying, for that nothing could be more
entertaining. "All this may be very true," said Matta;
"but for my part, I must confess, if I were married,
I should rather choose to inform myself who was the
real father of my children, than who were my wife's
grandfathers." The Marquis, smiling at this rudeness, did not leave off until he had traced back the
ancestors of his spouse, from line to line, as far as
Yolande de Senantes: after this he offered to prove, in
less than half an hour, that the Gramonts came originally from Spain. "Very well," said Matta, "and
pray what does it signify to us from whence the
Gramonts are descended? Do not you know, sir, that
it is better to know nothing at all, than to know too
much?"

The Marquis maintained the contrary with great
warmth, and was preparing a formal argument to
prove that an ignorant man is a fool; but the Chevalier
de Gramont, who was thoroughly acquainted with
Matta, saw very clearly that he would send the logician
to the devil before he should arrive at the conclusion
of his syllogism: for which reason, interposing as
soon as they began to raise their voices, he told them
it was ridiculous to quarrel about an affair in itself so
trivial, and treated the matter in a serious light, that
it might make the greater impression. Thus supper
terminated peaceably, owing to the care he took to
suppress all disputes, and to substitute plenty of wine
in their stead.

The next day Matta went to the chase, the Chevalier
de Gramont to the bagnio, and the Marquis to his
country-house. While the latter was making the
necessary preparations for his guests, not forgetting
the music, and Matta pursuing his game to get an
appetite, the Chevalier was meditating on the execution of his project.

As soon as he had regulated his plan of operations in his own mind, he privately sent anonymous intelligence to the officer of the guard at the palace that the Marquis de Senantes had had some words with Monsieur de Matta the preceding night at supper; that the one had gone out in the morning, and the other could not be found in the city.

Madame Royale, alarmed at this advice, immediately sent for the Chevalier de Gramont. He appeared surprised when her Highness mentioned the affair: he confessed, indeed, that some high words had passed between them, but that he did not believe either of them would have remembered them the next day. He said that if no mischief had yet taken place, the best way would be to secure them both until the morning, and that if they could be found, he would undertake to reconcile them, and to obliterate all grievances. In this there was no great difficulty. On inquiry at the Marquis's they were informed that he was gone to his country-house: there certainly he was, and there they found him; the officer put him under an arrest, without assigning any reason for so doing, and left him in very great surprise.

Immediately upon Matta's return from hunting, her Royal Highness sent the same officer to desire him to give her his word that he would not stir out that evening. This compliment very much surprised him, more particularly as no reason was assigned for it. He was expected at a good entertainment; he was dying with hunger, and nothing appeared to him more unreasonable than to oblige him to stay at home in a situation like the present; but he had given his word, and not knowing to what this might tend, his only resource was to send for his friend. But his friend did not come to him until his return from the country. He had there found the Marquis in the midst of his

fiddlers, and very much vexed to find himself a prisoner in his own house on account of Matta, whom he
was waiting for in order to feast him. He complained
of him bitterly to the Chevalier de Gramont. He said
that he did not believe that he had offended him; but
that, since he was very desirous of a quarrel, he desired
the Chevalier to acquaint him, if he felt the least
displeasure on the present occasion, he should, on the
very first opportunity, receive what is called satisfaction. The Chevalier de Gramont assured him that
no such thought had ever entered the mind of Matta;
that, on the contrary, he knew that he very greatly
esteemed him; that all this could alone arise from the
extreme tenderness of his lady, who, being alarmed
upon the report of the servants who waited at table,
must have gone to her Royal Highness, in order to
prevent any unpleasant consequences; that he thought
this the more probable, as he had often told the
Marchioness, when speaking of Matta, that he was
the best swordsman in France; for in truth the poor
gentleman had never fought without having the misfortune of killing his man.

The Marquis, being a little pacified, said he was
very much obliged to him, that he would severely chide
his wife for her unseasonable tenderness, and that he
was extremely desirous of again enjoying the pleasure
of his dear friend Matta's company.

The Chevalier de Gramont assured him that he
would use all his endeavours for that purpose, and at
the same time gave strict charge to the guards not
to let him escape without orders from the Court, as
he seemed fully bent upon fighting, and they would
be responsible for him. There was no occasion to say
more to have him strictly watched, though there was
no necessity for it.

One being thus safely lodged, his next step was

to secure the other.   He returned immediately to
town: and as soon as Matta saw him, "What the
devil," said he, "is the meaning of this farce which I
am obliged to act?   For my part, I cannot understand
the foolish customs of this country; how comes it that
they make me a prisoner upon my parole?"   "How
comes it?" said the Chevalier de Gramont; "it is
because you yourself are far more unaccountable than
all their customs; you cannot help disputing with a
peevish fellow, whom you ought only to laugh at;
some officious footman has no doubt been talking of
your last night's dispute; you were seen to go out of
town in the morning, and the Marquis soon after;
was not this sufficient to make her Royal Highness
think herself obliged to take these precautions?   The
Marquis is in custody; they have only required your
parole; so far, therefore, from taking the affair in the
sense you do, I should send very humbly to thank
her Highness for the kindness she has manifested
towards you in putting you under arrest, since it is
only on your account that she interests herself in the
affair.   I shall take a walk to the palace, where I will
endeavour to unravel this mystery; in the meantime,
as there is but little probability that the matter should
be settled this evening, you would do well to order
supper, for I shall come back to you immediately."

Matta charged him not to fail to express to her
Royal Highness the grateful sense he had of her
favour, though in truth he as little feared the Marquis
as he loved him; and it is impossible to express the
degree of his fortitude in stronger terms.

The Chevalier de Gramont returned in about half
an hour with two or three gentlemen whom Matta had
got acquainted with at the chase, and who, upon the
report of the quarrel, waited upon him and each
offered him separately his services against the unas-

sisted and pacific Marquis. Matta, having returned them his thanks, insisted upon their staying supper, and put on his *robe de chambre*.

As soon as the Chevalier de Gramont perceived that everything coincided with his wishes, and that towards the end of the entertainment the toasts went merrily round, he knew he was sure of his man till next day: then taking him aside with the permission of the company, and making use of a false confidence in order to disguise a real treachery, he acquainted him, after having sworn him several times to secrecy, that he had at last prevailed upon the little Saint-Germain to grant him an interview that night; for which reason he would take his leave, under pretence of going to play at Court. He therefore desired him fully to satisfy the company that he would not have left them on any other account, as the Piedmontese are naturally mistrustful. Matta promised he would manage this point with discretion; that he would make an apology for him, and that there was no occasion for his personally taking leave. Then, after congratulating him upon the happy posture of his affairs, he sent him away with all the expedition and secrecy imaginable; so great was his fear lest his friend should lose the present opportunity.

Matta then returned to the company, much pleased with the confidence which had been placed in him, and with the share he had in the success of this adventure. He put himself into the best humour imaginable in order to divert the attention of his guests; he severely satirised those, whose rage for gaming induced them to sacrifice to it every other consideration; he loudly ridiculed the folly of the Chevalier upon this article, and secretly laughed at the credulity of the Piedmontese, whom he had deceived with so much ingenuity.

It was late at night before the company broke up, and Matta went to bed, very well satisfied with what he had done for his friend; and, if we may credit appearances, this friend enjoyed the fruit of his perfidy. The amorous Marchioness received him[8] like one who wished to enhance the value of the favour she bestowed; her charms were far from being neglected; and if there are any circumstances in which we may detest the traitor while we profit by the treason, this was not one of them; and however cautious the Chevalier de Gramont was in his intrigues, it was not owing to him that the contrary was not believed; but be that as it may, being convinced that in love whatever is gained by address is gained fairly, it does not appear that he ever showed the smallest degree of repentance for this trick. But it is now time for us to take him from the Court of Savoy, to see him shine in that of France.

[8] Attired (Vizetelly's translation).

CHAPTER V

THE Chevalier de Gramont, upon his return to France, sustained, with the greatest success, the reputation he had acquired abroad. Alert in play, active and vigilant in love; sometimes successful, and always feared, in his intrigues; in war alike prepared for the events of good or ill fortune; possessing an inexhaustible fund of pleasantry in the former, and full of expedients and dexterity in the latter.

Zealously attached to the Prince de Condé[1] from inclination, he was a witness, and, if we may be

---

[1] Louis of Bourbon, Duke d'Enghien (born 1620). By the death of his father in 1646, Prince de Condé. Of this great man Cardinal de Retz says: "He was born a general, which never happened but to Cæsar, to Spinola, and to himself. He has equalled the first: he has surpassed the second. Intrepidity is one of the least shining strokes in his character. Nature had formed him with a mind as great as his courage. Fortune, in setting him out in a time of wars, has given this last a full extent to work in: his birth, or rather his education, in a family devoted and enslaved to the court, has kept the first within too straight bounds. He was not taught time enough the great and general maxims which alone are able to form men to think always consistently. He never had time to learn them of himself, because he was prevented from his youth, by the great affairs that fell unexpectedly to his share, and by the continual success he met with. This defect in him was the cause, that with the soul in the world the least inclined to evil, he has committed injuries; that with the heart of an Alexander, he has, like him, had his failings; that with a wonderful understanding, he has acted imprudently; that having all the qualities which the Duke Francis of Guise had, he has not served the state in some occasions so well as he ought; and that having likewise all the qualities of the Duke Henry of Guise, he has not carried faction so far as he might. He could not come up to the height of his

allowed to say it, his companion, in the glory he had acquired at the celebrated battles of Lens, Nordlinguen, and Fribourg;[2] and the details he so frequently gave of them were far from diminishing their lustre.

So long as he had only some scruples of conscience, and a thousand interests to sacrifice, he quitted all to follow a man, whom strong motives and resentments, which in some manner appeared excusable, had withdrawn from the paths of rectitude. He adhered to him in his first disgrace, with a constancy of which there are few examples; but he could not submit to the injuries which he afterwards received, and which such an inviolable attachment so little merited. Therefore, without fearing any reproach for a conduct which sufficiently justified itself, as he had formerly deviated from his duty by entering into the service of the Prince de Condé, he thought he had a right to leave him to return again to his duty.

His peace was soon made at Court, where many, far more culpable than himself, were immediately received

merit; which, though it be a defect, must yet be owned to be very uncommon, and only to be found in persons of the greatest abilities" (*Memoirs*, vol. i. p. 248, edit. 1723). He retired from the army, soon after the death of Turenne, to Chantilly, " from whence," says Voltaire, "he very rarely came to Versailles, to behold his glory eclipsed in a place where the courtier never regards anything but favour. He passed the remainder of his days, tormented with the gout, relieving the severity of his pains, and employing the leisure of his retreat in the conversation of men of genius of all kinds, with which France then abounded. He was worthy of their conversation; as he was not unacquainted with any of those arts and sciences in which they shone. He continued to be admired even in his retreat; but at last that devouring fire, which, in his youth, had made him a hero, impetuous, and full of passions, having consumed the strength of his body, which was naturally rather fragile than robust, he declined before his time; and the strength of his mind decaying with that of his body, there remained nothing of the great Condé during the last two years of his life. He died in 1686" (*Age of Louis XIV*. chap. xi.).

[2] These were fought in the years 1648, 1645, and 1644.

into favour, when they desired it; for the Queen,[*] still terrified at the dangers into which the civil wars had plunged the State at the commencement of her regency, endeavoured by lenient measures to conciliate the minds of the people. The policy of the minister[*] was neither sanguinary nor revengeful. His favourite maxim was rather to appease the minds of the discontented by lenity than to have recourse to violent measures; to be content with losing nothing by the war, without being at the expense of gaining any advantage from the enemy; to suffer his character to be very severely handled, provided he could amass much wealth, and to spin out the minority to the greatest possible extent.

His avidity to heap up riches was not alone confined to the thousand different means, with which he was

[*] Anne of Austria, daughter of Philip III. of Spain, widow of Louis XIII., to whom she was married in 1615, and mother of Louis XIV. She died in 1666. Cardinal de Retz speaks of her in the following terms: " The Queen had more than anybody whom I ever knew, of that sort of wit which was necessary for her not to appear a fool to those that did not know her. She had in her more of harshness than haughtiness; more of haughtiness than of greatness; more of outward appearance than reality; more regard to money than liberality; more of liberality than of self-interest; more of self-interest than disinterestedness: she was more tied to persons by habit than by affection; she had more of insensibility than of cruelty; she had a better memory for injuries than for benefits; her intention towards piety was greater than her piety; she had in her more of obstinacy than of firmness; and more incapacity than of all the rest which I mentioned before" (*Memoirs*, vol. i. p. 247).

[*] Cardinal Mazarin, who, during a few of the latter years of his life, governed France. He died at Vincennes the 9th of March 1661, aged fifty-nine, leaving as heir to his name and property the Marquis de la Meilleraye, who married his niece, and took the title of Duke of Mazarin. On his death, Louis XIV. and the court appeared in mourning, an honour not common, though Henry IV. had shown it to the memory of Gabrielle d'Estrées. Voltaire, who appears unwilling to ascribe much ability to the Cardinal, takes an opportunity, on occasion of his death, to make the following observation: "We cannot refrain from combating the opinion, which supposes prodigious abilities, and a genius

furnished by his authority, and the situation in which
he was placed. His whole pursuit was gain. He was
naturally fond of gaming; but he only played to enrich
himself, and therefore, whenever he found an opportunity, he cheated.

As he found the Chevalier de Gramont possessed a
great deal of wit, and a great deal of money, he was
a man according to his wishes, and soon became one
of his set. The Chevalier soon perceived the artful-
ness and dishonesty of the Cardinal, and thought it
was allowable in him to put in practice those talents
which he had received from nature, not only in his
own defence, but even to attack him whenever an
opportunity offered. This would certainly be the place
to mention these particulars; but who can describe
them with such ease and elegance as may be expected
by those who have heard his own relation of them?
Vain is the attempt to endeavour to transcribe these
entertaining anecdotes : their spirit seems to evaporate
upon paper; and in whatever light they are exposed
the delicacy of their colouring and their beauty is lost.

It is then enough to say, that upon all occasions
where address was reciprocally employed, the Chevalier gained the advantage; and that if he paid his court
badly to the minister, he had the consolation to find,
that those who suffered themselves to be cheated, in
the end gained no great advantage from their complaisance; for they always continued in an abject submission, while the Chevalier de Gramont, on a thou-

almost divine, in those who have governed empires with some
degree of success. It is not a superior penetration that makes
statesmen; it is their character. All men, how inconsiderable
soever their share of sense may be, see their own interest nearly
alike. A citizen of Bern or Amsterdam, in this respect, is equal
to Sejanus, Ximenes, Buckingham, Richelieu, or Mazarin; but
our conduct and our enterprises depend absolutely on our natural
dispositions, and our success depends upon fortune" (*Age of
Louis XIV*. chap. v.).

The Chevalier was so agreeable and diverting, that he made his mistress almost die with laughing.

—p. 38

From the painting by C. Delort.

sand different occasions, never put himself under the
least restraint, of which the following is one instance:

The Spanish army, commanded by the Prince de
Condé and the Archduke,[5] besieged Arras. The Court
was advanced as far as Peronne.[6] The enemy, by the
capture of this place, would have procured a reputation for their army of which they were in great need;
as the French, for a considerable time past, had evinced
a superiority in every engagement.

The Prince supported a tottering party, as far as
their usual inactivity and irresolution permitted him;
but as in the events of war it is necessary to act in-
dependently on some occasions, which, if once suffered
to escape, can never be retrieved, for want of this
power it frequently happened that his great abilities
were of no avail. The Spanish infantry had never
recovered itself since the battle of Rocroi;[7] and he
who had ruined them by that victory, by fighting
against them, was the only man who now, by commanding their army, was capable of repairing the
mischief he had done them. But the jealousy of the
generals, and the distrust attendant upon their counsels, tied up his hands.

Nevertheless, the siege of Arras[8] was vigorously
carried on. The Cardinal was very sensible how dishonourable it would be to suffer this place to be taken
under his nose, and almost in sight of the King. On

[5] Leopold, brother of the Emperor Ferdinand III.
[6] A small town, standing among marshes on the river Somme,
in Picardy.
[7] This famous battle was fought and won 19th May 1643, five
days after the death of Louis XIII.
[8] Voltaire observes, that it was the fortune of Turenne and
Condé to be always victorious when they fought at the head of
the French, and to be vanquished when they commanded the
Spaniards. This was Condé's fate before Arras, 25th August 1654,
when he and the Archduke besieged that city. Turenne attacked
them in their camp, and forced their lines: the troops of the
Archduke were cut to pieces; and Condé, with two regiments

the other hand, it was very hazardous to attempt its relief, the Prince de Condé being a man who never neglected the smallest precaution for the security of his lines; and if lines are attacked and not forced, the greatest danger threatens the assailants, for, the more furious the assault, the greater is the disorder in the retreat; and no man in the world knew so well as the Prince de Condé how to make the best use of an advantage. The army, commanded by Monsieur de Turenne, was considerably weaker than that of the enemy; it was, likewise, the only resource they had to depend upon. If this army was defeated, the loss of Arras was not the only misfortune to be dreaded.

The Cardinal, whose genius was happily adapted to such junctures, where deceitful negotiations could extricate him out of difficulties, was filled with terror at the sight of imminent danger, or of a decisive event. He was of opinion to lay siege to some other place, the capture of which might prove an indemnification for the loss of Arras; but Monsieur de Turenne, who was altogether of a different opinion from the Cardinal, resolved to march towards the enemy, and did not acquaint him with his intentions until he was upon his march. The courier arrived in the midst of his distress, and redoubled his apprehensions and alarms; but there was then no remedy.

The Marshal, whose great reputation had gained him the confidence of the troops, had determined upon his measures before an express order from the Court could prevent him. This was one of those occasions

of French and Lorrainers, alone sustained the efforts of Turenne's army; and, while the Archduke was flying, he repulsed the Marshal de la Ferté, and retreated victoriously himself, by covering the retreat of the vanquished Spaniards. The King of Spain, in his letter to him after this engagement, had these words: " I have been informed that everything was lost, and that you have recovered everything."

in which the difficulties you encounter heighten the glory of success. Though the general's capacity, in some measure, afforded comfort to the Court, they nevertheless were upon the eve of an event, which in one way or other must terminate both their hopes and their fears. While the rest of the courtiers were giving various opinions concerning the issue, the Chevalier de Gramont determined to be an eye-witness of it; a resolution which greatly surprised the Court; for those who had seen as many actions as he had, seemed to be exempted from such eagerness; but it was in vain that his friends opposed his resolutions.

The King was pleased with his intention; and the Queen appeared no less satisfied. He assured her that he would bring her good news; and she promised to embrace him, if he was as good as his word. The Cardinal made the same promise. To the latter, however, he did not pay much attention; yet he believed it sincere, because the keeping of it would cost him[9] nothing.

He set out in the dusk of the evening with Caseau, whom Monsieur de Turenne[10] had sent express to their Majesties. The Duke of York,[11] and the Marquis d'Humières,[12] commanded under the Marshal. The

[9] The Cardinal.

[10] Vicomte de Turenne, the great French Commander, born in 1611, is perhaps most famous for his extraordinary campaign in Alsace in 1674-75. His defence of the frontiers of the Rhine showed his remarkable genius as a tactician. The spot where he was struck down by a spent cannon-ball at the battle of Sassbach in the Grand-Duchy of Baden (on 27th July 1675) is marked by a monument.

[11] Priorato, in his *Memoirs of Cardinal Mazarin*, mentions other Englishmen besides the Duke of York being present; as Lords Gerrard, Barclay, and Jermyn, with others (*Memoirs*, 12mo, 1673, vol. i. part iii. p. 365).

[12] Marshal d'Humières, *b.* 1628, *ob.* 1694. Voltaire says of him, that he was the first who, at the siege of Arras, in 1658, was served on silver in the trenches, and had ragoûts and entremets served up to his table.

latter was upon duty when the Chevalier arrived, it being scarce daylight. The Duke of York did not at first recollect him; but the Marquis d'Humières, running to him with open arms, "I thought," said he, "if any man came from Court to pay us a visit upon such an occasion as this, it would be the Chevalier de Gramont. Well," continued he, "what are they doing at Peronne?" "They are in great consternation," replied the Chevalier. "And what do they think of us?" "They think," said he, "that if you beat the Prince, you will do no more than your duty; if you are beaten, they will think you fools and madmen, thus to have risked everything, without considering the consequences." "Truly," said the Marquis, "you bring us very comfortable news. Will you now go to Monsieur de Turenne's quarters, to acquaint him with it; or will you choose rather to repose yourself in mine, for you have been riding post all last night, and perhaps did not experience much rest in the preceding?" "Where have you heard that the Chevalier de Gramont had ever any occasion for sleep?" replied he. "Only order me a horse, that I may have the honour to attend the Duke of York; for, most likely, he is not in the field so early, except to visit some posts."

The advanced guard was only at cannon-shot from that of the enemy. As soon as they arrived there, "I should like," said the Chevalier de Gramont, "to advance as far as the sentry which is posted on that eminence. I have some friends and acquaintance in their army, whom I should wish to inquire after: I hope the Duke of York will give me permission." At these words he advanced. The sentry, seeing him come forward directly to his post, stood upon his guard. The Chevalier stopped as soon as he was within shot of him. The sentry answered the sign which was

made to him, and made another to the officer, who had
begun to advance as soon as he had seen the Chevalier
come forward, and was soon up with him; but seeing
the Chevalier de Gramont alone, he made no difficulty
to let him approach. He desired leave of this officer
to inquire after some relations he had in their army,
and at the same time asked if the Duke d'Arscot was at
the siege. "Sir," said he, "there he is, just alighted
under those trees, which you see on the left of our
grand guard: it is hardly a minute since he was here
with the Prince d'Aremberg, his brother, the Baron
de Limbec, and Louvigny." "May I see them upon
parole?" said the Chevalier. "Sir," said he, "if I were
allowed to quit my post, I would do myself the honour
of accompanying you thither; but I will send to
acquaint them that the Chevalier de Gramont desires
to speak to them." And, after having despatched one
of his guard towards them, he returned. "Sir," said
the Chevalier de Gramont, "may I take the liberty to
inquire how I came to be known to you?" "Is it possible," said the other, "that the Chevalier de Gramont
should forget La Motte, who had the honour to serve
so long in his regiment?" "What! is it you my good
friend La Motte? Truly, I was to blame for not
remembering you, though you are in a dress very different from that which I first saw you in at Brussels,
when you taught the Duchess of Guise to dance the
'triolets'; and I am afraid your affairs are not in so
flourishing a condition as they were the campaign after
I had given you the company you mention." They
were talking in this manner, when the Duke d'Arscot,
followed by the gentlemen above mentioned, came up
on full gallop. The Chevalier de Gramont was saluted
by the whole company before he could say a word.
Soon after arrived an immense number of others of
his acquaintance, with many people out of curiosity

on both sides, who seeing him upon the eminence, assembled together with the greatest eagerness; so that the two armies, without design, without truce, and without fraud, were going to join in conversation, if, by chance, Monsieur de Turenne had not perceived it at a distance. The sight surprised him. He hastened that way; and the Marquis d'Humières acquainted him with the arrival of the Chevalier de Gramont, who wished to speak to the sentry before he went to the headquarters. He added, that he could not comprehend how the devil he had managed to assemble both armies around him, for it was hardly a minute since he had left him. "Truly," said Monsieur de Turenne, "he is a very extraordinary man; but it is only reasonable that he should let us now have a little of his company, since he has paid his first visit to the enemy." At these words he despatched an aide-de-camp, to recall the officers of his army, and to acquaint the Chevalier de Gramont with his impatience to see him.

This order arrived at the same time, with one of the same nature, to the enemy's officers. The Prince de Condé being informed of this peaceable interview, was not the least surprised at it, when he heard that it was occasioned by the arrival of the Chevalier de Gramont. He only gave Lussan orders to recall the officers, and to desire the Chevalier to meet him at the same place the next day; which the Chevalier promised to do, provided Monsieur de Turenne should approve of it, as he made no doubt he would.

His reception in the King's army was equally agreeable as that which he had experienced from the enemy. Monsieur de Turenne esteemed him no less for his frankness than for the poignancy of his wit. He took it very kindly that he was the only courtier who came to see him in a time so critical as the present: the ques-

tions which he asked him about the Court were not so
much for information, as to divert himself with his
manner of relating their different apprehensions and
alarms. The Chevalier de Gramont advised him to
beat the enemy, if he did not choose to be answerable
for an enterprise which he had undertaken without
consulting the Cardinal. Monsieur de Turenne promised him he would exert himself to the utmost to follow his advice, and assured him, that if he succeeded,
he would make the Queen keep her word with him;
and concluded with saying, that he was not sorry the
Prince de Condé had expressed a desire to see him.
His measures were taken for an attack upon the lines:
on this subject he discoursed in private with the Chevalier de Gramont, and concealed nothing from him except the time of execution; but this was all to no
purpose, for the Chevalier had seen too much, not to
judge, from his own knowledge, and the observations
he had made, that from the situation of the army, the
attack could be no longer deferred.

He set out the next day for his rendezvous, attended
by a trumpet, and found the Prince at the place which
Monsieur de Lussan had described to him the evening
before. As soon as he alighted: "Is it possible," said
the Prince, embracing him, "that this can be the Chevalier de Gramont, and that I should see him in the
contrary party?" "It is you, my lord, whom I see
there," replied the Chevalier, "and I refer it to yourself, whether it was the fault of the Chevalier de
Gramont, or your own, that we now embrace different
interests." "I must confess," said the Prince, "that if
there are some who have abandoned me like base, ungrateful wretches, you have left me, as I left myself,
like a man of honour, who thinks himself in the right.
But let us forget all cause of resentment, and tell me
what was your motive for coming here, you, whom I

thought at Peronne with the Court?" "Must I tell you?" said he:[13] "why, faith then, I came to save your life. I know that you cannot help being in the midst of the enemy in a day of battle; it is only necessary for your horse to be shot under you, and to be taken in arms, to meet with the same treatment from this Cardinal as your uncle Montmorency[14] did from the other. I come, therefore, to hold a horse in readiness for you in case of a similar misfortune, that you may not lose your head." "It is not the first time," said the Prince, smiling, "that you have rendered me this service, though the being taken prisoner at that time could not have been so dangerous to me as now."

From this conversation they passed to more entertaining subjects. The Prince asked him many questions concerning the Court, the ladies, play, and about his amours; and returning insensibly to the present situation of affairs, the Chevalier having inquired after some officers of his acquaintance, who had remained with him, the Prince told him that if he chose he might go to the lines, where he would have an opportunity not only of seeing those whom he inquired after, but likewise the disposition of the quarters and entrenchments. To this he consented, and the Prince having shown him all the works and attended him back to their rendezvous, "Well, Chevalier," said he, "when do you think we shall see you again?" "Faith," replied he, "you have used me so handsomely, that I shall conceal nothing from you. Hold yourself in readiness an hour before daybreak; for, you may depend upon it, we shall attack you to-morrow morning. I would not have acquainted you with this, perhaps, had I been entrusted with the secret, but, nevertheless, in the pres-

[13] Gramont.

[14] Henry, Duke of Montmorency, who was taken prisoner 1st September 1692, and had his head struck off at Toulouse in the month of November following.

ent case you may believe me." "You are still the same man," said the Prince, again embracing him. The Chevalier returned to Monsieur de Turenne's camp towards night; every preparation was then making for the attack of the lines, and it was no longer a secret among the troops.

"Well, Monsieur le Chevalier, were they all very glad to see you?" said Monsieur de Turenne; "the Prince, no doubt, received you with the greatest kindness, and asked a great number of questions?" "He showed me all the civility imaginable," replied the Chevalier; "and, to convince me he did not take me for a spy, he led me round the lines and entrenchments, and showed me the preparations he had made for your reception." "And what is his opinion?" said the Marshal.

"He is persuaded that you will attack him to-night, or to-morrow by daybreak; for you great captains," continued the Chevalier, "see through each other's designs in a wonderful manner."

Monsieur de Turenne with pleasure received this commendation from a man who was not indiscriminately accustomed to bestow praise. He communicated to him the disposition of the attack; and at the same time acquainted him that he was very happy that a man who had seen so many actions was to be present at this; and that he esteemed it no small advantage to have the benefit of his advice; but as he believed that the remaining part of the night would be hardly sufficient for his repose, after having passed the former without any refreshment, he consigned him to the Marquis d'Humières, who provided him with a supper and a lodging.

The next day the lines of Arras were attacked, wherein Monsieur de Turenne, being victorious, added additional lustre to his former glory; and the Prince de

Condé, though vanquished, lost nothing of his former reputation.

There are so many accounts of this celebrated battle, that to mention it here would be altogether superfluous. The Chevalier de Gramont, who, as a volunteer, was permitted to go into every part, has given a better description of it than any other person. Monsieur de Turenne reaped great advantage from that activity which never forsook the Chevalier either in peace or war; and that presence of mind which enabled him to carry orders, as coming from the General, so very àpropos, that Monsieur de Turenne, otherwise very particular in such matters, thanked him, when the battle was over, in the presence of all his officers, and despatched him to Court with the first news of his success.

All that is generally necessary in these expeditions is to be accustomed to hard riding, and to be well provided with fresh horses, but he had a great many other obstacles to surmount. In the first place, the parties of the enemy were dispersed over all the country, and obstructed his passage. Then he had to prepare against greedy and officious courtiers, who, on such occasions, post themselves in all the roads, in order to cheat the poor courier out of his news. However, his address preserved him from the one, and deceived the others.

He had taken eight or ten troopers, commanded by an officer of his acquaintance, to escort him half way to Bapaume,[15] being persuaded that the greatest danger would lie between the camp and the first stage. He had not proceeded a league before he was convinced of the truth of what he suspected, and turning to the

[15] A fortified town in Artois, seated in a barren country, without rivers or springs, and having an old palace, which gave rise to the town, with a particular governor of its own, a royal and forest court. In 1641 the French took it from the Spaniards.

officer, who followed him closely, "If you are not well mounted," said he, "I would advise you to return to the camp; for my part, I shall set spurs to my horse, and make the best of my way." "Sir," said the officer, "I hope I shall be able to keep you company, at whatever rate you go, until you are out of all danger." "I doubt that," replied the Chevalier, "for those gentlemen there seem prepared to pay us a visit." "Don't you see," said the officer, "they are some of our own people who are grazing their horses?" "No," said the Chevalier; "but I see very well that they are some of the enemy's troopers." Upon which, observing to him that they were mounting, he ordered the horsemen that escorted him to prepare themselves to make a diversion, and he himself set off full speed towards Bapaume.

He was mounted upon a very swift English horse; but having entangled himself in a hollow way where the ground was deep and miry, he soon had the troopers at his heels, who, supposing him to be some officer of rank, would not be deceived, but continued to pursue him, without paying any attention to the others. The best mounted of the party began to draw near him; for the English horses, swift as the wind on even ground, proceeded but very indifferently in bad roads; the trooper presented his carbine, and cried out to him, at some distance, "Good quarter." The Chevalier de Gramont, who perceived that they gained upon him and that whatever efforts his horse made in such heavy ground, he must be overtaken at last, immediately quitted the road to Bapaume, and took a causeway to the left, which led quite a different way. As soon as he had gained it, he drew up, as if to hear the proposal of the trooper, which afforded his horse an opportunity of recovering; while his enemy, mistaking his intention, and thinking that he only waited to surrender, immediately exerted every effort, that he might take him before the rest of his companions, who were following, could arrive, and by this means almost killed his horse.

One minute's reflection made the Chevalier consider what a disagreeable adventure it would be, thus coming from so glorious a victory, and the dangers of a battle so warmly disputed, to be taken by a set of scoundrels who had not been in it, and, instead of being received in triumph, and embraced by a great queen for the important news with which he was charged, to see himself stripped by the vanquished.

During this short meditation, the trooper who followed him was arrived within shot, and still presenting his carbine, offered him good quarter, but the Chevalier de Gramont, to whom this offer, and the manner in which it was made, were equally displeasing, made a sign to him to lower his piece; and perceiving his horse to be in wind, he lowered his hand, rode off like lightning, and left the trooper in such astonishment that he even forgot to fire at him.

As soon as he arrived at Bapaume, he changed horses; the commander of this place showed him the greatest respect, assuring him that no person had yet passed; that he would keep the secret, and that he would retain all that followed him, except the couriers of Monsieur de Turenne.

He now had only to guard against those who would be watching for him about the environs of Peronne, to return as soon as they saw him, and carry his news to Court, without being acquainted with any of the particulars. He knew very well that Marshal du Plessis, Marshal de Villeroy, and Gaboury, had boasted of this to the Cardinal before his departure. Wherefore, to elude this snare, he hired two well-mounted horsemen at Bapaume, and as soon as he had got a league from that place, and after giving them each two louis d'ors, to secure their fidelity, he ordered them to ride on before, to appear very much terrified, and to tell all those who should ask them any questions, "that all was lost; that the Chevalier de Gramont had stopped at Bapaume, having no great inclination to be the messenger of ill news; and that as for themselves, they had been pursued by the enemy's troopers, who were spread over the whole country since the defeat."

Everything succeeded to his wish: the horsemen were intercepted by Gaboury, who in his eagerness had outstripped the two marshals; but whatever questions were asked them, they acted their parts so well, that Peronne was already in consternation, and rumours of the defeat were whispered among the courtiers, when the Chevalier de Gramont arrived.

Nothing so enhances the value of good news as when a false alarm of bad has preceded; yet, though the Chevalier's was accompanied with this advantage, none but their Majesties received it with that transport of joy it deserved.

The Queen kept her promise to him in the most fascinating manner: she embraced him before the whole Court; the King appeared no less delighted; but the Cardinal, whether with the view of lessening the merit of an action which deserved a handsome reward, or whether it was from a return of that insolence which always accompanied him in prosperity, appeared at first not to pay any attention to what he said, and being afterwards informed that the lines had been forced, that the Spanish army was beaten, and that Arras was relieved: "Is the Prince de Condé taken?" said he. "No," replied the Chevalier de Gramont. "He is dead, then, I suppose?" said the Cardinal. "Not so, neither," answered the Chevalier. "Fine news indeed!" said the Cardinal, with an air of contempt; and at these words he went into the Queen's cabinet with their Majesties. And happy it was for the Chevalier that he did so, for without doubt he would have given him some severe reply,[16] in resentment for those two fine questions, and the conclusion he had drawn from them.

The Court was filled with the Cardinal's spies: the Chevalier, as is usual on such an occasion, was surrounded by a crowd of courtiers and inquisitive people, and he was very glad to ease himself of some part of the load which laid heavy on his heart, within the hearing of the Cardinal's creatures, and which he would perhaps have told him to his face. "Faith, gentlemen," said he, with a sneer, "there is nothing like being zealous and eager in the service of kings and great princes: you have seen what a gracious reception his Majesty has given me; you are likewise witnesses in what an obliging manner the Queen kept her promise with me, but as for the Cardinal, he has received my news as if he gained no more by it than he did by the death of Peter Mazarin.'"[17]

This was sufficient to terrify all those who were sincerely attached to him; and the best established fortune would have been ruined at some period by a jest much less severe; for it was delivered in the presence of witnesses, who were only desirous of having an opportunity of representing it in its utmost malignancy, to make a merit of their vigilance with a power-

[16] This spirit seems not always to have attended him in his transactions with the Cardinal. On occasion of the entry of the King in 1660, " Le Chevalier de Gramont, Rouville, Bellefonds, and some other courtiers, attended in the Cardinal's suite, a degree of flattery which astonished everybody who knew him. I was informed that the Chevalier wore a very rich orange coloured dress on that occasion" (*Letters de Maintenon*, vol. i. p. 32).

[17] Peter Mazarin was the Cardinal's father. He was a native of Palermo in Sicily, which place he left in order to settle at Rome, where he died in the year 1654.

ful and absolute minister. Of this the Chevalier de
Gramont was thoroughly convinced; yet whatever
detriment he foresaw might arise from it, he could
not help being much pleased with what he had said.

The spies very faithfully discharged their duty;
however, the affair took a very different turn from
what they expected. The next day, when the Chevalier
de Gramont was present while their Majesties were at
dinner, the Cardinal came in, and coming up to him,
everybody making way for him out of respect: "Chevalier," said he, "the news which you have brought is
very good; their Majesties are very well satisfied with
it; and to convince you it is more advantageous to
me than the death of Peter Mazarin, if you will come
and dine with me we will have some play together;
for the Queen will give us something to play for, over
and above her first promise."

In this manner did the Chevalier de Gramont dare
to provoke a powerful minister, and this was all the
resentment which the least vindictive of all statesmen
expressed on the occasion. It was indeed very unusual for so young a man to reverence the authority
of ministers no farther than as they were themselves
respectable by their merit; for this his own breast, as
well as the whole Court, applauded him, and he enjoyed the satisfaction of being the only man who durst
preserve the least shadow of liberty in a general state
of servitude. But it was perhaps owing to the Cardinal's passing over this insult with impunity, that he
afterwards drew upon himself some difficulties, by
other rash expressions less fortunate in the event.

In the meantime, the Court returned. The Cardinal,
who was sensible that he could no longer keep his
master in a state of tutelage—being himself worn
out with cares and sickness, and having amassed treasures he knew not what to do with, and being suffi-

ciently loaded with the weight of public odium,—
turned all his thoughts towards terminating, in a manner the most advantageous for France, a ministry
which had so cruelly shaken that kingdom. Thus,
while he was earnestly laying the foundations of a
peace so ardently wished for, pleasure and plenty
began to reign at Court.

The Chevalier de Gramont experienced for a long
time a variety of fortune in love and gaming: he was
esteemed by the courtiers, beloved by beauties whom
he neglected, and a dangerous favourite of those whom
he admired; more successful in play than in his
amours; but the one indemnifying him for want of
success in the other, he was always full of life and
spirits; and in all transactions of importance, always a
man of honour.

It is a pity that we must be forced here to interrupt
the course of his history, by an interval of some years,
as has been already done at the commencement of
these *Memoirs*. In a life where the most minute
circumstances are always singular and diverting, we
can meet with no chasm which does not afford regret;
but whether he did not think them worthy of holding
a place among his other adventures, or that he has only
preserved a confused idea of them, we must pass to
the parts of these fragments which are better ascer-
tained, that we may arrive at the subject of his journey
to England.

The peace of the Pyrenees,[18] the King's marriage,[19]
the return of the Prince de Condé,[20] and the death of

---

[18] This treaty was concluded 7th November 1659.
[19] Louis XIV. with Maria, the Infanta Theresa of Spain
(daughter of King Philip IV. and Maria-Theresa of Austria, who
was born 20th September 1638, married 1st June 1660, and
entered Paris 26th August following. She died at Versailles 30th
July 1683, and was buried at St. Denis.
[20] 11th April (see De Retz's *Memoirs,* vol. iii. p. 119).

the Cardinal, gave a new face to the State.[21] The eyes
of the whole nation were fixed upon their King, who,
for nobleness of mien, and gracefulness of person, had
no equal; but it was not then known that he was
possessed of those superior abilities, which, filling his
subjects with admiration, in the end made him so
formidable to Europe. Love and ambition, the invis-
ible springs of the intrigues and cabals of all courts,
attentively observed his first steps: pleasure promised
herself an absolute empire over a prince who had been
kept in ignorance of the necessary rules of government,
and ambition had no hopes of reigning in the Court
except in the minds of those who were able to dispute
the management of affairs; when men were surprised
to see the King on a sudden display such brilliant
abilities, which prudence, in some measure necessary,
had so long obliged him to conceal.

An application, inimical to the pleasures which generally attract that age, and which unlimited power very
seldom refuses, attached him solely to the cares of
government. All admired this wonderful change, but
all did not find their account in it: the great lost their
consequence before an absolute master and the courtiers approached with reverential awe the sole object
of their respects and the sole master of their fortunes:
those who had conducted themselves like petty tyrants
in their provinces, and on the frontiers, were now no
more than governors: favours, according to the King's
pleasure, were sometimes conferred on merit, and
sometimes for services done the State; but to impor-
tune, or to menace the Court, was no longer the
method to obtain them.

The Chevalier de Gramont regarded his master's
attention to the affairs of state as a prodigy: he could
not conceive how he could submit at his age to the

[21] *Ob.* 9th March 1661, *aet.* 59.

rules he prescribed himself, or that he should give up
so many hours of pleasure, to devote them to the
tiresome duties and laborious functions of government; but he blessed the Lord that henceforward no
more homage was to be paid, no more court to be
made, but to him alone to whom they were justly due.
Disdaining as he did the servile adoration usually paid
to a minister, he could never crouch before the power
of the two Cardinals who succeeded each other:
he neither worshipped the arbitrary power of the
one, nor gave his approbation to the artifices of the
other; he had never received anything from Cardinal Richelieu but an abbey, which on account of his
rank, could not be refused him; and he never acquired anything from Mazarin but wnat he won of
him at play.

By many years' experience under an able general he
had acquired a talent for war; but this during a general peace was of no further service to him. He therefore thought that, in the midst of a Court flourishing
in beauties and abounding in wealth, he could not
employ himself better than in endeavouring to gain
the good opinion of his master, in making the best
use of those advantages which nature had given him
for play, and in putting in practice new stratagems
in love.

He succeeded very well in the two first of these
projects, and as he had from that time laid it down
as the rule of his conduct to attach himself solely to
the King in all his views of preferment, to have no
regard for favour unless when it was supported by
merit, to make himself beloved by the courtiers and
feared by the minister, to dare to undertake anything
in order to do good, and to engage in nothing at the
expense of innocence, he soon became one in all the
King's parties of pleasure, without gaining the ill-will

of the courtiers. In play he was successful, in love
unfortunate; or, to speak more properly, his restless-
ness and jealousy overcame his natural prudence, in a
situation wherein he had most occasion for it. La
Motte Argencourt[22] was one of the maids of honour to
the Queen Dowager, and though no sparkling beauty,
she had drawn away lovers from the celebrated Méneville.[23] It was sufficient in those days for the King
to cast his eye upon a young lady of the Court to inspire her with hopes, and often with tender sentiments;
but if he spoke to her more than once, the courtiers
took it for granted, and those who had either pretensions to, or love for her, respectfully withdrew both
the one and the other, and afterwards only paid her
respect. But the Chevalier de Gramont thought fit to
act quite otherwise, perhaps to preserve a singularity
of character, which upon the present occasion was of
no avail.

He had never before thought of her, but as soon as
he found that she was honoured with the King's attention, he was of opinion that she was likewise deserving of his. Having attached himself to her, he
soon became very troublesome, without convincing her
he was much in love. She grew weary of his persecutions, but he would not desist, neither on account of her
ill-treatment nor of her threats. This conduct of his
at first made no great noise, because she was in hopes
that he would change his behaviour; but finding him
rashly persist in it, she complained of him; and then it
was that he perceived that if love renders all conditions

[22] Should be La Motte Houdancourt, a niece of Marshal
Houdancourt. Louis XIV. is said to have paid addresses to this
beauty in 1662, with less success than her rival, La Vallière. She
married the Marquis de la Vieuville. Mademoiselle de la Mothe-
Argencourt was the mistress of the Marquis de Richelieu (see
Vizetelly's edition of the *Memoirs,* vol. i. p. 118, note).
[23] Mademoiselle de Méneville, notorious for her gallantries.

equal, it is not so between rivals. He was banished the Court, and not finding any place in France which could console him for what he most regretted—the presence and sight of his Prince—after having made some slight reflections upon his disgrace, and bestowed a few imprecations against her who was the cause of it, he at last formed the resolution of visiting England.

CHAPTER VI

CURIOSITY to see a man equally famous for his crimes and his elevation, had once before induced the Chevalier de Gramont to visit England. Reasons of state assume great privileges. Whatever appears advantageous is lawful, and everything that is necessary is honourable in politics. While the King of England sought the protection of Spain in the Low Countries, and that of the States-General in Holland, other powers sent splendid embassies to Cromwell.

This man, whose ambition had opened him a way to sovereign power by the greatest crimes, maintained himself in it by accomplishments which seemed to render him worthy of it by their lustre. The nation of all Europe the least submissive patiently bore a yoke which did not even leave her the shadow of that liberty of which she is so jealous; and Cromwell, master of the Commonwealth, under the title of Protector, feared at home, but yet more dreaded abroad, was at his highest pitch of glory when he was seen by the Chevalier de Gramont; but the Chevalier did not see any appearance of a court. One part of the nobility proscribed, the other removed from employments; an affectation of purity of manners, instead of the luxury which the pomp of courts displays, all taken together presented nothing but sad and serious objects in the finest city in the world; and therefore the Chevalier acquired nothing by this voyage but the idea of some merit in a profligate man, and the admiration of some concealed beauties he had found means to discover.

Affairs wore quite a different appearance at his second voyage. The joy for the Restoration of the Royal Family still appeared in all parts. The nation, fond of change and novelty, tasted the pleasure of a natural government, and seemed to breathe again after a long oppression. In short, the same people who, by a solemn abjuration, had excluded even the posterity of their lawful sovereign, exhausted themselves in festivals and rejoicings for his return.[1]

The Chevalier de Gramont arrived about two years after the Restoration. The reception he met with in this Court soon made him forget the other; and the engagements he in the end contracted in England lessened the regret he had in leaving France.

This was a desirable retreat for an exile of his disposition. Everything flattered his taste, and if the adventures he had in this country were not the most considerable, they were at least the most agreeable of his life. But before we relate them it will not be improper to give some account of the English Court as it was at that period.

[1] Bishop Burnet confirms this account. " With the restoration of the King," says he, "a spirit of extravagant joy spread over the nation, that brought on with it the throwing off the very professions of virtue and piety. All ended in entertainments and drunkenness which overrun the three kingdoms to such a degree, that it very much corrupted all their morals. Under the colour of drinking the King's health, there were great disorders, and much riot everywhere: and the pretences of religion, both in those of the hypocritical sort, and of the more honest, but no less pernicious enthusiasts, gave great advantages, as well as they furnished much matter to the profane mockers of true piety" (*History of his Own Time,* vol. i. p. 127, 8vo edit.). Voltaire says King Charles "was received at Dover by twenty thousand of his subjects, who fell upon their knees before him; and I have been told by some old men who were of this number, that hardly any of those who were present could refrain from tears" (*Age of Louis XIV.* chap. v.).

The necessity of affairs had exposed Charles II. from his earliest youth to the toils and perils of a bloody war. The fate of the King, his father, had left him for inheritance nothing but his misfortunes and disgraces. They overtook him everywhere; but it was not until he had struggled with his ill-fortune to the last extremity that he submitted to the decrees of Providence.

All those who were either great on account of their birth or their loyalty had followed him into exile; and all the young persons of the greatest distinction having afterwards joined him, composed a Court worthy of a better fate.

Plenty and prosperity, which are thought to tend only to corrupt manners, found nothing to spoil in an indigent and wandering Court. Necessity, on the contrary, which produces a thousand advantages whether we will or no, served them for education; and nothing was to be seen among them but an emulation in glory, politeness, and virtue.

With this little Court, in such high esteem for merit, the King of England returned two years prior to the period we mention, to ascend a throne which, to all appearances, he was to fill as worthily as the most glorious of his predecessors. The magnificence displayed on this occasion was renewed at his coronation.[2]

The death of the Duke of Gloucester,[3] and of the

[2] Pepys gives a graphic account of the Coronation festivities, etc., in his *Diary*, 22nd to 24th April 1661.

[3] Henry, Duke of Gloucester, youngest child of Charles I., born 1640. He died of the smallpox 3rd September 1660, and, according to Pepys, in a great measure owing to the negligence of his doctors. Both the King and his brother James were much affected by his loss. "He was a prince," says James, "of the greatest hopes, undaunted courage, admirable parts, and a clear understanding." He had a particular talent at languages. Besides the Latin, he was master of the French, the Spanish, the Italian, and Low Dutch. He was, in short, possessed of all the natural qualities, as well as acquired accomplishments, necessary to make

Princess Royal,[4] which followed soon after, had interrupted the course of this splendour by a tedious mourning, which the Court quitted at last to prepare for the reception of the Infanta of Portugal.[5]

It was in the height of the rejoicings they were

a great prince (Macpherson's *History of Great Britain,* ch. i.). Bishop Burnet's character of this young prince is also very favourable (see *History of His Own Time,* vol. i. p. 238).

[4] Mary, eldest daughter of Charles I. and mother of William III., born 4th November 1631, married to the Prince of Orange 2nd May 1641, who died 27th October 1650. She arrived in England 23rd September, and died of the smallpox 24th December 1660—according to Burnet, not much lamented. "She had lived," says the Bishop, "in her widowhood for some years with great reputation, kept a decent Court, and supported her brothers very liberally; and lived within bounds. But her mother, who had the art of making herself believe anything she had a mind to, upon a conversation with the Queen Mother of France, fancied the King of France might be inclined to marry her. So she wrote to her to come to Paris. In order to that, she made an equipage far above what she could support. So she ran her self into debt, sold all her jewels, and some estates that were in her power as her son's guardian; and was not only disappointed of that vain expectation, but fell into some misfortunes that lessened the reputation she had formerly lived in" (*History of his Own Time,* vol. i. p. 238).

[5] Catherine of Braganza (*b.* 1638, *ob.* 1705). "The Infanta of Portugal landed 14th May 1662 at Portsmouth. The King went thither, and was married privately by Lord Aubigny, a secular priest, and almoner to the Queen, according to the rites of Rome, in the Queen's chamber; none present but the Portuguese Ambassador, three more Portuguese of quality, and two or three Portuguese women. What made this necessary was that the Earl of Sandwich did not marry her by proxy, as usual, before she came away. How this happened, the Duke knows not, nor did the Chancellor know of this private marriage. The Queen would not be bedded till pronounced man and wife by Sheldon, Bishop of London" (James II.'s Journal; Macpherson's *State Papers,* vol. i.). Though Charles told Colonel Legge that at the first sight of his wife "he thought they had brought him a *bat* instead of a woman," his letter to Lord Clarendon, dated from Portsmouth 21st May, records that he was not unfavourably impressed upon the first meeting. "She hath as much agreeableness in her looks as ever I saw," he says, "and if I have any skill in physiognomy, which I think I have, she must be a good woman as ever was born. Her conversation, as much as I can perceive, is very good; for she has wit enough, and a most

making for this new queen, in all the splendour of a
brilliant court, that the Chevalier de Gramont arrived
to contribute to its magnificence and diversions.[6]

Accustomed as he was to the grandeur of the Court
of France, he was surprised at the politeness and splendour of the Court of England. The King was inferior
to none,[7] either in shape or air; his wit was pleasant;
his disposition easy and affable; his soul, susceptible
of opposite impressions, was compassionate to the un-
happy, inflexible to the wicked, and tender even to
excess; he showed great abilities in urgent affairs,
but was incapable of application to any that were not
so: his heart was often the dupe, but oftener the
slave, of his engagements.

The character of the Duke of York[8] was entirely
different: he had the reputation of undaunted courage,

agreeable voice. You will wonder to see how well we are
acquainted already: in a word, I think myself very happy, for I
am confident our two humours will agree very well together."

In the register of St. Thomas à Becket, Portsmouth, may be
seen the entry of the King's marriage with his Portuguese wife.

[6] Charles and his bride arrived at Hampton Court 29th May
1662, and the Court removed to London probably some time in
June.

[7] Charles II. was born 29th May 1630, and died 6th February
1684-5. His character is very amply detailed and accurately
depicted by George Saville, Marquis of Halifax. See also Evelyn,
Burnet, Clarendon, and Sheffield, Duke of Buckingham, etc.

[8] James, Duke of York, afterwards King James II. He was
born 15th October 1633; succeeded his brother 6th February
1684-5; abdicated the crown in 1688; and died 6th September
1701. Bishop Burnet's character of him appears not very far
from the truth. "He was," says this writer, "very brave in his
youth; and so much magnified by Monsieur Turenne, that till
his marriage lessened him, he really clouded the King, and
passed for the superior genius. He was naturally candid and
sincere, and a firm friend, till affairs and his religion wore out
all his first principles and inclinations. He had a great desire to
understand affairs; and in order to that he kept a constant
journal of all that passed, of which he showed me a great deal.
The Duke of Buckingham gave me once a short but severe
character of the two brothers. It was the more severe, because
it was true; the King (he said) could see things if he would:

an inviolable attachment for his word, great economy in his affairs, hauteur, application, arrogance, each in their turn. A scrupulous observer of the rules of duty and the laws of justice, he was accounted a faithful friend, and an implacable enemy.

His morality and justice, struggling for some time with prejudice, had at last triumphed, by his acknowl- edging for his wife Miss Hyde,[9] maid of honour to the Princess Royal, whom he had secretly married in

and the Duke would see things if he could. He had no true judgment, and was soon determined by those whom he trusted: but he was obstinate against all other advices. He was bred with high notions of kingly authority, and laid it down for a maxim, that all who opposed the King were rebels in their hearts. He was perpetually in one amour or other, without being very nice in his choice: upon which the King once said, he believed his brother had his mistress given him by his priests for penance. He was naturally eager and revengeful: and was against the taking off any that set up in an opposition to the measures of the Court, and who by that means grew popular in the House of Commons. He was for rougher methods. He continued many years dissembling his religion, and seemed zealous for the Church of England, but it was chiefly on design to hinder all propositions that tended to unite us among our- selves. He was a frugal prince, and brought his Court into method and magnificence, for he had £100,000 a year allowed him. He was made High Admiral, and he came to understand all the concerns of the sea very particularly" (*History of his Own Time.*)

[9] Anne Hyde, eldest daughter of Lord Chancellor Clarendon (*b.* 1637, *ob.* 1671). James himself mentions his marriage in these terms: "The King at first refused the Duke of York's marriage with Miss Hyde. Many of the Duke's friends and servants opposed it. The King at last consented, and the Duke of York privately married her, and soon after owned the marriage. Her want of birth was made up by endowments; and her car- riage afterwards became her acquired dignity." Again: "When his sister, the Princess Royal, came to Paris to see the Queen Mother, the Duke of York fell in love with Mrs. Anne Hyde, one of her maids of honour. Besides her person, she had all the qualities proper to inflame a heart less apt to take fire than his; which she managed so well as to bring his passion to such an height, that, between the time he first saw her and the winter before the King's restoration, he resolved to marry none but her; and promised her to do it: and though, at first, when the Duke asked the King his brother for his leave, he refused, and

Holland.   Her father,[10] from that time Prime[11] Minister of England, supported by this new interest, soon rose to the head of affairs, and had almost ruined them: not that he wanted capacity, but he was too self-sufficient.

dissuaded him from it, yet at last he opposed it no more; and the Duke married her privately, owned it some time after, and was ever after a true friend to the Chancellor for several years" (Macpherson's *State Papers*, vol. i.).   Pepys in his *Diary*, 7th October 1660, says: "To my Lord's, and dined with him; he all dinner-time talking French to me, and telling me the story how the Duke of York hath got the Lord Chancellor's daughter with child, and that she do lay it to him, and that for certain he did promise her marriage, and had signed it with his blood, but that he by stealth had got the paper out of her cabinet. And that the King would have him to marry her, but that he will not.   So that the thing is very bad for the Duke and them all; but my Lord do make light of it, as a thing that he believes is not a new thing for the Duke to do abroad."   Again, 23rd February 1660-1: "Mr. Hartlett told me how my Lord Chancellor had lately got the Duke of York and Duchesse and her woman, my Lord Ossory, and a doctor, to make oath before most of the judges of the kingdom, concerning all the circumstances of the marriage.   And in fine, it is confessed that they were not fully married till about a month or two before she was brought to bed; but that they were contracted long before, and time enough for the child to be legitimate.   But I do not hear that it was put to the judges to determine whether it was so or no."   She was contracted to the Duke at Breda, 24th November 1659, and married at Worcester House, 3rd September 1660, in the night, between eleven and two, by Dr. Joseph Crowther, the Duke's chaplain; the Lord Ossory giving her in marriage (Kennet's *Register*, p. 246).

[10] Edward Hyde, Earl of Clarendon (*b*. 1608, *ob*. 1674), "for his comprehensive knowledge of mankind, styled the Chancellor of Human Nature.   His character, at this distance of time, may and ought to be impartially considered.   Designing or blinded contemporaries heaped the most unjust abuse upon him.   The subsequent age, when the partisans of prerogative were at least the loudest, if not the most numerous, smit with a work that deified their martyr, have been unbounded in their encomium" (*Catalogue of Noble Authors*, vol. ii. p. 18).   Lord Orford, who professes to steer a middle course, and separate his great virtues as a man from his faults as an historian, acknowledges that he possessed almost every virtue of a minister which could make his character venerable.

[11] Then already a minister (Vizetelly's translation).

The Duke of Ormonde[12] possessed the confidence and esteem of his master: the greatness of his services, the splendour of his merit and his birth, and the fortune he had abandoned in adhering to the fate of his Prince, rendered him worthy of it: nor durst the courtiers even murmur at seeing him Grand Steward of the Household, First Lord of the Bedchamber, and Lord-Lieutenant of Ireland. He exactly resembled the Marshal de Gramont, in the turn of his wit and the nobleness of his manners, and like him was the honour of his master's court.

The Duke of Buckingham[13] and the Earl of St. Albans[14] were the same in England as they appeared in

[12] James Butler, Duke of Ormonde (b. 1610, ob. 1688). This distinguished Royalist succeeded his grandfather as twelfth Earl in 1632, and was created Duke at the Restoration. During the Civil War he held Ireland for the King when Charles fell into the hands of the Parliament, when he retired to France. Bishop Burnet says of him: "He was a man every way fitted for a court; of a graceful appearance, a lively wit, and a cheerful temper; a man of great expense; decent even in his vices, for he always kept up the form of religion. He had gone through many transactions in Ireland with more fidelity than success. He had made a treaty with the Irish, which was broken by the great body of them, though some few of them adhered still to him. But the whole Irish nation did still pretend, that though they had broke the agreement first, yet he, or rather the King, in whose name he had treated with them, was bound to perform all the articles of the treaty. He had miscarried so in the siege of Dublin, that it very much lessened the opinion of his military conduct. Yet his constant attendance on his master, his easiness to him, and his great suffering for him, raised him to be Lord-Steward of the Household, and Lord-Lieutenant of Ireland. He was firm to the Protestant religion, and so far firm to the laws, that he always gave good advices; but when bad ones were followed, he was not for complaining too much of them" (History of his Own Time, vol. i. p. 230). An interesting detailed account of Ormonde's last days is given by his friend, Sir Robert Southwell (see Hist. MS. Com. Rep. 7, App. pp. 757-758).

[13] "The Duke of Buckingham is again one hundred and forty thousand pounds in debt, and by this prorogation his creditors have time to tear all his lands to pieces" (Andrew Marvell's Works, 4to edit. vol. i. p. 406).

France: the one, full of wit and vivacity, dissipated, without splendour, an immense estate upon which he had just entered: the other, a man of no great genius, had raised himself a considerable fortune from nothing, and by losing at play, and keeping a great table, made it appear greater than it was.

Sir George Berkeley,[15] afterwards Earl of Falmouth,

[14] Henry Jermyn, younger son of Sir Thomas Jermyn, was attached at an early age to the Court of Charles I., and during the Civil War acted as Secretary to the Queen, to whose favour he owed his advancement. In 1643 he was created Baron Jermyn of Bury St. Edmunds, and in the following year was appointed Governor of Jersey. His rival and enemy, Lord Clarendon, records that out of the scanty finances of the exiled court Jermyn managed to live luxuriously. When the young King left France for the Netherlands, Jermyn remained at Paris with the queen mother, to whom, by current report, he was secretly married, and treated far from well (*vide* Pepys, Reresby, and Burnet). In 1660 he was created Earl of St. Albans, and acted as English Ambassador at the Court of France, where he had great influence, and helped in a great measure the secret treaty with Louis XIV. In 1671 he was appointed Lord Chamberlain of the King's Household. Jermyn died at his house in St. James's Square in January 1683-4 (*aet.* about eighty). [This square was originally planned by him.] Evelyn, who saw the Earl a few months before his death, says that though he was nearly blind he was as great a gambler as ever and had to have "some one that sits by him to name the spots on the cards. He ate and drank with extraordinary appetite, though he could not see to take his food" (*vide* Evelyn's *Diary,* 18th August 1683). For many years Cowley acted as his private secretary. Andrew Marvell does not allude to him in flattering terms: he speaks of his "drayman's shoulders and butcher's mien" ("Last Instructions to a Painter," see *Dict. of Nat. Biography.* vol. xxix. pp. 342-344). The old seat of the Jermyns, Rushbrooke Hall, near Bury St. Edmunds, is full of memories of the Stuarts—relics, portraits, etc. The rooms, with their quaint old furniture, are in their original state.

[15] This was not George, but Charles Berkeley, second son of Sir Charles Berkeley (who, like his brother, Sir John Berkeley of Stratton [the author of the *Berkeley Memoirs*] was eminently loyal to Charles I.). He was the principal favourite and companion of the Duke of York in all his campaigns. He was created Baron Berkeley of Rathdown, and Viscount (1663) Fitzharding of Ireland, and Earl of Falmouth in 1665. Lord Clarendon calls him "a fellow of great wickedness," and says, "he was one in

was the confidant and favourite of the King: he commanded the Duke of York's regiment of guards, and governed the Duke himself. He had nothing very remarkable either in his wit or his person; but his sentiments were worthy of the fortune which awaited him, when, on the very point of his elevation, he was killed at sea. Never did disinterestedness so perfectly characterise the greatness of the soul: he had no views but what tended to the glory of his master: his credit was never employed but in advising

whom few other men (except the King) had ever observed any virtue or quality, which they did not wish their best friends without. He was young and of an unsatiable ambition, and a little more experience might have taught him all things which his weak parts were capable of" (Clarendon's *Life*, pp. 34, 267). Bishop Burnet is rather more favourable. "Berkeley," says he, "was generous in his expense; and it was thought if he had outlived the lewdness of that time and come to a more sedate course of life, he would have put the King on great and noble designs" (*History*, vol. i. p. 137). While Pepys says he owed his greatness to being "a pimp to the King and my Lady Castlemaine," being able to bring the former to the latter from the Council Chamber whenever he pleased (*Diary*, 15th Dec. 1662 and 31st July 1663). He lost his life in the action at Southwold Bay, 2nd June 1665 by a shot, which, at the same time, killed Lord Muskerry and Mr. Boyle, as they were standing on the quarter-deck, near the Duke of York. Pepys thus records the fact: "The Earl of Falmouth, Muskerry, and Mr. Boyle killed on board the Duke's ship, *The Royal Charles*, with one shot; their blood and brains flying in the Duke's face, and the head of Mr. Boyle striking down the Duke as some say" (*Diary*, 8th June 1665). "He was," says Clarendon, "lamented by the King with floods of tears, to the amazement of all who had seen how unshaken he stood on other assaults of fortune" (*Clarendon's Life*, p. 269). Even his death did not save him from Marvell's satire.

> "Falmouth was there, I know not what to act,
> Some say, 'twas to grow duke too by contract;
> An untaught bullet, in its wanton scope,
> Dashes him all to pieces, and his hope:
> Such was his rise, such was his fall unpraised,—
> A chance shot sooner took him than chance raised;
> His shattered head the fearless duke disdains,
> And gave the last first proof that he had brains."
> *Advice to a Painter*, p. 1.

him to reward services, or to confer favours on merit: so polished in conversation, that the greater his power, the greater was his humility; and so sincere in all his proceedings, that he would never have been taken for a courtier.

The Duke of Ormonde's sons and his nephews had been in the King's Court during his exile, and were far from diminishing its lustre after his return. The Earl of Arran[16] had a singular address in all kinds of exercises, played well at tennis and on the guitar, and was pretty successful in gallantry. His elder brother, the Earl of Ossory,[17] was not so lively, but of the most liberal sentiments, and of great brobity.

[16] Richard Butler, Earl of Arran, fifth son of James Butler, the first Duke of Ormonde (*b.* 1639, *ob.* 1686). Created Earl of Arran 1662. He married in 1664 Lady Mary Stuart, only surviving daughter of James, Duke of Richmond and Lennox, by Mary, only daughter of the great Duke of Buckingham (she died three years later, aged 18). In 1673 he married, secondly, Dorothy, daughter of John Ferrers of Tamworth. His only daughter, Charlotte, married Charles, Lord Cornwallis. Pepys speaks of his "glorious dancing" at the masquerade of 2nd February 1664 (*vide* chap. vii. of these *Memoirs*), when the Earl of Mulgrave was disgraced for paying his addresses to the Princess Anne, of whom he was also an admirer (vide *Hist. MS. Com. Rep.* 7, App. p. 480).

[17] Thomas, Earl of Ossory, eldest son of the first, and father of the last Duke of Ormonde (*b.* 1634, *ob.* 1680). At the age of twenty-one years he had so much distinguished himself that Sir Robert Southwell then drew the following character of him: "He is a young man with a very handsome face; a good head of hair; well set; very good natured; rides the great horse very well; is a very good tennis-player, fencer, and dancer; understands music, and plays on the guitar and lute; speaks French elegantly; reads Italian fluently; is a good historian; and so well versed in romances that if a gallery be full of pictures and hangings he will tell the stories of all that are there described. He shuts up his door at eight o'clock in the evening and studies till midnight: he is temperate, courteous, and excellent in all his behaviour. Lord Ossory married in 1659 Emilie de Nassau, eldest daughter of Louis de Nassau, Lord Beverwaert, in Holland, the illegitimate son of Maurice, Prince of Orange. Her sister married Lord Arlington.

The elder of the Hamiltons,[18] their cousin, was the man who of all the Court dressed best: he was well made in his person, and possessed those happy talents which lead to fortune, and procure success in love: he was a most assiduous courtier, had the most lively wit, the most polished manners, and the most punctual attention to his master imaginable. No person danced better, nor was any one a more general lover: a merit of some account in a court entirely devoted to love and gallantry.

It is not at all surprising, that with these qualities he succeeded my Lord Falmouth in the King's favour; but it is very extraordinary that he should have experienced the same destiny, as if this sort of war had been declared against merit only, and as if this sort of combat was fatal to none but such as had certain hopes of a splendid fortune. This, however, did not happen till some years afterwards.

The beau Sidney,[19] less dangerous than he appeared to be, had not sufficient vivacity to support the impression which his figure made; but little Jermyn was on all sides successful in his intrigues. The old Earl of St. Albans, his uncle, had for a long time adopted him, though the youngest of all his nephews. It is well known what a table the good[20] man kept at Paris, while the King, his master, was starving at Brussels,

[18] James Hamilton, eldest son of Sir George Hamilton. He and his younger brother George are the two Hamiltons who figure in the *Memoirs*. *Ob.* 1673, *vide* Prefatory Notice.

[19] Henry Sidney (*ob.* 1704), youngest son of Robert Sidney, second Earl of Leicester, and brother of Algernon and Colonel Robert (the reputed father of the Duke of Monmouth [vide *King Monmouth*]). He attended Charles II. in exile, and was Master of the Horse to Anne Hyde, Duchess of York. He was created Earl of Romney in 1694 (*vide* his *Diary and Correspondence*, 1843). Burnet says he was much addicted to pleasure, and that some of his adventures became very public.

[20] *Old*, not good (Vizetelly's translation).

and the Queen Dowager, his mistress,[21] lived not over
well in France.

160795

[21] To what a miserable state the Queen was reduced may be
seen in the following extract from De Retz: "Four or five
days before the King removed from Paris, I went to visit the
Queen of England, whom I found in her daughter's chamber, who
hath been since Duchess of Orleans. At my coming in she said:
'You see I am come to keep Henrietta company. The poor
child could not rise to-day for want of a fire.' The truth is, that
the Cardinal for six months together had not ordered her any
money towards her pension; that no tradespeople would trust
her for anything; and that there was not at her lodgings in the
Louvre one single billet. You will do me the justice to suppose
that the Princess of England did not keep her bed the next day
for want of a faggot; but it was not this which the Princess
of Condé meant in her letter. What she spoke about was, that
some days after my visiting the Queen of England, I remembered the condition I had found her in, and had strongly represented the shame of abandoning her in that manner, which caused
the Parliament to send 40,000 livres to Her Majesty. Posterity
will hardly believe that a Princess of England, granddaughter
of Henry the Great, had wanted a faggot, in the month of
January, to get out of bed in the Louvre, and in the eyes of a
French court. We read in histories, with horror, of baseness less
monstrous than this; and the little concern I have met with
about it in most people's minds has obliged me to make, I believe,
a thousand times, this reflection: that examples of times past
move men beyond comparison more than those of their own
times. We accustom ourselves to what we see; and I have
sometimes told you, that I doubted whether Caligula's horse
being made a consul would have surprised us so much as we
imagine" (*Memoirs*, vol. i. p. 261). As for the relative situation
of the King and Lord Jermyn (afterwards St. Albans), Lord
Clarendon says, that the "Marquis of Ormonde was compelled
to put himself in prison, with other gentlemen, at a pistole a
week for his diet, and to walk the streets a-foot, which was no
honourable custom in Paris, whilst the Lord Jermyn kept an
excellent table for those who courted him, and had a coach of
his own, and all other accommodations incident to the most full
fortune: and if the King had the most urgent occasion for the
use but of twenty pistoles, as sometimes he had, he could not
find credit to borrow it, which he often had experiment of"
(*History of the Rebellion*, vol. iii. p. 2). Lord Dartmouth, in a
note to Burnet's *History of his Own Time*, mentions a story of
how the Duke of Hamilton was upon one occasion an unwilling
witness to some love passage between Jermyn and the Queen,
and in an old MS. volume in the possession of the Earl of
Egmont is the following curious entry: "*Queen Henrietta Maria*

Jermyn,[22] supported by his uncle's wealth, found it no difficult matter to make a considerable figure upon his arrival at the Court of the Princess of Orange: the poor courtiers of the King her brother could not vie with him in point of equipage and magnificence; and these two articles often produce as much success in love as real merit.   There is no necessity for any other example than the present; for though Jermyn was brave, and certainly a gentleman, yet he had neither brilliant actions nor distinguished rank to set him off; and as for his figure, there was nothing advantageous in it.   He was little: his head was large and his legs small; his features were not disagreeable, but he was affected in his carriage and behaviour.   All his wit consisted in expressions learnt by rote, which he occasionally employed either in raillery or in love. This was the whole foundation of the merit of a man so formidable in amours.

—Thomas Carew, Gentleman of the Privy Chamber, going to light King Charles into her chamber, saw Jermyn, Lord St. Albans, with his arm round her neck; he stumbled and put out the light; Jermyn escaped; Carew never told the King, and the King never knew it.   The Queen heaped favours on Carew. She quarrelled with Jermyn and tore her will; after reconciliation she made another will in his favour; he brought it to her to sign, but she being asleep he deferred it till the next morning, when she was found dead of a dose of laudanum she had taken, 1669. My authority [says the writer] is old G. Clarke, Esq., formerly Lord of the Admiralty and Secretary to Prince George of Denmark" (*Hist. MS. Com. Rep.* 7, App. p. 244).

As to the Queen Dowager's will, we learn something further from the Verney MSS. W. Denton, writing to Sir Ralph Verney says: "*September* 7, 1669—The night the Queen Mother died she called for her will, said she did not like it, tore off the seals, said she would alter it to-morrow.   She complained much of want of sleep, so an opiate was ordained her, and her physician who watched with her to give or not give it to her, he did not like to give it her, but her impatiency extorted it from him, but she died that night" (*Hist. MS. Com. Rep.* 7, App. p. 448).

[22] Henry Jermyn, first Baron Dover, second son of Thomas Jermyn of Rushbrooke Hall, near Bury St. Edmunds, nephew of Henry Jermyn, Earl of St. Albans, and younger brother of

The Princess Royal was the first who was taken with him.[23] Miss Hyde seemed to be following the steps of her mistress: this immediately brought him into credit, and his reputation was established in England before his arrival. Prepossession in the minds of women is sufficient to find access to their hearts; Jermyn found them in dispositions so favourable for him, that he had nothing to do but to speak.

It was in vain they perceived that a reputation so lightly established was still more weakly sustained: the prejudice remained. The Countess of Castlemaine,[24] a woman lively and discerning, followed the delusive shadow; and though undeceived in a reputation which promised so much, and performed so little, she never-

Thomas, who succeeded his uncle as second Baron Jermyn in 1683-4. Attached to the household of the Duke of York prior to the Restoration. Charles II.'s sister Mary, the widowed Princess of Orange, was on such intimate terms with Jermyn that the rumor got abroad that he was secretly married to her as his uncle was said to be to her mother. After the Restoration, when Master of the Horse to the Duke of York, he became notorious for gambling and debauchery. His amorous intrigues are fully dealt with in these *Memoirs*. With the accession of James, he was made Lord-Lieutenant of Cambridgeshire, appointed Privy Councillor and created Baron Dover, and became one of the King's chief Catholic advisers in 1688, when he was entrusted with the care of the little Prince of Wales. At the battle of the Boyne he also commanded a troop for the ab cated King, but was induced eventually to accept overtures from William III., to whom he became reconciled about 1692 (*vide* Evelyn, 7th November 1692). In 1703 he succeeded his brother Thomas, as third Baron Jermyn of Bury St. Edmunds, and died at his country house, Cheveley Park, near Newmarket, where Charles II. occasionally used to stop during the races (vide *King Monmouth*). *Ob.* 1708. He was buried at Bruges. By his wife, Judith Pooley, he had an only daughter, who died young. The peerage therefore became extinct. (See *Dict. of Nat. Biography*, vol. xxix. pp. 344-345).

[23] It was suspected of this princess to have had a similar engagement with the Duke of Buckingham as the Queen with Jermyn, and that was the cause she would not see the Duke on his second voyage to Holland, in the year 1652.

[24] *Vide* her Memoir in the Appendix.

theless continued in her infatuation; she even persisted in it, until she was upon the point of embroiling herself with the King; so great was this first instance of her constancy.

Such were the heroes of the Court. As for the beauties, you could not look anywhere without seeing them: those of the greatest reputation were this same Countess of Castlemaine, afterwards Duchess of Cleveland, Lady Chesterfield, Lady Shrewsbury,[25] Mrs. Roberts, Mrs. Middleton,[26] the Misses Brooke,[27] and a thousand others, who also shone at Court with equal

[25] Anna Maria, Countess of Shrewsbury, eldest daughter of Robert Brudenel, second Earl of Cardigan, and wife of Francis Talbot, eleventh Earl of Shrewsbury, married 10th January 1658-9. The duel in which he was killed by the Duke of Buckingham, 16th January 1667-8, is mentioned later on in the *Memoirs* (see p. 348). After living for some years as the victor's paramour, the Countess married, secondly, in 1680, George Rodney Bridges, Esq. (of Keynsham and Avington), second son of Sir Thomas Bridges (vide *King Monmouth*). A pension of £1600 granted her by Charles II. was stopped in William III.'s reign (see petition of her husband, March 1697, State Papers Dom. Petition Book 20).

By her first husband she had two sons—Charles, afterwards created Duke of Shrewsbury (*ob. s. p.*), and John Talbot, who was killed in a duel, 2nd February 1685, by Henry, Duke of Grafton. By her second husband she left a son George, who died without issue in 1751. He was found drowned in the lake at Avington Park. The old Jacobean mansion of Avington (Hants), which came into the Countess's possession through her second marriage, still retains the "old Banqueting Hall" and "Nell Gwyn's closet," associated with the pleasure visits of the "Merry Monarch."

The Countess of Shrewsbury died in 1702. Her husband survived her eleven years, and was buried in the same grave at St. Giles in the Fields.   [26] See footnote, p. 112.

[27] The three Misses Brooke, Hill, Frances, and Margaret,[1] were the daughters of Sir William Brooke (the grandson of William Brooke, Lord Cobham), *ob.* in Cromwell's service, 30th September 1643. Their mother, Penelope (daughter of Sir Moyses Hill, Kt., of Hillsborough, Co. Down), married, secondly, Hon. Edward Russell, son of Francis, fourth Earl of Bedford. The Earl of Bristol mentioned in the *Memoirs* as having introduced the Misses Brooke to the King (see p. 189) was their stepfather's

[1] She is sometimes named Elizabeth *in error*.

lustre; but it was Miss Hamilton and Miss Stewart
who were its chief ornaments. The new Queen gave
but little additional brilliancy to the Court,[28] either in
her person or in her retinue, which was then composed

brother-in-law, he having married Lady Anne Russell, the Earl
of Bedford's sister.

Hill, the eldest girl, married Sir William Boothby, second Baronet of Ashbourn, Derbyshire; Frances, the second, married Sir
Thomas Whitmore of Buildwas, Salop, second son of Sir Thomas
Whitmore of Apley Park, Stockton, Salop. Frances Whitmore,
the daughter of Lady Whitmore *née* Brooke, married twice, her
second husband being Sir Richard Middleton of Chirk Castle,
Denbighshire (the nephew of the famous Mrs. Middleton's husband). She also was a great beauty (*vide* her full-length portrait
at Hampton Court). Lady Whitmore married, secondly, Mat-
thew Harvey of Twickenham (nephew of the great physician),
where her tomb may be seen bearing the arms of Harvey im-
paling Brooke. The husband survived her and died in 1690.
There is no date of the wife's death.

[28] Lord Clarendon confirms, in some measure, this account.
" There was a numerous family of men and women, that were
sent from Portugal, the most improper to promote that conformity in the Queen that was necessary for her condition and future
happiness that could be chosen; the women, for the most part,
old and ugly, and proud, incapable of any conversation with
persons of quality and a liberal education: and they desired, and
indeed had conspired so far to possess the Queen themselves, that
she should neither learn the English language nor use their habit,
nor depart from the manners and fashions of her own country
in any particulars: which resolution," they told, " would be for
the dignity of Portugal, and would quickly induce the English
ladies to conform to Her Majesty's practice. And this imagination had made that impression, that the tailor who had been sent
into Portugal to make her clothes could never be admitted to
see her or receive any employment. Nor when she came to
Portsmouth, and found there several ladies of honour and prime
quality to attend her in the places to which they were assigned
by the King, did she receive any of them till the King himself
came; nor then with any grace, or the liberty that belonged to
their places and offices. She could not be persuaded to be dressed
out of the wardrobe that the King had sent to her, but would
wear the clothes which she had brought, until she found that
the King was displeased, and would be obeyed; whereupon she
conformed, against the advice of her women, who continued their
opiniatrety, without any one of them receding from their own
mode, which exposed them the more to reproach" (*Continuation
of Clarendon's Life*, p. 168).

of the Countess de Panétra, who came over with her
in quality of lady of the bedchamber; six frights, who
called themselves maids of honour, and a duenna, another monster, who took the title of governess to those
extraordinary beauties.[29]

Among the men were Francisco de Melo, brother to
the Countess de Panétra; one Taurauvèdez, who called
himself Don Pedro Francisco Correo de Silva, extremely handsome, but a greater fool than all the Portuguese put together: he was more vain of his names
than of his person: but the Duke of Buckingham, a
still greater fool than he, though more addicted to
raillery, gave him the additional name of Peter of the
Wood. He was so enraged at this, that after many
fruitless complaints and ineffectual menaces, poor
Pedro de Silva was obliged to leave England, while
the happy Duke kept possession of a Portuguese
nymph more hideous than the Queen's maids of
honour, whom he had taken from him, as well as two
of his names. Besides these, there were six chaplains,
four bakers, a Jew perfumer, and a certain officer,
probably without an office, who called himself her
Highness's barber.[30] Catharine of Braganza was far
from appearing with splendour in the charming Court
where she came to reign; however, in the end she was
pretty successful.[31] The Chevalier de Gramont, who

[29] These ladies were soon afterwards sent back to Portugal.

[30] A suggestion as to this post is mentioned by Walpole in his
Strawberry Hill edition of the *Memoirs*.

[31] " The Queen arrived with a train of Portuguese ladies," says
Evelyn, 30th May 1662, " in their monstrous fardingals or guard-
infantas, their complexions olivader and sufficiently unagreeable;
Her Majesty in the same habit, her foretop long and turned aside
very strangely. She was yet of the handsomest countenance of
all the rest, and though low of stature prettily shaped, languishing
and excellent eyes, her teeth wronging her mouth by sticking a
little too far out: for the rest, lovely enough."

Lord Clarendon says: " The Queen had beauty and wit enough
to make herself agreeable to him (the King) ; and it is very cer-

had been long known to the Royal Family, and to most of the gentlemen of the Court, had only to get acquainted with the ladies; and for this he wanted no interpreter: they all spoke French enough to explain themselves, and they all understood it sufficiently to comprehend what he had to say to them.

The Queen's Court was always very numerous; that of the Duchess was less so, but more select. This princess" had a majestic air, a pretty good shape, not much beauty, a great deal of wit, and so just a discernment of merit, that, whoever of either sex were possessed of it, were sure to be distinguished by her.

tain, that at their first meeting, and for some time after, the King had very good satisfaction in her. . . . Though she was of years enough to have had more experience of the world, and of as much wit as could be wished, and of a humour very agreeable at some seasons, yet she had been bred, according to the mode and discipline of her country, in a monastery, where she had only seen the women who attended her, and conversed with the religious who resided there; and, without doubt, in her inclinations, was enough disposed to have been one of that number: and from this restraint she was called out to be a great Queen, and to a free conversation in a Court that was to be upon the matter new formed, and reduced from the manners of a licentious age to the old rules and limits which had been observed in better times; to which regular and decent conformity the present disposition of men or women was not enough inclined to submit, nor the King enough disposed to exact" (*Continuation of Lord Clarendon's Life*, p. 167). After some struggle, she submitted to the King's licentious conduct, and from that time lived upon easy terms with him until his death. On the 30th March 1692 she left Somerset House, her usual residence, and retired to Lisbon, where she died, 31st December 1705.

⁸² Anne Hyde, Duchess of York. At the age of twelve she accompanied her mother (Frances, daughter of Sir Thomas Ailesbury) and brothers to Antwerp, and five years later was attached to the train of the Princess of Orange, Charles II.'s eldest sister. "The Duchess," says Bishop Burnet, "was a very extraordinary woman. She had great knowledge, and a lively sense of things. She soon understood what belonged to a princess, and took state on her rather too much. She wrote well, and had begun the Duke's life, of which she showed me a volume. It was all drawn from his journal; and he intended to have employed me

An air of grandeur in all her actions made her be considered as if born to support the rank which placed her so near the throne. The Queen Dowager returned after the marriage of the Princess Royal,[33] and it was in her Court that the two others met.

The Chevalier de Gramont was soon liked by all parties: those who had not known him before were surprised to see a Frenchman of his disposition. The King's restoration having drawn a great number of foreigners from all countries to the Court, the French were rather in disgrace; for, instead of any persons of distinction having appeared among the first who came over, they had only seen some insignificant puppies, each striving to outdo the other in folly and extravagance, despising everything which was not like themselves, and thinking they introduced the *bel air,* by treating the English as strangers in their own country.

in carrying it on. She was bred in great strictness in religion, and practised secret confession. Morley told me he was her confessor. She began at twelve years old, and continued under his direction till, upon her father's disgrace, he was put from the Court. She was generous and friendly, but was too severe an enemy" (*History of his Own Time,* vol. i. p. 237). She died 31st March 1671, having adopted the Roman Catholic faith three years previously.

[33] Queen Henrietta Maria arrived at Whitehall 2nd November 1660, after nineteen years' absence. She was received with acclamations; and bonfires were lighted on the occasion, both in London and Westminster. She returned to France with her daughter, the Princess Henrietta, 2nd January 1660-1. She arrived again at Greenwich 28th July 1662, and continued to keep her Court in England until July 1665, when she embarked for France, "and took so many things with her," says Lord Clarendon, "that it was thought by many that she did not intend ever to return into England. Whatever her intentions at that time were, she never did see England again, though she lived many years after" (*Continuation of Clarendon's Life,* p. 263). She died at Colombe, near Paris, in August 1669; and her son, the Duke of York, pronounces this eulogium on her: "She excelled in all the good qualities of a good wife, of a good mother, and a good Christian" (Macpherson's *Original Papers,* vol. i.).

The Chevalier de Gramont, on the contrary, was familiar with everybody: he gave in to their customs, ate of everything, and easily habituated himself to their manner of living, which he looked upon as neither vulgar nor barbarous; and as he showed a natural complaisance, instead of the impertinent affectation of the others, all the nation was charmed with a man who agreeably indemnified them for what they had suffered from the folly of the former.

He first of all made his court to the King, and was of all his parties of pleasure.[34] He played high, and lost but seldom. He found so little difference in the manners and conversation of those with whom he chiefly associated, that he could scarcely believe he was out of his own country. Everything which could agreeably engage a man of his disposition presented itself to his different humours, as if the pleasures of the Court of France had quitted it to accompany him in his exile.

He was every day engaged for some entertainment; and those who wished to regale him in their turn were obliged to take their measures in time, and to invite him eight or ten days beforehand. These importunate civilities became tiresome in the long run; but as they seemed indispensable to a man of his disposition, and as they were the most genteel people of the Court who loaded him with them, he submitted with a good grace; but always reserved to himself the liberty of supping at home.

His supper hour depended upon play, and was indeed very uncertain; but his supper was always served up with the greatest elegance, by the assistance of one or two servants, who were excellent caterers

[34] " He makes one in all the parties of the King, and has his say at Madame de Castlemaine's."—Comminges to King Louis, August 1663 (Jusserand's *Ambassador at the Court of Charles*, p. 93).

and good attendants, but understood cheating still better.

The company, at these little entertainments, was not numerous, but select: the first people of the Court were commonly of the party; but the man, who of all others suited him best on these occasions, never failed to attend: that was the celebrated Saint-Evremond, who with great exactness, but too great freedom, had written the history of the treaty of the Pyrenees: an exile like himself, though for very different reasons.

Happily for them both, fortune had, some time before the arrival of the Chevalier de Gramont, brought Saint-Evremond[35] to England, after he had had leisure to repent in Holland of the beauties of his famous satire.

[35] Charles de St. Denis, Seigneur de Saint-Evremond, was born at St. Denis le Guast, in Lower Normandy, on the 1st of April 1613. He was educated at Paris, with a view to the profession of the law; but he early quitted that pursuit, and went into the army, where he signalised himself on several occasions. At the time of the Pyrenean treaty, he wrote a letter censuring the conduct of Cardinal Mazarin, which occasioned his being banished France. He first took refuge in Holland; but in 1662 he removed into England, where he continued, with a short interval, during the rest of his life. In 1675 the Duchess of Mazarin came to reside in England; and with her Saint-Evremond passed much of his time. He preserved his health and cheerfulness to a very great age, and died 9th of September 1703, and was buried in Westminster Abbey. His biographer, Monsieur Des Maizeaux, describes him thus: " M. de Saint-Evremond had blue, lively, and sparkling eyes, a large forehead, thick eyebrows, a handsome mouth, and a sneering physiognomy. Twenty years before his death a wen grew between his eyebrows, which in time increased to a considerable bigness. He once designed to have it cut off, but as it was no ways troublesome to him, and he little regarded that kind of deformity, Dr. Le Fevre advised him to let it alone, lest such an operation should be attended with dangerous symptoms in a man of his age. He would often make merry with himself on account of his wen, his great leather cap, and grey hair, which he chose to wear rather than a periwig." The philosopher's character, as drawn by himself, is to be found in a letter to Gramont in Saint-Evremond's *Works*.

The Chevalier was from that time his hero: they had each of them attained to all the advantages which a knowledge of the world, and the society of people of fashion, could add to the improvement of good natural talents. Saint-Evremond, less engaged in frivolous pursuits, frequently gave little lectures to the Chevalier, and by making observations upon the past, endeavoured to set him right for the present, or to instruct him for the future. "You are now," said he, "in the most agreeable way of life a man of your temper could wish for: you are the delight of a youthful, sprightly, and gallant court: the King has never a party of pleasure to which you are not admitted. You play from morning to night, or, to speak more properly, from night to morning, without knowing what it is to lose. Far from losing the money y⏝u brought hither, as you have done in other places, you have doubled it, trebled it, multiplied it almost beyond your wishes, notwithstanding the exorbitant expenses you are imperceptibly led into. This, without doubt, is the most desirable situation in the world: stop here, Chevalier, and do not ruin your affairs by returning to your old sins. Avoid love, by pursuing other pleasures: love has never been favourable to you. You are sensible how much gallantry has cost you: every person here is not so well acquainted with that matter as yourself. Play boldly: entertain the Court with your wit: divert the King by your ingenious and entertaining stories; but avoid all engagements which can deprive you of this merit, and make you forget you are a stranger and an exile in this delightful country.

"Fortune may grow weary of befriending you at play. What would have become of you if your last misfortune had happened to you when your money had been at as low an ebb as I have known it? Attend carefully then to this necessary deity, and renounce the other. You will be missed at the Court of France before you grow weary of this; but be that as it may, lay up a good store of money: when a man is rich he consoles himself for his banishment. I know you well, my dear Chevalier: if you take it into your head to seduce a lady, or to supplant a lover, your gains at play will by no means suffice for presents and for bribes: no, let play be as productive to you as it can be, you will never gain so much by it as you will lose by love, if you yield to it.

"You are in possession of a thousand splendid qualifications which distinguish you here: generous, benevolent, elegant, and polite; and for your engaging wit, inimitable. Upon a strict examination, perhaps, all this would not be found literally true; but these are brilliant marks; and since it is granted that you possess them, do not show yourself here in any other light: for, in love, if your manner of paying your addresses can be so denominated, you do not in the least resemble the picture I have just now drawn."

"My little philosophical monitor," said the Chevalier de Gramont, "you talk here as if you were the Cato of Normandy." "Do I say anything untrue?" replied Saint-Evremond: "is it not a fact, that as soon as a woman pleases you, your first care is to find out whether she has any other lover, and your second how to plague her; for the gaining her affection is the last thing in your thoughts. You seldom engage in intrigues, but to disturb the happiness of others: a mistress who had no lovers would have no charms for you, and if she had, she would be invaluable. Do not all the places through which you have passed furnish me with a thousand examples? Shall I mention your *coup d'essai* at Turin? the trick you played at Fontainebleau, where you robbed the Princess Palatine's courier upon the highway? And for what purpose was this fine exploit, but to put you in possession of some proofs of her affection for another, in order to give her uneasiness and confusion by reproaches and menaces, which you had no right to use?

"Who but yourself ever took it into his head to place himself in ambush upon the stairs, to disturb a man in an intrigue, and to pull him back by the leg when he was half way up to his mistress's chamber? Yet did not you use your friend, the Duke of Buckingham, in this manner, when he was stealing at night to ——, although you were not in the least his rival? How many spies did not you send out after D'Olonne?[36] How many tricks, frauds, and persecutions did you not practise for the Countess de Fiesque, who perhaps might have been constant to you, if you had not yourself forced her to be otherwise? But, to conclude, for the enumeration of your iniquities would be endless, give me leave to ask you how you came here? Are not we obliged to that same evil genius of yours, which rashly inspired you to intermeddle even in the gallantries of your prince? Show some discretion then on this point here, I beseech you; all the beauties of the Court are already engaged; and however docile the English may be with respect to their wives, they can by no means bear the inconstancy of their mistresses, nor patiently suffer the advantages of a rival: suffer them therefore to remain in tranquillity, and do not gain their ill-will for no purpose.

[36] Mademoiselle de la Loupe, who is mentioned in De Retz's *Memoirs,* vol. iii. p. 95. She married the Count d'Olonne, and became famous for her gallantries. Her maiden name was Catherine Henrietta d'Angennes, and she was daughter to Charles d'Angennes, Lord of la Loupe, Baron d'Amberville, by Mary du Raynier. There is a long character of her by Saint-Evremond, in his works, vol. i. p. 17; vol. ii. p. 24. See also *Histoire Amoureuse des Gaules.*

"You certainly will meet with no success with such as are unmarried: honourable views, and good landed property, are required here; and you possess as much[37] of the one as the other. Every country has its customs: in Holland, unmarried ladies are of easy access, and of tender dispositions; but as soon as they are married, they become like so many Lucretias: in France, the women are great coquettes before marriage, and still more so afterwards; but here it is a miracle if a young lady yields to any proposal but that of matrimony: and I do not believe you yet so destitute of grace as to think of that."

Such were Saint-Evremond's lectures; but they were all to no purpose: the Chevalier de Gramont only attended to them for his amusement; and though he was sensible of the truth they contained, he paid little regard to them: in fact, being weary of the favours of fortune, he had just resolved to pursue those of love.

Mrs. Middleton[38] was the first whom he attacked: she was one of the handsomest women in town, though then little known at Court: so much of the coquette

[37] Should be *little* (Vizetelly's translation).

[38] Mrs. Middleton, *née* Jane Needham, was the daughter of Sir Robert Needham and his second wife Jane, the widow of Mr. Worfield. She was born at Lambeth, where her father resided, and baptized 23rd January 1645-6. The great beauty married, 18th June 1660 (at Lambeth), Charles Middleton, Esq. (born 1635), son of Sir Thomas Middleton, Kt., of Chirk Castle, Denbighshire. The old mansion, Plas Newydd, was rebuilt by Mr. Middleton, whose arms are still to be seen over the porch. There were two daughters by this marriage: Jane, baptized 21st December 1661, and Althamia. The family resided for a time, 1668-9, in Charles Street, St. Martin's in the Fields: the site of the house is now occupied by part of Regent Street. Mrs. Middleton for some years received a pension of £500 from the Privy Purse, and died in 1692 and was buried in Lambeth Church or Churchyard, but no stone records her interment.

Both Evelyn and the French Ambassador Courtin describe Mrs. Middleton as an incomparable beauty. The latter says (23rd November 1676): "I still hold to the opinion that she's the

as to discourage no one; and so great was her desire
of appearing magnificently, that she was ambitious to
vie with those of the greatest fortunes, though unable
to support the expense. All this suited the Chevalier
de Gramont; therefore, without trifling away his time
in useless ceremonies, he applied to her porter for
admittance, and chose one of her lovers for his
confidant.

This lover, who was not deficient in wit, was at
that time a Mr. Jones, afterwards Earl of Ranelagh.[39]
What engaged him to serve the Chevalier de Gramont
was to traverse the designs of a most dangerous rival,
and to relieve himself from an expense which began
to lie too heavy upon him. In both respects the
Chevalier answered his purpose.

Immediately spies were placed, letters and presents
flew about: he was received as well as he could wish:

sweetest woman I ever came across in any foreign country.
She's beautiful, has the air of high breeding, is full of talent,
and yet modest and unassuming." It appears from the French
despatches (Barillon to Pomponne, 25th July 1678), that "to
outdo the Duchess of Portsmouth, Mrs. Middleton and Lady
Harvey trust to get the King to honour Mrs. Middleton's daughter with his attentions." The Duchess of Portsmouth, however,
caused the King's cabinet to be inaccessible, for the mother took
her daughter there "intent on pleasing His Majesty"! (*Louise
de Keroualle,* p. 202). This was possibly Jane, mentioned above,
who married Charles May, Esq., of Frant, Sussex, only son of
Sir Algernon May, Kt., of Hampton, Middlesex. She was left a
widow in 1715, and died in 1740 and was buried at Hampton
Church.

(The above is mainly extracted from Steinman's *Althorp
Memoirs.*)

[39] Richard, first Earl of Ranelagh, was member of the English
House of Commons, and Vice Treasurer of Ireland 1674. He
held several offices under King William and Queen Anne, and
died 5th January 1711. Bishop Burnet says: "Lord Ranelagh was
a young man of great parts, and as great vices: he had a pleas-
antness in his conversation that took much with the King; and
had a great dexterity in business" (*History of his Own Time,*
vol. i. p. 373). His daughter Elizabeth became the King's mistress in 1679 (*vide* Reresby's *Memoirs*).

he was permitted to ogle: he was even ogled again: but this was all: he found that the fair one was very willing to accept, but was tardy in making returns.[40] This induced him, without giving up his pretensions to her, to seek his fortune elsewhere.

Among the Queen's maids of honour there was one called Warmester: she was a beauty very different from the other. Mrs. Middleton was well made, fair, and delicate; but had in her behaviour and discourse something precise and affected. The indolent, languishing airs she gave herself did not please everybody: people grew weary of those sentiments of delicacy, which she endeavoured to explain without understanding them herself, and instead of entertaining she became tiresome. In these attempts she gave herself so much trouble, that she made the company uneasy, and her ambition to pass for a wit only established her the reputation of being wearisome, which lasted much longer than her beauty.

Miss Warmester[41] was brown[42]: she had no shape

[40] The French Ambassador, Courtin, gives another story: "Mrs. Middleton is not at all mercenary; she once refused a purse containing fifteen hundred golden angels which Gramont offered her" (see Forneron's *Louise de Keroualle*, p. 156).

[41] Miss Warmester, or Warmestry, is referred to in *Gramont's Memoirs* under her real name, and not, as the previous annotators have it, under an assumed one. Similar circumstances in the career of the maid of honour Mary Kirke led the Earl of Arran to suppose that Warmester must have been a fictitious name; but such was not the case. This lady is referred to in a letter from Lord Cornbury to the Duchess of Bedford (10th June 1662) under her correct name, as maid of honour to Queen Catherine. Mary Kirke was maid of honour to the Duchess of York, but she did not resign her position until 1675, *six years after Gramont's departure from England;* whereas the Miss Warmester episode took place during his sojourn at the Court. The Warmestrys settled in Worcester prior to the reign of Edward VI., from which the members were registrars of the diocese, and the name is still retained in a narrow street leading from the Cathedral to the river Severn. The parentage of the lady of the *Memoirs* is not known, but it is not unlikely she was the daugh-

at all, and still less air; but she had a very lively complexion, very sparkling eyes, tempting looks, which spared nothing that might engage a lover, and promised everything which could preserve him. In the end, it very plainly appeared that her consent went along with her eyes to the last degree of indiscretion.

It was between these two goddesses that the inclinations of the Chevalier de Gramont stood wavering, and between whom his presents were divided. Perfumed gloves, pocket looking-glasses, elegant boxes, apricot paste, essences, and other small wares of love, arrived every week from Paris, with some new suit for himself: but, with regard to more solid presents, such as ear-rings, diamonds, brilliants, and bright guineas, all these were to be met with of the best sort in London, and the ladies were as well pleased with them as if they had been brought from abroad.

ter of Dr. Thomas Warmestry, Vicar of Bromsgrove and Dean of Worcester, a staunch royalist (b. 1610), who had lands at Paxford, County Worcester, lived prior to the Restoration at Chelsea, and was granted the mastership of the Savoy in June 1660. He died 30th October 1665, and was buried in the Cathedral of Worcester (see *Dict. of Nat. Biography,* vol. lix. p. 389, also *Notes and Queries,* Series i. vol. viii. p. 461, and the M.S. additions of Sir William Musgrave in a copy of the *Gramont Memoirs* in the British Museum).

Mary Kirke (the daughter of George Kirke, Groom of the Bedchamber to Charles II. and Keeper of Whitehall Palace, and sister to Colonel Percy Kirke of execrable fame) is mentioned in the Belvoir MSS. as being a mistress of the Duke of Monmouth (vide *King Monmouth,* p. 47) ; in any case she ultimately married Sir Thomas Vernon, who became a widower in June 1676, and who has hitherto been confused with Killigrew's cousin, who came most opportunely to the rescue of Miss Warmester. Lady Vernon survived her husband nearly thirty years, and died in great poverty at Greenwich, where she was buried. Her son, Sir Richard, was the last baronet, and the family became extinct in 1752.

[42] Dark, not brown (Vizetelly's translation).

Miss Stewart's[48] beauty began at this time to be celebrated. The Countess of Castlemaine perceived that the King paid attention to her; but, instead of being alarmed at it, she favoured, as far as she was able, this new inclination, whether from an indiscretion common to all those who think themselves superior to the rest of mankind, or whether she designed, by this pastime, to divert the King's attention from the commerce which she held with Jermyn. She was not satisfied with appearing without any degree of uneasiness at a preference which all the Court began

[48] Frances Theresa Stewart, or Stuart, afterwards Duchess of Richmond and Lennox, daughter of Walter Stuart, third son of Walter, Lord Blantyre, which family claimed to be related to the Royal House of Stuart. Born about the year 1647, and educated in France, she was in the train of Queen Henrietta when the Dowager came to England two years after the Restoration, shortly after which she became maid of honour to Queen Catherine of Braganza. Charles II., as had King Louis before him, soon became enslaved by her beauty, which resulted in a rivalry between her and Lady Castlemaine; and had the Queen's illness proved fatal, there is little doubt the King would have married her, for in vain he had solicited her favours.

There are frequent allusions to her by Pepys, who describes her as the greatest beauty at Court, with her "sweet eye, little Roman nose, and excellent taille." The well-known Hampton Court portrait by Lely is probably referred to in the following entry in the *Diary* of 15th July 1664:—"To Whitehall, where—in one of the Galleries—there comes out of the Chayre-room Mrs. Stewart in a most lovely form, with her hair all about her eares, having her picture taken there. There was the King and twenty more, I think, standing by all the while, and a lovely creature she, in this dress, seemed to be." On 26th August of the same year Pepys was taken to Huysman's studio, where he saw his portrait of Frances Stewart "in a buff doublet like a soldier." This painting is now in Buckingham Palace. John Roettier, the medallist, depicted *La Belle Stewart's* profile upon the reverse of a thin gold plate now in the British Museum. Referring to this, Pepys says (25th February 1666-7):—"At my goldsmith's did observe the King's new medall where, in little, there is Mrs. Steward's face as well done as ever I saw anything in my whole life, I think: and a pretty thing it is, that he should choose her face to represent Britannia by." She also sat for the Britannia of several medals struck in the year 1667, the original of the Britannia of our copper coinage.

to remark: she even affected to make Miss Stewart her favourite, invited her to all the entertainments she made for the King; and in confidence of her own charms, with the greatest indiscretion she often kept her to sleep.

The King, who seldom neglected to visit the Countess before she rose, seldom failed likewise to find Miss Stewart in bed with her. The most indifferent objects have charms in a new attachment: however, the imprudent Countess was not jealous of this rival's appearing with her in such a situation, being confident, that whenever she thought fit, she could triumph over all the advantages which these opportunities could afford Miss Stewart. But she was quite mistaken.

The Chevalier de Gramont took notice of this conduct, without being able to comprehend it; but, as he was attentive to the inclinations of the King, he began to make his court to him by enhancing the merit of this new mistress.[44]

Her figure was more showy than engaging: it was hardly possible for a woman to have less wit, or more beauty. All her features were fine and regular; but her shape was not good: yet she was slender, straight enough, and taller than the generality

[44] Between February and June 1663 several rumours were current that Frances Stewart had become the King's mistress (*vide* Pepy's *Diary*, 8th and 17th February, 18th May, and 4th June). The Marquis de Ruvigny, writing to Louis XIV. on 25th June, hints at her sins by saying that she did not take the communion at Whitsuntide, though, he adds, she is " one of the most modest girls to be seen." By this time Lady Castlemaine saw the danger of entertaining her rival. " There was a great row the other day among the ladies," says the Ambassador Comminges in a letter to King Louis (25th June 1663) ; " it was carried so far that the King threatened the lady at whose apartments he sups every evening that he would never set foot there again if he did not find the Demoiselle with her, and for this cause the lady is never without her " (see Jusserand's *French Ambassador at the Court of Charles II.* p. 90).

of women: she was very graceful, danced well,[45] and spoke French better than her mother tongue: she was well bred, and possessed in perfection that air of dress which is so much admired, and which cannot be attained, unless it be taken when young, in France. While her charms were gaining ground in the King's heart, the Countess of Castlemaine amused herself in the gratification of all her caprices.[46]

Mrs. Hyde[47] was one of the first of the beauties who were prejudiced with a blind prepossession in favour of Jermyn: she had just married a man whom she loved: by this marriage she became sister-in-law to the Duchess, brilliant by her own native lustre, and full of pleasantry and wit. However, she was of opinion, that so long as she was not talked of on account of Jermyn, all her other advantages would avail nothing for her glory: it was, therefore, to receive this finishing stroke that she resolved to throw herself into his arms.

She was of middle size, had a skin of a dazzling whiteness, fine hands, and a foot surprisingly beautiful, even in England: long custom had given such a languishing tenderness to her looks, that she never opened her eyes but like a Chinese; and, when she ogled, one would have thought she was doing something else.

Jermyn accepted of her at first; but, being soon puzzled what to do with her, he thought it best to

[45] " Mighty finely," according to Pepys, who, on the occasion of a Court ball, thought her "the beautifullest creature" he ever saw (see *Diary,* 15th November 1666).

[46] This is corroborated by Pepys (see *Diary,* 8th February 1662-3).

[47] Theodosia, daughter of Arthur, Lord Capel, first wife of Henry Hyde, Lord Cornbury, and sister-in-law of the Duchess of York.

She must not be confused with the wife of Laurence Hyde, afterwards Earl of Rochester.

sacrifice her to Lady Castlemaine. The sacrifice was
far from being displeasing to her; it was much to
her glory to have carried off Jermyn from so many
competitors; but this was of no consequence in the
end.

Jacob Hall, the famous rope-dancer,[48] was at that
time in vogue in London; his strength and agility
charmed in public, even to a wish to know what he
was in private; for he appeared, in his tumbling dress,
to be quite of a different make, and to have limbs
very different from the fortunate Jermyn. The tum-
bler did not deceive Lady Castlemaine's expectations,
if report may be believed, and as was intimated in
many a song, much more to the honour of the
rope-dancer than of the Countess; but she despised
all these rumours, and only appeared still more
handsome.

While satire thus found employment at her cost,
there were continual contests for the favours of another beauty, who was not much more niggardly in
that way than herself; this was the Countess of
Shrewsbury.

[48] The combination of Hercules and Adonis in the person of
Jacob Hall made him very popular with the fair sex. He attained
his greatest distinction in 1668 when he became a regular visitor
to Lady Castlemaine's house, and is said to have received a salary
from her. Hall's earliest entertainment was in a booth at Smith-
field, after which he set up a stage for his performances at Charing Cross, and in Lincoln's Inn Fields. His exhibition included
" excellent dancing and vaulting on the ropes with variety of
rare feats of activity and agility of body upon the stage, as doing
of somersets and flip-flaps, flying over thirty rapiers, and over
several men's heads, and also flying through several hoops." He
further challenged anybody to do the like for £20. (See *Notes
and Queries,* Second Series, vii. p. 62.) Pepys, who saw him in
August and September 1668, at Southwark Fair, describes him as
a " mighty strong man." In an interview with the diarist, the
athlete declared that though he had had many falls he had never
broken a limb (21st September). See also *Dict. of Nat. Biography,* vol. xxiv. p. 67.

The Earl of Arran,[40] who had been one of her first admirers, was not one of the last to desert her; this beauty, less famous for her conquests than for the misfortunes she occasioned, placed her greatest merits in being more capricious than any other. As no person could boast of being the only one in her favour, so no person could complain of having been ill received.

Jermyn was displeased that she had made no advances to him, without considering that she had no leisure for it; his pride was offended; but the attempt which he made to take her from the rest of her lovers was very ill-advised.

Thomas Howard, brother to the Earl of Carlisle,[50] was one of them: there was not a braver or finer man in England; and though he was of a modest demeanour, and his manners appeared gentle and pacific, no person was more spirited nor more passionate. Lady Shrewsbury, inconsiderately returning the first ogles of the invincible Jermyn, did not at all make herself more agreeable to Howard; that, however, she paid little attention to; yet, as she designed to keep fair with him, she consented to accept an entertainment which he had often proposed, and which she durst no longer refuse. A place of amusement called Spring Garden[51] was fixed upon for the scene of this entertainment.

[40] Richard Butler, second son of James, Duke of Ormonde, b. 1639, ob. 1686.
[50] Captain Thomas Howard, fourth son of Sir William Howard, and the third husband of Mary Villiers, daughter of the first Duke of Buckingham, whose second husband was James Lennox, third Duke of Richmond.
[51] Spring Garden, the scene of intrigue in many comedies of this time, derived its name from a mechanical spring or jet of water, a practical joke so contrived that a passer-by was doused as inadvertently he trod upon a hidden trap. These water springs date from Elizabeth's time: an example existed until a comparatively recent date at Chatsworth; another was at Enstone in Oxfordshire.

As soon as the party was settled, Jermyn was privately informed of it. Howard had a company in the regiment of guards, and one of the soldiers of his company played pretty well on the bagpipes. This soldier was, therefore, at the entertainment. Jermyn was at the garden, as by chance, and, puffed up with his former successes, he trusted to his victorious air for accomplishing this last enterprise; he no sooner appeared on the walks, than her ladyship showed herself upon the balcony.

I know not how she stood affected to her hero; but Howard did not fancy him much. This did not prevent his coming upstairs upon the first sign she made

In *A Character of England,* published in 1659 and attributed to Evelyn, is the following description:—"The manner is, as the company returns [from Hyde Park], to alight at the Spring Garden, so called in order to the Parke, as our Thuilleries is to the Course; the inclosure not disagreeable, for the solemness of the grove, the warbling of the birds, and as it opens into the spacious walks of St. James's; but the company walk in it at such a rate, you would think that all the ladies were so many Atalantas contending with their wooers; but as fast as they ran they stay there so long as if they wanted not time to finish the race; for it is usual here to find some of the young company till midnight; and the thickets of the garden seem to be contrived to all advantages of gallantry, after they have refreshed with the collation, which is here seldom omitted, at a certain cabaret in the middle of this paradise, where the forbidden fruits are certain trifling tarts, neats' tongues, salacious meats, and bad Rhenish, for which the gallants pay sauce, as indeed they do at all such houses throughout England."

In 1661 the *New* Spring Gardens at Foxhall, or Vauxhall, were set out with lawns, gravel walks, arbours, and hedges of gooseberry trees and roses, and were the forerunner of the famous Vauxhall Gardens. Pepys makes several allusions to this pleasure resort. "It is very pleasant and cheap going thither," says the diarist; "for a man may go to spend what he will or nothing, all as one. But to hear the nightingale and the birds, and here fiddles and there a harp, and here a Jew's trump, and here laughing and there fine people walking, is mighty divertising" (28th May 1667). But he was evidently grieved to see how the women were molested, and "how rude some of the young gallants of the town are become, to go into people's arbors where there are not men, and almost force the women."

to him; and not content with acting the petty tyrant, at an entertainment not made for himself, no sooner had he gained the soft looks of the fair one, than he exhausted all his commonplace, and all his stock of low irony, in railing at the entertainment, and ridiculing the music.

Howard possessed but little raillery, and still less patience; three times was the banquet on the point of being stained with blood; but three times did he suppress his natural impetuosity, in order to satisfy his resentment elsewhere with greater freedom.

Jermyn, without paying the least attention to his ill-humour, pursued his point, continued talking to Lady Shrewsbury, and did not leave her until the repast was ended.

He went to bed, proud of this triumph, and was awakened next morning by a challenge. He took for his second Giles Rawlings,[52] a man of intrigue and a deep player. Howard took Dillon,[53] who was dexterous and brave, much of a gentleman, and, unfortunately, an intimate friend to Rawlings.

In this duel fortune did not side with the votaries of love: poor Rawlings was left stone dead; and Jermyn, having received three wounds, was carried to his uncle's, with very little signs of life.[54]

[52] Colonel Giles Rawlings, gentleman of the Privy Purse to James, Duke of York. According to Rugge's *Diurnal* he used to live in great state, with six horses and three footmen to his coach.

[53] Colonel Cary Dillon, youngest son of Robert, second Earl of Roscommon.

[54] This took place in Pall Mall on 18th August 1662 (*vide* Pepys, 19th August 1662). A more detailed account appears in the Verney papers, 21st August 1662. "On Monday Tom Howard, brother to the Earl of Carlisle, and Mr. Dillon, brother to Lord Dillon, accosted H. Germaine [Jermyn] and Giles Rawlins, drew upon them before —— door coming from the tennis court, and Tom slew Giles dead in the place, and after that fell on Harry and wounded him in three or four places, which proved but slight

While the report of this event engaged the courtiers according to their several interests, the Chevalier de Gramont was informed by Jones, his friend, his confidant, and his rival, that there was another gentleman very attentive to Mrs. Middleton. This was Montagu,[55] no very dangerous rival on account of his person, but very much to be feared for his assiduity, the acuteness of his wit, and for some other talents which are of importance, when a man is once permitted to display them.

There needed not half so much to bring into action all the Chevalier's vivacity, in point of competition: vexation awakened in him whatever expedients the desire of revenge, malice, and experience could suggest, for troubling the designs of a rival, and tormenting a mistress. His first intention was to return her letters, and demand his presents, before he began to tease her; but, rejecting this project, as too weak a

hurts; which done Tom said, ' Now we have done justice, let's be gone.' And having their horses hard by, with pistols at the saddlebow, they presently fled, and 'tis thought Howard had some hurt, for he was seen to bear himself up on his pummell. The quarrel it's said was between Howard and Germaine about Lady Shrewsbury. It is also said that Howard was in buff, and that he cut off the heels of his boots, and so came fully prepared and took the other unawares, who because they had only the usual bodkins desired but their footmen's swords, but had them not; and yet Rawlins thrust so home that he bent his sword at the hilt, but buff or other armour would not suffer entrance. Dillon fought carelessly, as if willing neither to hurt nor be hurt, it being none of his quarrel." By Pepys's account it was Dillon who had protected himself against sword thrusts. From Rugge's *Diurnal* we learn that Howard and Dillon both fled, "but after a quarter of a year they came into England and were acquitted by law."

[55] Ralph Montagu, second son of Edward, second Lord Montagu of Boughton (*b.* 1636, *ob.* 1709), created Duke of Montagu by Queen Anne in 1705. In 1669 he was sent as Ambassador Extraordinary to France, and aided Louis XIV.'s interests, and afterwards was active in opposing King James in favour of William III. He married the widowed Countess of Northumberland, sister of Lady Rachael Russell.

revenge for the injustice done him, he was upon the point of conspiring the destruction of poor Mrs. Middleton, when, by accident, he met with Miss Hamilton.[56]

From this moment ended all his resentment against Mrs. Middleton and all his attachment to Miss Warmester: no longer was he inconstant; no longer were his wishes fluctuating; this object fixed them all; , and, of all his former habits, none remained, except uneasiness and jealousy.

Here his first care was to please; but he very plainly saw, that to succeed he must act quite in a different manner from that which he had been accustomed to.

The family of the Hamiltons, being very numerous, lived in a large and commodious house near the Court; the Duke of Ormonde's family was continually with them; and here persons of the greatest distinction in London constantly met. The Chevalier de Gramont was here received in a manner agreeable to his merit and quality, and was astonished that he had spent so much time in other places; for, after having made this acquaintance, he was desirous of no other.

[56] The Ambassador Comminges, who handles the Chevalier less leniently than Hamilton, writes to King Louis (August 1663) :— "He" (Gramont) "follows his usual style of life. He sees the ladies at the lawful hours, and a little also at the forbidden ones. . . . He continues his gallantries as is his wont—that is, making much noise and little progress." With regard to Mrs. Middleton he says: "He has just managed to have a very ridiculous affair with Madame Middleton, whose maid he bribed, but the maid kept to herself both the money and the love declarations of the Chevalier. When at length the lady heard of what was meant for her, as it was not conveyed, it seems, with all the eloquence Gramont had meant, she was nothing moved, but ordered him to keep quiet and look elsewhere. Gramont did not fail to take her at her word, and he is now, six months after his coming, in a fair way to marriage" (Jusserand's *Ambassador at the Court of Charles II.* pp. 93-94).

All the world agreed that Miss Hamilton[57] was worthy of the most ardent and sincere affection: nobody could boast a nobler birth, nothing was more charming than her person.

[57] Elizabeth, sister of the author of these *Memoirs,* and daughter of Sir George Hamilton, fourth son of James, the first Earl of Abercorn, by Mary, third daughter of Thomas, Viscount Thurles, eldest son of Walter, eleventh Earl of Ormonde, and sister to James, the first Duke of Ormonde. She married Philibert, Count of Gramont, the hero of these *Memoirs,* by whom she had a son, born in 1664 (who probably died young), and two daughters, Claude Charlotte, married (1694) to Henry, Earl of Stafford, and Mary Elizabeth, who became Abbess of St. Marie de Poussay in Lorraine. Dangeau describes her as "a most lively wit, the most extensive information, the greatest dignity, the utmost ease, and the most polished elegance at Court (Dangeau's *Journal,* vol. i. p. 241). The Duke of Richmond, the Earl of Arundel, Jermyn the invincible, the Earl of Falmouth, John Russell (son of the Duke of Bedford, William Russell (John's nephew), were among the aspirants to the hand of the beautiful Elizabeth Hamilton.

CHAPTER VII

THE Chevalier de Gramont, never satisfied in his amours, was fortunate without being beloved, and became jealous without having an attachment.

Mrs. Middleton, as we have said, was going to experience what methods he could invent to torment, after having experienced his powers of pleasing.

He went in search of her to the Queen's drawing-room, where there was a ball. There she was; but, fortunately for her, Miss Hamilton was there likewise. It had so happened, that of all the beautiful women at Court, this was the lady whom he had least seen, and whom he had heard most commended; this, therefore, was the first time that he had a close view of her, and he soon found that he had seen nothing at Court before this instant. He asked her some questions, to which she replied; as long as she was dancing, his eyes were fixed upon her; and from this time he no longer resented Mrs. Middleton's conduct. Miss Hamilton was at the happy age when the charms of the fair sex begin to bloom; she had the finest shape, the loveliest neck, and most beautiful arms in the world; she was majestic and graceful in all her movements; and she was the original after which all the ladies copied in their taste and air of dress.[1] Her forehead was open, white, and smooth; her hair was well set, and fell with ease into that natural order which it is so difficult to imitate. Her complexion was possessed of a certain freshness, not to be equalled by borrowed colours: her eyes were

[1] And arrangement of their hair (Vizetelly's translation).

not large, but they were lively, and capable of expressing whatever she pleased : her mouth was full of graces, and her contour uncommonly perfect : nor was her nose, which was small, delicate, and turned up, the least ornament of so lovely a face. In fine, her air, her carriage, and the numberless graces dispersed over her whole person, made the Chevalier de Gramont not doubt but that she was possessed of every other qualification. Her mind was a proper companion for such a form : she did not endeavour to shine in conversation by those sprightly sallies which only puzzle; and with still greater care she avoided that affected solemnity in her discourse which produces stupidity; but without any eagerness to talk, she just said what she ought, and no more. She had an admirable discernment in distinguishing between solid and false wit; and far from making an ostentatious display of her abilities, she was reserved, though very just in her decisions. Her sentiments were always noble, and even lofty to the highest extent, when there was occasion; nevertheless, she was less prepossesed with her own merit than is usually the case with those who have so much. Formed as we have described, she could not fail of commanding love; but so far was she from courting it, that she was scrupulously nice with respect to those whose merit might entitle them to form any pretensions to her.

The more the Chevalier de Gramont was convinced of these truths, the more did he endeavour to please and engage her in his turn. His entertaining wit, his conversation, lively, easy, and always distinguished by novelty, constantly gained him attention; but he was much embarrassed to find that presents, which so easily made their way in his former method of courtship, were no longer proper in the mode which, for the future, he was obliged to pursue.

He had an old valet-de-chambre, called Termes, a bold thief, and a still more impudent liar: he used to send this man from London every week, on the commissions we have before mentioned. But after the disgrace of Mrs. Middleton, and the adventure of Miss Warmester, Mr. Termes was only employed in bringing his master's clothes from Paris, and he did not always acquit himself with the greatest fidelity in that employment, as will appear hereafter.

The Queen was a woman of sense, and used all her endeavours to please the King, by that kind, obliging behaviour which her affection made natural to her: she was particularly attentive in promoting every sort of pleasure and amusement, especially such as she could be present at herself.

She had contrived, for this purpose, a splendid masquerade, where those whom she appointed to dance had to represent different nations. She allowed some time for preparation, during which, we may suppose, the tailors, the mantua-makers, and embroiderers were not idle.

Nor were the beauties, who were to be there, less anxiously employed; however, Miss Hamilton found time enough to invent two or three little tricks, in a conjuncture so favourable, for turning into ridicule the vain fools of the Court. There were two who were very eminently such: the one was Lady Muskerry,[2]

---

[2] Lady Margaret de Burgh, only child of Ulick, Marquis of Clanricarde, by Lady Anne Compton, daughter of William, Earl of Northampton. She was three times married: 1st, To Charles, Viscount Muskerry, eldest son of the Earl of Clancarty, and nephew of the Duke of Ormonde, who lost his life in the great sea-fight with the Dutch, 3rd June 1665. 2nd, In 1676, to Robert Villiers, third Viscount Purbeck, who was killed in a duel in 1684. 3rd, To Major-General Robert. better known as Beau Fielding.

who had married her cousin-german; and the other a
maid of honour to the Duchess, called Blague.[3]

The first, whose husband most assuredly never
married her for beauty, was made like the generality
of rich heiresses, to whom just Nature seems sparing of
her gifts, in proportion as they are loaded with those
of Fortune. She had the shape of a woman big with
child, without being so; but had a very good reason
for limping; for, of two legs uncommonly short, one
was much shorter than the other. A face suitable to
this description gave the finishing stroke to this disagreeable figure.

Miss Blague was another species of ridicule: her
shape was neither good nor bad: her countenance bore
the appearance of the greatest insipidity, and her complexion was the same all over; with two little hollow
eyes, adorned with white[4] eyelashes, as long as one's
finger. With these attractions she placed herself in
ambuscade to surprise unwary hearts; but she might
have done so in vain, had it not been for the arrival
of the Marquis de Brisacier.[5] Heaven seemed to have
made them for each other: he had in his person and
manners every requisite to dazzle a creature of her
character: he talked eternally, without saying anything,
and in his dress exceeded the most extravagant fashions. Miss Blague believed that all this finery was on
her account; and the Marquis believed that her long

[3] It appears, by Chamberlayne's *Angliæ Notitia*, 1669, that this
lady, or perhaps her sister, continued one of the Duchess's maids
of honour at that period. The list, at the time, was as follows:—
Mrs. Arabella Churchill, Mrs. Dorothy Howard, Mrs. Anne Ogle,
Mrs. Mary Blague, daughter of Colonel Blague, a devoted ad-
herent to Charles II. during exile. The Mother of the maids
then was Mrs. Lucy Wise.

[4] *Light*, not white (Vizetelly's translation).

[5] It was Henrietta Maria, the sister of Mary Blague, who had
the flirtation with the Marquis. She married afterwards Sir
Thomas Yarborough of Snaith, Yorkshire. Evelyn mentions another sister, Margaret.

eyelashes had never taken aim at any but himself:
everybody perceived their inclination for each other;
but they had only conversed by mute interpreters, when
Miss Hamilton took it into her head to intermeddle in
their affairs.

She was willing to do everything in order, and
therefore began with her cousin Muskerry on account
of her rank. Her two darling foibles were dress and
dancing. Magnificence of dress was intolerable with
her figure; and though her dancing was still more insupportable, she never missed a ball at Court; and the
Queen had so much complaisance for the public, as
always to make her dance. But it was impossible to
give her a part in an entertainment so important and
splendid as this masquerade.[6] However, she was dying
with impatience for the orders she expected.

It was in consequence of this impatience, of which
Miss Hamilton was informed, that she founded the
design of diverting herself at the expense of this silly
woman. The Queen sent notes to those whom she
appointed to be present, and described the manner in
which they were to be dressed. Miss Hamilton wrote
a note[7] exactly in the same manner to Lady Muskerry,
with directions for her to be dressed in the Babylonian
fashion.

She assembled her counsel to advise about the means
of sending it. This cabinet was composed of one of
her brothers and a sister, who were glad to divert
themselves at the expense of those who deserved it.
After having consulted some time, they at last resolved
upon a mode of conveying it into her own hands.
Lord Muskerry was just going out when she received
it: he was a man of honour, rather serious, very

[6] Both Evelyn and Pepys mention this masquerade under the
dates 2nd and 3rd February 1664-5 (*vide* Cunningham's "Chronology,"
[7] Had a note written (Vizetelly's translation).

severe, and a mortal enemy to ridicule. His wife's deformity was not so intolerable to him as the ridiculous figure she made upon all occasions. He thought that he was safe in the present case, not believing that the Queen would spoil her masquerade by naming Lady Muskerry as one of the dancers; nevertheless, as he was acquainted with the passion his wife had to expose herself in public, by her dress and dancing, he had just been advising her very seriously to content herself with being a spectator of this entertainment, even though the Queen should have the cruelty to engage her in it. He then took the liberty to show her what little similarity there was between her figure and that of persons to whom dancing and magnificence in dress were allowable. His sermon concluded at last, by an express prohibition to solicit a place at this entertainment, which they[8] had no thoughts of giving her. But, far from taking his advice in good part, she imagined that he was the only person who had prevented the Queen from doing her an honour she so ardently desired; and as soon as he was gone out, her design was to go and throw herself at her Majesty's feet to demand justice. She was in this very disposition when she received the billet : three times did she kiss it ; and without regarding her husband's injunctions, she immediately got into her coach in order to get information of the merchants who traded to the Levant, in what manner the ladies of quality dressed in Babylon.

The plot laid for Miss Blague was of a different kind. She had such faith in her charms, and was so confident of their effects, that she could believe anything. Brisacier, whom she looked upon as desperately smitten, had wit, which he set off with commonplace talk, and with little sonnets : he sung out of tune most methodically, and was continually exerting one or

[8] The Queen (*ibid.*).

other of these happy talents. The Duke of Buckingham did all he could to spoil him, by the praises he bestowed upon both his voice and upon his wit.

Miss Blague, who hardly understood a word of French, regulated herself upon the Duke's authority, in admiring the one and the other. It was remarked, that all the words which he sung to her were in praise of fair women, and that always taking this to herself, she cast down her eyes in acknowledgment and consciousness. It was upon these observations they resolved to make a jest of her the first opportunity.

While these little projects were forming, the King, who always wished to oblige the Chevalier de Gramont, asked him if he would make one at the masquerade, on condition of being Miss Hamilton's partner? He did not pretend to dance sufficiently well for an occasion like the present; yet he was far from refusing the offer: "Sire," said he, "of all the favours you have been pleased to show me since my arrival, I feel this more sensibly than any other; and to convince you of my gratitude, I promise you all the good offices in my power with Miss Stewart." He said this because they had just given her an apartment separate from the rest of the maids of honour, which made the courtiers begin to pay respect to her. The King was very well pleased at this pleasantry, and having thanked him for so necessary an offer: "Monsieur le Chevalier," said he, "in what style do you intend to dress yourself for the ball? I leave you the choice of all countries." "If so," said the Chevalier, "I will dress after the French manner, in order to disguise myself; for they already do me the honour to take me for an Englishman in your city of London. Had it not been for this, I should have wished to have appeared as a Roman; but for fear of embroiling myself with

Prince Rupert,[9] who so warmly espouses the interests of Alexander against Lord Thanet,[10] who declares himself for Cæsar, I dare no longer think of assuming the hero; nevertheless, though I may dance awkwardly, yet, by observing the tune, and with a little alertness, I hope to come off pretty well; besides, Miss Hamilton will take care that too much attention shall not be paid to me. As for my dress, I shall send Termes off to-morrow morning; and if I do not show you at his return the most splendid habit you have ever seen, look upon mine as the most disgraced nation in your masquerade."

Termes set out with ample instructions on the subject of his journey; and his master, redoubling his impatience on an occasion like the present, before the courier could be landed, began to count the minutes in expectation of his return. Thus was he employed until the very eve of the ball; and that was the day that Miss Hamilton and her little society had fixed for the execution of their project.

Martial[11] gloves were then very much in fashion. She had by chance several pairs of them: she sent one to Miss Blague, accompanied with four yards of yellow riband, the palest she could find, to which she added this note:

"You were the other day more charming than all the fair women in the world: you looked yesterday still more fair than you did the day before: if you go on, what will become of my heart? But it is a long

[9] See footnote, p. 312.
[10] Either John or Nicholas Tufton, the second and third Earls of Thanet. The second Earl died in 1664, and was succeeded by his eldest son Nicholas, b. 1631, ob. 1679. From the hardships the family suffered in the Royalist cause they adopted the motto "Fiel pero desdichado." In the Tufton chapel at Rainham, near Rochester, there are numerous ancestral tombs.
[11] Martial was a fashionable Paris glove-maker at the time (see Vizetelly's edition of the *Memoirs*, vol. i. p. 165).

time since that has been a prey to your pretty little *young wild boar's eyes.*[12] Shall you be at the masquerade to-morrow? But can there be any charms at an entertainment at which you are not present? It does not signify: I shall know you in whatever disguise you may be: but I shall be better informed of my fate by the present I send you. You will wear knots of this riband in your hair; and these gloves will kiss the most beautiful hands in the universe."

This billet, with the present, was delivered to Miss Blague with the same success as the other had been conveyed to Lady Muskerry. Miss Hamilton had just received an account of it, when the latter came to pay her a visit: something seemed to possess her thoughts very much, when, having stayed some time, her cousin desired her to walk into her cabinet. As soon as they were there: "I desire your secrecy for what I am going to tell you," said Lady Muskerry. "Do you not wonder what strange creatures men are? Do not trust to them, my dear cousin. My Lord Muskerry, who, before our marriage, could have passed whole days and nights in seeing me dance, thinks proper now to forbid me dancing, and says it does not become me. This is not all: he has so often rung in my ears the subject of this masquerade, that I am obliged to hide from him the honour the Queen has done me in inviting me to it. However, I am surprised I am not informed who is to be my partner: but if you knew what a plague it is to find out, in this cursed town, in what manner the people of Babylon dress, you would pity me for what I have suffered since the time I have been appointed. Besides, the cost which it puts me to is beyond all imagination."

[12]*Marcassin* is French for a wild boar: The eyes of this creature being remarkably small and lively, from thence the French say, "Des yeux marcassins," to signify *little, though roguish eyes;* or, as we say, *pigs' eyes.*

Here it was that Miss Hamilton's inclination to laugh, which had increased in proportion as she endeavoured to suppress it, at length overcame her, and broke out in an immoderate fit. Lady Muskerry took it in good humour, not doubting but it was the fantastical conduct of her husband that she was laughing at. Miss Hamilton told her that all husbands were much the same, and that one ought not to be concerned at their whims; that she did not know who was to be her partner at the masquerade; but that, as she was named, the gentleman named with her would certainly not fail to attend her; although she could not comprehend why he had not yet declared himself, unless he likewise had some fantastical spouse, who had forbid him to dance.

This conversation being finished, Lady Muskerry went away in great haste, to endeavour to learn some news of her partner. Those who were accomplices in the plot were laughing very heartily at this visit, when Lord Muskerry paid them one in his turn, and taking Miss Hamilton aside: "Do you know," said he, "whether there is to be any ball in the city to-morrow?" "No," said she; "but why do you ask?" "Because," said he, "I am informed that my wife is making great preparations of dress. I know very well she is not to be at the masquerade: that I have taken care of; but as the devil is in her for dancing, I am very much afraid that she will be affording some fresh subject for ridicule, notwithstanding all my precautions: however, if it was amongst the citizens, at some private party, I should not much mind it."

They satisfied him as well as they could, and having dismissed him, under pretence of a thousand things they had to prepare for the next day, Miss Hamilton thought herself at liberty for that morning, when in came Miss Price, one of the maids of honour to the Duchess."[13] This was just what she was wishing for. This lady and Miss Blague had been at variance some time, on account of Duncan,[14] whom Miss Price had drawn away from the other; and hatred still subsisted between these two divinities.

Though the maids of honour were not nominated for the masquerade, yet they were to assist at it; and, consequently, were to neglect nothing to set them-

[13] This lady was Goditha Price, the sister of Henrietta Maria Price, who was maid of honour to the Queen (the latter figures in the list of names in Chamberlayne's *Angliæ Notitia*).

According to Pepys, a Miss Price was the mistress of the Duke of York, but was not openly acknowledged as such, going to her assignations "up and down the privy stairs" (10th June 1666). The footnote to Scott's edition of the *Memoirs* points out that Miss Price was maid of honour to the Queen, not the Duchess, though her Christian name is not specified; but the fact of the lady being the Duke's mistress looks as if she was, as stated by Gramont, maid of honour to the Duchess, therefore we will take as conclusive Mr. Steinman's assertion that it was Goditha who died unmarried and was buried at St. Margaret's, Westminster, 7th September 1678.

On the other hand, there appears to be a similarity between Gramont's Miss (or rather *Mrs.*, as single ladies were called) Price and the lady correspondent of the Earl of Chesterfield in 1665 or 1666, who sent him a pair of gloves with a poem by Lord Rochester, the latter being endorsed by Chesterfield: "From Mrs. Prise, *Maid of Honour to Her Majesty*." The association of Rochester in both instances strengthens this supposition (*vide* the *Memoirs*).

The Queen's maid of honour, Henrietta Maria Price, became the second wife of Alexander Stanhope, son of Sir John Stanhope of Elvaston, Derbyshire. Her father was Sir Herbert Price, Bart., Master of the Household to Queen Henrietta Maria (hence perhaps his daughter's name), and afterwards to King Charles II. She was buried in Westminster Abbey, 23rd October 1674. There was also at Court a certain Lady Price *née* Warcup. Her father, Sir Edmond Warcup, belonged to an old Oxfordshire family, and wrote with pride that his daughter "was one night and t'other with the King, and very graciously received by him" (see Wood's *Fasti Oxon.* vol. ii. p. 184; also Grainger, vol. iv. p. 438. See also Steinman's *Memoir of Barbara, Duchess of Cleveland*, p. 73; Pepys's *Diary*, vol. v. p. 321; and *The Letters of Philip, Earl of Chesterfield*, pp. 136-137).

[14] Dongan (not Duncan). Lord Orford says of this house were the ancient Earls of Limerick.

selves off to advantage. Miss Hamilton had still another pair of gloves of the same sort as those she had sent to Miss Blague, which she made a present of to her rival, with a few knots of the same riband, which appeared to have been made on purpose for her, brown[15] as she was. Miss Price returned her a thousand thanks, and promised to do herself the honour of wearing them at the ball. "You will oblige me if you do," said Miss Hamilton, "but if you mention that such a trifle as this comes from me, I shall never forgive you. But," continued she, "do not go and rob poor Miss Blague of the Marquis Brisacier, as you already have of Duncan.[16] I know very well that it is wholly in your power: you have wit: you speak French: and were he once to converse with you ever so little, the other could have no pretensions to him." This was enough. Miss Blague was only ridiculous and coquettish: Miss Price was ridiculous, coquettish, and something else besides.

The day being come, the Court, more splendid than ever, exhibited all its magnificence at this masquerade. The company were all met except the Chevalier de Gramont: everybody was astonished that he should be one of the last at such a time, as his readiness was so remarkable on every occasion; but they were still more surprised to see him at length appear in an ordinary court-dress, which he had worn before. The thing was preposterous on such an occasion, and very extraordinary with respect to him: in vain had he the finest point-lace, with the largest and best-powdered peruke imaginable: his dress, magnificent enough for any other purpose, was not at all proper for this entertainment.

The King immediately took notice of it. "Chevalier," said he, "Termes is not arrived then?" "Pardon

[15] Dark.   [16] Dongan.

me, sire," said he; "God be thanked!" "Why God be thanked?" said the King; "has anything happened to him on the road?" "Sire," said the Chevalier de Gramont, "this is the history of my dress, and of Termes, my messenger." At these words the ball, ready to begin, was suspended: the dancers making a circle around the Chevalier de Gramont, he continued his story in the following manner:

"It is now two days since this fellow ought to have been here, according to my orders and his protestations; you may judge of my impatience all this day, when I found he did not come. At last, after I had heartily cursed him, about an hour ago he arrived, splashed all over from head to foot, booted up to the waist, and looking as if he had been excommunicated. 'Very well, Mr. Scoundrel,' said I, 'this is just like you; you must be waited for to the very last minute, and it is a miracle that you are arrived at all.' 'Yes, faith,' said he, 'it is a miracle. You are always grumbling: I had the finest suit in the world made for you, which the Duke de Guise himself was at the trouble of ordering.' 'Give it me then, scoundrel,' said I. 'Sir,' said he, 'if I did not employ a dozen embroiderers upon it, who did nothing but work day and night, I am a rascal: I never left them one moment.' 'And where is it, traitor?' said I: 'do not stand here prating, while I should be dressing.' 'I had,' continued he, 'packed it up, made it tight, and folded it in such a manner, that all the rain in the world could never have been able to reach it; and I rid post, day and night, knowing your impatience, and that you were not to be trifled with.' 'But where is it?' said I. 'Lost, sir,' said he, clasping his hands. 'How! lost,' said I, in surprise. 'Yes, lost, perished, swallowed up: what can I say more?' 'What! was the packet-boat cast away then?' said I. 'Oh! indeed, sir, a great deal worse, as you

shall see,' answered he: 'I was within half a league of
Calais yesterday morning, and I was resolved to go by
the seaside, to make greater haste; but, indeed, they
say very true, that nothing is like the highway; for I
got into a quicksand, where I sunk up to the chin.' 'A
quicksand,' said I, 'near Calais?' 'Yes, sir,' said he,
'and such a quicksand, that, the devil take me, if they
saw anything but the top of my head when they pulled
me out: as for my horse, fifteen men could scarce
get him out; but the portmanteau, where I had unfortunately put your clothes, could never be found: it
must be at least a league underground.' "

"This, sire," continued the Chevalier de Gramont,
"is the adventure, and the relation which this honest
gentleman[17] has given me of it. I should certainly have
killed him, but I was afraid of making Miss Hamilton
wait, and I was desirous of giving Your Majesty
immediate advice of the quicksand, that your couriers
may take care to avoid it."

The King was ready to split his sides with laughing,
when the Chevalier de Gramont, resuming the discourse: "Apropos, sire," said he, "I had forgot to tell
you, that, to increase my ill-humour, I was stopped,
as I was getting out of my chair, by the devil of
a phantom in masquerade, who would by all means
persuade me that the Queen had commanded me to
dance with her; and as I excused myself with the
least rudeness possible, she charged me to find out who
was to be her partner, and desired me to send him
to her immediately. So that Your Majesty will do
well to give orders about it; for she has placed herself
in ambush in a coach, to seize upon all those who pass
through Whitehall. However, I must tell you, that
it is worth while to see her dress, for she must have at
least sixty ells of gauze and silver tissue about her,

[17] Fellow (Vizetelly).

not to mention a sort of a pyramid upon her head, adorned with a hundred thousand baubles."

This last account surprised all the assembly, except those who had a share in the plot. The Queen assured them that all she had appointed for the ball were present; and the King, having paused some minutes, "I bet," said he, "that it is the Duchess of Newcastle,"[18] "And I," said Lord Muskerry, coming up to Miss Hamilton, "will bet it is another fool; for I am very much mistaken if it is not my wife."

The King was for sending to know who it was, and to bring her in. Lord Muskerry offered himself for that service, for the reason already mentioned; and it was very well he did so. Miss Hamilton was not sorry for this, knowing very well that he was not mistaken in his conjecture; the jest would have gone much farther than she intended, if the Princess of Babylon had appeared in all her glory.

The ball was not very well executed, if one may be allowed the expression, so long as they danced only

[18] Margaret, daughter of Sir Thomas Lucas of Colchester, and sister of John, Lord Lucas. She married William Cavendish, Marquis of Newcastle, created Duke in 1665. She had been one of the maids of honour to Charles the First's queen, whom she attended when forced to leave England. At Paris she married the Duke of Newcastle, and continued in exile with him until the Restoration. After her return to England, she lived entirely devoted to letters, and published many volumes of plays, poems, letters, etc. She died in 1673, and was buried in Westminster Abbey. There is a whole-length of this duchess at Welbeck, in a theatrical dress, which, tradition says, she generally wore. She had always a maid of honour in waiting during the night, who was often called up to register the Duchess's conceptions. These were all of a literary kind; for her Grace left no children. Pepys writes, 11th April 1667: "The whole story of this lady is a romance and all she do is romantick." Her antiquated appearance is thus described by him: "a velvet cap, her hair about her ears, many black patches, because of pimples about her mouth; naked-necked, without anything about it, and a black *just-au-corps*" (jacket). Wherever she went it appears she had a crowd following her. See Pepys's *Diary*, vol. vi. pp. 246, 269, 290, 299, 312.

slow dances; and yet there were as good dancers, and as beautiful women in this assembly, as were to be found in the whole world; but as their number was not great, they left the French and went to country dances. When they had danced some time, the King thought fit to introduce his auxiliaries, to give the others a little respite; the Queen's and the Duchess's maids of honour were therefore called in to dance[19] with the gentlemen.

Then it was that they were at leisure to take notice of Miss Blague, and they found that the billet they had conveyed to her on the part of Brisacier had its effect. She was more yellow than saffron: her[20] hair was stuffed with the citron-coloured riband, which she had put there out of complaisance; and, to inform Brisacier of his fate, she raised often to her head her victorious hands, adorned with the gloves we have before mentioned. But, if they were surprised to see her in a head-dress that made her look more wan than ever, she was very differently surprised to see Miss Price partake with her in every particular of Brisacier's present. Her surprise soon turned to jealousy; for her rival had not failed to join in conversation with him, on account of what had been insinuated to her the evening before; nor did Brisacier fail to return her first advances, without paying the least attention to the fair Blague, nor to the signs which she was

---

[19] The masquerade took place on 2nd February 1664-5. Under that date Evelyn says in his *Diary:* "I saw a masq perform'd at Court by 6 gentlemen and 6 ladys—surprizing His Majesty, it being Candlemas day." On the 3rd, Pepys says: There "were six women (my Lady Castlemayne and Duchesse of Monmouth being two of them) and six men (the Duke of Monmouth and Lord Arran and Monsieur Blanfort [Blanquefort, afterwards Earl of Feversham] being three of them) in vizards, but most rich and antique dresses, did dance admirably and most gloriously. God give us cause to continue the mirthe!"

[20] *Light* hair (Vizetelly).

tormenting herself to make him, to inform him of his happy destiny.

Miss Price was short and thick, and consequently no dancer. The Duke of Buckingham, who brought Brisacier forward as often as he could, came to desire him, on the part of the King, to dance with Miss Blague, without knowing what was then passing in that nymph's heart. Brisacier excused himself, on account of the contempt that he had for country dances. Miss Blague thought that it was herself that he despised; and seeing that he was engaged in conversation with her mortal enemy, she began to dance, without knowing what she was doing. Though her indignation and jealousy were sufficiently remarkable to divert the Court, none but Miss Hamilton and her accomplices understood the joke perfectly. Their pleasure was quite complete; for Lord Muskerry returned, still more confounded at the vision of which the Chevalier de Gramont had given the description. He acquainted Miss Hamilton that it was Lady Muskerry herself, a thousand times more ridiculous than she had ever been before, and that he had had an immense trouble to get her home, and place a sentry at her chamber door.

The reader may think, perhaps, that we have dwelt too long on these trifling incidents; perhaps he may be right. We will therefore pass to others.

Everything favoured the Chevalier de Gramont in the new passion which he entertained. He was not, however, without rivals; but, what is a great deal more extraordinary, he was without uneasiness. He was acquainted with their understandings, and no stranger to Miss Hamilton's way of thinking.

Among her lovers, the most considerable, though the least professedly so, was the Duke of York: it was in vain for him to conceal it, the Court was too well acquainted with his character to doubt of his inclinations for her. He did not think it proper to declare such sentiments as were not fit for Miss Hamilton to hear; but he talked to her as much as he could, and ogled her with great assiduity. As hunting was his favourite diversion, that sport employed him one part of the day, and he came home generally much fatigued; but Miss Hamilton's presence revived him, when he found her either with the Queen or the Duchess. There it was that, not daring to tell her of what lay heavy on his heart, he entertained her with what he had in his head; telling her miracles of the cunning of foxes and the mettle of horses; giving her accounts of broken legs and arms, dislocated shoulders, and other curious and entertaining adventures; after which, his eyes told her the rest, till such time as sleep interrupted their conversation; for these tender interpreters could not help sometimes composing[21] themselves in the midst of their ogling.

The Duchess was not at all alarmed at a passion which her rival was far from thinking sincere, and with which she used to divert herself, as far as respect would permit her; on the contrary, as Her Highness had an affection and esteem for Miss Hamilton, she never treated her more graciously than on the present occasion.

The two Russells, uncle[22] and nephew,[23] were two other of the Chevalier de Gramont's rivals. The

[21] Closing (Vizetelly).

[22] John Russell, third son of Francis, the fourth Earl of Bedford, and younger brother of the first Duke of Bedford, colonel of the first regiment of foot guards. He died unmarried, 1681. In 1664, at the time Gramont speaks of, Russell was fully twenty years younger than above described (see *Notes and Queries,* Series I. vol. ix. p. 584). Pepys mentions him at a Court ball 15th November 1666.

[23] William, eldest son of Hon. Edward Russell, who was the brother of Colonel John, mentioned above, and William, the fifth Earl of Bedford (afterwards created Duke), whose son Lord

uncle was full seventy,[24] and had distinguished himself by his courage and fidelity in the civil wars. His passions and intentions, with regard to Miss Hamilton, appeared both at once; but his magnificence only appeared by halves in those gallantries which love inspires.

It was not long since the fashion of high-crowned hats had been left off, in order to fall into the other extreme. Old Russell, amazed at so terrible a change, resolved to keep a medium, which made him remarkable. He was still more so, by his constancy for cut[25] doublets, which he supported a long time after they had been universally suppressed; but, what was more surprising than all was a certain mixture of avarice and liberality, constantly at war with each other, ever since he had entered the lists with love.

His nephew was only of a younger brother's family, but was considered as his uncle's heir; and though he was under the necessity of attending to his uncle for an establishment, and still more so of humouring him, in order to get his estate, he could not avoid his fate. Mrs. Middleton showed him a sufficient degree of preference; but her favours could not secure him from the charms of Miss Hamilton. His person would have had nothing disagreeable in it if he had but left it to nature; but he was formal in all his actions, and silent even to stupidity; and yet rather more tiresome when he did speak.

William Russell was beheaded for implication in the Rye House Plot. A portrait of the last mentioned has been given in three of the illustrated editions of De Gramont, though he was a cousin of the William Russell described above, and had no connection with the adventures recorded in the *Memoirs*. The Chevalier's youthful rival was half-brother to the Misses Brooke. He died unmarried in 1674.

[24] In the original French it is sixty (see Vizetelly's edition), but to give the uncle's real age at this time, forty would be more correct.   [25] Slashed (Vizetelly).

The Chevalier de Gramont, very much at his ease in all these competitions, engaged himself more and more in his passion, without forming other designs, or conceiving other hopes, than to render himself agreeable. Although his passion was openly declared, no person at Court regarded it otherwise than as a habit of gallantry, which goes no farther than to do justice to merit.

His monitor, Saint-Evremond, was quite of a different opinion, and finding that, besides an immense increase of magnificence and assiduity, he regretted those hours which he bestowed on play; that he no longer sought after those long and agreeable conversations they used to have together; and that this new attachment everywhere robbed him of himself:

"Monsieur le Chevalier," said he, "methinks that for some time you have left the town beauties and their lovers in perfect repose. Mrs. Middleton makes fresh conquests with impunity, and wears your presents, under your nose, without your taking the smallest notice. Poor Miss Warmester has been very quietly brought to bed in the midst of the Court, without your having even said a word about it. I foresaw it plain enough, Monsieur le Chevalier, you have got acquainted with Miss Hamilton, and—what has never before happened to you—you are really in love. But let us consider a little what may be the consequence. In the first place, then, I believe you have not the least intention of seducing her; such is her birth and merit, that if you were in possession of the estate and title of your family, it might be excusable in you to offer yourself upon honourable terms, however ridiculous marriage may be in general; for, if you only wish for wit, prudence, and the treasures of beauty, you could not pay your addresses to a more proper person. But for you, who possess only a very moderate share of those of fortune, you cannot pay your addresses more improperly.

"For your brother Toulongeon,[26] whose disposition I am acquainted with, will not have the complaisance to die to favour your pretensions. But suppose you had a competent fortune for you both,—and that is supposing a good deal,—are you acquainted with the delicacy not to say capriciousness, of this fair one about such an engagement? Do you know that she has had the choice of the best matches in England? The Duke of Richmond paid his addresses to her first; but though he was in love with her, still he was mercenary. However, the King, observing that want of fortune was the only impediment to the match, took that article upon himself, out of regard to the Duke of Ormonde, to the merit and birth of Miss Hamilton, and to her father's services; but resenting that a man, who pretended to be in love, should bargain like a merchant, and likewise reflecting upon his character in the world, she did not think that being Duchess of Richmond was a sufficient recompense for the danger that was to be feared from a brute and a debauchee.

"Has not little Jermyn, notwithstanding his uncle's great estate, and his own brilliant reputation, failed in his suit to her? And has she ever so much as vouchsafed to look at Henry Howard,[27] who is upon

[26] Count de Toulongeon, elder brother of the Count de Gramont, *ob.* 1679.

[27] Henry Howard (*b.* 1628, *ob.* 1684) succeeded his brother Thomas in the Dukedom of Norfolk (revived 1664) in 1677, before which (1672) he was created Earl of Norwich and constituted Earl Marshal of England. He bequeathed the library made by his grandfather, Thomas, Earl of Arundel, to the Royal Society, and the famous Arundel marbles to Oxford university.

Evelyn says, 23rd January 1678: "Din'd with the Duke of Norfolk, being the first time I had seene him since the death of his elder brother, who died at Padoa in Italy, where he resided above 30 yeares. The Duke had now newly declar'd his marriage to his concubine, whom he promis'd me he never would marry."

the point of being the first duke in England, and who is already in actual possession of all the estates of the house of Norfolk? I confess that he is a clown, but what other lady in all England would not have dispensed with his stupidity and his disagreeable person to be the first duchess in the kingdom, with twenty-five thousand a year?

"To conclude, Lord Falmouth has told me himself that he has always looked upon her as the only acquisition wanting to complete his happiness; but, that even at the height of the splendour of his fortune, he never had had the assurance to open his sentiments to her; that he either felt in himself too much weakness, or too much pride, to be satisfied with obtaining her solely by the persuasion of her relations; and that, though the first refusals of the fair on such occasions are not much minded, he knew with what an air she had received the addresses of those whose persons she did not like. After this, Monsieur le Chevalier, consider what method you intend to pursue: for if you are in love, the passion will still increase, and the greater the attachment, the less capable will you be of making those serious reflections that are now in your power."

"My poor philosopher," answered the Chevalier de Gramont, "you understand Latin very well, you can

This was his second wife, Jane Bickerton, the actress daughter of a Scotch gentleman, Robert Bickerton, gentleman of the wine cellar to Charles II. Evelyn speaks of the Duke's "Palace" (Ham House, Weybridge), newly built at great expense, and of its costly fittings, pictures, etc. It was afterwards sold to James II.'s mistress, the Countess of Dorchester, and through her daughter descended to the Earls of Portmore. Nothing now remains but the (restored) piers of the entrance gate (for further particulars see *Secret Chambers and Hiding Places*, pp. 214-216). The Duke of Norfolk appears to have parted with most of his valuable pictures. Evelyn asked whether he would part with his Raphael cartoons and drawings (on 9th March 1683), and was told "the late Sir Peter Lely had gotten some of his best" (Evelyn's *Diary*). These were dispersed at that artists's famous sale of pictures.

make good verses, you understand the course, and are acquainted with the nature of the stars in the firmament; but, as for the luminaries of the terrestrial globe, you are utterly unacquainted with them. You have told me nothing about Miss Hamilton but what the King told me three days ago. That she has refused the savages you have mentioned is all in her favour: if she had admitted their addresses, I would have had nothing to say to her, though I love her to distraction. Attend now to what I am going to say: I am resolved to marry her, and I will have my tutor Saint-Evremond himself to be the first man to commend me for it. As for an establishment, I shall make my peace with the King, and will solicit him to make her one of the ladies of the bed-chamber to the Queen. This he will grant me. Toulongeon will die, without my assistance, and notwithstanding all his care; and Miss Hamilton will have Semeac,[28] with the Chevalier de Gramont, as an indemnification for the Norfolks and Richmonds. Now, have you anything to advance against this project? For I will bet you an hundred louis that everything will happen as I have foretold it."

At this time the King's attachment to Miss Stewart was so public, that every person perceived, that if she was but possessed of art, she might become as absolute a mistress over his conduct as she was over his heart.[29] This was a fine opportunity for those who

[28] Séméac, a country seat belonging to the Gramonts.
[29] 8th February 1662-3. Pepys mentions a story, related by one Captain Ferrers, of an entertainment given by Lady Castlemaine, "a frolique that they two must be married. Married they were with ring and all other ceremonies of Church service, and ribbands and a sack posset in bed and flinging the stocking; but in the close, it is said that my Lady Castlemaine, who was the bridegroom, rose, and the King came and took her place with pretty Mrs. Stuart." This story, however, is unsubstantiated, though it was certainly rumoured that Frances Stewart had become the King's mistress (vide Pepys, 17th February 1662-3, 18th May 1663, and 15th April 1666). That these were only

had experience and ambition. The Duke of Buckingham formed the design of governing her, in order to
ingratiate himself with the King: God knows what a
governor he would have been, and what a head he was
possessed of, to guide another. However, he was the
properest man in the world to insinuate himself with
Miss Stewart; she was childish in her behaviour, and
laughed at everything, and her taste for frivolous
amusements, though unaffected, was only allowable in
a girl about twelve or thirteen years old. A child,
however, she was, in every other respect, except playing with a doll. Blindman's buff was her most favourite amusement. She was building castles of cards,
while the deepest play was going on in her apartments, where you saw her surrounded by eager courtiers, who handed her the cards, or young architects,
who endeavoured to imitate her.

She had, however, a passion for music, and had
some taste for singing. The Duke of Buckingham,

rumours may be gathered from an entry on 6th November 1663.
Lord Sandwich here tells Pepys "how he and Sir H. Bennet, the
Duke of Buckingham and his Duchesse, was of a committee with
somebody else for the getting of Mrs. Stewart for the King; but
that she proves a common slut, and is advised at Somerset House
by the Queen Mother and by her mother, and so all the plot is
spoiled and the whole committee broke." Three days later,
Pierce, the surgeon, tells Pepys "how the King is now become
besotted upon Mrs. Stewart, that he gets into corners, and will
be with her half an hour together kissing her to the observation
of all the world; and she now stays by herself and expects it";
and on 20th January 1663-4, the diarist records from the same
source that the King "do doat upon Mrs. Stewart only" and
"dallies with her openly, and then privately in his chamber below,
where the very sentrys observe his going in and out, and that so
commonly that the Duke or any of the nobles when they would
ask where the King is, they will ordinarily say, 'Is the King
above or below?' meaning with Mrs. Stewart." On 8th February
1663-4, again from Pierce, Pepys learns how the Queen "will of
herself stop before she goes sometimes into her dressing-room
till she knows whether the King be there, for fear he should be
as she hath sometimes taken him with Mrs. Stewart."

who built the finest towers of cards imaginable, had
an agreeable voice. She had no aversion to scandal;
and the Duke was both the father and the mother of
scandal. He made songs, and invented old women's
stories, with which she was delighted; but his particular talent consisted in turning into ridicule whatever
was ridiculous in other people, and in taking them off,
even in their presence, without their perceiving it. In
short, he knew how to act all parts with so much grace
and pleasantry, that it was difficult to do without him,
when he had a mind to make himself agreeable; and
he made himself so necessary to Miss Stewart's amusement, that she sent all over the town to seek for him,
when he did not attend the King to her apartments.

He was extremely handsome,[30] and still thought
himself much more so than he really was. Although
he had a great deal of discernment, yet his vanity made

[30] George Villiers, the second Duke of Buckingham, was born
30th January 1627. Lord Orford observes: "When this extraordinary man, with the figure and genius of Alcibiades, could
equally charm the presbyterian Fairfax and the dissolute Charles;
when he alike ridiculed that witty king and his solemn chancellor;
when he plotted the ruin of his country with a cabal of bad ministers, or, equally unprincipled, supported its cause with bad
patriots,—one laments that such parts should have been devoid
of every virtue; but when Alcibiades turns chemist; when he is
a real bubble and a visionary miser; when ambition is but a
frolic; when the worst designs are for the foolishest ends,—contempt extinguishes all reflection on his character."

"The portrait of this duke has been drawn by four masterly
hands. Burnet has hewn it out with his rough chisel; Count
Hamilton touched it with that slight delicacy that finishes while
it seems but to sketch; Dryden caught the living likeness; Pope
completed the historical resemblance" (*Royal Authors,* vol. ii.
p. 78).

Bishop Burnet says, he "was a man of noble presence. He
had a great liveliness of wit, and a peculiar faculty of turning
all things into ridicule, with bold figures, and natural descriptions.
He had no sort of literature, only he was drawn into chemistry;
and for some years he thought he was very near the finding
the philosopher's stone, which had the effect that attends on all
such men as he was when they are drawn in, to lay out for it.

him mistake some civilities as intended for his person, which were only bestowed on his wit and drollery. In short, being seduced by too good an opinion of his own merit, he forgot his first project and his Portuguese mistress, in order to pursue a fancy in which he mistook himself; for he no sooner began to act a serious part with Miss Stewart, than he met with so severe a repulse that he abandoned at once all his

He had no principles of religion, virtue, or friendship—pleasure, frolic, or extravagant diversion was all that he laid to heart. He was true to nothing; for he was not true to himself. He had no steadiness nor conduct: he could keep no secret, nor execute any design without spoiling it. He could never fix his thoughts, nor govern his estate, though then the greatest in England. He was bred about the King, and for many years he had a great ascendency over him; but he spake of him to all persons with that contempt, that at last he drew a lasting disgrace upon himself. And he at length ruined both body and mind, fortune and reputation equally. The madness of vice appeared in his person in very eminent instances; since at last he became contemptible and poor, sickly, and sunk in his parts, as well as in all other respects; so that his conversation was as much avoided as ever it had been courted."—*History of his Own Time,* vol. i. p. 137.

Reresby speaks of Buckingham as "the finest gentleman of person and wit I think I ever saw" (*Memoirs* p. 40). Like the first Duke, he had a particularly graceful mien, and in horsemanship, fencing, or dancing, nobody could surpass him. Profligacy, vanity, and restless ambition were perhaps Buckingham's chief characteristics; but with all his faults he is said to have been charitable, good-natured, and forgiving, and, like his rival Arlington, always courteous. His chief amusements, especially in the latter part of his life, were racing and hunting, and it was while following the hounds that he caught a chill which resulted in his death, at the house of a tenant at Kirkby Moorside, on 16th April 1687. With the death of Charles II., Buckingham had retired from the political arena, and lived peacefully in Yorkshire. He had fallen into disgrace in 1674, but was again received into favour towards the end of Charles's reign. His wife, Mary Fairfax, survived him seventeen years, and was buried with her husband in Henry VII.'s Chapel, Westminster. Among the Duke of Buckingham's satirical poems, lampoons, and plays, *The Rehearsal,* published in 1672, is by far the best. See Buckingham's *Miscellaneous Works,* 1704-5; also *Dict. of Nat. Biography,* vol. lviii. pp. 337-345.

designs upon her. However, the familiarity she had procured him with the King opened the way to those favours to which he was afterwards advanced.

"The Duke of Bucks is one," says Samuel Butler, "that has studied the whole body of vice. His parts are disproportionate to the whole, and, like a monster, he has more of some, and less of others, than he should have. He has pulled down all that nature raised in him, and built himself up again after a model of his own. He has dammed up all those lights that nature made into the noblest prospects of the world, and opened other little blind loopholes backward, by turning day into night, and night into day. His appetite to his pleasures is diseased and crazy, like the pica in a woman, that longs to eat that which was never made for food, or a girl in the green sickness, that eats chalk and mortar. Perpetual surfeits of pleasure have filled his mind with bad and vicious humours (as well as his body with a nursery of diseases), which makes him affect new and extravagant ways, as being sick and tired with the old. Continual wine, women, and music, put false value upon things, which, by custom, become habitual, and debauch his understanding so, that he retains no right notion nor sense of things. And as the same dose of the same physic has no operation on those that are much used to it, so his pleasures require larger proportion of excess and variety, to render him sensible of them. He rises, eats, and goes to bed by the Julian account, long after all others that go by the new style, and keeps the same hours with owls and the antipodes. He is a great observer of the Tartar customs, and never eats till the great cham, having dined, makes proclamation that all the world may go to dinner. He does not dwell in his house, but haunts it like an evil spirit, that walks all night, to disturb the family, and never appears by day. He lives perpetually benighted, runs out of his life, and loses his time as men do their ways in the dark; and as blind men are led by their dogs, so is he governed by some mean servant or other, that relates to his pleasures. He is as inconstant as the moon which he lives under; and although he does nothing but advise with his pillow all day, he is as great a stranger to himself as he is to the rest of the world. His mind entertains all things very freely that come and go, but, like guests and strangers, they are not welcome if they stay long. This lays him open to all cheats, quacks, and impostors, who apply to every particular humour while it lasts, and afterwards vanish. Thus, with St. Paul, though in a different sense, he dies daily, and only lives in the night. He deforms nature, while he intends to adorn her, like Indians that hang jewels in their lips and noses. His ears are perpetually drilled with a fiddlestick. He endures pleasures with less patience than other men do their pains" (Butler's *Posthumous Works,* vol. ii. p. 72).

Lord Arlington[31] took up the project which the
Duke of Buckingham had abandoned, and endeavoured to gain possession of the mind of the mistress,
in order to govern the master. A man of greater merit
and higher birth than himself might, however, have
been satisfied with the fortune he had already acquired.

[31] Henry Bennet, Earl of Arlington, second son of Sir John
Bennet of Harlington, Middlesex, born 1618. He was secretary
to the Duke of York in France before the Restoration. When
Charles came to the throne he was made Keeper of the Privy
Purse, and, according to Burnet (vol. i. p. 182, 1833 edit.), with
his friend Sir Charles Berkeley, had the management of the Royal
mistresses; no easy task, one would imagine, but his easy principles, natural cunning, and dissimulation, combined with his
courtly manner and good breeding, peculiarly adapted him for
such an office. "He was little calculated for bold measures on
account of his natural timidity," says Macpherson (*Original
Papers,* vol. i.), "and that defect created an opinion of his moderation that was ascribed to virtue. His facility to adopt new
measures was forgotten in his readiness to acknowledge the
errors of the old. The deficiency of his integrity was forgiven
in the decency of his dishonesty." He managed to keep in the
King's good graces until his retirement towards the end of
Charles's reign. His solemn face and formal gait, his official
white staff and the ungainly black patch across the bridge of
his nose made him the object of much mimicry among the
younger generation of courtiers (see *Echard,* p. 369).
   He was made Secretary of State, October 1662, and in the
following year was created Viscount Thetford and Earl of
Arlington: by an error at the Heralds' College the H was
omitted. It was at his seat, Euston Hall, where Louise Keroualle,
afterwards Duchess of Portsmouth, became the King's mistress
(see Evelyn's *Diary,* 9th October 1671). Both Pepys and Evelyn
mention his town residence "Goring House," which occupied the
site of the present Buckingham Palace. The latter speaks of the
costly interior decorations—pictures, cabinets, hangings, etc.—
"the most princely furniture that any subject had in England,"
which, with the mansion, were destroyed by fire in September
1674; Pepys, 12th July 1666; Evelyn, 7th April 1673 and 21st September 1674; also *Hist. M.S. Com. Rep.* 7, App. p. 492).
   The Earl died 28th July 1685 (and was buried at Euston),
leaving an only daughter, Isabella, who married (1672) Henry,
Earl of Euston, afterwards Duke of Grafton, Charles II.'s son
by the Duchess of Cleveland. See Cunningham's *London; Dict.
of Nat. Biography,* vol. iv. pp. 230-233; Macpherson's *Original
Papers,* vol. i.; *Works* of John Sheffield, Duke of Buckingham, etc.

His first negotiations were during the treaty of the Pyrenees; and though he was unsuccessful in his proceedings for his employer, yet he did not altogether lose his time: for he perfectly acquired in his exterior the serious air and profound gravity of the Spaniards, and imitated pretty well their tardiness in business. He had a scar across his nose, which was covered by a long patch, or rather by a small plaister, in form of a lozenge.

Scars in the face commonly give a man a certain fierce and martial air, which sets him off to advantage; but it was quite the contrary with him, and this remarkable plaister so well suited his mysterious looks, that it seemed an addition to his gravity and self-sufficiency.

Arlington, under the mask of this compound countenance, where great earnestness passed for business, and impenetrable stupidity for secrecy, had given himself the character of a great politician; and no one having leisure to examine him, he was taken at his word, and had been made minister and secretary of state, upon the credit of his own importance.

His ambition soaring still above these high stations, after having provided himself with a great number of fine maxims, and some historical anecdotes, he obtained an audience of Miss Stewart, in order to display them; at the same time offering her his most humble services, and best advice, to assist her in conducting herself in the situation to which it had pleased God and her virtue to raise her. But he was only in the preface of his speech, when she recollected that he was at the head of those whom the Duke of Buckingham used to mimic; and as his presence and his language exactly revived the ridiculous ideas that had been given her of him, she could not forbear bursting out into a fit of laughter in his face, so much the more violent as she had for a long time struggled to suppress it.

The minister was enraged: his pride became his post, and his punctilious behaviour merited all the ridicule which could be attached to it. He quitted her abruptly, with all the fine advice he had prepared for her, and was almost tempted to carry it to Lady Castlemaine, and to unite himself with her interests; or immediately to quit the Court party, and declaim freely in Parliament against the grievances of the State, and particularly to propose an Act to forbid the keeping of mistresses. But his prudence conquered his resentments; and only thinking how to enjoy with pleasure the blessings of fortune, he sent to Holland for a wife,[32] in order to complete his felicity.

Hamilton[33] was, of all the courtiers, the best qualified to succeed in an enterprise in which the Duke of Buckingham and Lord Arlington had miscarried. He was thinking upon it; but his natural coquetry traversed his intentions, and made him neglect the most advantageous prospects in the world, in order unnecessarily to attend to the advances and allurements thrown out to him by the Countess of Chesterfield. This was one of the most agreeable women in the world. She had a most exquisite shape, though she was not very tall. Her complexion was extremely fair, with all the expressive charms of a brunette. She had large blue eyes, very tempting and alluring; her manners were engaging; her wit lively and amusing; but her heart, ever open to tender sentiments, was

[32] This lady was Isabella, daughter to Lewis de Nassau, Lord Beverwaert, son to Maurice, Prince of Orange, and Count Nassau. Her daughter Isabella, previously mentioned (note, p. 153), married, secondly, Sir Thomas Hanmer, Bart. She assisted at the coronation of King George I., as Countess of Arlington, in her own right, and died 7th February 1722-3. Her portrait, by Kneller, is among the "Hampton Court Beauties."

[33] James Hamilton.

neither scrupulous in point of constancy, nor nice in point of sincerity. She was daughter to the Duke of Ormonde,[34] and Hamilton, being her cousin-german, they might be as much as they pleased in each other's company without being particular; but as soon as her eyes gave him some encouragement, he entertained no other thoughts than how to please her, without considering her fickleness, or the obstacles he had to encounter. His intention, which we mentioned before, of establishing himself in the confidence of Miss Stewart no longer occupied his thoughts: she now was of opinion that she was capable of being the mistress of her own conduct. She had done all that was necessary to inflame the King's passions, without exposing her virtue by granting the last favours; but the eagerness of a passionate lover, blessed with favourable opportunities, is difficult to withstand, and still more difficult to vanquish; and Miss Stewart's virtue was almost exhausted, when the Queen was attacked with a violent fever, which soon reduced her to extreme danger.

Then it was that Miss Stewart was greatly pleased with herself for the resistance she had made, though she had paid dearly for it. A thousand flattering hopes of greatness and glory filled her heart, and the additional respect that was universally paid her contributed not a little to increase them. The Queen was given over by her physicians:[35] the few Portuguese

[34] Elizabeth Butler, the second wife of Philip, second Earl of Chesterfield, the daughter of James Butler, first Duke of Ormonde. She died in July 1665, aged twenty-five. The portrait of the Countess in Jameson's *Beauties of the Court of Charles II.* represents the Earl's *third* wife, who does not figure in the *Memoirs.*

[35] This happened in October 1663. Lord Arlington, in a letter to the Duke of Ormonde, dated the 17th of that month, says: "The condition of the Queen is much worse, and the physicians give us but little hopes of her recovery; by the next you will hear she is either in fair way to it, or dead: to-morrow is a very

women that had not been sent back to their own country filled the Court with doleful cries; and the good nature of the King was much affected with the situation in which he saw a princess, whom, though he did not love her, yet he greatly esteemed. She loved him tenderly, and thinking that it was the last time she should ever speak to him, she told him, that the concern he showed for her death was enough to make her quit life with regret; but that, not possessing charms sufficient to merit his tenderness, she had at least the consolation in dying to give place to a consort who might be more worthy of it, and to whom heaven, perhaps, might grant a blessing that had been refused to her. At these words, she bathed his hands with some tears, which he thought would be her last. He mingled his own with hers; and without supposing she would take him at his word, he conjured her to live for his sake. She had never yet disobeyed him; and, however dangerous sudden impulses may be, when one is between life and death, this transport of joy, which might have proved fatal to her, saved her life, and the King's wonderful tenderness had an effect for which every person did not thank Heaven in the same manner.

critical day with her: God's will be done. The King is coming to see her this morning, she told him she willingly left all the world but him; which hath very much afflicted His Majesty, and all the Court with him" (Brown's *Miscellanea Aulica*, 1702, p. 306). "Though she has some little respite from time to time," writes Comminges to King Louis (1st November 1663), "I despair of her recovery. . . . The King seems to me deeply affected. Well! he supped none the less yesterday with Madame de Castlemaine, and had his usual talk with Mlle. Stewart, of whom he is excessively fond. There is already a talk of his marrying again, and everybody gives him a new wife according to his own inclination; and there are some who do not look beyond England to find one for him" (see Jusserand's *French Ambassador at the Court of Charles II.* 1892, p. 88; see also Pepys's *Diary*, 19th-25th October 1663).

Jermyn had now for some time been recovered of his wounds. However, Lady Castlemaine, finding his health in as deplorable a condition as ever, resolved to regain the King's heart, but in vain; for notwithstanding the softness of her tears, and the violence of her passions, Miss Stewart wholly possessed it. During this period the Court was variously entertained: sometimes there were promenades, and at others the Court beauties sallied out on horseback, and to make attacks with their charms and graces, sometimes successfully, sometimes otherwise, but always to the best of their abilities[36] at other seasons there were such shows on the river as the city of London alone can afford.

The Thames washes the sides of a large though not a magnificent palace of the kings of Great Britain.[37]

[36] On 13th July 1663 Pepys gives a vivid picture of the above. "Hearing that the King and Queen are rode abroad with the Ladies of Honour to the Park, and seeing a great crowd of gallants staying here to see their return, I also staid walking up and down. By and by the King and Queen, who looked in this dress (a white laced waistcoat and a crimson short pettycoat, and her hair dressed *à la négligence*) mighty pretty; and the King rode hand in hand with her. Here was also my Lady Castlemaine rode among the rest of the ladies; but the King took, methought, no notice of her; nor when they 'light did anybody press (as she seemed to expect, and staid for it) to take her down, but was taken down by her own gentleman. She looked mighty out of humour, and had a yellow plume in her hat (which all took notice of), and yet is very handsome, but very melancholy; nor did anybody speak to her, or she so much as smile or speak to anybody. I followed them up into White Hall, and into the Queen's presence, where all the ladies walked, talking and fiddling with their hats and feathers, and changing and trying one another's by one another's heads, and laughing. But it was the finest sight to me, considering their great beautys and dress, that ever I did see in all my life. But above all Mrs. Stewart in this dress with her hat cocked and a red plume."

[37] The Palace of Whitehall extended from the Thames to St. James's Park, and from old Scotland Yard to Canon Row, Westminster, a public road running through the two gateways, known as Whitehall Gate and King Street Gate, from Charing Cross to Westminster. The original mansion of Henry VIII.'s time was in the style of Hampton Court, with a series of galleries and

From the stairs of this palace the Court used to take water in the summer evenings, when the heat and dust prevented their walking in the park. An infinite number of open boats, filled with the Court and city beauties, attended the barges, in which were the royal family. Collations, music, and fireworks completed the scene. The Chevalier de Gramont always made one of the company, and it was very seldom that he did not add something of his own invention, agreeably to surprise by some unexpected stroke of magnificence and gallantry. Sometimes he had complete concerts of vocal and instrumental music, which he privately brought from Paris, and which struck up on a sudden in the midst of these parties; sometimes he gave banquets, which likewise came from France, and which, in the midst of London, surpassed the King's collations. These entertainments sometimes exceeded, as others fell short of his expectations, but they always cost him an immense deal of money.

Lord Falmouth was one of those who had the greatest friendship and esteem for the Chevalier de Gramont. This profusion gave him concern, and as he often used to go and sup with him without ceremony,

courts, and Hall, Chapel, Tennis Court, Cockpit, Orchard, and Banqueting House. The last-named building is the only portion that was re-erected, in the reign of James I., by Inigo Jones, who was to have reconstructed the whole Palace, but the idea was never carried out. This excepted, the whole was burned down in William III.'s reign: first, by a fire on 10th April 1691 (when all the buildings over the Stone Gallery to the water side, including the more recently rebuilt apartments of the Duchess of Portsmouth, at the end of the Long Gallery, where the fire originated, were destroyed) ; and, secondly, by the greater fire of 4th January 1697-8, of the various apartments Pepys refers occasionally to, Henry VIII.'s Gallery, the Boarded Gallery, the Matted Gallery, the Shield Gallery, the Stone Gallery, and the Vane Room. There were also the Guard Room, the Adam and Eve Gallery. Fisher's Ground Plan of about 1670 (*not* 1680) mentions the names of those to whom the several apartments were allotted. See Cunningham's *London,* pp. 549-550

one day finding only Saint-Evremond there, and a
supper fit for half a dozen guests, who had been invited in form: "You must not," said he, addressing
himself to the Chevalier de Gramont, "be obliged to
me for this visit. I come from the King's *coucher*,
where all the discourse was about you; and I can
assure you that the manner in which the King spoke
of you, could not afford you so much pleasure as I
myself felt upon the occasion. You know very well,
that he has long since offered you his good offices
with the King of France; and for my own part," continued he, smiling, "you know very well that I would
solicit him so to do, if it was not through fear of
losing you as soon as your peace is made; but, thanks
to Miss Hamilton, you are in no great haste. However,
I am ordered by the King, my master, to acquaint you,
that, while you remain here until you are restored to
the favour of your sovereign, he presents you with a
pension of fifteen hundred Jacobuses.[38] It is indeed a
trifle, considering the figure the Chevalier de Gramont
makes among us, but it will assist him," said he, embracing him, "to give us sometimes a supper."

The Chevalier de Gramont received, as he ought,
the offer of a favour he did not think proper to accept.
"I acknowledge," said he, "the King's bounty in this
proposal, but I am still more sensible of Lord Falmouth's generosity in it, and I request him to assure
his Majesty of my perfect gratitude. The King, my
master, will not suffer me to want, when he thinks fit
to recall me; and while I continue here I will let you
see that I have wherewithal to give my English
friends, now and then, a supper."

At these words, he called for his strong-box, and
showed him seven or eight thousand guineas in solid
gold. Lord Falmouth, willing to improve to the

[38] £1875.

Chevalier's advantage the refusal of so advantageous
an offer, gave Monsieur de Comminges,[39] then Ambassador at the English Court, an account of it;
nor did Monsieur de Comminges fail to represent
properly the merit of such a refusal to the French
Court.[40]

Hyde Park, every one knows, is the promenade
of London:[41] nothing was so much in fashion, during
the fine weather, as that promenade, which was the
rendezvous of magnificence and beauty. Every one,
therefore, who had either sparkling eyes, or a splendid

[39] Comminges was Ambassador in London, from the Court of
France, during the years 1663, 1664, and 1665. Lord Clarendon,
speaking of him, describes him as somewhat capricious in his
nature, which made him hard to treat with, and not always
vacant at the hours himself assigned; being hypochondriac, and
seldom sleeping without opium (*Continuation of Clarendon's
Life*, p. 263).

[40] "The Chevalier de Gramont," writes Comminges to Louis
XIV. (10th-20th December 1663), "was delighted with the news
I gave him, and repeated to me a thousand times that he preferred to serve Your Majesty for nothing than all the Kings in
the world for all their treasures. He is preparing to take his
leave of the Sovereign of Great Britain, to whom he is doubtless
under great obligations for the gracious manner in which he has
been received and treated."

[41] "I did frequently, in the spring, accompany my Lord N——
into a field near the town, which they call Hyde Park; the place
is not unpleasant, and which they use as our course; but with
nothing of that order, equipage, and splendour; being such an
assembly of wretched jades, and hackney coaches, as, next a
regiment of carmen, there is nothing approaches the resemblance.
This park was (it seems) used by the late king and nobility for
the freshness of the air and the goodly prospect; but it is that
which now (besides all other excises) they pay for here, in
England, though it be free in all the world besides; every coach
and horse which enters buying his mouthful, and permission
of the publican who has purchased it; for which the entrance
is guarded with porters and long staves" (*A Character of England, as it was lately presented to a Nobleman of France*, 12mo,
1659, p. 54). Evelyn, writing in April 1653, says: "A fee of
a shilling was charged for every coach and sixpence for every
horse. The Park became the resort of fashion for drives and
promenades in Charles II.'s reign. It was then first walled in
with brick."

equipage, constantly repaired thither; and the King seemed pleased with the place.

Coaches with glasses[42] were then a late invention. The ladies were afraid of being shut up in them. They greatly preferred the pleasure of showing almost their whole persons, to the conveniences of modern coaches. That which was made for the King not being remarkable for its elegance, the Chevalier de Gramont was of opinion that something ingenious might be invented, which should partake of the ancient fashion, and likewise prove preferable to the modern. He therefore sent away Termes privately with all the necessary instructions to Paris. The Duke of Guise[43] was likewise charged with this commission; and the courier, having by the favour of Providence escaped the quicksand, in a month's time brought safely over to England the most elegant and magnificent calash that had ever been seen, which the Chevalier presented to the King.

The Chevalier de Gramont had given orders that fifteen hundred louis should be expended upon it; but the Duke of Guise, who was his friend, to oblige him,

[42] Coaches were first introduced into England in the year 1564. Taylor, the Water Poet (*Works*, 1630, p. 240), says: "One William Boonen, a Dutchman, brought first the use of coaches hither; and the said Boonen, was Queen Elizabeth's coachman; for, indeed, a coach was a strange monster in those days, and the sight of them put both horse and man into amazement." Dr. Percy observes, they were first drawn by two horses, and that it was the favourite Buckingham who, about 1619, began to draw with six horses. About the same time, he introduced the sedan. *The Ultimum Vale of John Carleton*, 4to, 1663, p. 23, will, in a great measure, ascertain the time of the introduction of glass coaches. He says: "I could wish her (*i.e.* Mary Carleton's) coach (which she said my Lord Taff bought for her in England, and sent it over to her, made of *the new fashion, with glasse*, very stately; and her pages and lacquies were of the same livery) was come for me," etc.

[43] Henry de Lorraine, Duke de Guise, Count d'Eu, Prince de Joinville, *b.* 1614, *ob.* 1664.

laid out two thousand. All the Court was in admiration at the magnificence of the present; and the King, charmed with the Chevalier's attention to everything which could afford him pleasure, failed not to acknowledge it. He would not, however, accept a present of so much value, but upon condition that the Chevalier should not refuse another from him.

The Queen, imagining that so splendid a carriage might prove fortunate for her, wished to appear in it first, with the Duchess of York. Lady Castlemaine, who had seen them in it, thinking that it set off a fine figure to greater advantage than any other, desired the King to lend her this wonderful calash to appear in it the first fine day in Hyde Park. Miss Stewart had the same wish, and requested to have it on the same day. As it was impossible to reconcile these two goddesses, whose former union was turned into mortal hatred, the King was very much perplexed.

The Queen Dowager, who, though she had no share in these broils, had no objection to them, and as usual being diverted with this circumstance, she took occasion to joke with the Chevalier de Gramont, for having thrown this bone of contention among such competitors; and did not fail to give him, in the presence of the whole Court, those praises which so magnificent a present deserved. "But how comes it," said she, "that you have no equipage yourself, although you are at so great an expense? for I am told that you do not keep even a single footman, and that one of the common runners in the streets lights you home with a stinking link.'"[44] "Madam," said he, "the Chevalier de Gramont hates pomp: my link-boy, of whom you speak, is faithful to my service; and besides, he is

[44] "A street urchin lights you home with one of those pitch torches which makes the whole town stink" (Vizetelly's translation).

one of the bravest fellows in the world. Your Majesty is unacquainted with the nation of link-boys: it is a charming one, I can assure you: a man cannot step out in the night without being surrounded by a dozen of them. The first time I became acquainted with them, I retained all that offered me their services; so that when I arrived at Whitehall, I had at least two hundred about my chair. The sight was new; for those who had seen me pass with this illumination, asked whose funeral it was. These gentlemen, however, began fighting about some dozen shillings I had thrown among them then; and he whom your Majesty mentions, having beaten three or four of his companions, I retained him for his valour. As for the parade of coaches and footmen, I despise it: I have sometimes had five or six valets-de-chambre at once, without having a single servant in livery, except my chaplain Poussatin." "How!" said the Queen, bursting out laughing, "a chaplain in your livery! he surely was not a priest?" "Pardon me, madam," said he, "and the first priest in the world for the Biscayan jig." "Chevalier," said the King, "pray tell us the history of your chaplain Poussatin."

CHAPTER VIII

"SIRE," said the Chevalier de Gramont, "the Prince de Condé besieged Lerida :[1] the place in itself was nothing; but Don Gregorio Brice, who defended it, was something. He was one of those Spaniards of the old stamp, as valiant as the Cid, as proud as all the Guzmans put together, and more gallant than all the Abencerrages of Grenada. He suffered us to make our first approaches to the place without the least molestation. The Marshal de Gramont[2]—whose maxim it was that a governor who at first makes a great blustering, and burns his suburbs in order to make a noble defence, generally makes a very bad one—looked upon Gregorio de Brice's politeness as no good omen for us; but the Prince, covered with glory, and elated with the campaigns of Rocroi, Nordlingen, and Fribourg, to insult both the place and the governor, ordered the trenches to be mounted at noon-day by his own regiment, at the head of which marched four-and-twenty fiddlers, as if it had been to a wedding.

"Night approaching, we were all in high spirits: our violins were playing soft airs, and we were com-

[1] This was in 1647. Voltaire says: "He, Condé, was accused, upon this occasion, in certain books, of a bravado, in having opened the trenches to the music of violins; but these writers were ignorant that this was the custom of Spain" (*Age of Louis XIV.* chap. ii.).

[2] Anthony, Maréchal of France. He appears to have quitted the army in 1672. "Le Duc de la Feuillade est colonel du régiment des gardes sur la démission volontaire du Maréchal de Gramont" (Hénault's *History of France*). He died 1678.

fortably regaling ourselves. God knows how we were joking about the poor governor and his fortifications, both of which we promised ourselves to take in less than twenty-four hours. This was going on in the trenches, when we heard an ominous cry from the ramparts, repeated two or three times, of 'Alert on the walls!' This cry was followed by a discharge of cannon and musketry, and this discharge by a vigorous sally, which, after having filled up[*] the trenches, pursued us as far as our grand guard.

"The next day Gregorio Brice sent by a trumpet a present of ice and fruit to the Prince de Condé, humbly beseeching his Highness to excuse his not returning the serenade which he was pleased to favour him with, as unfortunately he had no violins; but that if the music of last night was not disagreeable to him, he would endeavour to continue it as long as he did him the honour to remain before the place. The Spaniard was as good as his word; and as soon as we heard, 'Alert on the walls,' we were sure of a sally, that cleared our trenches, destroyed our works, and killed the best of our officers and soldiers. The Prince was so piqued at it, that, contrary to the opinion of the general officers, he obstinately persisted in carrying on a siege which was like to ruin his army, and which he was at last forced to quit in a hurry.

"As our troops were retiring, Don Gregorio, far from giving himself those airs which governors generally do on such occasions, made no other sally than sending a respectful compliment to the Prince. Signor Brice set out not long after for Madrid, to give an account of his conduct, and to receive the recompense he had merited. Your Majesty perhaps will be desirous to know what reception poor Brice met with, after having performed the most brilliant action the

[*] Emptied (Vizetelly's translation).

Spaniards could boast of in all the war—he was confined by the Inquisition."

"How!" said the Queen Dowager, "confined by
the Inquisition for his services!" "Not altogether for
his services," said the Chevalier; "but without any
regard to his services, he was treated in the manner I
have mentioned for a little affair of gallantry, which
I shall relate to the King presently.

"The campaign of Catalonia being thus ended, we
were returning home, not overloaded with laurels; but
as the Prince de Condé had laid up a great store on
former occasions, and as he had still great projects in
his head, he soon forgot this trifling misfortune. We
did nothing but joke with one another during the
march, and the Prince was the first to ridicule the
siege. We made some of those rhymes on Lerida,
which were sung all over France, in order to prevent
others more severe; however, we gained nothing by
it, for notwithstanding we treated ourselves freely
in our own ballads, others were composed in Paris
in which we were ten times more severely handled.
At last we arrived at Perpignan upon a holiday: a
company of Catalans, who were dancing in the middle
of the street, out of respect to the Prince came to
dance under his windows. Monsieur Poussatin, in a
little black jacket, danced in the middle of this company, as if he was really mad. I immediately recognised him for my countryman, from his manner of
skipping and frisking about. The Prince was charmed
with his humour and activity. After the dance, I sent
for him, and inquired who he was. 'A poor priest, at
your service, my lord,' said he: 'my name is Poussatin,
and Bearn is my native country. I was going into
Catalonia to serve in the infantry, for, God be praised,
I can march very well on foot; but since the war is
happily concluded, if your lordship pleases to take me

into your service, I would follow you everywhere, and serve you faithfully.' 'Monsieur Poussatin,' said I, 'my lordship has no great occasion for a chaplain; but since you are so well disposed towards me, I will take you into my service.'

"The Prince de Condé, who was present at this conversation, was overjoyed at my having a chaplain. As poor Poussatin was in a very tattered condition, I had no time to provide him with a proper habit at Perpignan; but giving him a spare livery of one of the Marshal de Gramont's servants, I made him get up behind the Prince's coach, who was like to die with laughing every time he looked at poor Poussatin's uncanonical mien in a yellow livery.

"As soon as we arrived at Paris, the story was told to the Queen, who at first expressed some surprise at it. This, however, did not prevent her from wishing to see my chaplain dance; for in Spain it is not altogether so strange to see ecclesiastics dance, as to see them in livery.

"Poussatin performed wonders before the Queen; but as he danced with great sprightliness, she could not bear the odour which his violent motions diffused around her room. The ladies likewise began to pray for relief; for he had almost entirely got the better of all the perfumes and essences with which they were fortified. Poussatin, nevertheless, retired with a great deal of applause, and some louis d'or.

"Some time afterwards I procured a small benefice in the country for my chaplain, and I have since been informed that Poussatin preached with the same ease in his village as he danced at the wedding of his parishioners."

The King was exceedingly diverted at Poussatin's history; and the Queen was not much hurt at his having been put in livery. The treatment of Gregorio

Brice offended her far more; and being desirous to justify the Court of Spain, with respect to so cruel a proceeding: "Chevalier de Gramont," said she, "what heresy did Governor Brice wish to introduce into the state? What crime against religion was he charged with, that he was confined in the Inquisition?" "Madam," said he, "the history is not very proper to be related before your Majesty: it was a little amorous frolic, ill-timed indeed; but poor Brice meant no harm: a school-boy would not have been whipped for such a fault, in the most severe college in France; as it was only for giving some proofs of his affection to a young Spanish fair one, who had fixed her eyes upon him on a solemn occasion."

The King desired to know the particulars of the adventure; and the Chevalier gratified his curiosity, as soon as the Queen and the rest of the Court were out of hearing. It was very entertaining to hear him tell a story; but it was very disagreeable to differ with him, either in competition, or in raillery. It is true that at that time there were few persons at the English Court who had merited his indignation. Russell was sometimes the subject of his ridicule, but he treated him far more tenderly than he usually did a rival.

This Russell was one of the most famous dancers in all England, I mean, for country dances. He had a collection of two or three hundred in print, all of which he danced at sight; and to prove that he was not an old man, he sometimes danced until he was almost exhausted. His mode of dancing was like that of his clothes, for they both had been out of fashion full twenty years.

The Chevalier de Gramont was very sensible that he was very much in love; but though he saw very well that it only rendered him more ridiculous, yet he felt some concern at the information he received, of his intention of demanding Miss Hamilton in marriage; but his concern did not last long.

Russell, being upon the point of setting out on a journey, thought it was proper to acquaint his mistress with his intentions before his departure. The Chevalier de Gramont was a great obstacle to the interview he was desirous of obtaining of her; but being one day sent for, to go and play at Lady Castlemaine's, Russell seized the opportunity, and addressing himself to Miss Hamilton with less embarrassment than is usual on such occasions, he made his declaration to her in the following manner: "I am brother to the Earl of Bedford: I command the regiment of guards: I have three thousand pounds* a year, and fifteen thousand in ready money: all which, madam, I come to present to you, along with my person. One present, I agree, is not worth much without the other, and therefore I put them together. I am advised to go to some of the watering-places for something of an asthma, which, in all probability, cannot continue much longer, as I have had it for these last twenty years. If you look upon me as worthy of the happiness of belonging to you, I shall propose it to your father, to whom I did not think it right to apply before I was acquainted with your sentiments. My nephew William is at present entirely ignorant of my intention; but I believe he will not be sorry for it, though he will thereby see himself deprived of a pretty considerable estate; for he has great affection for me, and besides, he has a pleasure in paying his respects to you since he has perceived my attachment. I am very much pleased that he should make his court to me, by the attention he pays to you; for he did nothing but squander his money upon that coquette Middleton, while at present

* " Jacobuses " (Vizetelly's translation).

he is at no expense, though he frequents the best company in England."

Miss Hamilton had much difficulty to suppress her laughter during this harangue. However, she told him that she thought herself much honoured by his intentions towards her, and still more obliged to him for consulting her, before he made any overtures to her relations. "It will be time enough," said she, "to speak to them upon the subject at your return from the waters; for I do not think it is at all probable that they will dispose of me before that time, and in case they should be urgent in their solicitations, your nephew William will take care to acquaint you; therefore, you may set out whenever you think proper; but take care not to injure your health by returning too soon."

The Chevalier de Gramont, having heard the particulars of this conversation, endeavoured, as well as he could, to be entertained with it; though there were certain circumstances in the declaration, notwithstanding the absurdity of others, which did not fail to give him some uneasiness. Upon the whole, he was not sorry for Russell's departure; and, assuming an air of pleasantry, he went to relate to the King how Heaven had favoured him by delivering him from so dangerous a rival. "He is gone then, Chevalier?" said the King. "Certainly, sire," said he; "I had the honour to see him embark in a coach, with his asthma, and country equipage, his *perruque à calotte,* neatly tied with a yellow riband, and his old-fashioned hat covered with oil-skin, which becomes him uncommonly well. Therefore I have only to contend with William Russell, whom he leaves as his resident with Miss Hamilton; and as for him, I neither fear him upon his own account, nor his uncle's; he is too much in love himself to pay attention to the interests of another;

and as he has but one method of promoting his own, which is by sacrificing the portrait, or some love-letters of Mrs. Middleton, I have it easily in my power to counteract him in such kind of favours, though I confess I have pretty well paid for them."

"Since your affairs proceed so prosperously with the Russells," said the King, "I will acquaint you that you are delivered from another rival, much more dangerous, if he were not already married: my brother has lately fallen in love with Lady Chesterfield." "How many blessings at once!" exclaimed the Chevalier de Gramont. "I have so many obligations to him for this inconstancy, that I would willingly serve him in his new amour, if Hamilton was not his rival: nor will your Majesty take it ill, if I promote the interests of my mistress's brother, rather than those of your Majesty's brother." "Hamilton, however," said the King, "does not stand so much in need of assistance, in affairs of this nature, as the Duke of York; but I know Lord Chesterfield is of such a disposition, that he will not suffer men to quarrel about his wife with the same patience as the complaisant Shrewsbury; though he well deserves the same fate." Here follows a true description of Lord Chesterfield.[5]

[5] Philip Stanhope, second Earl of Chesterfield, born 1633, succeeded to the earldom in 1656. He was committed to the Tower in 1658-9 for duelling and on suspect of being implicated in Sir George Booth's royalist rising. He fled to France, 17th January 1660, for killing an adversary in a duel. The same year he married Lady Elizabeth Butler, who figures in Gramont's *Memoirs*. His first wife, Lady Anne Percy, daughter of Algernon, Earl of Northumberland, died in 1653. In July 1665 he again became a widower, and married, four years later, Lady Elizabeth Dormer, daughter of the Earl of Carnarvon, by whom he had two sons and two daughters. (His daughter by his second wife married Lord Lyon, Earl of Strathmore.) The Earl of Chesterfield accompanied Charles II. to Dover at the Restoration and was appointed Lord Chamberlain to the Queen in 1662. He succeeded the Duke of Monmouth in 1679 as Lord Warden of the King's

He had a very agreeable face, a fine head of hair, an indifferent shape, and a worse air; he was not, however, deficient in wit. A long residence in Italy had made him ceremonious in his commerce with men, and jealous in his connection with women. He had been much hated by the King, because he had been much beloved by Lady Castlemaine. It was reported that he had been in her good graces prior to her marriage; and as neither of them denied it, it was the more generally believed.

He had paid his devoirs to the eldest daughter of the Duke of Ormonde, while his heart was still taken up with his former passion. The King's love for Lady Castlemaine, and the advancement he expected from such an alliance, made him press the match with as much ardour as if he had been passionately in love. He had therefore married Lady Chesterfield without loving her, and had lived some time with her in such coolness as to leave her no room to doubt of his indifference. As she was endowed with great sensibility and delicacy, she suffered at this contempt. She was at first much affected with his behaviour, and afterwards enraged at it; and, when he began to give her proofs of his affection, she had the pleasure of convincing him of her indifference.

They were upon this footing, when she resolved to cure Hamilton, as she had lately done her husband, of

Forests South of the Trent, and in 1680 was admitted into the Privy Council in acknowledgment of his opposing the Bill of Exclusion. Throughout his life the Earl was a staunch Royalist, and resolutely refused any appointments under William of Orange. After the abdication of James II. he lived peacefully in retirement at his newly erected house at Bretby in Derbyshire, and died at his house in Bloomsbury Square in 1713. In his earlier days Chesterfield was a notorious rake. Sufficient evidence of his gallantries may be found in his Letter Book, which was acquired by the British Museum in 1852. The Earl's memoirs, with his correspondence, were published in 1829.

all his remaining tenderness for Lady Castlemaine. For her it was no difficult undertaking. The conversation of the one was disagreeable, from the unpolished state of her manners, her ill-timed pride, her uneven temper, and extravagant humours. Lady Chesterfield, on the contrary, knew how to heighten her charms with all the bewitching attractions in the power of a woman to invent, who wishes to make a conquest.

Besides all this, she had greater opportunities of making advances to him than to any other. She lived at the Duke of Ormonde's, at Whitehall, where Hamilton, as was said before, had free admittance at all hours. Her extreme coldness, or rather the disgust which she showed for her husband's returning affection, wakened his natural inclination to jealousy; he suspected that she could not so very suddenly pass from anxiety to indifference for him, without some secret object of a new attachment; and according to the maxim of all jealous husbands, he immediately put in practice all his experience and industry, in order to make a discovery, which was to destroy his own happiness.

Hamilton, who knew his disposition, was, on the other hand, upon his guard, and the more he advanced in his intrigue, the more attentive was he to remove every degree of suspicion from the Earl's mind. He pretended to make him his confidant, in the most unguarded and open manner, of his passion for Lady Castlemaine:[1] he complained of her caprice, and most earnestly desired his advice how to succeed with a person whose affections he alone had entirely possessed.

Chesterfield, who was flattered with this discourse, promised him his protection with greater sincerity than it had been demanded. Hamilton, therefore, was no further embarrassed than to preserve Lady Chester-

[1] See Pepys's *Diary,* 20th January 1663-4.

field's reputation, who, in his opinion, declared herself rather too openly in his favour; but whilst he was diligently employed in regulating, within the rules of discretion, the partiality she expressed for him, and in conjuring her to restrain her glances within bounds, she was receiving those of the Duke of York, and, what is more, made them favourable returns.

He thought that he had perceived it, as well as every one besides; but he thought likewise, that all the world was deceived as well as himself: how could he trust his own eyes, as to what those of Lady Chesterfield betrayed for this new rival? He could not think it probable that a woman of her disposition could relish a man whose manners had a thousand times been the subject of their private ridicule; but what he judged still more improbable was that she should begin another intrigue before she had given the finishing stroke to that in which her own advances had engaged her. However, he began to observe her with more circumspection, when he found by his discoveries, that if she did not deceive him, at least the desire of doing so was not wanting. This he took the liberty of telling her of; but she answered him in so high a strain, and treated what he said so much like a phantom of his own imagination, that he appeared confused without being convinced. All the satisfaction he could procure from her, was her telling him, in a haughty manner, that such unjust reproaches as his ought to have had a better foundation.

Lord Chesterfield had taken the same alarm; and being convinced, from the observations he had made that he had found out the happy lover who had gained possession of his lady's heart, he was satisfied; and without teasing her with unnecessary reproaches, he only waited for an opportunity to confound her, before he took his measures.

After all, how can we account for Lady Chesterfield's conduct, unless we attribute it to the disease incident to most coquettes, who, charmed with superiority, put in practice every art to rob another of her conquest, and spare nothing to preserve it.

But before we enter into the particulars of this adventure, let us take a retrospect of the amours of his Royal Highness, prior to the declaration of his marriage, and particularly of what immediately preceded this declaration. It is allowable sometimes to drop the thread of a narrative, when real facts, not generally known, give such a variety upon the digression as to render it excusable. Let us see then how those things happened.

The Duke of York's marriage,[8] with the Chancellor's daughter, was deficient in none of those circumstances which render contracts of this nature valid in the eye of Heaven: the mutual inclination, the formal ceremony, witnesses, and every essential point of matrimony, had been observed.

Though the bride was no perfect beauty, yet, as there were none at the Court of Holland who eclipsed her, the Duke, during the first endearments of matrimony, was so far from repenting of it, that he seemed only to wish for the King's restoration that he might have an opportunity of declaring it with splendour; but when he saw himself enjoying a rank which placed him so near the throne; when the possession of Miss Hyde afforded him no new charms; when England, so abounding in beauties, displayed all that was charming and lovely in the Court of the King his brother; and when he considered he was the only prince, who,

[8] The material facts in this narrative are confirmed by Lord Clarendon (*Continuation of his Life*, p. 33). It is difficult to speak of the persons concerned in this infamous transaction without some degree of asperity, notwithstanding they are, by a strange perversion of language, styled, *all men of honour.*

from such superior elevation, had descended so low, he began to reflect upon it. On the one hand, his marriage appeared to him particularly ill suited in every respect. He recollected that Jermyn had not engaged him in an intimacy with Miss Hyde, until he had convinced him, by several different circumstances, of the facility of succeeding. He looked upon his marriage as an infringement of that duty and obedience he owed to the King; the indignation with which the Court, and even the whole kingdom, would receive the account of his marriage presented itself to his imagination, together with the impossibility of obtaining the King's consent to such an act, which for a thousand reasons he would be obliged to refuse. On the other hand, the tears and despair of poor Miss Hyde presented themselves; and still more than that, he felt a remorse of conscience, the scruples of which began from that time to rise up against him.

In the midst of this perplexity he opened his heart to Lord Falmouth, and consulted with him what method he ought to pursue. He could not have applied to a better man for his own interests, nor to a worse for Miss Hyde's; for at first Falmouth maintained not only that he was not married, but that it was even impossible that he could ever have formed such a thought; that any marriage was invalid for him, which was made without the King's consent, even if the party was a suitable match; but that it was a mere jest, even to think of the daughter of an insignificant lawyer, whom the favour of his sovereign had lately made a peer of the realm, without any noble blood, and chancellor, without any capacity; that as for his scruples, he had only to give ear to some gentlemen whom he could introduce, who would thoroughly inform him of Miss Hyde's conduct before he became acquainted with her; and provided he did not tell them that he really was married, he would soon have sufficient grounds to come to a determination.

The Duke of York consented, and Lord Falmouth, having assembled both his council and his witnesses, conducted them to his Royal Highness's cabinet, after having instructed them how to act. These gentlemen were the Earl of Arran, Jermyn, Talbot, and Killegrew,[9] all men of honour; but who infinitely preferred

[9] Henry or "Harry" Killigrew, eldest son of Thomas Killigrew, by Cecilia Crofts, daughter of Sir John Crofts (Maid of Honour to Queen Henrietta Maria), the court wit and dramatic author, Groom of the Bedchamber to the Duke of York, and afterwards to Charles II., whom he attended the night before the fatal apoplectic seizure (vide *King Monmouth*). Both he and his brother Charles (born December 1655) succeeded their father as Master of the Revels. Henry Killigrew was born 9th April 1637. He married, in 1662, Lady Mary Savage, daughter of John, second Earl Rivers of Rock Savage, Cheshire (Maid of the Privy Chamber to the Queen). Pepys describes him as one of the most notorious rogues in town, and the King, writing to his sister Henrietta (17th October 1668), warns her to "believe not one word he sayes of us heere, for he is a most notorious lyar and does not want witt to sett forth his storyes pleasantly enough" (*Madame*, by Julia Cartwright, pp. 273-274). One of these stories procured his disgrace at Court, in October 1666. He was banished for "raw words spoken against a lady of pleasure" (*Hist. M.S. Com. Rep.* 7, App. p. 485. See also Pepys's *Diary*, 21st October 1666. In the Verney Papers of 19th March 1667-8 a story is current of Killigrew opiating a mother and daughter and ravishing the latter for which he was condemned to be hanged, but by the intercession of the Queen Mother, and Madame (Duchess of Orleans), it was altered to banishment, evidently to France, for we find him returning to England with the Duke of Monmouth shortly afterwards, though not to favour at Court. Pepys encountered him among some boon companions at Fox Hall, 30th May 1668, "ready to take hold of every woman that came by them"—"their mad bawdy talk did make my heart ake."

A fray between Buckingham and Killigrew in the Duke's Theatre on the 20th July 1667 is mentioned by Pepys on the 22nd; "The Duke of Buckingham did soundly beat and take away his sword, and make a fool of, till the fellow prayed him to spare his life." Further particulars appear in the Verney MSS. "H. Killigrew being in the next box to the Duke of Buckingham at a play, drolled with him and made fun at him, and spake scurry language at him, insomuch that the Duke told him he might

the Duke of York's interest to Miss Hyde's reputation, and who, besides, were greatly dissatisfied, as well as the whole Court, at the insolent authority of the Prime Minister.

The Duke having told them, after a sort of preamble, that although they could not be ignorant of his affection for Miss Hyde, yet they might be unacquainted with the engagements his tenderness for her had induced him to contract; that he thought himself obliged to perform all the promises he had made her; but as the innocence of persons of her age was generally exposed to Court scandal, and as certain reports, whether false or true, had been spread abroad on the subject of her conduct, he conjured them as his friends, and charged them upon their duty, to tell him sincerely everything they knew upon the subject, since he was resolved to make their evidence the rule of his conduct towards her. They all appeared rather reserved at first, and seemed not to dare to give their opinions upon an affair of so serious and delicate a nature; but the Duke of York having renewed his entreaties, each

govern his tongue and his face better. Killigrew went out of the box and would have had one Vaughan to have carried him a challenge, but he refusing to do it in that place, he returned and stroke the Duke twice on the head with his sword in the scabbard, and then ran away most nobly over the boxes and forms, and the Duke after him, and cut him well favouredly, he crying, ' Good your Grace, spare my life,' and fell down, some say, to beg for his life, but certainly the Duke kicked him. The Duke lost his wig in the pursuit for a while " (*Hist. MS. Com. Rep.* 7, App. p. 486). From the same we learn that Killigrew was suspected of stabbing his servant while drunk in a room next the King's (ibid. p. 468), 8th February 1676-7.

The attack upon Killigrew in May 1669, owing to his boasted favours of the Countess of Shrewsbury, is mentioned later (p. 346.)

He is said to have left two sons by a second and third wife: Henry, a major in the Dragoons, and Thomas, an ensign or lieutenant (see *Althorp Memoirs*, p. 28). The date of his death is unknown. He was living in 1694, when he still held the post of Master of the Revels.

began to relate the particulars of what he knew, and perhaps of more than he knew, of poor Miss Hyde; nor did they omit any circumstance necessary to strengthen the evidence. For instance the Earl of Arran, who spoke first, deposed, that in the gallery at Honslaerdyk, where the Countess of Ossory, his sister-in-law, and Jermyn, were playing at nine-pins, Miss Hyde, pretending to be sick, retired to a chamber at the end of the gallery; that he, the deponent, had followed her, and having cut her lace, to give a greater probability to the pretence of the vapours, he had acquitted himself to the best of his abilities, both to assist and to console her.

Talbot[10] said, that she had made an appointment with him in the Chancellor's cabinet, while he was in council; and that, not paying so much attention to what was upon the table as to what they were engaged in, they had spilled a bottle full of ink upon a despatch of four pages, and that the King's monkey, which was blamed for this accident, had been a long time in disgrace.

[10] Richard (usually called "Dick") Talbot, Earl and titular Duke of Tyrconnel, the youngest son of Sir William Talbot, born 1630. When in the service of the Duke of York prior to the Restoration, he was concerned in royalist plots, indeed, suspected of being implicated in a scheme to assassinate Cromwell, by whom he was arrested, but he effected his escape to Brussels, and many believed he had purchased his freedom by treachery to his original cause. At the Restoration he was made Gentleman of the Bedchamber to the Duke of York, whose amours, according to Burnet (*Own Time*, i, 227), he assisted. On James's accession he took command of the army in Ireland, and was created Earl, made Privy Councillor in January 1686-7, and Viceroy and Lord Deputy. After the abdication, when James landed at Kinsale, Talbot escorted him in state to Dublin Castle, and strongly advised him to continue in the capital. During James's sojourn he was created Duke. After the siege of Limerick, he followed the exiled King to France, afterwards returning to Ireland as Lord Lieutenant (January 1690-1), and died of apoplexy six months afterwards (14th August). He was buried in Limerick Cathedral, but there is no commemorative stone. In appear-

Jermyn mentioned many places where he had received long and favourable audiences; however, all these articles of accusation amounted only to some delicate familiarities, or at most, to what is generally denominated the innocent part of an intrigue; but Killigrew, who wished to surpass these trivial depositions, boldly declared that he had had the honour of being upon the most intimate terms with her. He was of a sprightly and witty humour, and had the art of telling a story in the most entertaining manner, by the graceful and natural turn he could give it.

The Duke of York found this last accusation greatly out of bounds, being convinced he himself had sufficient proofs of the contrary; he therefore returned thanks to these officious informers for their frankness, ordered them to be silent for the future upon what they had been telling him, and immediately passed into the King's apartment.

As soon as he had entered the cabinet, Lord Falmouth, who had followed him, related what had passed to the Earl of Ossory, whom he met in the presence chamber. They strongly suspected what was the subject of the conversation of the two brothers, as it was long; and the Duke of York appeared to be in such agitation when he came out, that they no longer doubted that the result had been unfavourable for poor Miss Hyde. Lord Falmouth began to be affected for her disgrace, and to relent that he had been concerned in it, when the Duke of York told him and the Earl of

ance he was tall, handsome, and commanding, but grew corpulent and unwieldy in later life. He had no genius for arms, but was unmistakably brave, and had plenty of common-sense, though he was both vain and cunning (see *Memoirs of Duke of Berwick,* also *Clarendon and Rochester Correspondence*). Lord Clarendon says he had the Duke of York's confidence to such a degree, and in his secret services so many scandalous circumstances were the result, that he (Clarendon) persuaded the Duke to withdraw his patronage (see *Dict. of Nat. Biography,* vol. lv. pp. 331-332).

Ossory to meet him in about an hour's time at the Chancellor's.

They were rather surprised that he should have the cruelty himself to announce such a melancholy piece of news. They found his Royal Highness at the appointed hour in Miss Hyde's chamber: a few tears trickled down her cheeks, which she endeavoured to restrain. The Chancellor, leaning against the wall, appeared to them to be puffed up with something, which they did not doubt was rage and despair. The Duke of York said to them, with that serene and pleasant countenance with which men generally announce good news: "As you are the two men of the Court whom I most esteem, I am desirous you should first have the honour of paying your compliments to the Duchess of York: there she is."

Surprise was of no use, and astonishment was unseasonable on the present occasion. They were, however, so greatly possessed with both surprise and astonishment, that in order to conceal it they immediately fell on their knees to kiss her hand, which she gave to them with as much majesty as if she had been used to it all her life.[11]

The next day the news was made public,[12] and the whole Court was eager to pay her that respect, from a sense of duty, which in the end became very sincere.

The petits-maîtres who had spoken against her, seeing their intentions disappointed, were not a little embarrassed. Women are seldom accustomed to forgive injuries of this nature; and, if they promise them-

[11] Clarendon, says Lord Falmouth (then Sir Charles Berkeley), declared " for the Duke's sake he would be content to marry her, though he well knew the familiarity the Duke had with her. This he afterwards declared to be false, and prayed for forgiveness on the plea that the assertion was made out of pure devotion to the Duke." See also Pepys's *Diary,* 10th December 1660.

[12] See footnote, p. 92.

selves the pleasure of revenge, when they gain the power they seldom forget it. In the present case, however, the fears of these petits-maîtres were their only punishment.

The Duchess of York, being fully informed of all that was said in the cabinet concerning her, instead of showing the least resentment, studied to distinguish, by all manner of kindness and good offices, those who had attacked her in so sensible a part; nor did she ever mention it to them, but in order to praise their zeal, and to tell them "that nothing was a greater proof of the attachment of a man of honour, than his being more solicitous for the interest of his friend or master than for his own reputation": a remarkable example of prudence and moderation, not only for the fair sex, but even for those men who value themselves most upon their philosophy.

The Duke of York, having quieted his conscience by the declaration of his marriage, thought that he was entitled, by this generous effort, to give way a little to his inconstancy. He therefore immediately seized upon whatever he could first lay his hands upon: this was Lady Carnegy,[13] who had been in several other hands. She was still tolerably handsome, and her dis-

---

[13] Anne, daughter of William, fourth Marquis and second Duke of Hamilton, who was mortally wounded at the battle of Worcester. She was one of five daughters. Her mother was Elizabeth, daughter of James, Earl of Dirleton. Philip, second Earl of Chesterfield, undoubtedly was carrying on an intrigue with this lady in 1657, at the same time as his liaison with Barbara Villiers, afterwards Lady Castlemaine. A letter addressed for these two, making an appointment at Ludgate Hill, is among the Earl's letters, (see "Letters of Philip, Earl of Chesterfield"). It appears from another letter that the mother sent her daughter Anne to Windsor owing to some discovery in which Chesterfield was involved. The following year Lady Anne sent the Earl an intimation that she could not bid him farewell as she would have wished, but points out that, "you may give me some adieus with your eyes, since it is to be done noe other way" (ibid.). She afterwards became the wife of Lord Carnegie, who, on his father's

position, naturally inclined to tenderness, did not oblige her new lover long to languish. Everything coincided with their wishes for some time. Lord Carnegy, her husband, was in Scotland; but his father dying suddenly, he as suddenly returned with the title of Southesk, which his wife detested; but which she took more patiently than she received the news of his return. Some private intimation had been given him of the honour that was done him in his absence; nevertheless, he did not show his jealousy at first; but as he was desirous to be satisfied of the reality of the fact, he kept a strict watch over his wife's actions.

The Duke of York and her ladyship had, for some time, been upon such terms of intimacy, as not to pass their time in frivolous amusements; however, the husband's return obliged them to maintain some decorum. He therefore never went to her house, but in form, that is to say, always accompanied by some friend or other, to give his amours at least the appearance of a visit.

About this time Talbot[14] returned from Portugal. This connection had taken place during his absence; and without knowing who Lady Southesk was, he had been informed that his master was in love with her.

A few days after his arrival, he was carried, merely to keep up appearances, to her house by the Duke; and after being introduced, and some compliments having been paid on both sides, he thought it his duty to give his Royal Highness an opportunity to pay his compliments, and accordingly retired into the ante-chamber,

death, became Earl of Southesk. Pepys mentions seeing her at the Duke of York's playhouse on 3rd December 1668: "We sat under the boxes and saw the fine ladies; among others my Lady Kerneguy, who is most devilishly painted. She died in 1681.
[14] Afterwards Duke of Tyrconnel (see note, p. 180).

which looked into the street, and placed himself at the window to view the people as they passed.

He was one of the best-meaning men in the world on such occasions; but was so subject to forgetfulness, and absence of mind, that[15] he once forgot, and left behind him at London, a complimentary letter which the Duke had given him for the Infanta of Portugal, and never recollected it till he was going to his audience.

He stood sentry, as we have before said, very attentive to his instructions, when he saw a coach stop at the door, without being in the least concerned at it, and still less, at a man whom he saw get out of it, and whom he immediately heard coming upstairs.

The devil, who ought to be civil[16] upon such occasions, forgot himself in the present instance,' and brought up Lord Southesk *in propriâ personâ.* His Royal Highness's equipage had been sent home, because my lady had assured him that her husband was gone to see a bear and a bull baiting, an entertainment in which he took great delight,[17] and from whence he seldom returned until it was very late; so that Southesk, not seeing any equipage at the door, little imagined that he had such good company in his house; but if he was surprised to see Talbot carelessly lolling in his wife's ante-chamber, his surprise was soon over. Talbot, who had not seen him since they were in Flanders, and never supposing that he had changed his name: "Welcome, Carnegy, welcome, my good fellow," said he, giving him his hand; "where the devil have you been, that I have never been able to set eyes

[15] Upon a journey to Lisbon (Vizetelly's translation).

[16] Cautious (*ibid.*).

[17] Evelyn and Pepys give a good description of the bull-baiting in the Bear Garden at Southwark. Both diarists appear to have been disgusted at this brutal sport (see Evelyn, 16th June 1670, and Pepys, 14th August 1666).

on you since we were at Brussels? What business brought you here? Do you likewise wish to see Lady Southesk? If this is your intention, my poor friend, you may go away again; for I must inform you, the Duke of York is in love with her, and I will tell you in confidence, that, at this very time, he is in her chamber."

Southesk, confounded, as one may suppose, had no time to answer all these fine questions. Talbot, therefore, attended him downstairs as his friend; and, as his humble servant, advised him to seek for a mistress elsewhere. Southesk, not knowing what else to do at that time, returned to his coach; and Talbot, overjoyed at the adventure, impatiently waited for the Duke's return, that he might acquaint him with it; but he was very much surprised to find that the story afforded no pleasure to those who had the principal share in it; and his greatest concern was, that Carnegy had changed his name, as if only to draw him into such a confidence.

This accident broke off a commerce which the Duke of York did not much regret; and indeed it was happy for him that he became indifferent; for the traitor Southesk meditated a revenge,[18] whereby, without

[18] Referring to this Pepys says: "Her (Lady Carnegy's) Lord finding her and the Duke of York, at the King's first coming in, too kind, did get it out of her that he did dishonour him, and so bid her continue, . . . which is the most pernicious and full piece of revenge that ever I heard of: and he at this day owns it with great glory, and lookes upon the Duke of York and the world with great content in the ampleness of his revenge" (*Diary*, 6th April 1668). A similar story is related by Oldys in his MS. Annotations on Langbaine's *Dramatic Poets* of Sir John Denham. Burnet, however, refers to the episode as follows: "A story was set about, and generally believed, that the Earl of Southesk, that had married a daughter of the Duke of Hamilton's suspecting some familiarities between the Duke and his wife, had taken a sure method to procure a disease to himself, which he communicated to his wife, and was, by that means, sent

using either assassination or poison, he would have obtained some satisfaction upon those who had injured him, if the connection had continued any longer.

Lady Robarts[18] was then in the zenith of her glory. Her beauty was striking; yet, notwithstanding the brightness of the finest complexion, with all the bloom of youth, and with every requisite for inspiring desire, she nevertheless was not attractive. The Duke of York, however, would probably have been successful, if difficulties, almost insurmountable, had not disappointed his good intentions. Lord Robarts,[20] her husband, was an old, snarling, troublesome, peevish fellow, in love with her to distraction, and, to complete her misery, a perpetual attendant on her person.

She perceived his Royal Highness's attachment to her and seemed as if she was inclined to be grateful. This redoubled his eagerness, and every outward mark

round till it came to the Duchess. Lord Southesk was, for some years, not ill pleased to have this believed. It looked like a peculiar strain of revenge, with which he seemed much delighted. But I know he has, to some of his friends, denied the whole of the story very solemnly " (*History of His Own Time*, vol. i. p. 319). [The Earl of Southesk informs me there is no allusion to this evident fiction in any of the letters or papers in the charter room at Kinnaird Castle.—A. F.]

[19] Probably Letitia Isabella, second wife of John, second Lord Robartes, eldest son of John Earl of Radnor, whom he succeeded. She was the daughter of Sir John Smith. Pepys mentions her (27th April 1668) and her daughter, "a very fine-skinned lady," with whom he danced at Lord Crewe's.

[20] John, second Lord Robartes, afterwards Viscount Bodmin and Earl of Radnor (1679), Lord Privy Seal from 1661 to 1673, Deputy, and afterwards Lord Lieutenant of Ireland. Pepys frequently mentions him, and speaks of him as a bad business man and a taskmaster. Clarendon says Lord Robartes was proud, imperious, and morose by nature. " He had parts, which in council and parliament were very troublesome; for, of all the men alive, who had so few friends, he had the most followers. They who conversed most with him knew him to have many humours which were very intolerable; they who were but little acquainted with him took him to be a man of much knowledge, and called his morosity gravity " (*Continuation of Clarendon,* p. 102.)

of tenderness he could possibly show her; but the watchful husband redoubling his zeal and assiduity, as he found the approaches advance, every art was practised to render him tractable. Several attacks were made upon his avarice and his ambition. Those who possessed the greatest share of his confidence, insinuated to him that it was his own fault if Lady Robarts, who was so worthy of being at Court, was not received into some considerable post, either about the Queen or the Duchess. He was offered to be made Lord Lieutenant of the county where his estate was; or to have the management of the Duke of York's revenues in Ireland, of which he should have the entire disposal, provided he immediately set out to take possession of his charge; and having accomplished it, he might return as soon as ever he thought proper.

He perfectly well understood the meaning of these proposals, and was fully apprised of the advantages he might reap from them. In vain did ambition and avarice hold out their allurements; he was deaf to all their temptations, nor could ever the old fellow be persuaded to be made a cuckold. It is not always an aversion to, or a dread of this distinction, which preserves us from it. Of this her husband was very sensible; therefore, under the pretence of a pilgrimage to Saint Winifred, the virgin and martyr, who was said to cure women of barrenness, he did not rest until the highest mountains in Wales were between his wife and the person who had designed to perform this miracle in London, after his departure.

The Duke was for some time entirely taken up with the pleasures of the chase, and only now and then engaged in those of love; but his taste having undergone a change in this particular, and the remembrance of Lady Robarts wearing off by degrees, his eyes and wishes were turned towards Miss Brooke;

and it was in the height of this pursuit that Lady Chesterfield threw herself into his arms, as we shall see by resuming the sequel of her adventures.

The Earl of Bristol,[21] ever restless and ambitious,

[21] George Digby, second Earl of Bristol, born 1612, succeeded to the title in 1653 (the first Earl, James I.'s Ambassador to Madrid, endeavoured in vain to bring about the Spanish match with Prince Charles in 1623).

There are several allusions in Pepys to the Earl's deadly animosity to Clarendon and of his unsuccessful impeachments against the Lord Chancellor in the House of Lords, by which he incurred the King's displeasure. On 17th March 1663-4 the diarist records how a guard was sent to arrest him at his house at Wimbledon, but he had effected his escape. This mansion was sold to him by the Queen Mother in 1661, and Evelyn went there on 17th February 1662 "to help contrive the garden after the moderne." The library, according to Evelyn, 20th December 1677, consisted much of "judicial astrologie, romances, and trifles." The house was pulled down about 1717. Digby sold this Wimbledon House to the Lord Treasurer and purchased Buckingham House, Chelsea (afterwards known as Beaufort House, and pulled down in 1740), when the fine Inigo Jones gateway was removed to Chiswick. Evelyn describes the latter as "large but ill-contrived." and speaks of the fine collection of pictures by Titian and Vandyke (among the latter the portrait of the Earl now at Althorp and reproduced here). His town house in Queen Street, Lincoln's Inn, with its long gallery and gardens, is also mentioned by the diarist (26th May 1671).

Though a man of extraordinary ability, Digby was utterly void of principle. Clarendon says he pandered to the tastes of "the Merry Monarch" by doing all that might be acceptable, and contriving such meetings and jollities as he was pleased with, which description quite accords with Gramont's account (Clarendon's *Continuation*, p. 208). In his *Royal and Noble Authors,* Walpole says: "His life was one contradiction. He wrote against popery and embraced it; he was a zealous opposer of the Court and a sacrifice to it. . . . With great parts he always hurt himself and his friends; with romantic bravery he was always an unsuccessful commander. He spoke for the Test Act, though a Roman Catholic, and addicted himself to astrology on the birthday of true philosophy" (vol. ii. p. 25). He certainly was one of the greatest orators of the day, and was the author of several plays and poems of note (see *Dict. of Nat. Biography,* xv. 52-55). The Earl died (20th March 1677) at his house in Chelsea, but there is no record in the church register of his burial (Lysons' *Environs*). With the death of the Earl's elder son, John, third Earl, the titles of Digby and Bristol became extinct.

had put in practice every art to possess himself of the King's favour. As this is the same Digby whom Count Bussy[22] mentions in his annals, it will be sufficient to say that he was not at all changed: he knew that love and pleasure had possession of a master, whom he himself governed, in defiance of the Chancellor;[23] thus he was continually giving entertainments at his house; and luxury and elegance seemed to rival each other in those nocturnal feasts, which always lead to other enjoyments. The two Miss Brookes,[24] his relations, were always of those parties; they were both formed by nature to excite love in others, as well as to be susceptible of it themselves; they were just what the King wanted. The Earl, from this commencement, was beginning to entertain a good opinion of his project, when Lady Castlemaine, who had lately gained entire possession of the King's heart, was not in a humour, at that time, to share it with another, as she did very indiscreetly afterwards, despising Miss Stewart. As soon, therefore, as she received intimation of these secret practices, under pretence of attending the King in his parties, she entirely disconcerted them; so that the Earl was obliged to lay aside his projects, and Miss Brooke to discontinue her advances. The King did not even dare to think any more on this subject; but his brother was pleased to look after what he neglected; and Miss Brooke accepted the offer of his heart, until it pleased Heaven to dispose of her otherwise, which happened soon after, in the following manner.

Sir John Denham,[25] loaded with wealth as well as years, had passed his youth in the midst of those

[22] Roger de Bussi-Rabutin.

[23] See *Continuation of Life,* by Lord Clarendon, p. 208.

[24] See footnote, p. 102.

[25] Sir John Denham, *b.* 1615, *ob.* 1669, Surveyor to the Crown, 'n which position he succeeded Inigo Jones. Burlington House

pleasures which people at that age indulge in without restraint; he was one of the brightest geniuses England ever produced, for wit and humour, and for brilliancy of composition: satirical and free in his poems, he spared neither frigid writers, nor jealous husbands, nor even their wives: every part abounded with the most poignant wit, and the most entertaining stories; but his most delicate and spirited raillery turned generally against matrimony; and, as if he wished to confirm, by his own example, the truth of what he had written in his youth, he married, at the age of seventy-nine, this Miss Brooke of whom we are speaking, who was only eighteen.[26]

The Duke of York had rather neglected her for some time before; but the circumstance of so unequal a match rekindled his ardour; and she, on her part, suffered him to entertain hopes of an approaching bliss, which a thousand considerations had opposed before her marriage. She wished to belong to the Court; and for the promise of being made lady of the bedchamber to the Duchess, she was upon the point of making him another promise, or of immediately performing it, if required, when, in the middle of this treaty, Lady Chesterfield was tempted, by her evil genius, to rob her of her conquest, in order to disturb all the world.

However, as Lady Chesterfield could not see the

was built by him for Lord Burlington (*vide* Pepys' *Diary*, 28th September 1668), who afterwards made extensive alterations. Sir John was a poet of some distinction (*vide* his " Cooper's Hill," and *Poems on State Affairs*).

[26] Sir John Denham's union with Margaret[1] Brooke (his second wife) took place 25th May 1665 (register Westminster Abbey). Far from being seventy-nine, his age was fifty at this time. About 1767 he had a period of madness, from which he afterwards recovered (*vide* Temple's *Works,* vol. i. p. 484, and Butler's *Posthumous Works,* vol. ii. p. 155).

[1] She is sometimes named Elizabeth *in error*.

Duke of York, except in public assemblies, she was under the necessity of making the most extravagant advances, in order to seduce him from his former connection; and as he was the most unguarded ogler of his time, the whole Court was informed of the intrigue before it was well begun.

Those who appeared the most attentive to their conduct were not the least interested in it. Hamilton and Lord Chesterfield watched them narrowly; but Lady Denham, vexed that Lady Chesterfield should have stepped in before her, took the liberty of railing against her rival with the greatest bitterness. Hamilton had hitherto flattered himself that vanity alone had engaged Lady Chesterfield in this adventure; but he was soon undeceived, whatever her indifference might have been when she first commenced this intrigue. We often proceed farther than we at first intended, when we indulge ourselves in trifling liberties which we think of no consequence; for though perhaps the heart takes no part at the beginning, it seldom fails to be engaged in the end.

The Court, as we have mentioned before, was an entire scene of gallantry and amusements, with all the politeness and magnificence which the inclinations of a Prince naturally addicted to tenderness and pleasure could suggest. The beauties were desirous of charming, and the men endeavoured to please: all studied to set themselves off to the best advantage. Some distinguished themselves by dancing; others by show and magnificence; some by their wit, many by their amours, but few by their constancy. There was a certain Italian at Court, famous for the guitar.[21] He had a genius for music, and he was the only man who could make anything of the guitar; his style of play was so full of grace and tenderness, that he would

[21] Francesco Corbetta (Vizetelly's translation).

have given harmony to the most discordant instruments. The truth is, nothing was so difficult as to play like this foreigner. The King's relish for his compositions had brought the instrument so much into vogue, that every person played upon it, well or ill; and you were as sure to see a guitar on a lady's toilet as rouge or patches. The Duke of York played upon it tolerably well, and the Earl of Arran like Francisco himself. This Francisco had composed a saraband, which either charmed or infatuated every person; for the whole *guitarery* at Court were trying at it; and God knows what an universal strumming there was. The Duke of York, pretending not to be perfect in it, desired Lord Arran to play it to him. Lady Chesterfield had the best guitar in England. The Earl of Arran, who was desirous of playing his best, conducted his Royal Highness to his sister's apartments: she was lodged at Court, at her father's, the Duke of Ormonde's; and this wonderful guitar was lodged there to. Whether this visit had been preconcerted or not, I do not pretend to say; but it is certain that they found both the lady and the guitar at home: they likewise found there Lord Chesterfield, so much surprised at this unexpected visit, that it was a considerable time before he thought of rising from his seat to receive them with due respect.

Jealousy, like a malignant vapour, now seized upon his brain: a thousand suspicions, blacker than ink, took possession of his imagination, and were continually increasing; for, whilst the brother played upon the guitar to the Duke, the sister ogled and accompanied him with her eyes, as if the coast had been clear, and no enemy to observe them. This saraband was at least repeated twenty times. The Duke declared it was played to perfection. Lady Chesterfield found fault with the composition; but her husband, who clearly perceived that he was the person played upon, thought it a most detestable piece. However, though he was in the last agony at being obliged to curb his passion while others gave a free scope to theirs, he was resolved to find out the drift of the visit; but it was not in his power; for having the honour to be Chamberlain to the Queen, a messenger came to require his immediate attendance on her Majesty. His first thought was to pretend sickness; the second to suspect that the Queen, who sent for him at such an unseasonable time, was in the plot; but at last, after all the extravagant ideas of a suspicious man, and all the irresolutions of a jealous husband, he was obliged to go.

We may easily imagine what his state of mind was when he arrived at the Palace. Alarms are to the jealous what disasters are to the unfortunate: they seldom come alone, but form a series of persecution. He was informed that he was sent for to attend the Queen at an audience she gave to seven or eight Muscovite ambassadors.[28] He had scarce begun to curse the Muscovites, when his brother-in-law appeared, and drew upon himself all the imprecations he bestowed upon the embassy. He no longer doubted his being in the plot with the two persons he had left together, and in his heart sincerely wished him such recompense for his good offices as such good offices deserved. It was with great difficulty that he restrained himself from immediately acquainting him what was his opinion of such conduct. He thought that what he had already seen was a sufficient proof of his wife's infidelity; but before the end of the very same day, some circumstances occurred which increased his suspicions, and persuaded him that they had taken

[28] They arrived towards the end of the year 1662 (see Evelyn's *Diary*, 29th December 1662, and Pepys' *Diary*, 5th January 1662-3).

advantage of his absence, and of the honourable officiousness of his brother-in-law. He passed, however, that night with tranquillity; but the next morning, being reduced to the necessity either of bursting or giving vent to his sorrows and conjectures, he did nothing but think and walk about the room until Park-time. He went to Court, seemed very busy, as if seeking for some person or other, imagining that people guessed at the subject of his uneasiness; he avoided everybody, but at length meeting with Hamilton, he thought he was the very man that he wanted; and, having desired him to take an airing with him in Hyde Park, he took him up in his coach, and they arrived at the Ring,[29] without a word having passed between them.

Hamilton, who saw him as yellow as jealousy itself, and particularly thoughtful, imagined that he had just discovered what all the world had perceived long before; when Chesterfield, after a broken, insignificant preamble, asked him how he succeeded with Lady Castlemaine. Hamilton, who very well saw that he meant nothing by this question, nevertheless thanked him; and as he was thinking of an answer: "Your cousin," said the Earl, "is extremely coquettish, and I have some reason to suppose she is not so prudent as she ought to be." Hamilton thought the last charge a little too severe; and as he was endeavouring to refute it: "Good God!" said my lord, "you see, as well as the whole Court, what airs she gives herself. Husbands are always the last people that are spoken to about those affairs that concern them the most; but they are not always the last to perceive it themselves. Though you have made me your confidant in other matters,

[29] A circular ride and promenade surrounded by trees (several of which still remain) made in Charles I.'s reign, and partially destroyed when the Serpentine was formed in George II.'s time (see Cunningham's *London*).

yet I am not at all surprised you have concealed this from me; but as I flatter myself with having some share in your esteem, I should be sorry you should think me such a fool as to be incapable of seeing, though I am so complaisant as not to express my sentiments: nevertheless, I find that affairs are now carried on with such barefaced boldness, that at length I find I shall be forced to take some course or other. God forbid that I should act the ridiculous part of a jealous husband: the character is odious; but then I do not intend, through an excess of patience, to be made the jest of the town. Judge, therefore, from what I am going to tell you, whether I ought to sit down unconcerned, or whether I ought to take measures for the preservation of my honour.

"His Royal Highness honoured me yesterday by a visit to my wife." Hamilton started at this beginning. "Yes," continued the other, "he did give himself that trouble, and Lord Arran took upon himself that of bringing him. Do not you wonder that a man of his birth should act such a part? What advancement can he expect from one who employs him in such base services? But we have long known him to be one of the silliest c_eatures in England, with his guitar, and his other whims and follies." Chesterfield, after this short sketch of his brother-in-law's merit, began to relate the observations he had made during the visit, and asked Hamilton what he thought of his cousin Arran, who had so obligingly left them together. "This may appear surprising to you," continued he, "but hear me out, and judge whether I have reason to think that the close of this pretty visit passed in perfect innocence. Lady Chesterfield is amiable, it must be acknowledged; but she is far from being such a miracle of beauty as she supposes herself. You know she has ugly feet; but perhaps you are not acquainted that she has still worse legs." "Pardon me," said Hamilton, within himself; and the other, continuing the description: "Her legs," said his lordship, "are short and thick; and, to remedy these defects as much as possible, she seldom wears any other than green stockings."

Hamilton could not for his life imagine the drift of all this discourse, and Chesterfield, guessing his thoughts: "Have a little patience," said he. "I went yesterday to Miss Stewart's after the audience of those damned Muscovites. The King arrived there just before me; and as if the Duke had sworn to pursue me wherever I went that day, he came in just after me. The conversation turned upon the extraordinary appearance of the ambassadors. I know not where that fool Crofts[30] had heard that all these Muscovites had handsome wives; and that all their wives had handsome legs. Upon this the King maintained that no woman ever had such handsome legs as Miss Stewart; and she, to prove the truth of his Majesty's assertion, with the greatest imaginable ease, immediately showed her legs above the knee. Some were ready to prostrate themselves, in order to adore its beauty; for indeed none can be handsomer; but the Duke alone began to criticise upon it. He contended that it was too slender, and that as for himself he would give nothing for a leg that was not thicker and shorter, and concluded by saying that no leg was worth anything without green stockings. Now this, in my opinion, was a sufficient demonstration that he had just seen green stockings,[31] and had them fresh in his remembrance."

Hamilton was at a loss what countenance to put on

[30] William, Lord Crofts of Saxham, *b.* 1658, *ob.* 1677 (*vide* footnote, p. 329).

[31] "There is nothing neater," says the French Ambassador Courtin, "than the feet and ankles of the English ladies, in their well-fitting shoes and silk stockings. They wear their skirts short; and I often see legs so well turned that a sculptor would

during a narrative which raised in him nearly the same conjectures; he shrugged up his shoulders, and faintly said that appearances were often deceitful; that Lady Chesterfield had the foible of all beauties, who place their merit on the number of their admirers; and whatever airs she might imprudently have given herself, in order not to discourage his Royal Highness, there was no ground to suppose that she would indulge him in any greater liberties to engage him. But in vain was it that he endeavoured to give that consolation to his friend which he did not feel himself. Chesterfield plainly perceived he did not think of what he was saying; however, he thought himself much obliged to him for the interest he seemed to take in his concerns.

Hamilton was in haste to go home to vent his spleen and resentment in a letter to his cousin. The style of this billet was very different from those which he formerly was accustomed to write to her. Reproaches, bitter expostulations, tenderness, menaces, and all the effusions of a lover who thinks he has reason to complain, composed this epistle, which, for fear of accident, he went to deliver himself.

Never did she before appear so lovely, and never did her eyes speak so kindly to him as at this moment. His

like to mould them. *Green silk* stockings are modish. The garter, of which glimpses are often afforded, is below the knee, and in black velvet, with diamond buckles. Those who have no silk stockings to wear show a white skin smooth as satin. English women prefer being stockingless to wearing clumsy disfiguring hosiery."—According to the Mss. *Relation d'Angleterre,* vol. cxxxvii. fol. 400. A foreign ambassador arriving in England called on Frances Stewart and asked to be allowed to see her leg, that he might report to his master that the fame of her calf and ankle had not been overrated (see Forneron's *Louise de Keroualle*), pp. 28, 161-2. Bolingbroke gives a glimpse of the freedom of the times (when it was no unusual thing for a maid of honour to receive her suitor in her bedroom) by saying that, when Churchill was courting the beautiful Sarah Jennings, one of his duties was to tie and untie her garters (see Wolseley's *Marlborough*).

heart quite relented; but he was determined not to lose all the fine things he had said in his letter. In receiving it, she squeezed his hand: this action completely disarmed him, and he would have given his life to have had his letter again. It appeared to him at this instant that all the grievances he complained of were visionary and groundless. He looked upon her husband as a madman and an impostor, and quite the reverse of what he supposed him to be a few minutes before; but this remorse came a little too late. He had delivered his billet, and Lady Chesterfield had shown such impatience and eagerness to read it as soon as she had got it that all circumstances seemed to conspire to justify her, and to confound him. She managed to get quit, some way or other, of some troublesome visitors, to slip into her closet. He thought himself so culpable that he had not the assurance to wait her return. He withdrew with the rest of the company; but he did not dare to appear before her the next day, to have an answer to his letter. However, he met her at Court; and this was the first time, since the commencement of their amour, that he did not seek for her. He stood at a distance, with downcast looks, and appeared in such terrible embarrassment that his condition was sufficient to raise laughter or to cause pity, when Lady Chesterfield approaching, thus accosted him: "Confess," said she, "that you are in as foolish a situation as any man of sense can be. You wish you had not written to me; you are desirous of an answer; you hope for none; yet you equally wish for and dread it. I have, however, written you one." She had not time to say more; but the few words she had spoken were accompanied with such an air, and such a look, as to make him believe that it was Venus with all her graces, who had addressed him. He was near her when she sat down to cards, and as he was puzzling himself to devise by what means he should get this answer, she desired him to lay her gloves and fan down somewhere. He took them, and with them the billet in question; and as he had perceived nothing severe or angry in the conversation he had with her, he hastened to open her letter, and read as follows:

"Your transports are so ridiculous that it is doing you a favour to attribute them to an excess of tenderness, which turns your head. A man, without doubt, must have a great inclination to be jealous to entertain such an idea of the person you mention. Good God! what a lover to have caused uneasiness to a man of genius, and what a genius to have got the better of mine! Are not you ashamed to give any credit to the visions of a jealous fellow who brought nothing else with him from Italy? It is possible that the story of the green stockings, upon which he has founded his suspicions, should have imposed upon you, accompanied as it is with such pitiful circumstances? Since he has made you his confidant, why did not he boast of breaking in pieces my poor harmless guitar? This exploit, perhaps, might have convinced you more than all the rest. Recollect yourself, and if you are really in love with me, thank fortune for a groundless jealousy, which diverts to another quarter the attention he might pay to my attachment for the most amiable and the most dangerous man at Court."

Hamilton was ready to weep for joy at these endearing marks of kindness, of which he thought himself so unworthy. He was not satisfied with kissing, in raptures, every part of this billet; he also kissed several times her gloves and her fan. Play being over, Lady Chesterfield received them from his hands, and read in his eyes the joy that her billet had raised in his heart. Nor was he satisfied with expressing his raptures only by looks. He hastened home, and wrote

to her at least four times as much. How different was
this letter from the other! Though perhaps not so
well written; for one does not show so much wit in
suing for pardon, as in venting reproaches, and it
seldom happens that the soft languishing style of a
love-letter is so penetrating as that of invective.

Be that as it may, his peace was made. Their past
quarrel gave new life to their correspondence; and
Lady Chesterfield, to make him as easy as he had
before been distrustful, expressed on every occasion a
feigned contempt for his rival, and a sincere aversion
for her husband.

So great was his confidence in her, that he consented
she should show in public some marks of attention to
the Duke, in order to conceal as much as possible their
private intelligence. Thus, at this time nothing disturbed his peace of mind, but his impatience of finding
a favourable opportunity for the completion of his
desires. He thought it was in her power to command
it; but she excused herself on account of several difficulties which she enumerated to him, and which she
was desirous he should remove by his industry
and attentions.

This silenced his complaints; but whilst he was
endeavouring to surmount these obstacles, still wondering how it was possible that two persons who were
so well disposed to each other, and who were agreed
to make each other happy, could not put their designs
in execution, accident discovered an unexpected adventure, which left him no room to doubt, either of the
happiness of his rival, or of the perfidy of his mistress.

Misfortunes often fall light when most feared; and
frequently prove heaviest when merited, and when
least suspected. Hamilton was in the middle of the
most tender and passionate letter he had ever written
to Lady Chesterfield, when her husband came to an-

nounce to him the particulars of this last discovery. He came so suddenly upon him, that he had only just time to conceal his amorous epistle among his other papers. His heart and mind were still so full of what he was writing to his cousin, that her husband's complaints against her, at first, were scarce attended to; besides, in his opinion, he had come in the most unfortunate moment on all accounts.

He was, however, obliged to listen to him, and he soon entertained quite different sentiments. He appeared almost petrified with astonishment, while the Earl was relating to him circumstances of such an extravagant indiscretion, as seemed to him quite incredible, notwithstanding the particulars of the fact. "You have reason to be surprised at it," said my lord, concluding his story; "but if you doubt the truth of what I tell you, it will be easy for you to find evidence that will convince you; for the scene of their tender familiarities was no less public than the room where the Queen plays at cards, which, while her Majesty was at play, was, God knows, pretty well crowded. Lady Denham was the first who discovered what they thought would pass unperceived in the crowd; and you may very well judge how secret she would keep such a circumstance. The truth is, she addressed herself to me first of all, as I entered the room, to tell me that I should give my wife a little advice, as other people might take notice of what I might see myself, if I pleased."[32]

"Your cousin was at play, as I before told you. The Duke was sitting next to her. I know not what

[32] Dates come in useful here to prove that Lady Denham could not have made this discovery. The Earl knew of his wife's intrigue with the Duke of York before 1st Jan. 1662-3 (see Pepys, 19th January 1662-3). Margaret Brooke also was not married until 25th May 1665 (see also footnote relating Lady Chesterfield's removal from Court, p. 206).

was become of his hand; but I am sure that no one could see his arm below the elbow. I was standing behind them, just in the place that Lady Denham had quitted. The Duke, turning round, perceived me, and was so much disturbed at my presence, that he almost undressed my lady in pulling away his hand. I know not whether they perceived that they were discovered; but of this I am convinced, that Lady Denham will take care that everybody shall know it. I must confess to you, that my embarrassment is so great, that I cannot find words to express what I now feel. I should not hesitate one moment what course to take, if I might be allowed to show my resentment against the person who has wronged me. As for her, I could manage her well enough, if, unworthy as she is of any consideration, I had not still some regard for an illustrious family, that would be distracted were I to resent such an injury as it deserves. In this particular you are interested yourself. You are my friend, and I make you my confidant in an affair of the greatest imaginable delicacy: let us then consult together what is proper to be done in so perplexing and disagreeable a situation."

Hamilton, if possible, more astonished, and more confounded than himself, was far from being in a proper state to afford him advice on the present occasion. He listened to nothing but jealousy, and breathed nothing but revenge; but these emotions being somewhat abated, in hopes that there might be calumny, or at least exaggeration in the charges against Lady Chesterfield, he desired her husband to suspend his resolutions, until he[33] was more fully informed of the fact; assuring him, however, that if he found the circumstances such as he had related, he should regard and consult no other interest than his.

[33] Hamilton.

Upon this they parted; and Hamilton found, on the first inquiry, that almost the whole Court was informed of the adventure, to which every one added something in relating it. Vexation and resentment inflamed his heart, and by degrees extinguished every remnant of his former passion.

He might easily have seen her, and have made her such reproaches as a man is generally inclined to do on such occasions; but he was too much enraged to enter into any detail which might have led to an explanation. He considered himself as the only person essentially injured in this affair; for he could never bring his mind to think that the injuries of the husband could be placed in competition with those of the lover.

He hastened to Lord Chesterfield, in the transport of his passion, and told him that he had heard enough to induce him to give such advice as he should follow himself in the same situation, and that if he wished to save a woman so strongly prepossessed, and who perhaps had not yet lost all her innocence, though she had totally lost her reason, he ought not to delay one single instant, but immediately to carry her into the country with the greatest possible expedition, without allowing her the least time to recover her surprise.

Lord Chesterfield readily agreed to follow his advice, which he had already considered as the only counsel a friend could give him; but his lady, who did not suspect he had made this last discovery of her conduct, thought he was joking with her when he told her to prepare for going into the country in two days. She was the more induced to think so as it was in the very middle of an extremely severe winter; but she soon perceived that he was in earnest; she knew from the air and manner of her husband that he thought he had sufficient reason to treat her in this imperious

style; and finding all her relations serious and cold to
her complaint, she had no hope left in this universally
abandoned situation but in the tenderness of Hamilton.
She imagined she should hear from him the cause of
her misfortunes, of which she was still totally ignorant,
and that his love would invent some means or other to
prevent a journey, which she flattered herself would be
even more affecting to him than to herself; but she
was expecting pity from a crocodile.

At last, when she saw the eve of her departure was
come; that every preparation was made for a long
journey; that she was receiving farewell visits in
form, and that still she heard nothing from Hamilton,
both her hopes and her patience forsook her in this
wretched situation. A few tears perhaps might have
afforded her some relief, but she chose rather to deny
herself that comfort than to give her husband so much
satisfaction. Hamilton's conduct on this occasion appeared to her unaccountable; and as he still never came
near her, she found means to convey to him the following billet:

"Is it possible that you should be one of those, who,
without vouchsafing to tell me for what crime I am
treated like a slave, suffer me to be dragged from
society? What means your silence and indolence in a
juncture wherein your tenderness ought most particularly to appear, and actively exert itself? I am upon
the point of departing, and am ashamed to think that
you are the cause of my looking upon it with horror,
as I have reason to believe that you are less concerned
at it than any other person. Do, at least, let me know
to what place I am to be dragged; what is to be done
with me within a wilderness; and on what account you,
like all the rest of the world, appear changed in your
behaviour towards a person whom all the world could
not oblige to change with regard to you, if your weak-

ness or your ingratitude did not render you unworthy
of her tenderness."

This billet did but harden his heart, and make him
more proud of his vengeance. He swallowed down
full draughts of pleasure in beholding her reduced to
despair, being persuaded that her grief and regret for
her departure were on account of another person. He
felt uncommon satisfaction in having a share in tormenting her, and was particularly pleased with the
scheme he had contrived to separate her from a rival,
upon the very point perhaps of being made happy.
Thus fortified as he was against his natural tenderness,
with all the severity of jealous resentment, he saw her
depart with an indifference which he did not even endeavour to conceal from her. This unexpected treatment, joined to the complication of her other misfortunes, had almost in reality plunged her into
despair.

The Court was filled with the story of this adventure; nobody was ignorant of the occasion of this
sudden departure,[34] but very few approved of Lord

[34] On 3rd November 1662 Pepys hears from the Duke of York's
surgeon Pierce, "how the Duke of York is smitten in love with
my Lady Chesterfield (a virtuous lady, daughter to my Lord of
Ormond), and so much that the Duchess of York hath complained to the King and her father about it, and my Lady
Chesterfield is gone into the country for it." It must have been
only a temporary removal from London, for, according to Gramont, she was in town when the Russian Ambassador was in
London in December (1662) and the following January. On 19th
January 1662-3 Pepys says: "This day by Dr. Clarke I was told
the occasion of my Lord Chesterfield's going and taking his lady
(my Lord Ormond's daughter) from Court. It seems he not
only hath been long jealous of the Duke of York, but did find
them two talking together, though there were others in the room,
and the lady by all opinions a most good, virtuous woman. He,
the next day (of which the Duke was warned by somebody that
saw the passion my Lord Chesterfield was in the night before)
went and told the Duke how much he did apprehend himself
wronged, in his picking out his lady of the whole Court to be
the subject of his dishonour; which the Duke did answer with

Chesterfield's conduct. In England they looked with astonishment upon a man who could be so uncivil as to be jealous of his wife; and in the city of London it was a prodigy, till that time unknown, to see a husband have recourse to violent means to prevent what jealousy fears, and what it always deserves. They endeavoured, however, to excuse poor Lord Chesterfield, as far as they could safely do it, without incurring the public odium, by laying all the blame on his bad education. This made all the mothers vow to God that none of their sons should ever set a foot in Italy, lest they should bring back with them that infamous custom of laying restraint upon their wives.

As this story for a long time took up the attention of the Court, the Chevalier de Gramont, who was not thoroughly acquainted with all the particulars, inveighed more bitterly than all the citizens of London put together against this tyranny; and it was upon this occasion that he produced new words to that fatal saraband which had unfortunately so great a share in the adventure. The Chevalier passed for the author; but if Saint-Evremond had any part in the composition, it certainly was greatly inferior to his other performances, as the reader will see in the following chapter.

great calmness, not seeming to understand the reason of complaint, and that was all that passed: but my Lord did presently pack his lady into the country in Derbyshire near the Peake, which is become a proverb at Court to send a man's wife to the Devil's-Peake when she vexes him." Lord Chesterfield and his wife set out for his country seat (Bretby) 12th May 1663 (*vide* books in the Lord Steward's office), where he remained with his wife throughout the summer (see *Letters of Philip, Earl of Chesterfield*, p. 25).

CHAPTER IX

EVERY man who believes that his honour depends upon that of his wife is a fool who
torments himself, and drives her to despair;
but he who, being naturally jealous, has the additional
misfortune of loving his wife, and who expects that
she should only live for him, is a perfect madman,
whom the torments of hell have actually taken hold
of in this world, and whom nobody pities. All reasoning and observation on these unfortunate circumstances attending wedlock concur in this, that precaution is vain and useless before the evil, and revenge
odious afterwards.

The Spaniards, who tyrannise over their wives,
more by custom than from jealousy, content themselves with preserving the niceness of their honour by
duennas, grates, and locks. The Italians, who are
wary in their suspicions, and vindictive in their resentments, pursue a different line of conduct: some satisfy
themselves with keeping their wives under locks which
they think secure; others by ingenious precautions exceed whatever the Spaniards can invent for confining
the fair sex; but the generality are of opinion, that in
either unavoidable danger or in manifest transgres-
sion, the surest way is to assassinate.

But, ye courteous and indulgent nations, who, far
from admitting these savage and barbarous customs,
give full liberty to your dear ribs,[1] and commit the
care of their virtue to their own discretion, you pass

[1] And better halves (Vizetelly's translation).

your peaceful days without alarms or strife, in all the enjoyments of domestic indolence!

It was certainly some evil genius that induced Lord Chesterfield to distinguish himself from his patient and good-natured countrymen, and ridiculously to afford the world an opportunity of examining into the particulars of an adventure which would perhaps never have been known beyond the precincts of the Court, and which would everywhere have been forgotten in less than a month; but now, as soon as ever he had turned his back, in order to march away with his prisoner, and the ornaments she was supposed to have bestowed upon him, God only knows what a terrible attack there was made upon his rear. Rochester,[2]

[2] John Wilmot, second Earl of Rochester, son of Henry Wilmot, first Earl, who followed King Charles in his adventurous wanderings after the battle of Worcester.[1] John's mother (his father's second wife) was the widow of Sir F. H. Lee, of Ditchley Park, Oxfordshire, where John was born, 10th April 1647 (the seat of the Wilmots was at Adderbury, in the same county[2]). He succeeded to the title, 9th February 1657-8. Educated at Burford, he was admitted a Fellow of Wadham College, Oxford, in January 1659-60, and created M.A. in 1661. On leaving the University he travelled in France and Italy under the care of Dr. Balfour, who encouraged his love of literature. On returning from his travels in 1664, he made his appearance at Court, where his natural brilliancy and wit had free scope for development. Though at first modest, he soon became corrupted by the King and his dissolute companions, whom soon he rivalled in debauchery. Two years afterwards he was made Gentleman of the King's Bedchamber, and in 1674, Keeper of Woodstock Park, where (at the High Lodge) he died 26th July 1681,[3] after two years' failing health, resulting from his debauched way of living. Bishop Burnet was with him for four days prior to his death, and, according to the book he published afterwards, brought him to a right way of thinking (see Burnet's *Life of Rochester*). His wife, "La triste héritière," survived him a little over a year, and his son[4] Charles, the third Earl of the Wilmots (then aged ten years) only five months. (Some of Rochester's letters to his wife and son have been published in Chambers's *English Literature*). Cibber records the fact that Rochester wrote a scandalous

[1] See *The Flight of the King*.   [2] *Ibid.*
[3] Buried at Spilsbury Church, near Ditchley (see *Picturesque Old Houses*, pp. 143-144).   [4] There were three daughters.

Middlesex,[3] Sedley,[4] Etherege,[5] and all the whole band of wits, exposed him in numberless ballads, and diverted the public at his expense.

history of contemporary Court intrigues, which was burnt by his mother's directions after his death. He gained most of his in-information from a footman whom he disguised as a sentinel to keep nocturnal watch at the apartments of the various Court ladies of whom he had his suspicions (*vide* Burnet's *Own Time*). Most of his poems and plays are mentioned in the article in the *Dict. of Nat. Biography,* from which much of the above has been quoted (vol. lxii. pp. 63-67). There are various stories of Rochester's wild exploits, disguised as a beggar, porter, mountebank, etc., as the freak might require, and on one occasion he and Buckingham took an inn near Newmarket, where they had many opportunities for amorous intrigues (*vide* Works of the Earls of Rochester and Roscommon).

[3] At this time the Earl of Middlesex was Lionel, who died in 1674. The person intended by our author was Charles, then Lord Buckhurst, eldest son of Richard, fifth Earl of Dorset, afterwards Earl of Middlesex, and, lastly, Duke of Dorset, *b.* 1637, *ob.* January 1705-6. Bishop Burnet says he "was a generous, good-natured man. He was so oppressed with phlegm, that, till he was a little heated with wine, he scarce ever spoke; but he was, upon that exaltation, a very lively man. Never was so much ill-nature in a pen as in his, joined with so much good-nature as was in himself, even to excess; for he was against all punishing, even of malefactors. He was bountiful, even to run himself into difficulties, and charitable to a fault; for he commonly gave all he had about him when he met an object that moved him. But he was so lazy, that, though the King seemed to court him to be a favourite, he would not give himself the trouble that belonged to that post. He hated the Court, and despised the King, when he saw he was neither generous nor tender-hearted" (*History of his Own Time,* vol. i. p. 370). Lord Orford says of him, that "he was the finest gentleman of the voluptuous Court of Charles the Second, and in the gloomy one of King William. He had as much wit as his first master, or his contemporaries, Buckingham and Rochester, without the royal want of feeling, the Duke's want of principles, or the Earl's want of thought. The latter said, with astonishment, 'that he did not know how it was, but Lord Dorset might do anything and yet was never to blame.' It was not that he was free from the failings of humanity, but he had the tenderness of it too, which made everybody excuse whom everybody loved; for even the asperity of his verses seems to have been forgiven too.

" 'The best good man, with the worst-natured muse.' "

Noble Authors, vol. ii. p. 96.

The Chevalier de Gramont was highly pleased with these lively and humorous compositions; and wherever this subject was mentioned, never failed to produce his supplement upon the occasion. "It is strange," said he, "that the country, which is little better than a gallows or a grave for young people, is allotted in this land only for the unfortunate, and

Pepys records (13th July 1667) that my Lord Buckhurst hath got Nell away from the King's House, and gives her £100 a year. Next day, at the King's Head, Epsom, he hears that the two are lodging in the next house with Sedley. In the following August (26th), Nell had left Buckhurst, and was back at the playhouse again (Diary). [The house at Epsom above alluded to is occupied as a grocer's shop. The rooms Nelly occupied, according to the tradition, are those with little bay windows, looking into the street. The interior has been modernised.]

⁴ Sir Charles Sedley, son of Sir John Sedley of Southfleet, and Elizabeth, daughter of Sir Henry Savile, was born at Aylesford, Kent, about the year 1639. Sedley married, in 1657, Catherine, daughter of John Savage, Earl Rivers, by whom he had one daughter, Catherine, who became James II.'s mistress, and was created Countess of Dorchester. Sir Charles retired from town life after the death of Charles II., and warmly espoused the cause of William of Orange at the Revolution. Pepys gives glimpses of Sedley's debaucheries, for which he was notorious. As a wit and author of amorous lyrics he was less sparkling and obscene than Rochester. Charles II. dubbed him "Apollo's Viceroy," and Dryden—"The Tibullus of the Age." His plays are, *Anthony and Cleopatra, The Mulberry Garden*, and *Bellamira or the Mistress*. He died 20th August 1701. Rochester's lines on Sedley's seductive verse are well known. (See also *Dict. of Nat. Biography*.)

⁵ Sir George Etherege, born 1634, knighted 1680, author of the Comedies, *The Comical Revenge, She Would if She Could,* and *Sir Flopling Flutter*. The hero of the last, according to Dean Lockier, was an exact portrait of Etherege himself. while the character of Dorinant, in the same play, was a picture of Etherege's boon companion, John Wilmot, Earl of Rochester. These two libertines, with William Jepson and Mr. Downes, were concerned in a midnight brawl with the watch at Epsom, in 1676, wherein the last was killed, and they had to abscond. When James came to the throne, Etherege was sent as Ambassador to Vienna, Hamburgh, and Ratisbon. His letter book of the last place gives an insight into his loose way of living. He, however, was loyal to his master, as may be seen from two interesting letters (preserved at Netherby Hall, Cumberland) to Lord Preston, at the time of the King's abdication. From Ratisbon, Etherege removed

not for the guilty! Poor Lady Chesterfield, for some
unguarded looks, is immediately seized upon by an
angry husband, who will oblige her to spend her
Christmas at a country-house a hundred and fifty miles
from London; while here there are a thousand ladies
who are left at liberty to do whatever they please, and
who indulge in that liberty, and whose conduct, in
short, deserves a daily bastinado. I name no person
—God forbid I should; but Lady Middleton, Lady
Denham, the Queen's and the Duchess's maids of
honour, and a hundred others, bestow their favours to
the right and to the left, and not the least notice is
taken of their conduct. As for Lady Shrewsbury,[6] she
is conspicuous. I would take a wager she might have
a man killed for her every day, and she would only
hold her head the higher for it. One would suppose
she imported from Rome plenary indulgences for her
conduct. There are three or four gentlemen who wear
an ounce of her hair made into bracelets, and no person finds any fault; and yet shall such a cross-grained
fool as Chesterfield be permitted to exercise an act of
tyranny, altogether unknown in this country, upon the
prettiest woman in England, and all for a mere trifle.
But I am his humble servant; his precautions will avail

to Paris, where his death occurred, like his contemporary Lord
Lovelace, from a tumble downstairs while in a state of intoxica-
tion (January 1690-1). He left a widow, but no legitimate issue.
He is said to have left a legacy to a natural daughter, by the
actress, Elizabeth Barry. According to Rochester, Etherege had
as much "fancy, sense, judgment, and wit," as any writer of the
day. (See *Dict. of Nat. Biography*, vol. xviii. p. 44; Add. MSS.
(B.M.), No. 11,513; Gosse's *Seventeenth Century Studies*, and
Hist. MS. Com. Rep. 7, App., p. 428, 467.)

[6] At this time, when Louis XIV. was negotiating his second
Secret Treaty with Charles II. (February 1670-1), by the Earl
of Arlington's suggestion, the Countess of Shrewsbury was
bribed with 10,000 livres "in order to fix Buckingham the
better." Upon the receipt the lady said "she would make Buckingham comply with King Charles in all things" (*vide* Dal-
rymple's *Memoirs*, 1773, App., pp. 81-82).

him nothing; on the contrary, very often a woman,
who had no bad intentions when she was suffered to
remain in tranquillity, is prompted to such conduct by
revenge, or reduced to it by necessity: this is as true
as the gospel. Hear now what Francisco's saraband
says on the subject:

> " Tell me, jealous-pated swain,
>   What avail thy idle arts,
>   To divide united hearts?
>   Love, like the wind, I trow,
>   Will, where it listeth, blow;
> So, prithee, peace, for all thy cares are vain.

> " When you are by,
> Nor wishful look, be sure, nor eloquent sigh,
>   Shall dare those inward fires discover,
>   Which burn in either lover:
> Yet Argus' self, if Argus were thy spy,
>   Should ne'er, with all his mob of eyes,
>   Surprise.

> " Some joys forbidden,
>   Transports hidden,
> Which love, through dark and secret ways,
> Mysterious love, to kindred souls conveys."

The Chevalier de Gramont passed for the author
of this sonnet. Neither the justness of the sentiment,
nor turn of it, are surprisingly beautiful; but as it
contained some truths that flattered the genius of the
nation, and pleased those who interested themselves
for the fair sex, the ladies were all desirous of having
them to teach them to their children.

During all this time the Duke of York, not being
in the way of seeing Lady Chesterfield, easily forgot
her. Her absence, however, had some circumstances
attending it which could not but sensibly affect the
person who had occasioned her confinement; but there
are certain fortunate tempers to which every situation
is easy; they feel neither disappointment with bitterness, nor pleasure with acuteness. In the meantime,

as the Duke could not remain idle, he had no sooner forgotten Lady Chesterfield, but he began to think of her whom he had been in love with before, and was upon the point of relapsing into his old passion for Miss Hamilton.

There was in London a celebrated portrait-painter named Lely,[7] who had greatly improved himself by studying the famous Vandyke's pictures, which were

[7] Sir Peter Lely, the principal painter of Charles II.'s reign, was born at Soest in Holland, and studied under Grebber at Haerlem. His real name was Van der Faes, his father being a captain in the infantry. He came to England in 1643, and was received with favour at Court, where he painted many portraits; but it was in the reign of the second Charles that he became particularly famous for his portraits of the ladies of the Court, some of the best examples of which are the well-known *Beauties* at Hampton Court. Althorp also possesses some of his best work. In comparing Lely's painting with Vandyke's, Walpole contrasts the formal drapery of the latter with the fantastic night-gown raiments of the former. "Whether the age was improved in beauty or in flattery," he adds, "Lely's women are certainly much handsomer than those of Vandyck. They please as much more as they evidently meaned to please." But for all that, there is a sameness in the Court painter's women which is unmistakable; whether it is the "sleepy eye and melting soul," of which doubtless Lady Castlemaine set the fashion, that was of more importance than any particular characteristic expression in a face; or whether the great demand for the painter's work introduced into his portraits so striking a similarity, we cannot undertake to say. Undoubtedly, many inferior pictures attributed to Lely are not by him at all, and for this reason he has been blamed for executing some very indifferent brushwork. Every house of any pretensions had to possess a few of the famous Court beauties, and doubtless there were many inferior artists to supply the demand and execute weak imitations in Lely's style.

Pepys records that Lely lived in great state and was "mighty proud." It is interesting to note that some of the best-known of the artist's portraits were seen in his studio at Covent Garden, or in the Royal apartments at Whitehall by the diarist, at the actual time the living representatives were giving the painter a sitting, and, with one or two exceptions, the likeness was approved by this somewhat captious critic. The last painting by Lely was the handsomest of all the "Beauties," the Duchess of Somerset. While engaged upon this, he died suddenly (in 1680). He was buried in Covent Garden Church, where his bust may be seen, carved by Grinling Gibbons.

dispersed all over England in abundance. Lely imitated Vandyke's manner, and approached the nearest to him of all the moderns. The Duchess of York, being desirous of having the portraits of the handsomest persons at Court, Lely painted them, and employed all his skill in the performance; nor could he ever exert himself upon more beautiful subjects. Every picture looked a masterpiece; and that of Miss Hamilton appeared the highest finished: Lely himself acknowledged that he had drawn it with particular pleasure.

The Duke of York took a delight in looking at it, and began again to ogle the original. He had very little reason to hope for success; and at the same time that his hopelesss passion alarmed the Chevalier de Gramont, Lady Denham thought proper to renew the negotiation which had so unluckily been interrupted. It was soon brought to a conclusion; for where both parties are sincere in a negotiation, no time is lost in cavilling.[8] Everything succeeded prosperously on one side; yet, I know not what fatality obstructed the pretensions of the other. The Duke was very urgent with the Duchess to put Lady Denham in possession of the place which was the object of her am-

    [8]Pepys (10th June 1666) says, on the authority of Pierce the surgeon, that "the Duke of York is wholly given up to his new mistress, my Lady Denham, going at noon-day with all his gentlemen with him to visit her in Scotland Yard, she declaring she will not be his mistress as Mrs. Price, to go up and down the privy stairs, but will be owned publicly, and so she is. Mr. Bruncker, it seems, was the pimp to bring it about." On 26th September (1666) he writes: "Here (Whitehall) I had the hap to see my Lady Denham, and at night went into the dining-room and saw several fine ladies, among others Castlemayne, but chiefly Denham again, and the Duke of York taking her aside and talking to her in the sight of all the world, all alone, which was strange, and what also I did not like. Here I met with good Mr. Evelyn, who cries out against it, and calls it bitchering, for the Duke of York talks a little to her, and then she goes away, and then he follows her again like a dog." There are other

bition; but as she was not guarantee for the performance of the secret articles of the treaty, though till this
time she had borne with patience the inconstancy of
the Duke, and yielded submissively to his desires; yet,
in the present instance, it appeared hard and dishonourable to her to entertain near her person a rival, who
would expose her to the danger of acting but a second
part in the midst of her own court. However, she
saw herself upon the point of being forced to it by
authority, when a far more unfortunate obstacle for
ever bereft poor Lady Denham of the hopes of possessing that fatal place, which she had solicited with
such eagerness.

Old Denham, naturally jealous, became more and
more suspicious, and found that he had sufficient
ground for such conduct. His wife was young and
handsome, he old and disagreeable: what reason then
had he to flatter himself that Heaven would exempt
him from the fate of husbands in the like circumstances? This he was continually saying to himself;
but when compliments were poured in upon him from
all sides, upon the place his lady was going to have
near the Duchess's person, he formed ideas of what
was sufficient to have made him hang himself, if he
had possessed the resolution. The traitor chose rather
to exercise his courage against another. He wanted
precedents for putting in practice his resentments in
a privileged country: that of Lord Chesterfield was
not sufficiently bitter for the revenge he meditated;
besides, he had no country-house to which he could

brief entries of the same nature, and on 10th November Pepys
says: "My Lady Denham is exceeding sick even to death, and
that she says and everybody else discourses that she is poisoned."
Though reported dead on 12th November, her ladyship rallied.
A month later (12th December) she was still ill, and on 7th
January Pepys records her death. She was buried at St. Margaret's, Westminster, in the middle of the chancel, but the stone
bears no inscription.

carry his unfortunate wife. This being the case, the old villain made her travel a much longer journey without stirring out of London. Merciless fate robbed her of life,[9] and of her dearest hopes, in the bloom of youth.

As no person entertained any doubt of his having poisoned her, the populace of his neighbourhood had a design of tearing him in pieces, as soon as he should come abroad, but he shut himself up to bewail her death, until their fury was appeased by a magnificent funeral, at which he distributed four times more burnt wine than had ever been drunk at any burial in England.

While the town was in fear of some great disaster, as an expiation for these fatal effects of jealousy, Hamilton[10] was not altogether so easy as he flattered himself he should be after the departure of Lady Chesterfield. He had only consulted the dictates of revenge in what he had done. His vengeance was satisfied; but such was far from being the case with his love; and having, since the absence of her he still admired, notwithstanding his resentments, leisure to

[9] The lampoons of the day, some of which are to be found in Andrew Marvell's *Works,* more than insinuate that she was deprived of life by a mixture infused into some chocolate. The slander of the times imputed her death to the jealousy of the Duchess of York. 7th January 1666-7: Lord Brouncker told Pepys "that my Lady Denham is at last dead. Some suspect her poisoned, but it will be best known when her body is opened to-day, she dying yesterday morning. The Duke of York is troubled for her, but hath declared he will never have another public mistress again, which I shall be glad of, and would the King do the like."

Aubrey says: "She was poisoned by the hands of the Co. of Roc. with chocolate." At the post-mortem examination, no trace of poison was found. She died a natural death. "My Lady Denham's body, at her own desire, was opened, but no sign of poison found" (Letter from Lord Orrery to the Duke of Ormonde, 25th January 1666-7, *Orrery State Papers,* 1742, p. 219). See Cunningham's "Chronology"

[10] James Hamilton.

make those reflections which a recent injury will not permit a man to attend to: "And wherefore," said he to himself, "was I so eager to make her miserable, who alone, however culpable she may be, has it in her power to make me happy? Cursed jealousy!" continued he, "yet more cruel to those who torment than to those who are tormented! What have I gained by having blasted the hopes of a more happy rival, since I was not able to perform this without depriving myself, at the same time, of her upon whom the whole happiness and comfort of my life was centred."

Thus, clearly proving to himself, by a great many reasonings of the same kind, and all out of season, that in such an engagement it was much better to partake with another than to have nothing at all, he filled his mind with a number of vain regrets and unprofitable remorse, when he received a letter from her who occasioned them, but a letter so exactly adapted to increase them, that, after he had read it, he looked upon himself as the greatest scoundrel in the world. Here it follows:

"You will, no doubt, be as much surprised at this letter as I was at the unconcerned air with which you beheld my departure. I am led to believe that you had imagined reasons which, in your own mind, justified such unseasonable conduct. If you are still under the impression of such barbarous sentiments, it will afford you pleasure to be made acquainted with what I suffer in the most horrible of prisons. Whatever the country affords most melancholy in this season presents itself to my view on all sides. Surrounded by impassable roads, out of one window I see nothing but rocks, out of another nothing but precipices; but wherever I turn my eyes within doors I meet those of a jealous husband, still more insupportable than the sad objects that encompass me. I should add to the

misfortunes of my life that of seeming criminal in
the eyes of a man who ought to have justified me,
even against convincing appearances, if by my avowed
innocence I had a right to complain or to expostulate.
But how is it possible for me to justify myself at such
a distance; and how can I flatter myself that the description of a most dreadful prison will not prevent
you from believing me? But do you deserve that I
should wish you did? Heavens! how I must hate you
if I did not love you to distraction. Come, therefore,
and let me once again see you, that you may hear my
justification; and I am convinced that if after this
visit you find me guilty it will not be with respect to
yourself. Our Argus sets out to-morrow for Chester,
where a lawsuit will detain him a week. I know not
whether he will gain it; but I am sure it will be entirely your fault if he does not lose one, for which he
is at least as anxious as that he is now going after."

This letter was sufficient to make a man run blind-
fold into an adventure still more rash than that which
was proposed to him, and that was rash enough in all
respects. He could not perceive by what means she
could justify herself; but as she assured him he should
be satisfied with his journey, this was all he desired
at present.

There was one of his relations with Lady Chesterfield, who, having accompanied her in her exile, had
gained some share in their mutual confidence; and it
was through her means he received this letter, with all
the necessary instructions about his journey and his
arrival. Secrecy being the soul of such expeditions,
especially before an amour is accomplished, he took
post, and set out in the night, animated by the most
tender and flattering wishes, so that, in less than no
time almost, in comparison with the distance and the
badness of the roads, he had travelled a hundred and

fifty tedious miles. At the last stage he prudently dismissed the post-boy. It was not yet daylight, and therefore, for fear of the rocks and precipices mentioned in her letter, he proceeded with tolerable discretion, considering he was in love.

By this means he fortunately escaped all the dangerous places, and, according to his instructions, alighted at a little hut adjoining the park wall. The place was not magnificent; but, as he only wanted rest, it did well enough for that. He did not wish for daylight, and was even still less desirous of being seen; wherefore, having shut himself up in this obscure retreat, he fell into a profound sleep, and did not wake until noon. As he was particularly hungry when he awoke, he ate and drank heartily; and, as he was the neatest man at Court, and was expected by the neatest lady in England, he spent the remainder of the day in dressing himself, and in making all those preparations which the time and place permitted, without deigning once to look around him, or to ask his landlord a single question. At last the orders he expected with great impatience were brought him, in the beginning of the evening, by a servant, who, attending him as a guide, after having led him for about half an hour in the dirt, through a park of vast extent, brought him at last into a garden, into which a little door[11] opened. He was posted exactly opposite to this door, by which, in a short time, he was to be introduced to a more agreeable situation; and here his conductor left him. The night advanced, but the door never opened.

Though the winter was almost over, the cold weather seemed only to be beginning. He was dirtied up to his knees in mud, and soon perceived that if he continued much longer in this garden it would all be

[11] The door of a low building opened (Vizetelly's translation).

frozen. This beginning of a very dark and bitter night would have been unbearable to any other; but it was nothing to a man who flattered himself to pass the remainder of it in the height of bliss. However, he began to wonder at so many precautions in the absence of a husband. His imagination, by a thousand delicious and tender ideas, supported him some time against the torments of impatience and the inclemency of the weather; but he felt his imagination, notwithstanding, cooling by degrees; and two hours, which seemed to him as tedious as two whole ages, having passed, and not the least notice being taken of him, either from the door or from the window, he began to reason with himself upon the posture of his affairs, and what was the fittest conduct for him to pursue in this emergency. "What if I should rap at this cursed door," said he; "for if my fate requires that I should perish, it is at least more honourable to die in the house than to be starved to death[12] in the garden. But then," continued he, "I may, thereby, perhaps, expose a person whom some unforeseen accident may, at this very instant, have reduced to greater perplexity than even I myself am in." This thought supplied him with a necessary degree of patience and fortitude against the enemies he had to contend with; he therefore began to walk quickly to and fro, with resolution to wait, as long as he could keep alive, the end of an adventure which had such an uncomfortable beginning. All this was to no purpose; for though he used every effort to keep himself warm, and though muffled up in a thick cloak, yet he began to be benumbed in all his limbs, and the cold gained the ascendancy over all his amorous vivacity and eagerness. Daybreak was not far off, and judging now that, though the accursed door should even be opened, it would be

[12] Perish of cold (Vizetelly's translation).

to no purpose, he returned, as well as he could, to the place from whence he had set out upon this wonderful expedition.

All the faggots that were in the cottage were hardly able to unfreeze him. The more he reflected on his adventure, the circumstances attending it appeared still the more strange and unaccountable; but so far from accusing the charming Countess, he suffered a thousand different anxieties on her account. Sometimes he imagined that her husband might have returned unexpectedly; sometimes, that she might suddenly have been taken ill; in short, that some insuperable obstacle had unluckily interposed, and prevented his happiness, notwithstanding his mistress's kind intentions towards him. "But wherefore," said he, "did she forget me in that cursed garden? Is it possible that she could not find a single moment to make me at least some sign or other, if she could neither speak to me nor give me admittance?" He knew not which of these conjectures to rely upon, or how to answer his own questions; but as he flattered himself that everything would succeed better the next night, after having vowed not to set foot again into that unfortunate garden, he gave orders to be awakened as soon as any person should inquire for him. Then he laid himself down in one of the worst beds in the world, and slept as sound as if he had been in the best. He supposed that he should not be awakened, except either by a letter or a message from Lady Chesterfield; but he had scarce slept two hours when he was aroused by the sound of the horn and the cry of the hounds. The hut which afforded him a retreat, joining, as we before said, to the park wall, he called his host, to know what was the occasion of that hunting, which made a noise as if the whole pack of hounds had been in his bedchamber. He was told that it was my lord hunting a hare in his park. "What lord?" said he, in great surprise. "The Earl of Chesterfield," replied the peasant. He was so astonished at this that at first he hid his head under the bedclothes, under the idea that he already saw him entering with all his hounds; but as soon as he had a little recovered himself he began to curse capricious fortune, no longer doubting but this jealous fool's return had occasioned all his tribulations in the preceding night. It was not possible for him to sleep again, after such an alarm; he therefore got up that he might revolve in his mind all the stratagems that are usually employed either to deceive, or to remove out of the way, a jealous scoundrel of a husband, who thought fit to neglect his lawsuit in order to plague his wife. He had just finished dressing himself, and was beginning to question his landlord, when the same servant who had conducted him to the garden delivered him a letter, and disappeared, without waiting for an answer. This letter was from his relation, and was to this effect:

"I am extremely sorry that I have innocently been accessory to bringing you to a place, to which you were only invited to be laughed at. I opposed this journey at first, though I was then persuaded it was wholly suggested by her tenderness; but she has now undeceived me. She triumphs in the trick she has played you: her husband has not stirred from hence, but stays at home, out of complaisance to her. He treats her in the most affectionate manner; and it was upon their reconciliation that she found out that you had advised him to carry her into the country. She has conceived such hatred and aversion against you for it, that I find, from her discourse, she has not yet wholly satisfied her resentment. Console yourself for the hatred of a person whose heart never merited your tenderness. Return: a longer stay in this place will but draw upon you some fresh misfortune. For my part, I shall soon leave her. I know her, and I thank God for it. I do not repent having pitied her at first; but I am disgusted with an employment which but ill agrees with my way of thinking."

Upon reading this letter, astonishment, shame, hatred, and rage, seized at once upon his heart; then menaces, invectives, and the desire of vengeance, broke forth by turns, and excited his passion and resentment; but, after he deliberately considered the matter, he resolved that it was now the best way quietly to mount his horse, and to carry back with him to London a severe cold, instead of the soft wishes and tender desires he had brought from thence. He quitted this perfidious place with much greater expedition than he had arrived at it, though his mind was far from being occupied with such tender and agreeable ideas. However, when he thought himself at a sufficient distance to be out of danger of meeting Lord Chesterfield and his hounds, he chose to look back, that he might at least have the satisfaction of seeing the prison where this wicked enchantress was confined; but what was his surprise, when he saw a very fine house, situated on the banks of a river, in the most delightful and pleasant country imaginable.[13] Neither rock nor precipice was here to be seen; for, in reality, they were

[13] Of the once splendid Inigo Jones mansion (partly constructed out of the remains of the ancient castle which stood in Queen Elizabeth's reign) of the Earls of Chesterfield at Bretby, near Repton, in South Derbyshire, only a few scanty ruins remain. When the older seat at Shelford, Nottinghamshire, was destroyed by the Parliamentary army, the family removed to Bretby and resided there until about the year 1780, when, under the belief that the building was unsafe, the Earl of Chesterfield of that day caused it to be pulled down and a new structure erected. Like many houses of the period, the house was long and narrow, with projecting wings. A paved courtyard was entered through massy iron gates. From here you entered a portico which led to the great hall, staircase, and numerous rich apartments,

only in the letter of his perfidious mistress. This furnished fresh cause for resentment and confusion to a man who thought himself so well acquainted with all the wiles, as well as weaknesses, of the fair sex; and who now found himself the dupe of a coquette, who was reconciled to her husband in order to be revenged on her lover.

adorned with painted ceilings and valuable tapestry and pictures. A chapel of later date stood at right angles with the east wing. The old gardens, designed after the style of Versailles, were " full of old buildings, fountains, and leaden images in the shape of wild beasts," etc. A series of fish ponds extended down a glen on the east side of the park, and to the north-east were long avenues of elm and chestnut trees. A description of the house is given in an old MS. relative to Derbyshire:—" The seat of the Earl of Chesterfield is situated in the midst of a very large park, well wooded and stored with several kinds of deer and exotic beasts. There are several fine avenues of trees leading to the house, which is of stone, though not of the modern architecture, yet very regular, convenient, and noble, with a very curious chapel and very good out-buildings. But the gardens, fountains, labyrinths, groves, greenhouses, grottoes, aviaries, but more especially the carpet walks, and situations of the orange-trees and water-works before the marble summer-house, are all noble and peculiarly curious and pleasant, suitable to the genius of the owner, who has also been the chief contriver of them, the present Earl of Chesterfield—Philip Stanhope, the third—who, now about eighty years of age, retains a great deal of that vigour and capacity which has hitherto rendered him the glory of the nation " (see Lysons' *Derbyshire*, p. 240). The Earl above alluded to was the same who figures in the *Memoirs*, and is wrongly described as the third Earl. Considerable alterations were made to the mansion by him in 1670, and in 1680 further alterations and improvements were added. The house as it was completed appears in Kip's engraving. A description of Bretby in 1787 is given in *A Tour from London to the Western Highlands of Scotland*, as follows: " Nothing scarce is left of that former grandeur, those shades, those sylvan scenes that everywhere graced the most charming of all parks. The baneful hand of luxury hath with rude violence laid them all waste. About ten years ago the venerable and lofty pile was standing, and exhibited delightful magnificence to its frequent visitors; its painted roofs and walls, besides a large collection of pictures, afforded much entertainment to the fond admirer of antique beauties; and the whole stood as a lasting monument of fame and credit to its lordly owner."

At last he reached London, well furnished with arguments to maintain that a man must be extremely weak to trust to the tenderness of a woman who has once deceived him, but that he must be a complete fool to run after her.

This adventure not being much to his credit, he suppressed, as much as possible, both the journey and the circumstances attending it; but, as we may easily suppose, Lady Chesterfield made no secret of it. The King came to the knowledge of it; and, having complimented Hamilton upon it, desired to be informed of all the particulars of the expedition. The Chevalier de Gramont happened to be present at this recital; and, having gently inveighed against the treacherous manner in which he had been used, said: "If she is to be blamed for carrying the jest so far, you are no less to be blamed for coming back so suddenly, like an ignorant novice. I dare lay an hundred guineas, she has more than once repented of a resentment which you pretty well deserved for the trick you had played her. Women love revenge; but their resentments seldom last long; and if you had remained in the neighbourhood till the next day, I will be hanged if she would not have given you satisfaction for the first night's sufferings." Hamilton being of a different opinion, the Chevalier de Gramont resolved to maintain his assertion by a case in point; and, addressing himself to the King: "Sire," said he, "your Majesty, I suppose, must have known Marion de l'Orme,[14] the most charming creature in all France. Though she was as witty as an angel, she was as capricious as a devil.

[14] Marion de l'Orme, born at Chalons, in Champagne, was esteemed the most beautiful woman of her times. It is believed that she was secretly married to the unfortunate Monsieur Cinqmars. After his death, she became the mistress of Cardinal Richelieu, and, at last, of Monsieur d'Emery, Superintendent of the Finances.

This beauty having made me an appointment, a whim
seized her to put me off, and to give it to another;
she therefore wrote me one of the tenderest billets in
the world, full of the grief and sorrow she was in,
by being obliged to disappoint me, on account of a
most terrible headache, that obliged her to keep her
bed, and deprived her of the pleasure of seeing me
till the next day. This headache coming all of a sudden, appeared to me very suspicious; and, never
doubting but it was her intention to jilt me: 'Very well,
mistress coquette,' said I to myself, 'if you do not
enjoy the pleasure of seeing me this day, you shall not
enjoy the satisfaction of seeing another.'

"Hereupon, I detached all my servants, some of
whom patrolled about her house, whilst others watched
her door. One of the latter brought me intelligence
that no person had gone into her house all the after-
noon; but that a foot-boy had gone out as it grew
dark; that he followed him as far as the Rue Saint
Antoine, where this boy met another, to whom he only
spoke two or three words. This was sufficient to confirm my suspicions, and make me resolve either to
make one of the party, or to disconcert it.

"As the bagnio where I lodged was at a great distance from the Marais, as soon as the night set in I
mounted my horse, without any attendant. When I
came to the Place-Royale, the servant, who was
sentry there, assured me that no person was yet gone
into Mademoiselle de l'Orme's house. I rode forward
towards the Rue Saint Antoine; and, just as I was
going out of the Place-Royale, I saw a man on foot
coming into it, who avoided me as much as he possibly
could; but his endeavour was all to no purpose; I
knew him to be the Duke de Brissac,[15] and I no longer

[15] Louis de Cosse Brissac, who at this time had not yet succeeded to the Dukedom (Vizetelly's edition, vol. ii. p. 60).

doubted but he was my rival that night. I then approached towards him, seeming as if I feared I mistook my man; and, alighting with a very busy air: 'Brissac, my friend,' said I, 'you must do me a service of the very greatest importance. I have an appointment, for the first time, with a girl who lives very near this place; and, as this visit is only to concert measures, I shall make but a very short stay. Be so kind, therefore, as to lend me your cloak, and walk my horse about a little, until I return; but, above all, do not go far from this place. You see that I use you freely like a friend; but you know it is upon condition that you may take the same liberty with me.' I took his cloak, without waiting for his answer, and he took my horse by the bridle, and followed me with his eye; but he gained no intelligence by this; for, after having pretended to go into a house opposite to him, I slipped under the piazzas to Mademoiselle de l'Orme's, where the door was opened as soon as I knocked. I was so much muffled up in Brissac's cloak that I was taken for him. The door was immediately shut, not the least question asked me; and having none to ask myself I went straight to the lady's chamber. I found her upon a couch in the most agreeable and genteelest déshabille imaginable: she never in her life looked so handsome, nor was so greatly surprised; and, seeing her speechless and confounded: 'What is the matter, my fair one?' said I, 'methinks this is a headache very elegantly set off; but your headache, to all appearance, is now gone?' 'Not in the least,' said she, 'I can scarce support it, and you will oblige me in going away that I may go to bed.' 'As for your going to bed, to that I have not the least objection,' said I, 'but as for my going away, that cannot be, my little princess: the Chevalier de Gramont is no fool; a woman does not dress herself with so much care for nothing.' 'You will find, however,' said she, 'that it is for nothing; for you may depend upon it that you shall be no gainer by it.' 'What!' said I, 'after having made me an appointment!' 'Well,' replied she hastily, 'though I had made you fifty, it still depends upon me, whether I chose to keep them or not, and you must submit if I do not.' 'This might do very well,' said I, 'if it was not to give it to another.' Mademoiselle de l'Orme, as haughty as a woman of the greatest virtue, and as passionate as one who has the least, was irritated at a suspicion which gave her more concern than confusion; and seeing that she was beginning to put herself in a passion: 'Madam,' said I, 'pray do not talk in so high a strain; I know what perplexes you: you are afraid lest Brissac should meet me here; but you may make yourself easy on that account. I met him not far from this place, and God knows that I have so managed the affair as to prevent his visiting you soon.' Having spoken these words in a tone somewhat tragical, she appeared concerned at first, and, looking upon me with surprise: 'What do you mean about the Duke de Brissac?' said she. 'I mean,' replied I, 'that he is at the end of the street, walking my horse about; but, if you will not believe me, send one of your own servants thither, or look at his cloak which I left in your ante-chamber.' Upon this she burst into a fit of laughter, in the midst of her astonishment, and, throwing her arms around my neck, 'My dear Chevalier,' said she, 'I can hold out no longer; you are too amiable and too eccentric not to be pardoned.' I then told her the whole story. She was ready to die with laughing; and, parting very good friends, she assured me my rival might exercise horses as long as he pleased, but that he should not set his foot within her doors that night.

"I found the Duke exactly in the place where I

had left him. I asked him a thousand pardons for having made him wait so long, and thanked him a thousand times for his complaisance. He told me I jested, that such compliments were unusual among friends; and to convince me that he had cordially rendered me this piece of service, he would, by all means, hold my horse while I was mounting. I returned him his cloak, bade him good-night, and went back to my lodgings, equally satisfied with my mistress and my rival. This," continued he, "proves that a little patience and address are sufficient to disarm the anger of the fair, to turn even their tricks to a man's advantage."

It was in vain that the Chevalier de Gramont diverted the Court with his stories, instructed by his example, and never appeared there but to inspire universal joy; for a long time he was the only foreigner in fashion. Fortune, jealous of the justice which is done to merit, and desirous of seeing all human happiness depend on her caprice, raised up against him two competitors for the pleasure he had long enjoyed of entertaining the English Court; and these competitors were so much the more dangerous, as the reputation of their several merits had preceded their arrival, in order to dispose the suffrages of the Court in their favour.

They came to display, in their own persons, whatever was the most accomplished either among the men of the sword, or of the gown. The one was the Marquis de Flamarens,[16] the sad object of the sad elegies of the Countess de la Suse,[17] the other was the

[16] François de Grossoles, *ob.* 1706. It is said to have been at his suggestion that Henrietta, Duchess of Orleans, came over to England with the object of influencing Charles in favour of the French alliance (see Vizetelly, vol. ii. p. 281).

[17] This lady was the daughter of Gaspar de Coligny, Marshal of France, and was celebrated in her time for her wit and her

President Tambonneau,[18] the most humble and most obedient servant and admirer of the beauteous Luynes.[19] As they arrived together, they exerted every endeavour to shine in concert. Their talents were as different as their persons; Tambonneau, who was tolerably ugly, founded his hopes upon a great store of wit, which, however, no person in England could find out; and Flamarens, by his air and mien, courted admiration, which was flatly denied him.

They had agreed mutually to assist each other, in order to succeed in their intentions; and therefore, in their first visits, the one appeared in state, and the other was the spokesman. But they found the ladies in England of a far different taste from those who had rendered them famous in France. The rhetoric of the one had no effect on the fair sex, and the fine mien of the other distinguished him only in a minuet, which he first introduced into England, and which he danced with tolerable success. The English Court had been too long accustomed to the solid wit of Saint-Evremond, and the natural and singular charms of his hero, to be seduced by appearances; however, as the English have, in general, a sort of predilection in favour of anything that has the appearance of bravery, Flamarens was better received on account of a duel,

elegies. She was one of the few women with whom Christina, Queen of Sweden, condescended to become intimate. Though educated a Protestant, she embraced the Roman Catholic religion, less from a motive of devotion, than to have a pretence for parting from her husband, who was a Protestant, and for whom she had an invincible abhorrence, which occasioned the Queen to say, "The Countess of Suse became a Catholic, that she might neither meet her husband in this world nor the next." —See Lacombe's *Life of Queen Christina*. The Countess died in 1673.

[18] President of the *Chambre des Comptes,* where the financial business of the State was transacted from the year 1302 until 1790, when it was abolished.

[19] Jane Mary, eldest daughter of Colbert, the French Minister. She married the Duke de Luynes (Vizetelly, ii. p. 64).

which, obliging him to leave his own country, was a recommendation to him in England.

Miss Hamilton had, at first, the honour of being distinguished by Tambonneau, who thought she possessed a sufficient share of wit to discover the delicacy of his; and, being delighted to find that nothing was lost in her conversation, either as to the turn, the expression, or beauty of the thought, he frequently did her the favour to converse with her; and, perhaps, he would never have found out that he was tiresome, if, contenting himself with the display of his eloquence, he had not thought proper to attack her heart. This was carrying the matter a little too far for Miss Hamilton's complaisance, who was of opinion that she had already shown him too much for the tropes of his harangues; he was therefore desired to try somewhere else the experiment of his seducing tongue, and not to lose the merit of his former constancy by an infidelity which would be of no advantage to him.

He followed this advice like a wise and tractable man; and some time after, returning to his old mistress in France, he began to lay in a store of politics for those important negotiations in which he has since been employed.

It was not till after his departure that the Chevalier de Gramont heard of the amorous declaration he had made. This was a confidence of no great importance; it, however, saved Tambonneau from some ridicule which might have fallen to his share before he went away. His colleague, Flamarens, deprived of his support, soon perceived that he was not likely to meet in England with the success he had expected, both from love and fortune; but Lord Falmouth, ever attentive to the glory of his master, in the relief of illustrious men in distress, provided for his subsistence, and Lady Southesk for his pleasures; he obtained a pension from the King, and from her everything he desired; and most happy was it for him that she had no other present to bestow but that of her heart.

It was at this time that Talbot, whom we have before mentioned, and who was afterwards created Duke of Tyrconnel, fell in love with Miss Hamilton. There was not a more genteel man[20] at Court. He was indeed but a younger brother, though of a very ancient family, which, however, was not very considerable either for its renown or its riches; and though he was naturally of a careless disposition, yet, being intent upon making his fortune, and much in favour with the Duke of York, and fortune likewise favouring him at play, he had improved both so well that he was in possession of about forty thousand pounds[21] a year in land. He offered himself to Miss Hamilton, with this fortune, together with the almost certain hopes of being made a peer of the realm, by his master's credit; and, over and above all, as many sacrifices as she could desire of Lady Shrewsbury's letters, pictures, and hair: curiosities which, indeed, are reckoned for nothing in housekeeping, but which testify strongly in favour of the sincerity and merit of a lover.

Such a rival was not to be despised; and the Chevalier de Gramont thought him the more dangerous, as he perceived that Talbot was desperately in love; that he was not a man to be discouraged by a first repulse; that he had too much sense and good breeding to draw upon himself either contempt or coldness by too great eagerness; and, besides this, his brothers began to frequent the house. One of these brothers was Almoner to the Queen,[22] an intriguing

[20] Man of better appearance (Vizetelly's translation).
[21] Livres (*ibid.*). This is less than £2000.
[22] Peter Talbot, Almoner to the Queen, born 1620, second son of Sir William Talbot, and elder brother of Richard, Duke of Tyrconnel. Consecrated in 1669 at Antwerp. He lived upon friendly terms with his brothers' patrons the Duke and Duchess

Jesuit, and a great match-maker; the other was what was called a lay-monk,[23] who had nothing of his order but the immorality and infamy of character which is ascribed to them, and withal, frank and free, and sometimes entertaining, but ever ready to speak bold and offensive truths, as to do good offices.

When the Chevalier de Gramont reflected upon all these things, there certainly was strong ground for uneasiness; nor was the indifference which Miss Hamilton showed for the addresses of his rival sufficient to remove his fears; for being absolutely dependent on her father's will, she could only answer for her own intentions; but Fortune, who seemed to have taken him under her protection in England, now delivered him from all his uneasiness.

Talbot had for many years stood forward as the patron of the distressed Irish. This zeal for his countrymen was certainly very commendable in itself; at the same time, however, it was not altogether free from self-interest; for, out of all the estates he had, through his credit, procured the restoration of to their primitive owners, he had always obtained some small compensation for himself; but as each owner found his advantage in it, no complaint was made. Nevertheless, as it is very difficult to use fortune and favour with moderation, and not to swell with the gales of prosperity, some of his proceedings had an air of haughtiness and independence, which offended the Duke of Ormonde,[24] then Lord Lieutenant of Ireland, as in-

of York, residing latterly at Poole Hall, Cheshire (which is still in good preservation). He died in 1680. Clarendon speaks of him in his *Continuation* in not too favourable terms.

[23] Thomas Talbot, a Franciscan friar, "of wit enough," says Lord Clarendon, "but of notorious debauchery" (*Continuation of Clarendon*, p. 363.)

[24] A minute account of this transaction is given by Lord Clarendon, by which it appears that Talbot was committed to the Tower for threatening to assassinate the Duke of Ormonde (*Continuation of Clarendon*. p. 362).

jurious to his Grace's authority. The Duke resented this behaviour with great spirit. As there certainly was a great difference between them, both as to their birth and rank, and to their credit, it had been prudent in Talbot to have had recourse to apologies and submission; but such conduct appeared to him base, and unworthy for a man of his importance to submit to. He accordingly acted with haughtiness and insolence; but he was soon convinced of his error; for, having inconsiderately launched out into some arrogant expressions, which it neither became him to utter nor the Duke of Ormonde to forgive, he was sent prisoner to the Tower, from whence he could not be released until he had made all necessary submissions to his Grace. He therefore employed all his friends for that purpose, and was obliged to yield more to get out of this scrape than would have been necessary to have avoided it. By this imprudent conduct he lost all hopes of marrying into a family which, after such a proceeding, was not likely to listen to any proposal from him.

It was with great difficulty and mortification that he was obliged to suppress a passion which had made far greater progress in his heart than this quarrel had done good to his affairs. This being the case, he was of opinion that his presence was necessary in Ireland, and that he was better out of the way of Miss Hamilton, to remove those impressions which still troubled his repose. His departure, therefore, soon followed this resolution.

Talbot played deep, and was tolerably forgetful; the Chevalier de Gramont won three or four hundred guineas of him the very evening on which he was sent to the Tower. That accident had made him forget his usual punctuality in paying the next morning whatever he had lost over-night; and this debt had so far escaped his memory, that it never once occurred to him after he was enlarged. The Chevalier de Gramont, who saw him at his departure, without taking the least notice of the money he owed him, wished him a good journey; and, having met him at Court, as he came to take his leave of the King: "Talbot," said he, "if my services can be of any use to you during your absence, you have but to command them. You know old Russell has left his nephew as his resident with Miss Hamilton. If you please, I will act for you in the same capacity. Adieu, God bless you; be sure not to fall sick upon the road; but if you should, pray remember me in your will." Talbot, who, upon this compliment, immediately recollected the money he owed the Chevalier, burst out laughing, and embracing him: "My dear Chevalier," said he, "I am so much obliged to you for your offer, that I resign you my mistress, and will send you your money instantly." The Chevalier de Gramont possessed a thousand of these genteel ways of refreshing the memories of those persons who were apt to be forgetful in their payments. The following is the method he used some years after with Lord Cornwallis.[25] This lord had

---

[25] Charles Cornwallis, second Baron Cornwallis of Eye (born 1632) Gentleman of the Privy Chamber to Charles II., was son and heir of Sir Frederick Cornwallis, Bart. (created Baron, 20th April 1661), and Elizabeth, daughter of Sir John Ashburnham. He married Margaret, daughter of Sir Thomas Playsted, and died at St. Dunstans in the East, 13th April 1673.

Pepys mentions the visit of Charles II. to Lord Cornwallis at Culford Hall, near Bury St. Edmunds (an Elizabethan mansion, rebuilt in the eighteenth century), during a sojourn at Newmarket, when (by Creed's account) the King's host endeavoured to procure for his Majesty the parson's pretty daughter, who, however, escaped, "and leaped off of some high place killed herself, which," says the diarist, "if true is very sad" (*Diary*, 18th July 1668).

The third Lord Cornwallis, born 1655, son of the above, married, in the year 1688, the widow of the Duke of Monmouth (vide *King Monmouth*).

married the daughter of Sir Stephen Fox,[26] Treasurer of the King's Household, one of the richest and most regular men in England. His son-in-law, on the contrary, was a young spendthrift, was very extravagant, loved gaming, lost as much as any one would trust him, but was not quite so ready at paying. His father-in-law disapproved of his conduct, paid his debts, and gave him a lecture at the same time. The Chevalier de Gramont had won of him a thousand or twelve hundred guineas, which he heard no tidings of, although he was upon the eve of his departure, and he had taken leave of Cornwallis in a more particular manner than any other person. This obliged the Chevalier to write him a billet, which was rather laconic. It was this:

"MY LORD,
        "Pray remember the Count de Gramont, and do not forget Sir Stephen Fox."[27]

[26] Sir Stephen Fox, son of William Fox, of Farley, Wilts, born 1627, statesman and Royalist. He was employed on various secret missions to England prior to the Restoration, being attached to Charles II.'s Court in Holland, and was the first to bring the welcome news of Cromwell's death. He was knighted in 1665. Though he supported Clarendon and voted against the Chancellor's impeachment, he retained the King's friendship. From Clerk of the Green Cloth and Paymaster of the Forces he was promoted to one of the Lords Commissioners of the Treasury in 1679. At the Revolution he opposed William of Orange, though he was won over in 1689. He led the Commons at Queen Anne's Coronation. He died at his house in Chiswick in October 1716, and was buried at Farley. By his second wife Christian Hope, whom he married in his seventy-seventh year, he left two sons (afterwards Earl of Ilchester and Viscount Holland) and two daughters. By his first wife, Elizabeth Whittle (sister to Charles II.'s court surgeon), he left two sons and three daughters.
    Evelyn speaks of his good parts—kindness and benevolence. Much of the wealth he had amassed was spent in erecting churches and almshouses, and the idea of founding Chelsea Hospital was in reality his and not Nell Gwyn's, as is popularly believed (vide *Dictionary of National Biography*, vol. xx. pp. 134-135).
    [27] Going by the date of Lord Cornwallis's marriage, the

To return to Talbot: he went away more concerned than became a man who had voluntarily resigned his mistress to another; neither his stay in Ireland, nor his solicitude about his domestic affairs, perfectly cured him; and if at his return he found himself disengaged from Miss Hamilton's chains, it was only to exchange them for others. The alteration that had taken place in the two Courts occasioned this change in him, as we shall see in the sequel.

We have hitherto only mentioned the Queen's Maids of Honour, upon account of Miss Stewart and Miss Warmester. The others were Miss Bellenden, Mademoiselle de la Garde, and Mademoiselle Bardou, all maids of honour, as it pleased God.

Miss Bellenden[28] was no beauty, but was a good-natured girl, whose chief merit consisted in being plump and fresh-coloured; and who, not having a sufficient stock of wit to be a coquette in form, used all her endeavours to please every person by her complaisance.

Mademoiselle de la Garde, and Mademoiselle Bardou, both French, had been preferred to their places by the Queen Dowager: the first was a little brunette, who was continually meddling in the affairs of her companions; and the other by all means claimed the rank of a maid of honour, though she only lodged with the others, and both her title and services were constantly contested.

It was hardly possible for a woman to be more ugly, with so fine a shape; but as a recompense, her ugliness was set off with every art. The use she was put to was to dance with Flamarens, and sometimes, towards the conclusion of a ball, possessed of casta-

above incident cannot have happened before 27th December 1673.

[28] Possibly the daughter of William, created Lord Bellenden 1661, the son of Sir James Bellenden of Broughton.

nets and effrontery, she would dance some figured saraband or other, which amused the Court. Let us now see in what manner this ended.

As Miss Stewart was very seldom in waiting on the Queen, she was scarcely considered as a maid of honour. The others went off almost at the same time, by different adventures; and this is the history of Miss Warmester, whom we have before mentioned, when speaking of the Chevalier de Gramont.

Lord Taaffe, eldest son of the Earl of Carlingford,[29] was supposed to be in love with her; and Miss Warmester not only imagined it was so, but likewise persuaded herself that he would not fail to marry her the first opportunity; and in the meantime she thought it her duty to entertain him with all the civility imaginable.

Taaffe had made the Duke of Richmond[30] his con-

[29] Nicholas, third Viscount Taaffe, afterwards second Earl of Carlingford, was the son of Sir Theobald Taaffe, the second Viscount of that name, first Earl of Carlingford, and Mary, daughter of Sir Nicholas White of Leixlip, Co. Kildare. He was Privy Councillor, and served in the Spanish Army. Both he and his brother John were killed in the Jacobite cause, the former at the battle of the Boyne (1691) and the latter at the siege of Derry (1689). Nicholas was succeeded by his brother Francis, fourth Viscount Taaffe and third Earl of Carlingford, b. 1639, ob. 1704, who, dying without issue, was succeeded by his nephew (John's son) Theobald, the fourth and last Earl, who died in 1738, when the title became extinct.

"Old Lord Carlingford" of the *Memoirs,* the second Viscount Taaffe, was in all probability the father of the Duke of Monmouth's half-sister, Mary Walter (vide *King Monmouth,* chap. vi., and the Appendix of that work, pp. 403-406). He was created Earl, 17th June 1661, and died 31st December 1677. Charles II. had a great regard for the Taaffe family.

[30] Charles Stewart, fourth Duke of Richmond, only son of George Stewart (the fourth son of Esmé, third Duke of Lennox) and Catherine Howard, eldest daughter of the second Earl of Suffolk, born March 1639-40. He succeeded to the title in August 1660. He was sent as ambassador to Denmark, as Burnet says, upon a sleeveless errand, and died at Elsinore in

fidant: these two were particularly attached to each other; but still more so to wine. The Duke of Richmond, notwithstanding his birth, made but an indifferent figure at Court; and the King respected him still less than his courtiers did; and perhaps it was in order to court his Majesty's favour that he thought proper to fall in love with Miss Stewart. The Duke and Lord Taaffe made each other the confidants of their respective engagements; and these were the measures they took to put their designs in execution. Little Mademoiselle de la Garde[31] was charged to acquaint Miss Stewart that the Duke of Richmond was dying of love for her, and that when he ogled her in public it was a certain sign that he was ready to marry her, as soon as ever she would consent.

Taaffe had no commission to give the little ambassadress for Miss Warmester; for there everything was already arranged; but she was charged to settle and provide some conveniences which were still wanting for the freedom of their commerce, such as to have free egress and regress to her at all hours of the day or night. This appeared difficult to be obtained, but it was, however, at length accomplished.

The governess of the maids of honour, who for the world would not have connived at anything that was not fair and honourable, consented that they should

1672, and was buried in Westminster Abbey, 20th September 1673. The titles reverted to the King as nearest collateral heir, who bestowed them on his natural son by the Duchess of Portsmouth, Charles Lennox, first Duke of Richmond, in August 1675.

[31] Daughter of Charles Peliot, Lord de la Garde, whose eldest daughter married Sir Thomas Bond, Comptroller of the Household to the Queen Mother, and who had lent large sums of money to Charles II. before the Restoration. (Bond's second son married the niece of Jermyn, one of the heroes of these *Memoirs*).—See Collins's *Baronetage*. Miss de la Garde became the wife of Sir Gabriel Silvius, who married a second wife in 1677.

sup as often as they pleased in Miss Warmester's apartments, provided their intentions were honourable, and she one of the company. The good old lady was particularly fond of green oysters, and had no aversion to Spanish wine; she was certain of finding at every one of these suppers two barrels of oysters: one to be eaten with the party, and the other for her to carry away. As soon, therefore, as she had taken her dose of wine, she took her leave of the company .

It was much about the time that the Chevalier de Gramont had cast his eyes upon Miss Warmester that this kind of life was led in her chamber. God knows how many ham pies, bottles of wine, and other products of his lordship's liberality were there consumed!

In the midst of these nocturnal festivals, and of this innocent commerce, a relation of Killegrew's[32] came up to London about a lawsuit. He gained his cause, but nearly lost his senses.

He was a country gentleman, who had been a widower about six months, and was possessed of fifteen or sixteen thousand pounds[33] a-year. The good man, who had no business at Court, went thither merely to see his cousin Killegrew, who could have dispensed with his visits. He there saw Miss Warmester; and at first sight fell in love with her. His passion increased to such a degree that, having no rest either by day or night, he was obliged to have recourse to extraordinary remedies; he therefore early one morning called upon his cousin Killegrew, told him his case, and desired him to demand Miss Warmester in marriage for him.

[32] He has been confused with Sir Thomas Vernon, who married Miss Mary Kirke under similar circumstances after he became a widower in June 1676 (see note, p. 114).

[33] Livres (Vizetelly)—a livre was about equivalent to a franc, which reduces the above income considerably.

Killegrew was struck with wonder and astonishment when he heard his design: nor could he cease wondering at what sort of creature, of all the women in London, his cousin had resolved upon marrying. It was some time before Killegrew could believe that he was in earnest; but when he was convinced that he was, he began to enumerate the dangers and inconveniences attending so rash an enterprise.   He told him that a girl educated at Court was a terrible piece of furniture for the country; that to carry her thither against her inclination would as effectually rob him of his happiness and repose as if he was transported to hell; that if he consented to let her stay, he needed only to compute what it would cost him in equipage, table, clothes, and gaming-money, to maintain her in London according to her caprices; and then to cast up how long his fifteen thousand[34] a-year would last.

His cousin had already formed this computation; but, finding his reason less potent than his love, he remained fixed in his resolution; and Killegrew, yielding at length to his importunities, went and offered his cousin, bound hand and foot, to the victorious fair. As he dreaded nothing more than a compliance on her part, so nothing could astonish him more than the contempt with which she received his proposal.   The scorn with which she refused him, made him believe that she was sure of Lord Taaffe, and wonder how a girl like her could find out two men who would venture to marry her.   He hastened to relate this refusal, with all the most aggravating circumstances, as the best news he could carry to his cousin; but his cousin would not believe him.   He supposed that Killegrew disguised the truth, for the same reasons he had already alleged; and not daring to mention the matter any more to him, he resolved to wait upon her himself.   He summoned all

[34] Livres.

his courage for the enterprise, and got his compliment by heart; but as soon as he had opened his mouth for the purpose, she told him he might have saved himself the trouble of calling on her about such a ridiculous affair; that she had already given her answer to Kille-grew; and that she neither had, nor ever should have, any other to give, which words she accompanied with all the severity with which importunate demands are usually refused.

He was more affected than confounded at this re-pulse: everything became odious to him in London, and he himself more so than all the rest. He there-fore left town, without taking leave of his cousin, went back to his country seat, and thinking it would be impossible for him to live without the inhuman fair, he resolved to neglect no opportunity in his power to hasten his death.

But whilst, in order to indulge his sorrow, he had forsaken all intercourse with dogs and horses—that is to say, renounced all the delights and endearments of a country squire—the scornful nymph, who was cer-tainly mistaken in her reckoning, took the liberty of being brought to-bed in the face of the whole Court.

An adventure so public made no small noise, as we may very well imagine. All the prudes at Court at once broke loose upon it; and those principally, whose age or persons secured them from any such scandal, were the most inveterate, and cried most loudly for justice. But the governess of the maids of honour, who might have been called to an account for it, affirmed that it was nothing at all, and that she was possessed of cir-cumstances which would at once silence all censorious tongues. She had an audience of the Queen, in order to unfold the mystery; and related to her Majesty how everything had passed with her consent, that is to say, upon honourable terms.

The Queen sent to inquire of Lord Taaffe whether he acknowledged Miss Warmester for his wife. To which he most respectfully returned for answer, that he neither acknowledged Miss Warmester nor her child, and that he wondered why she should rather father it upon him than any other. The unfortunate Warmester, more enraged at this answer than at the loss of such a lover, quitted the Court as soon as ever she was able, with a resolution of quitting the world the first opportunity.

Killegrew, being upon the point of setting out upon a journey when this adventure happened, thought he might as well call upon his afflicted cousin in his way, to acquaint him with the circumstances; and as soon as he saw him, without paying any attention to the delicacy of his love, or to his feelings, he bluntly told him the whole story; nor did he omit any colouring that could heighten his indignation, in order to make him burst with shame and resentment.

We read that the gentle Tiridates quietly expired upon the recital of the death of Mariamne; but Killegrew's fond cousin, falling devoutly upon his knees, and lifting up his eyes to Heaven, poured forth this exclamation:

"Praised be the Lord for a small misfortune, which perhaps may prove the comfort of my life! Who knows but the beauteous Warmester will now accept of me for a husband; and that I may have the happiness of passing the remainder of my days with a woman I adore, and by whom I may expect to have heirs?" "Certainly," said Killegrew, more confounded than his cousin ought to have been on such an occasion, "you may depend upon having both. I make no manner of doubt but she will marry you as soon as ever she is recovered from her lying-in; and it would be a great ill-nature in her, who already knows the way, to

let you want children. However, in the meantime I
advise you to take that she has already, till you get
more."

Notwithstanding this raillery, all that was said did
take place. This faithful lover courted her, as if she
had been the chaste Lucretia, or the beauteous Helen.
His passion even increased after marriage, and the
generous fair, first out of gratitude, and afterwards
through inclination, never brought him a child of
which he was not the father; and though there have
been many a happy couple in England, this certainly
was the happiest.

Some time after, Miss Bellenden, not being terrified
by this example, had the prudence to quit the Court
before she was obliged so to do. The disagreeable
Bardou followed her soon after; but for different reasons. Every person was at last completely tired of
her saraband, as well as of her face; and the King,
that he might see neither of them any more, gave each
a small pension for her subsistence. There now only
remained little Mademoiselle de la Garde to be provided for. Neither her virtues nor her vices were
sufficiently conspicuous to occasion her being either
dismissed from Court, or pressed to remain there.
God knows what would have become of her, if a Mr.
Silvius,[35] a man who had nothing of a Roman in him

[35]Afterwards Sir Gabriel Silvius. In Chamberlayne's *Angliæ
Notitia*, 1669, Gabriel de Sylviis is put down as one of the car-
vers to the Queen, and Mrs. de Sylviis, one of the six chambriers
or dressers to the Queen. He was afterwards knighted, and, 30th
February 1680, was sent ambassador to the Dukes of Brunswick
and Lunenburgh. Lord Orford says he was a native of Orange,
and was attached to the Princess Royal, afterwards to the Duke
of York. He also says he was sent ambassador to Denmark.
In 1677 Sir Gabriel married, secondly, Anne Howard, daughter
of William, fourth son of the first Earl of Berkshire, and sister
to Craven, afterwards Earl. The same year she was made lady
of the bedchamber to the Princess Mary (see "Diary of Sir
Thomas Lake," Camden's *Miscellany*, vol. i. p. 13).

except the name, had not taken the poor girl to be his wife.

We have now shown how all these damsels deserved to be expelled, either for their irregularities, or for their ugliness; and yet, those who replaced them found means to make them regretted, Miss Wells[36] only excepted.

She was a tall girl, exquisitely shaped; she dressed very well, walked like a goddess; and yet, her face, though made like those that generally please the most, was unfortunately one of those that pleased the least: nature had spread over it a certain careless indolence[37] that made her look sheepish.[38] This gave but a bad opinion of her wit; and her wit had the ill-luck to make good that opinion. However, as she was fresh coloured, and appeared inexperienced, the King, whom the fair Stewart did not render over nice as to the perfections of the mind, resolved to try whether the senses would not fare better with Miss Wells's person than fine sentiments with her understanding. Nor was this experiment attended with much difficulty. She was of a loyal family; and her father having faithfully served Charles the First, she thought it her duty not to revolt against Charles the Second. But this connection was not attended with very advantageous circumstances for herself. Some pretended that she did not hold out long enough, and that she surrendered at discretion before she was vigorously attacked; and others said that his Majesty complained of certain other facilities still less pleasing. The Duke of Buckingham made a couplet upon this occasion, wherein the King, speaking to Progers,[39] the confidant of his intrigues, puns upon the name of the fair one.

---

[36] Winifred Wells was Maid of Honour to the Queen and belonged to a good royalist family.

[37] Vague look (Vizetelly).   [38] Like a musing sheep (ibid.).

[39] Edward Progers, or Proger, was a younger son of Colonel Philip Progers (of the family of Garreddin, in Monmouthshire).

Miss Wells, notwithstanding a species of anagram upon her name, and certain remarks upon her person, shone the brightest among her new companions.[40]

equerry to James I. He was early introduced to Court, and, after having been page to Charles I., was made Groom of the Bedchamber to the Prince of Wales. In the lampoons of the times, particularly in those of Andrew Marvell, he is described as one devoted to assist his master's pleasure; for which reason, perhaps, he was banished from the King's presence in 1650, by an act of the estates of Scotland, " as an evil instrument and bad counsellor of the King." In 1660, he was named, says Walpole, one of the knights of the Royal Oak, an order the King then intended to institute. Progers obtained permission from the King to build a house in Bushey Park, near Hampton Court, on condition that, after his death, it should revert to the Crown. This was the " Upper Lodge " which stood on the site of the house occupied by King William IV., and here some of the Merry Monarch's convivial meetings took place. He represented the county of Brecon in Parliament for seventeen years, but retired in 1679. On the death of Charles, he retired from public life. In James II.'s reign he was in low circumstances, and applied to the King for relief, with what effect is not known. Progers had a family by his wife Elizabeth Wells (possibly Winifred's sister) ; and the scandal-bearers of the time remarked that his eldest daughter Philippa, afterwards Mrs. Croxel, bore a strong resemblance to Charles II. (*Monumenta Anglicana*, 1717, p. 273). Mr. Progers died, says Le Neve, " 31st December, or 1st January 1713-14, aged ninety-six, of the anguish of cutting teeth, he having cut four new teeth, and had several ready to cut, which so inflamed his gums, that he died thereof." When the old church at Hampton was pulled down, Proger's tomb now in the new church, was discovered beneath the reading desk. It was Progers who managed to abduct the young Duke of Monmouth from his mother, Lucy Walter (vide *King Monmouth,* p. 20).

[40] At a Court ball some time in January 1662-3, and recorded by Pepys 8th February of that year, a child was dropped by one of the maids of honour, which was smuggled off in a handkerchief. The next day Miss Wells was missing, having fallen sick, says Pepys, so this misadventure was attributed to her. The King, who was supposed to be the father, according to the same authority, amused himself by dissecting this still-born boy! (*Diary,* 17th February 1662-3). On 12th June 1666 the diarist saw her in her riding garb, with coat, doublet, and deep skirt, hat and periwig exactly like a man's, the only distinction being a long petticoat dragging beneath the coat. It is needless to add that Mr. Pepys, so susceptible to beauty, did not approve of this costume.

In the last entry but one in Pepys' *Diary,* 30th May 1669, he

These were Miss Levingston,[41] Miss Fielding,[42] and Miss Boynton,[43] who little deserve to be mentioned in these *Memoirs;* therefore we shall leave them in obscurity until it please fortune to draw them out of it.

This was the new establishment of maids of honour to the Queen. The Duchess of York, nearly about the same time, likewise recruited hers; but showed, by a happier and more brilliant choice, that England possessed an inexhaustible stock of beauties. But before we begin to speak of them, let us see who were the first maids of honour to her Royal Highness, and on what account they were removed.

mentions meeting Miss Wells in Mr. Chevin's (Chiffinch) apartments at Whitehall. He speaks of her great beauty, and pretty conversation, which scarcely tallies with Gramont's description. "I had my full gaze upon her," says Pepys, "to my great content."

[41] Nothing appears to be known of this lady. It has been surmised, however, that it was to her that the Earl of Chesterfield (Philip, second Earl) wrote one of his amatory epistles. Under the initials " B. L." her portrait is thus described: " Your shape tho' neat deserves rather to be commended than admired. Your motions are easy and allways attended with an air, that is peculiar to persons of quality. Your complexion is none of those faint whits [whites] that represents a Venus in the green sickness, but such as Appollo favours and visits most. Your hair is like Mary Magdalain's, and a pretty sullenness commonly shades your face; but smiles from a new fashioned mouth doe disperse those clouds and shew such beauties of red and white, that all other mouths can never prayes enough. Your eyes (tho' not to big) are full of fire and seem to penetrat our thoughts, and sometimes allso to express your own; which leads me to a mind that I dare hardly mention, as never having had the honour of your company," etc. (*Letters of Philip, Earl of Chesterfield*, pp. 153-156).

[42] Beau Fielding's sister Anne. John Verney, writing to his son Ralph, 30th November 1676, says: " Sir Samuel Morland is lately married to handsome Fielding's sister, and saith he will not have a penny for portion. She is handsomer for a woman than he is for a man " (*Hist. MS. Com. Rep.* 7, App. p. 467). According to the poem, " Cullen with his Flock of Misses," she was among the applicants for the position held by the Duchess of Portsmouth when the French mistress was out of favour in 1679. She died February 1679-80.   [43] See note, p. 285.

Beside Miss Blague and Miss Price, who we have before mentioned, the establishment was composed of Miss Bagot and Miss Hobart, the president of the community.

Miss Blague, who never knew the true reason of her quarrel with the Marquis de Brisacier, took it up upon that fatal letter she had received from him, wherein, without acquainting her that Miss Price was to wear the same sort of gloves and yellow riband[44] as herself, he had only complimented her upon her hair, her fair complexion,[45] and her eyes *marcassins*. This word she imagined must signify something particularly wonderful, since her eyes were compared to it; and being desirous, some time afterwards, to know all the energy of the expression, she asked the meaning of the French word *marcassin*. As there are no wild boars in England, those to whom she addressed herself told her that it signified a young pig. This scandalous simile confirmed her in the belief she entertained of his perfidy. Brisacier, more amazed at her change than she was offended at his supposed calumny, looked upon her as a woman still more capricious than insignificant, and never troubled himself more about her; but Sir Thomas Yarborough,[46] of as fair a complexion as herself, made her an offer of marriage in the height of her resentment, and was accepted. Chance made up this match, I suppose, as an experiment to try what such a white-[47]haired union would produce.

Miss Price was witty; and as her person was not very likely to attract many admirers, which, however,

[44] Yellow gloves and ribands (Vizetelly's translation).

[45] Fair hair and complexion (*ibid.*).

[46] Son of Sir Nicholas Yarborough, of Snaith, Yorkshire, and cousin of Sir John Reresby. The character of *Sir Francis Wronghead* in Cibber's *Provoked Husband* is said to have been drawn from Sir Thomas (*vide* Reresby's *Memoirs* 1875 ed., note, p. 413).   [47] Pale (*ibid.*).

she was resolved to have, she was far from being coy
when an occasion offered; she did not so much as
make any terms. She was violent in her resentments,
as well as in her attachments, which had exposed her
to some inconveniences; and she had very indiscreetly
quarrelled with a young girl whom Lord Rochester
admired. This connection, which till then had been a
secret, she had the imprudence to publish to the whole
world, and thereby drew upon herself the most dangerous enemy in the universe. Never did any man write
with more ease, humour, spirit, and delicacy; but he
was at the same time the most severe satirist.

Poor Miss Price, who had thus voluntarily provoked his resentment, was daily exposed in some new
shape. There was every day some new song or other,
the subject of which was her conduct, and the burden
her name. How was it possible for her to bear up
against these attacks, in a Court where every person
was eager to obtain the most insignificant trifle that
came from the pen of Lord Rochester? The loss of
her lover, and the discovery that attended it, was only
wanting to complete the persecution that was raised
against her.

About this time died Dongan,[48] a gentleman of
merit, who was succeeded by Durfort, afterwards Earl
of Feversham,[49] in the post of lieutenant of the Duke's

[48] Robert Dongan, Dungan, or Duncan, one of Nell Gwyn's
early admirers, and possibly he who introduced her first to the
stage, lieutenant in the Duke of York's Life Guards, an appointment attributed by Etheridge to the influence of Nelly
(see Cunningham's *Story of Nell Gwyn*).

[49] Louis de Duras, Earl of Feversham, a native of France, being
son of the Duke de Duras, and brother to the last Duke of that
name, as also to the Duke de Lorge. His mother was sister to
the great Turenne, of the princely house of Bouillon. After the
Restoration he came to England, was naturalised, and behaved
with great gallantry in the sea-fight with the Dutch, in 1665.
He then bore the name of Durfort, and the title of Marquis of
Blancfort. By letters patent, 19th January 1672-3, he was created

Life Guards. Miss Price having tenderly loved him, his death plunged her into a gulf of despair; but the inventory of his effects almost deprived her of her senses. There was in it a certain little box sealed up on all sides; it was addressed in the deceased's own handwriting to Miss Price; but instead of receiving it, she had not even the courage to look upon it. The governess thought it became her in prudence to receive it, on Miss Price's refusal, and her duty to deliver it to the Duchess herself, supposing it was filled with many curious and precious commodities, of which perhaps she might derive some advantage. Though the Duchess was not altogether of the same opinion, she had the curiosity to see what was contained in a box sealed up in a manner so particularly carefully, and therefore caused it to be opened in the presence of some ladies, who happened then to be in her closet.

All kinds of love trinkets were found in it; and all these favours, it appeared, came from the tender-hearted Miss Price. It was difficult to comprehend how a single person could have furnished so great a collection; for, besides counting the pictures, there was hair of all descriptions, wrought into bracelets, lockets, and into various other different devices, wonderful to

Baron Duras of Holdenby, Northampton, and having married in 1676 Mary, the eldest daughter and co-heir of Sir George Sondes, of Lees Court, Kent, who had been created Earl of Feversham, the same title was limited to him, and he succeeded to it on the death of his father-in-law in April 1677. Besides these honours, King Charles preferred him to the command of the third troop of Horse Guards, afterwards promoted him to the second, and then to the first. In 1679 he was made Master of the Horse to Queen Catharine, and afterwards her Lord-Chamberlain. Upon King James's accession he was admitted into the Privy Council, and was Commander-in-Chief of the forces sent against the Duke of Monmouth (vide *King Monmouth*). After the Revolution he continued Lord-Chamberlain to the Queen Dowager. He died 8th April 1709, aged sixty-eight, and was buried in the Savoy, in the Strand, London; but removed, 21st March 1740, to Westminster Abbey.

see. After these were three or four packets of letters, of so tender a nature, and full of raptures and languors so naturally expressed, that the Duchess could not endure the reading of any more than the two first.

Her Royal Highness was sorry that she had caused the box to be opened in such good company; for being before such witnesses, she rightly judged it was impossible to stifle this adventure; and, at the same time, there being no possibility of retaining any longer such a maid of honour, Miss Price had her valuables restored to her, with orders to go and finish her lamentations, or to console herself for the loss of her lover, in some other place.[50]

Miss Hobart's[51] character was at that time as uncommon in England, as her person was singular, in a country where, to be young, and not to be in some degree handsome, is a reproach; she had a good shape, rather a bold air, and much wit, which was well cultivated, without having much discretion. She was likewise possessed of a considerable amount of vivacity, with an irregular fancy. There was a great deal of fire in her eyes, which, however, produced no effect upon the beholders; and she had a tender heart, whose sensibility some pretended was alone in favour of the fair sex.

Miss Bagot[52] was the first that gained her tenderness and affection, which she returned at first with equal

[50] Miss Price was Maid of Honour to the Queen, not the Duchess of York.

[51] The sister of Sir John and daughter of Sir Henry Hobart, of Blickling, Norfolk. Sir Henry (*ob.* 1625) left sixteen children, from one of whom descended John, first Earl of Buckinghamshire (vide *Dict. of Nat. Biog.*).

[52] Mary, daughter of Colonel Hervey Bagot, second son of Sir Hervey Bagot, maid of honour to the Duchess of York, born 1645.[1] She married, 1664, first, Charles Berkley, Earl of Falmouth, and, after his death (3rd June 1665), Charles Sackville, who became the first Duke of Dorset. From the pen of a satirist

[1] Her christian name has often been erroneously given as " Elizabeth."

warmth and sincerity; but perceiving that all her friendship was insufficient to repay that of Miss Hobart, she yielded the conquest to the governess's niece, who thought herself as much honoured by it as her aunt thought herself obliged by the care she took of the young girl.

Satirical ballads soon began to compliment her upon her new position; and upon the insinuations that were therein made, her companions began to fear her.

much dependence is not to be placed for the truth of facts. This lady's character is treated by Dryden and Mulgrave with very little respect, in the following lines, extracted from "The Essay on Satire":

> "Thus Dorset, purring like a thoughtful cat,
> Married; but wiser puss ne'er thought of that:
> And first he worried her with railing rhyme,
> Like Pembroke's mastiffs at his kindest time;
> Then for one night sold all his slavish life,
> A teeming widow, but a barren wife;
> Swell'd by contact of such a fulsome toad,
> He lugg'd about the matrimonial load;
> Till fortune, blindly kind as well as he,
> Has ill restored him to his liberty;
> Which he would use in his old sneaking way,
> Drinking all night, and dozing all the day;
> Dull as Ned Howard,[2] whom his brisker times
> Had famed for dulness in malicious rhymes."

Pepys (on 29th July 1667) says that there was a report that Henry Jermyn was going to marry Lady Falmouth, at which Lady Castlemaine, who at that time bestowed her favours upon him, was "mad." Jermyn, however, married the daughter of Sir Edward Poley. The diarist mentions her again on 4th March 1668-9. She died 12th September 1679, and was buried at Wythiam, Sussex. Lady Mary Berkeley, her only daughter by her first husband, died in 1693 and was buried in the chancel of Bexley Church. She married Sir Gilbert Gerard, second Baron Fiskerton, from whom she obtained a divorce in 1684 (see Banks's *Dormant and Extinct Peerage*).

Before the Countess of Falmouth married Sackville she had been spoken of as a possible wife of the Duke of York after the death of the Duchess in 1671. At Knole Park is preserved one of Sackville's love-letters containing a long lock of his (brown) hair.

[2] Edward Howard, fifth son of Thomas Howard, first Earl of Berkshire.

The governess, alarmed at these reports, consulted Lord Rochester upon the danger to which her niece was exposed. She could not have applied to a fitter person. He immediately advised her to take her niece out of the hands of Miss Hobart; and contrived matters so well that she fell into his own. The Duchess, who had too much generosity not to treat as visionary what was imputed to Miss Hobart, and too much justice to condemn her upon the faith of lampoons, removed her from the society of the maids of honour, to be an attendant upon her own person.

Miss Bagot was the only one who was really possessed of virtue and beauty among these maids of honour. She had beautiful and regular features, and that sort of brown complexion, which, when in perfection, is so particularly fascinating, and more especially in England, where it is uncommon. There was an involuntary blush almost continually upon her cheek, without having anything to blush for. Lord Falmouth cast his eyes upon her. His addresses were better received than those of Miss Hobart, and some time after Cupid raised her from the post of maid of honour to the Duchess, to a rank which might have been envied by all the young ladies in England.

The Duchess of York, in order to form her new Court, resolved to see all the young persons that offered themselves, and, without any regard to recommendations, to choose none but the handsomest.

At the head of this new assembly appeared Miss Jennings and Miss Temple; and indeed they so entirely eclipsed the other two, that we shall speak of them only.

Miss Jennings,[53] adorned with all the blooming treasures of youth, had the fairest and brightest com-

[53] Frances Jenyns (or Jennings), the elder sister of the more famous Sarah, Duchess of Marlborough, who, when maid of

plexion[54] that ever was seen. Her hair was of a most beauteous flaxen. There was something particularly lively and animated in her countenance, which preserved her from that insipidity which is frequently

honour to Mary of Modena, also received the Duke of York's unwelcome attentions (see *Louise de Keroualle,* p. 153). They were the daughters of Richard Jenyns of Sandridge, near St. Albans, at whose house they were brought up. Holywell House, in this vicinity, was afterwards built by the Duke of Marlborough, and pulled down in 1837. The wife of Richard Jenyns, Frances, daughter of Sir Gifford Thornhurst, a Kentish baronet, was far from a pleasant woman. Miss Strickland, in her *Lives of the Queens of England,* says she was not allowed to approach the Court on account of her infamous character, although she had laid Charles II. under some mysterious obligation (xii. p. 206). In the Belvoir MS., under date 23rd November 1676, however, it appears otherwise. Sarah and her mother, it is stated, actually came to blows, and the daughter threatened to run away if the mother was not ejected from St. James's, and when this was requested at the Duchess of York's instigation, she answered " with all her heart she should never dispute the Duke and Dutchesses commands, but with the grace of God she would take her daughter away with her, for two of the maids had had great bellies att Court, and she would not leave her child there to have a third, so rather than part with her, the mother must stay." But a month later it appears that " Sarah Jennings hath got the better of her mother, who is commanded to leave the Court and her daughter in itt, notwithstanding the mother's petition that she might have her girle with her, the girle saying she is a mad woman" (25th December).—*Hist. MS. Com. Rep.* 12, App. part v. vol. ii. pp. 32 and 34. Frances married, first, George Hamilton, and secondly, " Dick " Talbot, of whom full particulars are given in the *Memoirs.* By the latter she left two daughters. By Hamilton six children (the three daughters being Vicountesses Ross, Dillon, and Kingsland). Talbot, Duke of Tyrconnel, and wife were both staunch Jacobites, and directed James's affairs in Ireland when he visited that country prior to the battle of the Boyne. The royal fugitive and Talbot returned to Dublin Castle, where the Duchess received the Stuart monarch prior to his return to France. The story is told that James being the first to arrive, his Majesty ungraciously complimented Lady Tyrconnel on the running powers of her husband's countrymen, at which she retorted that his Majesty had the advantage of them (*Dict. of Nat. Biog.* vol. lv. p. 335). After her husband's death of apoplexy, August 1691, while preparing to defend Limerick against King William (by some accounts he was poisoned in a cup of ratafia), the titular Duchess joined the exiled Court

an attendant on a complexion so extremely fair. Her mouth was not the smallest, but it was the handsomest mouth in the world. Nature had endowed her with all those charms which cannot be expressed, and the graces had given the finishing stroke to them. The turn[55] of her face was exquisitely fine, and her swelling neck[56] was as fair and as bright as her face. In a word, her person gave the idea of Aurora, or the goddess of the spring, "such as youthful poets fancy when they love." But as it would have been unjust that a single person should have engrossed all the treasures of beauty without any defect, there was something wanting in her hands and arms to render them worthy of the rest; her nose was not the most elegant, and her eyes gave some relief, whilst her mouth and her other charms pierced the heart with a thousand darts.

With this amiable person she was full of wit and sprightliness, and all her actions and motions were unaffected and easy. Her conversation was bewitching, when she had a mind to please; piercing[57] and delicate when disposed to raillery; but as her imagination was subject to flights, and as she frequently began

at St. Germain, and received a pension with other needy Jacobites. When her brother, the Duke of Marlborough, was in Flanders, she had frequent access to him and acted as his agent. Walpole's story of the widowed Duchess selling haberdashery at a stall under the New Exchange is very doubtful (*vide* Pennant's *London*). She, however, returned to England in 1705, when Holywell House was put at her disposal by her brother-in-law, and afterwards, obtaining the restoration of some of her husband's property, she settled in Dublin, where she established a nunnery in King Street, and died 6th March 1730-1 (in her eighty-second year) in Paradise Row, near Phœnix Park. There is no monument to her memory in St. Patrick's Cathedral, but in the Scottish College at Paris (destroyed in 1860) there was a mural tablet to her memory, which is quoted in Steinman's *Althorp Memoirs*, pp. 72-73 (see also Jameson's *Beauties of the Court of Charles II*.)

[54] A skin of the most dazzling whiteness (Vizetelly's translation).   [55] Outline (Vizetelly).

[56] Budding bosom (*ibid*.).   [57] Subtle (*ibid*.).

to speak before she had done thinking, her expressions did not always convey what she wished; sometimes exceeding, and at others falling short of her ideas.[58]

Miss Temple,[59] nearly of the same age, was brown[60] compared with the other. She had a good shape, fine

[58] The French Ambassador Courtin describes her (4th May 1665) as "one of the fairest girls in England. . . . She is small but with a fine figure, a splendid complexion, the hair such as you [Lionne] remember Madame de Longueville's was, brilliant keen eyes, the whitest, smoothest skin I ever saw." The young Marquis di Berni (eldest son of Hugues de Lionne, Foreign Secretary to King Louis), having been sent by his father to the English Court under the wing of the French Ambassador that he might obtain some knowledge of the world, soon after his arrival fell a slave to the charms of Miss Jenyns, who on her part was far from indifferent. Under the watchful eye of the King, the Queen Mother, Duchess of York, and Court generally, the little romance is allowed to develop, while the father is assured by Courtin that he will check the liaison if necessary, saying "his intrigue is exactly at the point where it must be to make him a man of the world." There were daily meetings, and love tokens sent in the shape of strawberries to the fair one. At length, however, there is a tiff. Miss Jenyns refuses to have her hands kissed, and her lover retaliates by making advances to Miss Boynton (who also figures in the *Memoirs*), which has the desired effect and brings the former lady to reason. At the end of three months the love story is over; young Lionne's sojourn in London was at an end. On 27th July (1665) the father hears from Courtin that on "Thursday evening the King of England teased very much in my presence Mrs. Genins [Jenyns] on the subject of your son: the young girl reddened: she never appeared more beautiful. His Majesty told me that your son had asked M. Porter[1] to let him know how she looked on the day he was gone, and at the same time his Majesty assured me that he had never seen such a picture of sadness and desolation as the young gallant offered when on board the yacht of the Queen Mother. He was right, I can tell you, for the young lady loved him dearly, and if the one who reduced you to the taking of certain waters flavouring of turpentine had been as beautiful, your stomach would not have been easily restored to health" (see Jusserand's *Ambassador at the Court of Charles II.* pp. 153-157).

[59] Anne, daughter of Thomas Temple of Frankton, Warwickshire; by Rebecca, daughter of Sir Nicholas Carew, of Beddington, Surrey, knight. She became the second wife of Sir Charles Lyttelton, by whom she had five sons and eight daughters (*ob.*

[1] Probably Charles or Thomas Porter mentioned in Pepys's *Diary*

teeth, languishing eyes, a fresh complexion, an agreeable smile, and a lively air. Such was the outward form; but it would be difficult to describe the rest; for she was simple and vain, credulous and suspicious, coquettish and prudent,[61] very self-sufficient and very silly.

As soon as these new stars appeared at the Duchess's Court, all eyes were fixed upon them, and everyone formed some design upon one of them or the other, some with honourable, and others with dishonest intentions. Miss Jennings soon distinguished herself, and left her companions no other admirers but such as remained constant from hopes of success. Her brilliant charms attracted at first sight, and the charms of her wit secured her conquests.

The Duke of York having persuaded himself that she was part of his property, resolved to pursue his claim by the same title whereby his brother had appropriated to himself the favours of Miss Wells; but he did not find her inclined to enter into his service, though she had engaged in that of the Duchess. She would not pay any attention to the perpetual ogling with which he at first attacked her. Her eyes were always wandering on other objects, when those of his Royal Highness were looking for them; and if by chance he caught any casual glance, she did not even blush. This made him resolve to change his manner of attack: ogling having proved ineffectual, he took an opportunity to speak to her; and this was still worse. I know not in what strain he told his

1718). On the accession of James II., Sir Charles was made Brigadier-General. He succeeded to the baronetcy on the death of his brother, Sir Henry Lyttelton, who died in 1693. Sir Charles died at Hagley in 1716, aged eighty-six. His son Thomas married also a Miss Temple (maid of honour), the daughter of Sir Richard Temple of Stowe, Bucks.

[60] Dark (Vizetelly).   [61] Prudish (*ibid.*).

case; but it is certain the oratory of the tongue was not more prevailing than the eloquence of his eyes.

Miss Jennings had both virtue and pride, and the proposals of the Duke were consistent with neither the one nor the other. Although from her great vivacity one might suppose that she was not capable of much reflection, yet she had furnished herself with some very salutary maxims for the conduct of a young person of her age. The first was, that a lady ought to be young to enter the Court with advantage, and not old to leave it with a good grace; that she could not maintain herself there but by a glorious resistance, or by illustrious foibles; and that, in so dangerous a situation, she ought to use her utmost endeavours not to dispose of her heart until she gave her hand.

Entertaining such sentiments, she had far less trouble to resist the Duke's temptations than to disengage herself from his perseverance. She was deaf to all treaties for a settlement, with which her ambition was sounded; and all offers of presents succeeded still worse. What was then to be done to conquer an extravagant virtue that would not hearken to reason? He was ashamed to suffer a giddy young girl to escape, whose inclinations ought in some manner to correspond with the vivacity that shone forth in all her actions, and who nevertheless thought proper to be serious when no such thing as seriousness was required of her.

After he had attentively considered her obstinate behaviour, he thought that writing might perhaps succeed, though ogling, speeches, and embassies had failed. Paper receives everything, and it unfortunately happened that she would not receive the paper. Every day billets, containing the tenderest expressions, and most magnificent promises, were slipped into her pockets, or into her muff. This, however, could not be done unperceived; and the malicious little gipsy[62] took care that those who saw them slip in, should likewise see them fall out, unperused and unopened; she only shook her muff, or pulled out her handkerchief; as soon as ever his back was turned, his billets fell about her like hailstones, and whoever pleased might take them up. The Duchess was frequently a witness of this conduct, but could not find in her heart to chide her for her want of respect to the Duke. After this, the charms and prudence of Miss Jennings were the only subjects of conversation in the two Courts: the courtiers could not comprehend how a young creature, brought directly from the country to Court, should so soon become its ornament by her attractions, and its example by her conduct.

The King was of opinion that those who had attacked her had ill-concerted their measures; for he thought it unnatural that she should neither be tempted by promises, nor gained by importunity: she, especially, who in all probability had not imbibed such severe precepts from the prudence of her mother, who had never tasted anything more delicious than the plums and apricots of St. Albans.[63] Being resolved to try her himself, he was particularly pleased with the great novelty that appeared in the turn of her wit, and in the charms of her person; and curiosity, which at first induced him to make the trial, was soon changed into a desire of succeeding in the experiment. God knows what might have been the consequence, for he greatly excelled in wit, and besides he was king: two qualities of no small consideration. The resolutions of the fair Jennings were commendable, and very judicious; but yet she was wonderfully pleased with

[62] Creature (Vizetelly).
[63] Sandridge, where the Jennings family lived, is 2½ miles to the N. E. of St. Albans.

wit; and royal majesty prostrate at the feet of a young person is very persuasive. Miss Stewart, however, would not consent to the King's project.

She immediately took the alarm, and desired his Majesty to leave to the Duke, his brother, the care of tutoring the Duchess's maids of honour, and only to attend to the management of his own flock, unless his Majesty would in return allow her to listen to certain proposals of a settlement which she did not think disadvantageous. This menace being of a serious nature, the King obeyed; and Miss Jennings had all the additional honour which arose from this adventure; it both added to her reputation, and increased the number of her admirers. Thus she continued to triumph over the liberties of others without ever losing her own. Her hour was not yet come, but it was not far distant, the particulars of which we shall relate as soon as we have given some account of the conduct of her companion.

Though Miss Temple's person was particularly charming, it was nevertheless eclipsed by that of Miss Jennings; but she was still more excelled by the other's superior mental accomplishments. Two persons, very capable to impart understanding, had the gift been communicable, undertook at the same time to rob her of the little she really possessed: these were Lord Rochester and Miss Hobart. The first began to mislead her by reading to her all his compositions, as if she alone had been a proper judge of them. He never thought proper to flatter her upon her personal accomplishments; but told her that if Heaven had made him susceptible of the impressions of beauty, it would not have been possible for him to have escaped her chains; but not being, thank God, affected with anything but wit, he had the happiness of enjoying the most agreeable conversation in the world without

running any risk. After so sincere a confession he
either presented to her a copy of verses, or a new song,
in which whoever dared to come in competition in any
respect with Miss Temple was laid prostrate before her
charms, most humbly to solicit pardon. Such flattering insinuations so completely turned her head that
it was a pity to see her.

The Duchess took notice of it, and well knowing
the extent of both their geniuses, she saw the precipice
into which the poor girl was running headlong without perceiving it; but as it is no less dangerous to
forbid a connection that is not yet thought of, than it
is difficult to put an end to one that is already well
established, Miss Hobart was charged to take care,
with all possible discretion, that these frequent and
long conversations might not be attended with any
dangerous consequences. With pleasure she accepted
the commission, and greatly flattered herself with
achieving success.

She had already made all necessary advances to
gain possession of her confidence and friendship; and
Miss Temple, less suspicious of her than of Lord
Rochester, made all imaginable returns. She was
greedy of praise, and loved all manner of sweetmeats,
as much as a child of nine or ten years old: her taste
was gratified in both these respects. Miss Hobart
having the superintendence of the Duchess's baths, her
apartment joined them, in which there was a closet
stored with all sorts of sweetmeats and liqueurs. The
closet suited Miss Temple's taste, as exactly as it
gratified Miss Hobart's inclination, to have something
that could allure her.

Summer, being now returned, brought back with it
the pleasures and diversions that are its inseparable
attendants. One day, when the ladies had been taking
the air on horseback, Miss Temple, on her return from

riding, alighted at Miss Hobart's in order to recover her fatigue at the expense of the sweetmeats, which she knew were there at her service; but before she began she desired Miss Hobart's permission to undress herself, and change her linen in her apartment, which request was immediately complied with. "I was just going to propose it to you," said Miss Hobart, "not but that you are as charming as an angel in your riding habit; but there is nothing so comfortable as a loose dress, and being at one's ease. You cannot imagine, my dear Temple," continued she, embracing her, "how much you oblige me by this free unceremonious conduct; but, above all, I am enchanted with your particular attention to cleanliness. How greatly you differ in this, as in many other things, from that silly creature Jennings! Have you remarked how all our Court fops admire her for her brilliant complexion, which perhaps, after all, is not wholly her own; and for blunders, which are truly original, and which they are such fools as to mistake for wit. I have not conversed with her long enough to perceive in what her wit consists; but of this I am certain, that if it is not better than her feet, it is no great matter. What stories have I heard of her sluttishness. No cat ever dreaded water so much as she does: fie upon her! Never to wash for her own comfort, and only to attend to those parts which must necessarily be seen, such as the neck and hands."

Miss Temple swallowed all this with even greater pleasure than the sweetmeats; and the officious Hobart not to lose time, was helping her off with her clothes, while the chamber-maid was coming. She made some objections to this at first, being unwilling to occasion that trouble to a person who, like Miss Hobart, had been advanced to a place of dignity; but she was overruled by her, and assured that it was with the greatest pleasure she showed her that small mark of civility. The collation being finished and Miss Temple undressed: "Let us retire," said Miss Hobart, "to the bathing-closet, where we may enjoy a little conversation secure from any impertinent visit." Miss Temple consented, and both of them sitting down on a couch: "You are too young, my dear Temple," said she, "to know the baseness of men in general, and too short a time acquainted with the Court to know the character of its inhabitants. I will give you a short sketch of the principal persons[64] to the best of my knowledge, without injury to any one; for I abominate the trade of scandal.

"In the first place, then, you ought to set it down as an undoubted fact that all courtiers are deficient either in honesty, good sense, judgment, wit, or sincerity; that is to say, if any of them by chance possess some one of these qualities, you may depend upon it he is defective in the rest: sumptuous in their equipages, deep play, a great opinion of their own merit, and contempt of that of others, are their chief characteristics.

"Interest or pleasure are the motives of all their actions. Those who are led by the first would sell God Almighty, as Judas sold his Master, and that for less money. I could relate you a thousand noble instances of this, if I had time. As for the sectaries of pleasure, or those who pretend to be such, for they are not all so bad as they endeavour to make themselves appear, these gentlemen pay no manner of regard either to promises, oaths, law, or religion; that is to say, they are literally no respecters of persons; they care neither for God nor man, if they can but gain their ends. They look upon maids of honour only as amusements, placed expressly at Court for their entertainment; and the

[64] Gentlemen (Vizetelly).

more merit any one has, the more she is exposed to their impertinence, if she gives any ear to them; and to their malicious calumnies, when she ceases to attend to them. As for husbands, this is not the place to find them; for unless money or caprice make up the match, there is but little hope of being married: virtue and beauty in this respect here are equally useless. Lady Falmouth is the only instance of a maid of honour well married without a portion; and if you were to ask her poor weak husband for what reason he married her, I am persuaded that he can assign none, unless it be her great red ears and broad feet. As for the pale Lady Yarborough, who appeared so proud of her match, she is wife, to be sure, of a great country bumpkin, who, the very week after their marriage, bid her take her farewell of the town for ever, in consequence of five or six thousand[*] pounds a year he enjoys on the borders of Cornwall. Alas! poor Miss Blague! I saw her go away about this time twelve-month, in a coach with four such lean horses, that I cannot believe she is yet halfway to her miserable little castle. What can be the matter! all the girls seem afflicted with the rage of wedlock, and however small their portion of charms may be, they think it only necessary to show themselves at Court in order to pick and choose their men; but were this in reality the case, being a wife is the most wretched condition imaginable for a person of nice sentiments. Believe me, my dear Temple, the pleasures of matrimony are so inconsiderable in comparison with its inconveniences, that I cannot imagine how any reasonable creature can resolve upon it: rather fly, therefore, from this irksome engagement than court it. Jealousy, formerly a stranger to these happy isles, is now coming into fashion, with many recent examples of which you are ac-

[*] Some few hundred (Vizetelly's translation).

quainted. However brilliant the phantom may appear,
suffer not yourself to be caught by its splendour, and
never be so weak as to transform your slave into your
tyrant: as long as you preserve your own liberty, you
will be mistress of that of others. I will relate to you
a very recent proof of the perfidy of man to our sex,
and of the impunity they experience in all attempts
upon our innocence. The Earl of Oxford[66] fell in love
with a handsome, graceful actress belonging to the
Duke's Theatre, who performed to perfection, particularly the part of Roxana,[67] in a very fashionable
new play, insomuch that she ever after retained that
name. This creature being both very virtuous and
very modest, or, if you please, wonderfully obstinate,
proudly rejected the addresses and presents of the Earl
of Oxford. This resistance inflamed his passion. He

[66] This was Aubrey de Vere, the twentieth and last Earl of Oxford of that name. In the reign of Charles II. he was Chief
Justice in Eyre of the Royal Forests, Lord of the Bedchamber,
Privy Councillor, Colonel of the Royal Regiment of Horse
Guards, and Lord-Lieutenant of the County of Essex; and, in
the reign of William III., Lieutenant-General of the Forces. He
died 12th March 1702-3, aged seventy-five, and was buried in
Westminster Abbey (see Malone's edition of *Dryden*). From
1663 to 1676 the Earl lived in the Piazza, Covent Garden.

[67] This should be "Roxalana," a character in the *Siege of
Rhodes*, acted prior to 9th January 1661-2 by Betty Davenport,
the younger of two sisters of that name. Evelyn mentions having seen "ye faire and famous comedian" in the piece before
she was "taken to be the Earl of Oxford's misse," which sad
occurrence is bewailed by Pepys (18th February and 20th May
1661-2). The elder sister, Frances Davenport, remained on the
stage until 1668, when she also went "to be kept by somebody,
which I am glad of," says Pepys (7th April 1668), "she being a
very bad actor." "Roxalana" was aged eighteen (born 3rd
March 1642) at the time the scandalous mock-marriage removed
her from the Duke's Theatre. She had a son, afterwards called
Aubrey Vere, by the Earl of Oxford, born 17th April 1664. The
Countess of Dunois, who relates at some length the sad story
of Roxalana's seduction, says that when she discovered that
she had been duped, she tried to put an end to her life with
her betrayer's sword. She further says, Roxalana "attempted
to make her marriage good in law, but the power of the Earl

had recourse to invectives, and even to spells; but all in vain. This disappointment had such effect upon him that he could neither eat nor drink. This did not signify to him; but his passion at length became so violent, that he could neither play nor smoke. In this extremity Love had recourse to Hymen. The Earl of Oxford, one of the first peers of the realm, is, you know, a very handsome man: he is of the Order of the Garter, which greatly adds to an air naturally noble. In short, from his outward appearance, you would suppose he was really possessed of some sense; but soon as ever you hear him speak, you are perfectly convinced of the contrary. This passionate lover presented her with a promise of marriage, in due form, signed with his own hand. She would not, however, rely upon this, but the next day she thought there could be no danger, when the Earl himself came to her lodgings attended by a clergyman, and another man for a witness. The marriage was accordingly solemnised with all due ceremonies, in the presence of one of her fellow-players, who attended as a witness on her part. You will suppose, perhaps, that the new Countess had nothing to do but to appear at Court according to her rank, and to display the Earl's arms upon her carriage. This was far from being the case. When examination was made concerning the marriage, it was found to be a mere deception. It appeared that the pretended priest was one of my lord's trumpeters, and the witness his kettle-drummer.

carry'd it above the poor actress. However, he was forced to allow her a maintenance and to provide for a son she brought into the world" (see *Memoirs of the Court of England*, 1707, pp. 448-449). By an error in the translation of the *Memoirs*, the story has been associated with "Roxana" of *The Rival Queens*, produced and acted by the more famous actress, Mrs. Marshall, at the King's Theatre (see Sir Wm. Davenant's *Works*, 1873, iii. 252, etc.).

The parson and his companion never appeared after the ceremony was over; and as for the other witness, they endeavoured to persuade her, that the Sultana Roxana must have supposed, in some part or other of a play, that she was really married. It was all to no purpose that the poor creature claimed the protection of the laws of God and man, both which were violated and abused, as well as herself, by this infamous imposition. In vain did she throw herself at the King's feet to demand justice: she had only to rise up again without redress; and happy might she think herself to receive an annuity of one thousand crowns, and to resume the name of Roxana, instead of Countess of Oxford. You will say, perhaps, that she was only a player; that all men have not the same sentiments as the Earl; and, that one may at least believe them, when they do but render justice to such merit as yours. But still do not believe them, though I know you are liable to it, as you have admirers; for all are not infatuated with Miss Jennings. The handsome Sidney ogles you; Lord Rochester is delighted with your conversation; and the most serious Sir Charles Lyttelton forsakes his natural gravity in favour of your charms. As for the first, I confess his figure is very likely to engage the inclinations of a young person like yourself; but were his outward form attended with other accomplishments, which I know it is not, and that his sentiments in your favour were as real as he endeavours to persuade you they are, and as you deserve, yet I would not advise you to form any connections with him, for reasons which I cannot tell you at present.

"Sir Charles Lyttelton[68] is undoubtedly in earnest,

[68] Sir Charles Lyttelton, seventh son of Thomas Lyttelton and brother of Sir Henry Lyttelton, the second Baronet. He fought for the Royalist cause at the siege of Colchester, battle of Worces-

since he appears ashamed of the condition to which you have reduced him; and I really believe if he could get the better of those vulgar chimerical apprehensions, of being what is vulgarly called a cuckold, the good man would marry you, and you would be his representative in his little government, where you might merrily pass your days in casting up the weekly bills of housekeeping, and in darning old napkins. What a glory would it be to have a Cato for a husband, whose speeches are as many lectures, and whose lectures are composed of nothing but ill-nature and censure!

"Lord Rochester is, without contradiction, the most witty man in all England; but then he is likewise the most unprincipled, and devoid even of the least tincture of honour; he is dangerous to our sex alone; and that to such a degree that there is not a woman who gives ear to him three times, but she irretrievably loses her reputation. No woman can escape him, for he has her in his writings, if his other attacks be ineffectual; and in the age we live in, the one is as bad as the other in the eye of the public. In the meantime nothing is more dangerous than the artful insinuating manner with which he gains possession of the mind. He applauds your taste, submits to your sentiments, and at the very instant that he himself does not believe a single word of what he is saying, he makes you believe it all. I dare lay a wager, that from the conversation you have had with him, you thought him one of the most honourable and sincerest men living; for my part I cannot imagine what he means by the assiduity he pays you: not but your accomplishments are sufficient to excite the adoration and praise of the

ter, and in Sir George Booth's rising in Cheshire, and afterwards joined Charles II. in exile. Knighted 1662, afterwards colonel in the Duke of York's regiment. See also note, p. 257.

whole world;[69] but had he even been so fortunate as
to have gained your affections, he would not know
what to do with the loveliest creature at Court; for it
is a long time since his debauches, with the assistance
of the favours of all the common street-walkers, have
brought him to order.   See then, my dear Temple,
what horrid malice possesses him, to the ruin and
confusion of innocence!   A wretch! to have no other
design in his addresses and assiduities to Miss Temple,
but to give a greater air of probability to the calumnies
with which he has loaded her.   You look upon me with
astonishment, and seem to doubt the truth of what I
advance; but I do not desire you to believe me without evidence.   Here," said she, drawing a paper out
of her pocket, "see what a copy of verses he has made
in your praise, while he lulls your credulity to rest, by
flattering speeches and feigned respect."

After saying this, the perfidious Hobart showed her
half a dozen couplets full of strained invective and
scandal, which Rochester had made against the former
maids of honour.   This severe and stinging lampoon
was principally levelled against Miss Price, whose
person he cut to pieces in the most frightful and
hideous manner imaginable.   Miss Hobart had sub-
stituted the name of Temple instead of Price, which
she made to agree both with the measure and tune
of the song.   This effectually answered Hobart's
intentions.

The credulous Temple no sooner heard her sing the
lampoon, but she firmly believed it to be made upon
herself; and in the first transports of her rage, having
nothing so much at heart as to give the lie to the fic-
tions of the poet: "Ah! as for this, my dear Hobart,"
said she, "I can bear it no longer.   I do not pretend to

[69] You are formed in a way to deserve the homage of every
one (Vizetelly).

be so handsome as some others; but as for the defects that villain charges me with, I daresay, my dear Hobart, there is no woman more free from them. We are alone, and I am almost inclined to convince you by ocular demonstration." Miss Hobart was too complaisant to oppose this motion; but, although she soothed her mind by extolling all her beauties, in opposition to Lord Rochester's song, Miss Temple was almost driven to distraction by rage and astonishment, that the first man she had ever attended to, should, in his conversation with her, not even have made use of a single word of truth, but that he should likewise have the unparalleled cruelty falsely to accuse her of defects; and not being able to find words capable of expressing her anger and resentment, she began to weep like a child.[70]

Miss Hobart used all her endeavours to comfort her, and chid her for being so much hurt with the invectives of a person whose scandalous impostures were too well known to make any impression. She, however, advised her never to speak to him any more, for that was the only method to disappoint his designs; that contempt and silence were, on such occasions, much preferable to any explanation, and that if he could once obtain a hearing, he would be justified, but she would be ruined.

Miss Hobart was not wrong in giving her this counsel. She knew that an explanation would betray her, and that there would be no quarter for her if Lord Rochester had so fair an opportunity of renewing his former panegyrics upon her; but her precaution was in vain. This conversation had been heard from one end to the other by the governess's niece,[71] who was blessed with a most faithful memory; and having that

[70] Like one distracted (Vizetelly).
[71] Sarah Cooke. See note, p. 284.

very day an appointment with Lord Rochester, she conned it over three or four times, that she might not forget one single word, when she should have the honour of relating it to her lover. We shall show in the next chapter what were the consequences resulting from it.

CHAPTER X

THE conversation before related was agreeable only to Miss Hobart; for if Miss Temple was entertained with its commencement, she was so much the more irritated by its conclusion. This indignation was succeeded by the curiosity of knowing the reason why, if Sidney[1] had a real esteem for her, she should not be allowed to pay some attention to him. The tender-hearted Hobart, unable to refuse her any request, promised her this piece of confidence, as soon as she should be secure of her conduct towards Lord Rochester. For this she only desired a trial of her sincerity for three days, after which, she assured her, she would acquaint her with everything she wished to know. Miss Temple protested she no longer regarded Lord Rochester but as a monster of perfidiousness, and vowed, by all that was sacred, that she would never listen to him, much less speak to him, as long as she lived.

As soon as they retired from the closet, Miss Sarah came out of the bath, where, during all this conversation, she had been almost perished with cold, without daring to complain. This little gipsy[2] had, it seems, obtained leave of Miss Hobart's woman[3] to bathe herself unknown to her mistress; and having, I know not how, found means to fill one of the baths with cold water, Miss[4] Sarah had just got into it, when they were both alarmed with the arrival of the other two. A

---

[1] Henry ("the handsome") Sidney.　　[2] Creature (Vizetelly).
[3] Maid (*ibid.*).　　[4] Little Sarah (*ibid.*).

glass partition enclosed the room where the baths were, and Indian[5] silk curtains, which drew on the inside, screened those that were bathing. Miss Hobart's chamber-maid had only just time to draw these curtains that the girl might not be seen, to lock the partition door, and to take away the key, before her mistress and Miss Temple came in.

These two sat down on a couch placed along the partition, and Miss Sarah, notwithstanding her alarms, had distinctly heard, and perfectly retained the whole conversation. As the little girl was at all this trouble to make herself clean, only on Lord Rochester's account, as soon as ever she could make her escape she regained her garret; where Rochester, having repaired thither at the appointed hour, was fully informed of all that had passed in the bathing-room. He was astonished at the audacious temerity of Hobart, in daring to put such a trick upon him; but, though he rightly judged that love and jealousy were the real motives, he would not excuse her. Little Sarah desired to know whether he had a real affection for Miss Temple, as Miss Hobart said she supposed that was the case. "Can you doubt it," replied he, "since that oracle of sincerity has affirmed it? But then you know that I am not now capable of profiting by my perfidy, were I even to gain Miss Temple's compliance, since my debauches and the street-walkers have brought me to order."

This answer made Miss Sarah very easy, for she concluded that the first article was not true, since she knew from experience that the latter was false. Lord Rochester was resolved that very evening to attend the Duchess's Court, to see what reception he would meet with after the fine portrait Miss Hobart had been so kind as to draw of him. Miss Temple did not fail

[5] China (*ibid.*).

to be there likewise, with the intention of looking on him with the most contemptuous disdain possible, though she had taken care to dress herself as well as she could. As she supposed that the lampoon Miss Hobart had sung to her was in everybody's possession, she was under great embarrassment lest all those whom she met should think her such a monster as Lord Rochester had described her. In the meantime, Miss Hobart, who had not much confidence in her promises never more to speak to him, narrowly watched her. Miss Temple never in her life appeared so handsome: every person complimented her upon it; but she received all the civilities with such an air, that every one thought she was mad; for when they commended her shape, her fresh complexion, and the brilliancy of her eyes: "Pshaw," said she, "it is very well known that I am but a monster, and formed in no respect like other women: all is not gold that glisters; and though I may receive some compliments in public, it signifies nothing." All Miss Hobart's endeavours to stop her tongue were ineffectual; and continuing to rail at herself ironically, the whole Court was puzzled to comprehend her meaning.

When Lord Rochester came in, she first blushed, then turned pale, made a motion to go towards him, drew back again, pulled her gloves one after the other up to the elbow; and after having three times violently flirted her fan, she waited until he paid his compliments to her as usual, and as soon as he began to bow, the fair one immediately turned her back upon him. Rochester only smiled, and being resolved that her resentment should be still more remarked, he turned round, and posting himself face to face: "Madam," said he, "nothing can be so glorious as to look so charming as you do, after such a fatiguing day: to support a ride of three long hours, and Miss

Hobart afterwards, without being tired, shows indeed
a very strong constitution."

Miss Temple had naturally a tender look, but she
was transported with such a violent passion at his
having the audacity to speak to her, that her eyes
appeared like two fire-balls when she turned them
upon him. Hobart pinched her arm, as she perceived
that this look was likely to be followed by a torrent
of reproaches and invectives.

Lord Rochester did not wait for them, and delaying
until another opportunity the acknowledgments he
owed Miss Hobart, he quietly retired. The latter, who
could not imagine that he knew anything of their
conversation at the bath, was, however, much alarmed
at what he had said; but Miss Temple, almost choked
with the reproaches with which she thought herself
able to confound him and which she had not time
to give vent to, vowed to ease her mind of them
upon the first opportunity, notwithstanding the promise she had made; but never more to speak to him
afterwards.

Lord Rochester had a faithful spy[6] near these
nymphs: this was Miss Sarah, who, by his advice,
and with her aunt's consent, was reconciled with Miss
Hobart, the more effectually to betray her. He was
informed by this spy that Miss Hobart's maid, being
suspected of having listened to them in the closet,
had been turned away; that she had taken another,
whom in all probability she would not keep long,
because, in the first place, she was ugly, and, in the
second, she ate the sweetmeats that were prepared
for Miss Temple. Although this intelligence was not
very material, Sarah was nevertheless praised for her

[6] Burnet mentions one of Rochester's spy systems, a footman
disguised as a sentinel placed so as to keep watch upon the
nocturnal assignations of the Court ladies (*Own Time*, vol. i.
p. 372).

punctuality and attention; and a few days afterwards she brought him news of real importance.

Rochester was by her informed that Miss Hobart and her new favourite designed, about nine o'clock in the evening, to walk in the Mall, in the Park; that they were to change clothes with each other, to put on scarfs, and wear black masks; she added that Miss Hobart·had strongly opposed this project, but that she was obliged to give way at last, Miss Temple having resolved to indulge her fancy.

Upon the strength of this intelligence, Rochester concerted his measures. He went to Killegrew, complained to him of the trick which Miss Hobart had played him, and desired his assistance in order to be revenged. This was readily granted, and having acquainted him with the measures he intended to pursue, and given him the part he was to act in this adventure, they went to the Mall.

Presently after appeared our two nymphs in masquerade. Their shapes were not very different, and their faces, which were very unlike each other, were concealed with their masks. The company was but thin in the Park; and as soon as Miss Temple perceived them at a distance, she quickened her pace in order to join them, with the design, under her disguise, severely to reprimand the perfidious Rochester; when Miss Hobart stopping her, said: "Where are you running to? Have you a mind to engage in conversation with these two devils, to be exposed to all the insolence and impertinence for which they are so notorious?" These remonstrances were entirely useless. Miss Temple was resolved to try the experiment; and all that could be obtained from her was, not to answer any of the questions Rochester might ask her.

They were accosted just as they had done speaking.

Rochester fixed upon Hobart, pretending to take her for the other, at which she was overjoyed; but Miss Temple was extremely sorry she fell to Killegrew's share, with whom she had nothing to do. He perceived her uneasiness, and, pretending to know her by her clothes: "Ah! Miss Hobart," said he, "be so kind as to look this way if you please. I know not by what chance you both come hither, but I am sure it is very apropos for you, since I have something to say to you, as your friend and humble servant."

This beginning raising her curiosity, Miss Temple appeared more inclined to attend to him; and Killegrew perceiving that the other couple had insensibly proceeded some distance from them: "In the name of God," said he, "what do you mean by railing so against Lord Rochester, whom you know to be one of the most honourable men at Court, and whom you nevertheless described as the greatest villain to the person whom of all others he esteems and respects the most? What do you think would become of you, if he knew that you made Miss Temple believe she is the person alluded to in a certain song, which you know as well as myself was made upon the clumsy Miss Price, above a year before the fair Temple was heard of? Be not surprised that I know so much of the matter; but pay a little attention, I pray you, to what I am now going to tell you out of pure friendship: your passion and inclinations for Miss Temple are known to every one but herself; for whatever methods you used to impose upon her innocence, the world does her the justice to believe that she would treat you as Lady Falmouth did, if the poor girl knew the wicked designs you had upon her. I caution you, therefore, against making any further advances to a person too modest to listen to them. I advise you likewise to take back your maid again, in order to

silence her scandalous tongue; for she says everywhere
that she is with child, that you are the occasion of her
being in that condition, and accuses you of behaving
towards her with the blackest ingratitude, upon trifling
suspicions only. You know very well, these are no
stories of my own invention; but that you may not
entertain any manner of doubt that I had all this
from her own mouth, she has told me your conversation in the bathing-room, the characters you there
drew of the principal men at Court, your artful malice
in applying so improperly a scandalous song to one
of the loveliest women in all England; and in what
manner the innocent girl fell into the snare you had
laid for her, in order to do justice to her charms. But
that which might be of the most fatal consequences
to you in that long conversation is the revealing certain secrets, which, in all probability, the Duchess did
not entrust you with, to be imparted to the maids of
honour; reflect upon this, and neglect not to make
some reparation to Sir Charles Lyttelton for the ridicule with which you were pleased to load him. I
know not whether he had his information from your
femme de chambre, but I am very certain that he
has sworn he will be revenged, and he is a man that
keeps his word; for after all, that you may not be
deceived by his look, like that of a Stoic, and his
gravity, like that of a judge, I must acquaint you
that he is the most passionate man living. Indeed,
these invectives are of the blackest and most horrible
nature. He says it is most infamous that a wretch
like yourself should find no other employment than to
blacken the characters of gentlemen to gratify your
jealousy; that if you do not desist from such conduct
for the future, he will immediately complain of you;
and that if her Royal Highness will not do him justice, he is determined to do himself justice, and to

run you through the body with his own sword, though you were even in the arms of Miss Temple; and that it is most scandalous that all the maids of honour should get into your hands before they can look around them.

"These things, madam, I thought it my duty to acquaint you with. You are better able to judge than myself, whether what I have now advanced be true, and I leave it to your own discretion to make what use you think proper of my advice; but were I in your situation, I would endeavour to reconcile Lord Rochester and Miss Temple. Once more I recommend to you to take care that your endeavours to mislead her innocency, in order to blast his honour, may not come to his knowledge; and do not estrange from her a man who tenderly loves her, and whose probity is so great, that he would not even suffer his eyes to wander towards her, if his intention was not to make her his wife."

Miss Temple observed her promise most faithfully during this discourse. She did not even utter a single syllable, being seized with such astonishment and confusion, that she quite lost the use of her tongue.

Miss Hobart and Lord Rochester came up to her while she was still in amazement at the wonderful discoveries she had made; things in themselves, in her opinion, almost incredible, but to the truth of which she could not refuse her assent, upon examining the evidences and circumstances on which they were founded. Never was confusion equal to that with which her whole frame was seized by the foregoing recital.

Rochester and Killegrew took leave of them before she recovered from her surprise; but as soon as she had regained the free use of her senses, she hastened back to St. James's, without answering a single question that the other put to her; and having locked herself up in her chamber, the first thing she did was immediately to strip off Miss Hobart's clothes, lest she should be contaminated by them; for after what she had been told concerning her, she looked upon her as a monster, dreadful to the innocence of the fair sex, of whatever sex she might be. She blushed at the familiarities she had been drawn into with a creature, whose maid was with child, though she never had been in any other service but hers. She therefore returned her all her clothes, ordered her servant to bring back all her own, and resolved never more to have any connection with her. Miss Hobart, on the other hand, who supposed Killegrew had mistaken Miss Temple for herself, could not comprehend what could induce her to give herself such surprising airs since that conversation; but being desirous to come to an explanation, she ordered Miss Temple's maid to remain in her apartments, and went to call upon Miss Temple herself, instead of sending back her clothes; and being desirous to give her some proof of friendship before they entered upon expostulation, she slipt softly into her chamber, when she was in the very act of changing her linen, and embraced her. But Miss Temple, disengaging herself with the highest indignation from her arms, began to shriek and cry in the most terrible manner, calling both heaven and earth to her assistance.

The first whom her cries raised were the governess and her niece. It was near twelve o'clock at night. Miss Temple, in her shift, almost frightened to death, was pushing back with horror Miss Hobart, who approached her with no other intent than to know the occasion of those transports. As soon as the governess saw this scene, she began to lecture Miss Hobart with all the eloquence of a real duenna. She demanded

of her, whether she thought it was for her that her
Royal Highness kept the maids of honour? whether
she was not ashamed to come at such an unseasonable
time of night into their very apartments to commit
such violences? and swore that she would, the very
next day, complain to the Duchess. All this confirmed
Miss Temple in her mistaken notions; and Hobart
was obliged to go away at last, without being able
to convince or bring to reason creatures, whom she
believed to be either distracted or mad. The next
day Miss Sarah did not fail to relate this adventure to her lover, telling him how Miss Temple's
cries had alarmed the maids of honour's apartment,
and how herself and her aunt, running to her assistance, had almost surprised Miss Hobart in the
very act.

Two days after, the whole adventure, with the
addition of several embellishments, was made public.
The governess swore to the truth of it, and related in
every company what a narrow escape Miss Temple
had experienced, and that Miss Sarah, her niece, had
preserved her honour, because, by Lord Rochester's
excellent advice, she had forbidden her all manner of
connection with so dangerous a person. Miss Temple
was afterwards informed, that the song that had so
greatly provoked her alluded to Miss Price only. This
was confirmed to her by every person, with additional
execrations against Miss Hobart for such a scandalous
imposition. Such great coldness after so much familiarity made many believe that this adventure was not
altogether a fiction.

This had been sufficient to have disgraced Miss
Hobart at Court, and to have totally ruined her reputation in London, had she not been, upon the present,
as well as upon a former occasion, supported by the
Duchess.

Her Royal Highness pretended to treat the whole story as romantic and visionary, or as solely arising from private pique. She chid Miss Temple for her impertinent credulity; turned away the governess and her niece for the lies with which she pretended they supported the imposture; and did many improper things in order to re-establish Miss Hobart's honour, which, however, she failed in accomplishing. She had her reasons for not entirely abandoning her, as will appear in the sequel.

Miss Temple, who continually reproached herself with injustice, with respect to Lord Rochester, and who, upon the faith of Killegrew's word, thought him the most honourable man in England, was only solicitous to find out some opportunity of easing her mind, by making him some reparation for the rigour with which she had treated him. These favourable dispositions, in the hands of a man of his character, might have led to consequences of which she was not aware; but Heaven did not allow him an opportunity of profiting by them.

Ever since he had first appeared at Court he seldom failed being banished from it, at least once in the year; for whenever a word presented itself to his pen, or to his tongue, he immediately committed it to paper, or produced it in conversation, without any manner of regard to the consequences. The ministers, the mistresses, and even the King himself, were frequently the subjects of his sarcasms; and had not the Prince. whom he thus treated, been possessed of one of the most forgiving and gentle tempers, his first disgrace had certainly been his last.

Just at the time that Miss Temple was desirous of seeing him, in order to apologise for the uneasiness which the infamous calumnies and black aspersions of Miss Hobart had occasioned both of them, he was forbid the Court for the third time. He departed without having seen Miss Temple, carried the disgraced governess down with him to his country seat, and exerted all his endeavours to cultivate in her niece some dispositions which she had for the stage; but though she did not make the same improvement in this line as she had by his other instructions, after he had entertained both the niece and the aunt for some months in the country, he got her entered in the King's company of comedians the next winter; and the public was obliged to him for the prettiest, but, at the same time, the worst actress in the kingdom.[7]

About this time Talbot returned from Ireland. He soon felt the absence of Miss Hamilton, who was then in the country with a relation, whom we shall mention hereafter. A remnant of his former tenderness still subsisted in his heart, notwithstanding his absence, and the promises he had given the Chevalier de Gramont at parting. He now therefore endeavoured to banish her entirely from his thoughts, by fixing his desires upon some other object; but he saw no one in the Queen's new Court whom he thought worthy of

[7] Sarah Cooke, an actress of the King's House, who spoke the prologue on the first night of Rochester's *Valentinian,* and the new prologue on the second night.. She is mentioned in the *State Poems* (1703, p. 136) by Dryden (Malone, ii. p. 24) and Etherege (Add. MSS. No. 11,513). Prologues and epilogues were her particular province. The Annotations of early editions of the *Memoirs* have in error identified " Sarah " with Elizabeth Barry, who did not appear on the stage until 1673, whereas the incidents related by Gramont do not go beyond September 1669. Barry owed her introduction to the stage to Rochester, where she made her first appearance at the age of fifteen, before which she was maid to Lady Skelton. The Earl bet that in six months he would make her the most popular actress on the stage. Mary of Modena so approved her acting that she gave her her wedding and coronation robes. Rochester is said to have had a child by Barry, on whom he settled an annuity of £40 (vide *Dict. of Nat. Biography,* vol. iii. pp. 317-319).

his attention.   Miss Boynton,[8] however, thought him
worthy of hers.   Her person was slender and delicate,
to which a good complexion and large motionless eyes
gave at a distance an appearance of beauty that vanished upon nearer inspection.   She affected to lisp, to
languish, and to have two or three fainting-fits a day.
The first time that Talbot cast his eyes upon her she
was seized with one of these fits; he was told that she
swooned away upon his account: he believed it and
was eager to afford her assistance; and ever after that
accident showed her some kindness, more with the
intention of saving her life, than to express any affection he felt for her.   This seeming tenderness was well
received, and at first she was visibly affected by it.
Talbot was one of the tallest men in England, and in
all appearance one of the most robust; yet she showed
sufficiently that she was willing to expose the delicacy
of her constitution to whatever might happen, in order
to become his wife; which event perhaps might then
have taken place, as it did afterwards, had not the
charms of the fair Jennings at that time proved an
obstacle to her wishes.

I know not how it came to pass that he had not yet
seen her; though he had heard her much praised, and
her prudence, wit, and vivacity equally commended.
He believed all this upon the faith of common report.
He thought it very singular that discretion and
sprightliness should be so intimately united in a person so young, more particularly in the midst of a
Court where love and gallantry were so much in

[8] Katherine, eldest daughter and co-heir of Colonel Mathew
Boynton (killed Wigan fight, 1651), son of Sir Mathew Boynton,
Bart., of Barnston, Yorkshire, Maid of Honour to Queen Catherine (*vide* Pepys, 26th October 1664).   She was the first wife of
Colonel Richard Talbot, Groom of the Bedchamber to the Duke
of York.   She died 17th March 1678, and was buried in Christ-
church Cathedral, Dublin.   Her only daughter was buried in the
same grave in June 1684.

fashion; but he found her personal accomplishments greatly to exceed whatever fame had reported of them.

As it was not long before he perceived he was in love, neither was it long before he made a declaration of it. As his passion was likely enough to be real, Miss Jennings thought she might believe him, without exposing herself to the imputation of vanity. Talbot was possessed of a fine and brilliant exterior; his manners were noble and majestic: besides this, he was particularly distinguished by the favour and friendship of the Duke; but his most essential merit, with her, was his forty[9] thousand pounds a-year, landed property, besides his employments. All these qualities came within the rules and maxims she had resolved to follow with respect to lovers. Thus though he had not the satisfaction to obtain from her an entire declaration of her sentiments, he had at least the pleasure of being better received than those who had paid their addresses to her before him.

No person attempted to interrupt his happiness; and Miss Jennings, perceiving that the Duchess approved of Talbot's pretensions, and after having well weighed the matter, and consulted her own inclinations, found that her reason was more favourable to him than her heart, and that the most she could do for his satisfaction was to marry him without reluctance.

Talbot, too fortunate in a preference which no man had before experienced, did not examine whether it was to her heart or to her head that he was indebted for it, and his thoughts were solely occupied in hastening the accomplishment of his wishes. One would have sworn that the happy minute was at hand; but love would no longer be love, if he did not delight in obstructing, or in overturning the happiness of those who live under his dominion.

[9] Couple of thousand (Vizetelly's translation).

Talbot, who found nothing reprehensible either in the person, in the conversation, or in the reputation of Miss Jennings, was however rather concerned at a new acquaintance she had lately formed; and having taken upon him to give her some cautions upon this subject, she was much displeased at his conduct.

Miss Price, formerly maid of honour, that had been set aside, as we have before mentioned, upon her leaving the Duchess's service, had recourse to Lady Castlemaine's protection. She had a very entertaining wit: her complaisance was adapted to all humours, and her own humour was possessed of a fund of gaiety and sprightliness which diffused universal mirth and merriment wherever she came. Her acquaintance with Miss Jennings was prior to Talbot's.

As she was thoroughly acquainted with all the intrigues of the Court, she related them without any manner of reserve to Miss Jennings, and her own with the same frankness as the others. Miss Jennings was extremely well pleased with her stories; for though she was determined to make no experiment in love, but upon honourable terms, she however was desirous of knowing from her recitals all the different intrigues that were carrying on. Thus, as she was never wearied with her conversation, she was overjoyed whenever she could see her.

Talbot, who remarked the extreme relish she had for Miss Price's company, thought that the reputation such a woman had in the world might prove injurious to his mistress, more especially from the particular intimacy there seemed to exist between them. Whereupon, in the tone of a guardian rather than a lover, he took upon him to chide her for the disreputable company she kept. Miss Jennings was haughty beyond conception, when once she took it into her head; and as she liked Miss Price's conversation much better than Talbot's, she took the liberty of desiring him "to attend to his own affairs, and that if he only came from Ireland to read lectures about her conduct, he might take the trouble to go back as soon as he pleased." He was offended at a sally which he thought ill-timed, considering the situation of affairs between them, and went out of her presence more abruptly than became the respect due from a man greatly in love. He for some time appeared offended; but perceiving that he gained nothing by such conduct, he grew weary of acting that part, and assumed that of an humble lover, in which he was equally unsuccessful; neither his repentance nor submissions could produce any effect upon her, and the mutinous little gipsy[10] was still in her pouts when Jermyn returned to Court.

It was above a year since he had triumphed over the weakness of Lady Castlemaine, and above two since the King had been weary of his triumphs. His uncle, being one of the first who perceived the King's disgust, obliged him to absent himself from Court, at the very time that orders were going to be issued for that purpose; for though the King's affections for Lady Castlemaine were now greatly diminished, yet he did not think it consistent with his dignity that a mistress, whom he had honoured with public distinction, and who still received a considerable support from him, should appear chained to the car of the most ridiculous conqueror that ever existed. His Majesty had frequently expostulated with the Countess upon this subject; but his expostulations were never attended to. It was in one of these differences that, he advising her rather to bestow her favours upon Jacob Hall, the rope-dancer, who was able to return them, than lavish away her money upon Jermyn to no pur-

[10] Refractory little thing (Vizetelly).

pose, since it would be more honourable for her to pass for the mistress of the first, than for the very humble servant of the other, she was not proof against his raillery. The impetuosity of her temper broke forth like lightning; she told him "that it very ill became him to throw out such reproaches against one, who, of all the women in England, deserved them the least; that he had never ceased quarrelling thus unjustly with her, ever since he had betrayed his own mean, low inclinations; that to gratify such a depraved taste as his, he wanted only such silly things as Stewart, Wells, and that pitiful strolling[11] actress,[12] whom he had lately introduced into their society." Floods of tears, from rage, generally attended these storms; after which, resuming the part of Medea, the scene closed with menaces of tearing her children in pieces, and setting his palace on fire. What course could he pursue with such an outrageous fury, who, beautiful as she was, resembled Medea less than her dragons, when she was thus enraged?

The indulgent monarch loved peace; and as he seldom contended for it on these occasions without paying something to obtain it, he was obliged to be at great expense, in order to reconcile this last rapture. As they could not agree of themselves, and both parties equally complained, the Chevalier de Gramont was chosen, by mutual consent, mediator of the treaty. The grievances and pretensions on each side were communicated to him, and what is very extraordinary, he managed so as to please them both. Here follow the articles of peace, which they agreed to:

"That Lady Castlemaine should for ever abandon Jermyn; that as a proof of her sincerity, and the reality of his disgrace, she should consent to his being sent, for some time, into the country; that she should

[11] Beggarly little (Vizetelly). [12] Probably Nell Gwyn.

not rail any more against Miss Wells, nor storm any more against Miss Stewart; and this without any restraint on the King's behaviour towards her; that in consideration of these condescensions, his Majesty should immediately give her the title of duchess,[13] with all the honours and privileges thereunto belonging, and an addition to her pension, in order to enable her to support the dignity."

As soon as this peace was proclaimed, the political critics, who, in all nations, never fail to censure all state proceedings, pretended that the mediator of this treaty, being every day at play with Lady Castlemaine, and never losing, had for his own sake insisted a little too strongly upon this last article.

Some days after she was created Duchess of Cleveland, and little Jermyn repaired to his country-seat. However, it was in his power to have returned in a fortnight; for the Chevalier de Gramont, having procured the King's permission, carried it to the Earl of St. Albans. This revived the good old man; but it was to little purpose he transmitted it to his nephew; for whether he wished to make the London beauties deplore and lament his absence, or whether he wished them to declaim against the injustice of the age, or rail against the tyranny of the Prince, he continued above half a year in the country, setting up for a little philosopher, under the eyes of the sportsmen in the neighbourhood, who regarded him as an extraordinary instance of the caprice of fortune. He thought the part he acted so glorious, that he would have continued there much longer had he not heard of Miss Jennings. He did not, however, pay much attention to what his friends wrote to him concerning her charms, being persuaded he had seen equally as great

[13] The title of Duchess of Cleveland was conferred on her 3rd August 1670.

in others: what was related to him of her pride and resistance appeared to him of far greater consequence; and to subdue the last, he even looked upon as an action worthy of his prowess; and quitting his retreat for this purpose, he arrived in London at the time that Talbot, who was really in love, had quarrelled, in his opinion, so unjustly with Miss Jennings.

She had heard Jermyn spoken of as a hero in affairs of love and gallantry. Miss Price, in the recital of those of the Duchess of Cleveland, had often mentioned him, without in any respect diminishing the insignificancy with which fame insinuated he had conducted himself in those amorous encounters. She nevertheless had the greatest curiosity to see a man whose entire person, she thought, must be a moving trophy and monument of the favours and freedoms of the fair sex.

Thus Jermyn arrived at the right time to satisfy her curiosity by his presence; and though his brilliancy appeared a little tarnished by his residence in the country; though his head was larger, and his legs more slender than usual, yet the giddy girl[14] thought she had never seen any man so perfect; and yielding to her destiny, she fell in love with him, a thousand times more unaccountably than all the others had done before her. Everybody remarked this change of conduct in her with surprise; for they expected something more from the delicacy of a person who, till this time, had behaved with so much propriety in all her actions.

Jermyn was not in the least surprised at this conquest, though not a little proud of it; for his heart had very soon as great a share in it as his vanity. Talbot, who saw with amazement the rapidity of this triumph, and the disgrace of his own defeat, was ready

10—Memoirs   [14] Jennings (Vizetelly).

to die with jealousy and spite; yet he thought it would be more to his credit to die than to vent those passions unprofitably; and shielding himself under a feigned indifference, he kept at a distance to view how far such an extravagant prepossession would proceed.

In the meantime Jermyn quietly enjoyed the happiness of seeing the inclinations of the prettiest and most extraordinary creature in England declared in his favour. The Duchess, who had taken her under her protection ever since she had declined placing herself under that of the Duke, sounded Jermyn's intentions towards her, and was satisfied with the assurances she received from a man, whose probity infinitely exceeded his merit in love. He therefore let all the Court see that he was willing to marry her, though, at the same time, he did not appear particularly desirous of hastening the consummation. Every person now complimented Miss Jennings upon having reduced to this situation the terror of husbands, and the plague of lovers: the Court was in full expectation of this miracle, and Miss Jennings of a near approaching happy settlement; but in this world one must have fortune in one's favour, before one can calculate with certainty upon happiness.

The King did not generally let Lord Rochester remain so long in exile. He grew weary of it, and being displeased that he was forgotten, he posted up to London to wait till it might be his Majesty's pleasure to recall him.

He first took up his habitation in the city, among the capital tradesmen and rich merchants, where politeness indeed is not so much cultivated as at Court; but where pleasure, luxury, and abundance reign with less confusion, and more sincerity. His first design was only to be initiated into the mysteries of those fortunate and happy inhabitants: that is to say, by changing his name and dress, to gain admittance to their feasts and entertainments; and, as occasion offered, to those of their loving spouses. As he was able to adapt himself to all capacities and humours, he soon deeply insinuated himself into the esteem of the substantial wealthy aldermen, and into the affections of their more delicate, magnificent, and tender ladies. He made one in all their feasts, and at all their assemblies; and, whilst in the company of their husbands, he declaimed against the faults and mistakes of government; he joined their wives in railing against the profligacy of the Court ladies, and in inveighing against the King's mistresses. He agreed with them, that the industrious poor were to pay for these cursed extravagances; that the city beauties were not inferior to those of the other end of London, and yet a sober husband in this quarter of the town was satisfied with one wife; after which, to out-do their murmurings, he said that he wondered Whitehall was not yet consumed by fire from Heaven, since such rakes as Rochester, Killegrew, and Sidney were suffered there, who had the impudence to assert that all married men in the city were cuckolds, and all their wives painted. This conduct endeared him so much to the cits, and made him so welcome at their clubs, that at last he grew sick of their cramming and endless invitations.

But, instead of approaching nearer the Court, he retreated into one of the most obscure corners of the city, where, again changing both his name and his dress, in order to act a new part, he caused bills to be dispersed, giving notice of "The recent arrival of a famous German doctor,"[15] who, by long application and

[15] Bishop Burnet confirms this account. "Being under an unlucky accident, which obliged him to keep out of the way, he disguised himself so that his nearest friends could not have known him, and set up in Tower Street for an Italian mounte-

experience, had found out wonderful secrets, and infallible remedies." His secrets consisted in knowing what was past, and foretelling what was to come, by the assistance of astrology; and the virtue of his remedies principally consisted in giving present relief to unfortunate young women in all manner of diseases, and all kinds of accidents incident to the fair sex, either from too unbounded charity to their neighbours, or too great indulgence to themselves.

His first practice, being confined to his neighbourhood, was not very considerable; but his reputation soon extending to the other end of the town, there presently flocked to him the women attending on the Court; next, the chamber-maids of ladies of quality, who, upon the wonders they related concerning the German doctor, were soon followed by some of their mistresses.[16]

Among all the compositions of a ludicrous and satirical kind, there never existed any that could be compared to those of Lord Rochester, either for humour, fire, or wit; but, of all his works, the most ingenious and entertaining is that which contains a detail of the intrigues and adventures in which he was engaged while he professed medicine and astrology in the suburbs of London.[17]

bank, where he practised physic for some weeks, not without success. In his latter years he read books of history more. He took pleasure to disguise himself as a porter, or as a beggar; sometimes to follow some mean amours, which for the variety of them, he affected. At other times, merely for diversion, he would go about in odd shapes, in which he acted his part so naturally, that even those who were in the secret, and saw him in these shapes, could perceive nothing by which he might be discovered" (Burnet's *Life of Rochester*, ed. 1774, p. 14).

Rochester's speech, when he practised the mountebank, Alexander Bendo, at a goldsmith's house in Tower Street, " next door to the Black Swan," is given in detail in the above volume.

[16] This was probably prior to 26th May 1665.

[17] *Vide* footnote, p. 210.

The fair Jennings was very near getting a place in this collection; but the adventure that prevented her from it did not, however, conceal from the public her intention of paying a visit to the German doctor.

The first chamber-maids that consulted him were only those of the maids of honour, who had numberless questions to ask, and not a few doubts to be resolved, both upon their own and their mistresses' accounts. Notwithstanding their disguise, he recognised some of them, particularly Miss Temple's and Miss Price's maids, and the one whom Miss Hobart had lately discarded. These creatures all returned either filled with wonder and amazement, or petrified with terror and fear. Miss Temple's chamber-maid deposed that he assured her she and her mistress would have the smallpox, within two months at farthest, if her aforesaid mistress did not guard against a man in woman's clothes. Miss Price's woman affirmed that, without knowing her, and only looking in her hand, he told her at first sight that, according to the course of the stars, he perceived that she was in the service of some good-natured lady, who had no other fault than loving wine and men. In short, every one of them, struck with some particular circumstance relating to their own private affairs, had either alarmed or diverted their mistresses with the account, not failing, according to custom, to embellish the truth in order to enhance the wonder.

Miss Price, relating these circumstances one day to her new friend, the devil immediately tempted her to go in person, and see what sort of a creature this new magician was. This enterprise was certainly very rash; but nothing was too rash for Miss Jennings, who was of opinion that a woman might despise appearances, provided she was in reality virtuous. Miss Price was all compliance, and thus having fixed upon this glorious resolution, they only thought of the proper means of putting it into execution.

It was very difficult for Miss Jennings to disguise herself, on account of her excessive fair and bright complexion, and of something particular in her air and manner: however, after having well considered the matter, the best disguise they could think of was to dress themselves like orange girls.[18] This was no sooner resolved upon, but it was put in execution.

[18] These frolics appear to have been not unfrequent with persons of high rank at this period. In a letter from Mr. Henshaw to Sir Robert Paston, afterwards Earl of Yarmouth, dated 13th October 1670, we have the following account: "Last week, there being a faire neare Audley-end,[1] the Queen, the Dutchess of Richmond, and the Dutchess of Buckingham, had a frolick to disguise themselves like country lasses, in red petticoats, wastcotes, etc., and so goe see the faire. Sir Barnard Gascoign, on a cart jade, rode before the Queen; another stranger before the Dutchess of Buckingham; and Mr. Roper before Richmond. They had all so overdone it in their disguise, and looked so much more like antiques than country volk, that, as soon as they came to the faire, the people began to goe after them; but the Queen going to a booth, to buy a pair of yellow stockings for her sweet hart, and Sir Bernard asking for a pair of gloves sticht with blew, for his sweet hart, they were soon, by their gebrish, found to be strangers, which drew a bigger flock about them. One amongst them had seen the Queen at dinner, knew her, and was proud of her knowledge. This soon brought all the faire into a crowd to stare at the Queen. Being thus discovered, they, as soon as they could, got to their horses; but as many of the faire as had horses got up, with their wives, children, sweet harts, or neighbours, behind them, to get as much gape as they could, till they brought them to the Court gate. Thus, by ill conduct, was a merry frolick turned into a penance" (Ive's Select Papers, p. 39).

Bishop Burnet says, "At this time (1668) the Court fell into much extravagance in masquerading: both the King and Queen, all the Court, went about masked, and came into houses unknown, and danced there, with a great deal of wild frolic. In all this people were so disguised, that, without being in the secret, none could distinguish them. They were carried about in hackney chairs. Once the Queen's chairmen, not knowing who she was, went from her. So she was alone, and was much disturbed, and came to Whitehall in a hackney coach; some say in a cart" (Burnet's Own Time, vol. i. p. 368).

[1] Newport, Essex.

They attired themselves alike, and, taking each a basket of oranges under their arms, they embarked in a hackney coach, and committed themselves to fortune, without any other escort than their own caprice and indiscretion.

The Duchess was gone to the play with her sister. Miss Jennings had excused herself under pretence of indisposition : she was overjoyed at the happy commencement of their adventure; for they had disguised themselves, had crossed the Park, and taken their hackney coach at Whitehall gate, without the least accident. They mutually congratulated each other upon it, and Miss Price, taking a beginning so prosperous as a good omen of their success, asked her companion what they were to do at the fortune-teller's, and what they should propose to him.

Miss Jennings told her that, for her part, curiosity was her principal inducement for going thither; that, however, she was resolved to ask him, without naming any person, why a man, who was in love with a handsome young lady, was not urgent to marry her, since this was in his power to do, and by so doing he would have an opportunity of gratifying his desires. Miss Price told her, smiling, that, without going to the astrologer, nothing was more easy than to explain the enigma, as she herself had almost given her a solution of it in the narrative of the Duchess of Cleveland's adventures.

Having by this time nearly arrived at the playhouse, Miss Price, after a moment's reflection, said, that since fortune favoured them, a fair opportunity was now offered to signalise their courage, which was to go and sell oranges in the very playhouse, in the sight of the Duchess and the whole Court. The proposal being worthy of the sentiments of the one, and of the vivacity of the other, they immediately alighted, paid off their hack, and, running through the midst of an immense number of coaches, with great difficulty they reached the playhouse door. Sidney, more handsome than the beautiful Adonis, and dressed more gay than usual, alighted just then from his coach. Miss Price went boldly up to him, as he was adjusting his curls; but he was too much occupied with his own dear self to attend to anything else, and so passed on without deigning to give her an answer. Killegrew came next, and the fair Jennings, partly encouraged by the other's pertness, advanced towards him, and offered him her basket, whilst Price, more used to the language, desired him to buy her fine oranges. "Not now," said he, looking at them with attention; "but if thou wilt to-morrow morning bring this young girl to my lodgings, I will make it worth all the oranges in London to thee;" and while he thus spoke to the one he chucked the other under the chin. These familiarities making little Jennings forget the part she was acting, after having pushed him away with all the violence she was able, she told him with indignation that it was very insolent to dare—— "Ha! ha!" said he, "here's a rarity indeed! a young w——, who, the better to sell her goods, sets up for virtue, and pretends innocence!"

Price immediately perceived that nothing could be gained by continuing any longer in so dangerous a place; and, taking her companion under the arm, she dragged her away, while she was still in emotion[19] at the insult that had been offered to her.

Miss Jennings, resolving to sell no more oranges on these terms, was tempted to return, without accomplishing the other adventure; but Price having represented to her the disgrace of such cowardly behaviour, more particularly after having before manifested so much resolution, she consented to go and pay the as-

[19] Agitation (Vizetelly).

trologer a short visit, so as they might be enabled to regain the palace before the play was ended.

They had one of the doctor's bills for a direction, but there was no occasion for it; for the driver of the coach they had taken told them he knew very well the place they wanted, for he had already carried above a hundred persons to the German doctor's. They were within half a street of his house, when fortune thought proper to play them a trick.

Brounker[20] had dined by chance with a merchant in that part of the city, and just as he was going away they ordered their coach to stop, as ill-luck would have

[20] Henry Brouncker, son of William Brouncker, and younger brother of William, Viscount Brouncker, President of the Royal Society, Groom of the Bedchamber to the Duke of York and Cofferer (1671) to the King. Evelyn says he was ever noted for a hard, covetous, vicious man; for his craft and skill at gaming few excelled him. Pepys describes him as one of the shrewdest fellows in England and a dangerous man; he further adds, he was "a pestilent rogue and atheist that would have sold his King and country for 6d. almost, so covetous and wicked a rogue he is" (29th August 1667). He kept in the Duke's good graces by pandering to his vices, and, according to Pepys, it was he who brought about the intimacy between his master and Lady Denham (10th June 1666).

Clarendon says "he was never notorious for anything but the highest degree of impudence and stooping to the most infamous offices"—"his abominable nature had rendered him so odious that it was taken notice of in Parliament," and he was expelled from the House of Commons (see *Continuation of Clarendon*, p. 270; see also Lister's *Life of Clarendon*, ii. 334, 335). Pepys speaks of his impeachment and of his flight in consequence (21st April 1668), but, ere six months had elapsed, he was in favour again at Court (see 4th November 1668).

Brouncker's country house, mentioned in the *Memoirs*, was formerly a religious house of some note, viz. Sheen Abbey, Richmond. It stood in the Park a little distance north-west of the Palace, and close to the site of the present observatory. The Abbey was converted into a private residence in Evelyn's time. On 27th August 1678 the diarist "din'd at Mr. Hen. Brouncker's at the Abbey of Sheene, formerly a monastery of Carthusians, there yet remaining one of their solitary cells with a crosse. Within this ample inclosure are several pretty villas and fine gardens of the most excellent fruites." In course of time this

it, just opposite to him. Two orange girls in a hackney coach, one of whom appeared to have a very pretty
face, immediately drew his attention; besides, he had
a natural curiosity for such objects.

Of all the men at Court, he had the least regard for
the fair sex, and the least attention to their reputation.
He was not young, nor was his person agreeable; however, with a great deal of wit, he had a violent passion
for women. He did himself justice respecting his own
merit; and, being persuaded that he could only succeed
with those who were desirous of having his money, he
was at open war with all the rest. He had a little
country-house four or five miles from London always
well stocked with girls.[21] In other respects he was a
very honest man, and the best chess-player in England.

Price, alarmed at being thus closely examined by
the most dangerous enemy they could encounter,
turned her head the other way, bid her companion do
the same, and told the coachman to drive on. Brounker followed them unperceived on foot; and the coach
having stopped twenty or thirty yards further up the
street, they alighted. He was just behind them, and
formed the same judgment of them which a man much
more charitable to the sex must unavoidably have
done, concluding that Miss Jennings was a young
courtesan upon the look-out, and that Miss Price was
the mother-abbess. He was, however, surprised to

grew into the hamlet of West Sheen, of which there are now
no remains.

Brouncker (who was created Doctor of Medicine at Oxford,
23rd June 1646) married Rebecca Rodway, the widow of
Thomas Jermyn, the brother of the Earl of St. Albans. He died
at his residence, Sheen Abbey, 4th January 1687-8 (having succeeded his brother in 1684 as third Viscount Brouncker), when
the title became extinct (see *Dict. of Nat. Biography*, vol. vi.
pp. 469-470).

[21] " Brounker, Love's squire, through all the field array'd,
No troop was better clad, nor so well paid."
Andrew Marvell's Poems, vol. ii. p. 94.

see them have much better shoes and stockings than women of that rank generally wear, and that the little orange girl, in getting out of a very high coach, showed one of the handsomest legs he had ever seen: but as all this was no obstruction to his designs, he resolved to purchase her at any rate, in order to place her in his seraglio.[22]

He came up to them, as they were giving their baskets in guard to the coachman, with orders to wait for them exactly in that place. Brounker immediately pushed in between them. As soon as they saw him, they gave themselves up for lost; but he, without taking the least notice of their surprise, took Price aside with one hand, and his purse with the other, and began immediately to enter upon business, but was astonished to perceive that she turned away her face, without either answering or looking at him. As this conduct appeared to him unnatural, he stared her full in the face, notwithstanding all her endeavours to prevent him. He did the same to the other; and immediately recognised them, but determined to conceal his discovery.

The old fox possessed a wonderful command of temper on such occasions, and having teased them a little longer to remove all suspicions, he quitted them. Upon this he went back to his coach, whilst they blessed themselves, returning Heaven their most hearty thanks for having escaped this danger without being discovered.

[22] The date of this adventure, according to Pepys, who heard of it from Lady Sandwich, may be fixed at February 1664-5. "My Lady [Sandwich] tells me . . . what mad freaks the Maids of Honour at Court have: that Mrs. Jenings, one of the Duchess's mayds, the other day dressed herself like an orange wench, and went up and down and cried oranges, till falling down, or by such accident . . . her fine shoes were discerned and she put to a great deale of shame" (*Diary*, 21st February 1664-5.

Brounker, on the other hand, would not have taken a thousand guineas for this rencounter: he blessed the Lord that he had not alarmed them to such a degree as to frustrate their intention; for he made no doubt but Miss Price had managed some intrigue for Miss Jennings. He therefore immediately concluded, that at present it would be improper to make known his discovery, which would have answered no other end but to have overwhelmed them with confusion.

Upon this account, although Jermyn was one of his best friends, he felt a secret joy in not having prevented his being made a cuckold before his marriage; and the apprehension he was in of preserving him from that accident was his sole reason for quitting them with the precautions before mentioned.

Whilst they were under these alarms, their coachman was engaged in a squabble with some blackguard boys, who had gathered round his coach in order to steal the oranges. From words they came to blows. The two nymphs saw the commencement of the fray as they were returning to the coach, after having abandoned the design of going to the fortune-teller's. Their coachman being a man of spirit, it was with great difficulty they could persuade him to leave their oranges to the mob, that they might get off without any further disturbance. Having thus regained their hack, after a thousand frights, and after having received an abundant share of the most low and infamous abuse applied to them during the fracas, they at length reached St. James's, vowing never more to go after fortune-tellers, through so many dangers, terrors, and alarms, as they had lately undergone.

Brounker, who, from the indifferent opinion he entertained of the fair sex, would have staked his life that Miss Jennings did not return from this expedition in the same condition she went, kept his thoughts, how-

ever, a profound secret; since it would have afforded
him the highest satisfaction to have seen the all-
fortunate Jermyn marry a little street-walker, who
pretended to pass for a pattern of chastity, that he
might, the day after his marriage, congratulate him
upon his virtuous spouse; but Heaven was not disposed
to afford him that satisfaction, as will appear in the
sequel of these *Memoirs*.

Miss Hamilton was in the country, as we before
mentioned, at a relation's. The Chevalier de Gramont
bore this short absence of hers with great uneasiness,
since she would not allow him permission to visit her
there, upon any pretence whatever; but play, which
was favourable to him, was no small relief to his
extreme impatience.

Miss Hamilton, however, at last returned. Mrs.
Wetenhall[23] (for that was the name of her relation)
would by all means wait upon her to London, in
appearance out of politeness; for ceremony, carried
beyond all bearing, is the grand characteristic of country gentry: yet this mark of civility was only a pretence, to obtain a peevish husband's consent to his
wife's journey to town. Perhaps he would have done
himself the honour of conducting Miss Hamilton up
to London, had he not been employed in writing some
remarks upon the ecclesiastical history, a work in
which he had long been engaged. The ladies were
more civil than to interrupt him in his undertakings,
and besides, it would entirely have disconcerted all
Mrs. Wetenhall's schemes.

[23] Elizabeth, daughter of Sir Henry Bedingfield (*ob.* 1684),
and wife of Thomas Whetenhall, of Hextall Court, near East
Peckham, Kent (see Collins's *Baronetage*, p. 216). The family
of Whetenhall, or Whetnall, was possessed of this estate from
Henry VIII.'s reign. Henry Whetenhall, Esq., alienated it to
John Fane, Earl of Westmoreland, and it afterwards was purchased by Sir William Twisden.

This lady was what may be properly called a beauty, entirely English, made up of lilies and roses, of snow and milk, as to colour; and of wax, with respect to the arms, hands, neck, and feet; but all this without either animation or air. Her face was uncommonly pretty; but there was no variety, no change of countenance in it : one would have thought she took it in the morning out of a case, in order to put it up again at night, without using it in the smallest degree in the daytime. What can I say of her! nature had formed her a baby[24] from her infancy, and a baby[25] remained till death the fair Mrs. Wetenhall. Her husband had been destined for the Church; but his elder brother dying just at the time he had gone through his studies of divinity, instead of taking orders, he came to England, and took to wife Miss Bedingfield, the lady of whom we are now speaking.

His person was not disagreeable, but he had a serious contemplative air, very apt to occasion disgust : as for the rest, she might boast of having for her husband one of the greatest theologists in the kingdom. He was all day poring over his books, and went to bed soon, in order to rise early; so that his wife found him snoring when she came to bed, and when he arose he left her there sound asleep. His conversation at table would have been very brisk, if Mrs. Wetenhall had been as great a proficient in divinity, or as great a lover of controversy, as he was; but being neither learned in the former, nor desirous of the latter, silence reigned at their table, as absolutely as at a refectory.

She had often expressed a great desire to see London; but though they were only distant a very short day's journey from it, she had never been able to satisfy her curiosity. It was not therefore without reason that she grew weary of the life she was forced to lead

[24] Doll (Vizetelly). [25] *Ibid.*

at Peckham.[26] The melancholy retired situation of the place was to her insupportable; and as she had the folly, incident to many other women, of believing sterility to be a kind of reproach, she was very much hurt to see that she might fall under that suspicion; for she was persuaded, that although Heaven had denied her children, she nevertheless had all the necessary requisites on her part, if it had been the will of the Lord.

This had occasioned her to make some reflections, and then to reason upon those reflections; as for instance, that since her husband chose rather to devote himself to his studies than to the duties of matrimony, to turn over musty old books, rather than attend to the attractions of beauty, and to gratify his own pleasures, rather than those of his wife, it might be permitted her to relieve some necessitous lover, in neighbourly charity, provided she could do it conscientiously, and to direct her inclinations in so just a manner, that the evil spirit should have no concern in it. Mr. Wetenhall, a zealous partisan for the doctrine of the casuists, would not perhaps have approved of these decisions; but he was not consulted.

The greatest misfortune was, that neither solitary Peckham, nor its sterile neighbourhood, presented any expedients, either for the execution of the before-mentioned design, or for the relief of poor Mrs. Wetenhall. She was visibly pining away, when, through fear of dying either with solitude or of want, she had recourse to Miss Hamilton's commiseration.

[26] East Peckham lies about midway between Tonbridge and Maidstone, and the village is still very primitive. The church is perched upon high ground away from everywhere, and the roads leading from East and West Peckham are circuitous in the extreme. Hextall, which was occupied for many years as a farmhouse, has been rebuilt, but the stables and some old walls remain.

Their first acquaintance was formed at Paris, whither Mr. Wetenhall had taken his wife half a year after they were married, on a journey thither to buy books. Miss Hamilton, who from that very time greatly pitied her, consented to pass some time in the country with her, in hopes by that visit to deliver her, for a short time at least, out of her captivity, which project succeeded according to her wish.

The Chevalier de Gramont, being informed of the day on which they were to arrive, borne on the wings of love and impatience, had engaged George Hamilton[27] to go with him, and meet them some miles out of London.

The equipage he had prepared for the purpose corresponded with his usual magnificence; and on such an occasion, we may reasonably suppose he had not neglected his person. However, with all his impatience, he checked the ardour of the coachman, through fear of accidents, rightly judging that upon a road prudence is preferable to eagerness. The ladies at length appeared, and Miss Hamilton, being in his eyes ten or twelve times more handsome than before her departure from London, he would have purchased with his life so kind a reception as she gave her brother.

Mrs. Wetenhall had her share of the praises, which at this interview were liberally bestowed upon her beauty, for which her beauty was very thankful to those who did it so much honour; and as Hamilton regarded her with a tender attention, she regarded Hamilton as a man very well qualified for putting in execution the little projects she had concerted with her conscience.

As soon as she was in London, her head was almost turned, through an excess of contentment and felicity:

[27] George, second son of Sir George Hamilton.

everything appeared like enchantment to her in this superb city; more particularly, as in Paris she had never seen anything farther than the Rue Saint Jacques, and a few booksellers' shops. Miss Hamilton entertained her at her own house, and she was presented, admired, and well received at both Courts.

The Chevalier de Gramont, whose gallantry and magnificence were inexhaustible, taking occasion, from this fair stranger's arrival, to exhibit his grandeur, nothing was to be seen but balls, concerts, plays, excursions by land and by water, splendid collations and sumptuous entertainments. Mrs. Wetenhall was transported with pleasures, of which the greatest part were entirely new to her; she was greatly delighted with all, except now and then at a play, when tragedy was acted, which she confessed she thought rather wearisome: she agreed, however, that the show was very interesting, when there were many people killed upon the stage, but thought the players were very fine handsome fellows, who were much better alive than dead.

Hamilton, upon the whole, was pretty well treated by her, if a man in love, who is never satisfied until the completion of his wishes, could confine himself within the bounds of moderation and reason. He used all his endeavours to determine her to put in execution the projects she had formed at Peckham. Mrs. Wetenhall, on the other hand, was much pleased with him. This is the Hamilton who served in the French army with distinction;[28] he was both agreeable and hand-

28 Viz. George Hamilton, who married Miss Jennings. At the Restoration Charles brought over with him a number of Catholic officers and soldiers who had served with him abroad and incorporated them among his guards. Parliament, however, insisted upon their dismissal, and it was these men, with others enlisted in Ireland, who accompanied Hamilton to France, and whom Louis XIV. formed into a company of English gendarmes. The Spanish Ambassador complained to Arlington at the time

some.   All imaginable opportunities conspired to favour the establishment of an intimacy, whose commencement had been so brisk, that in all probability it would not languish for a conclusion; but the more he pressed her to it, the more her resolution began to fail, and a regard for some scruples, which she had not well weighed, kept her in suspense.   There was reason to believe that a little perseverance would have removed these obstacles; yet this at the present time was not attempted.   Hamilton, not able to conceive what could prevent her from completing his happiness, since in his opinion the first and greatest difficulties of an amour were already overcome with respect to the public, resolved to abandon her to her irresolutions, instead of endeavouring to conquer them by a more vigorous attack.   It was not consistent with reason to desist from an enterprise, where so many prospects of success presented themselves, for such inconsiderable obstacles; but he suffered himself to be intoxicated with chimeras and visions, which unseasonably cooled the vigour of his pursuit, and led him astray in another unprofitable undertaking.

I know not whether poor Mrs. Wetenhall took the blame upon herself; but it is certain, she was extremely mortified.   Soon after being obliged to return to her cabbages and turkeys at Peckham, she went nearly distracted.   That residence appeared a thousand

with reference to these Irish levies.   Arlington, writing to Lord Sandwich, October 1667, gives the reason of Hamilton's entering the French service as follows:—

"Concerning the reformadoes of the guards of horse, his Majesty thought fit the other day to have them dismissed according to his promise made to Parliament at the last session. Mr. Hamilton had a secret overture made him, that he with those men should be welcome into the French service; his Majesty at their dismission having declared they should have leave to go abroad whither they pleased.   They accepted of Mr. Hamilton's offer to carry them into France" (see Arlington's *Letters,* vol. i. p. 185, and Vizetelly's edition, ii. p. 149, note).

times more dreadful to her, since she had been initiated into the amusements of London; but as the Queen was to set out within a month for Tunbridge Wells, she was obliged to yield to necessity, and return to the philosopher, Wetenhall, with the consolation of having engaged Miss Hamilton to come and live at her house, which was within ten or twelve miles of Tunbridge, as long as the Court remained there.

Miss Hamilton promised not to abandon her in her retirement, and further engaged to bring the Chevalier de Gramont along with her, whose humour and conversation extremely delighted her. The Chevalier de Gramont, who on all occasions started agreeable raillery, engaged on his part to bring George Hamilton, which words overwhelmed her with blushes.

The Court set out soon after to pass about two months in the place of all Europe the most rural and simple, and yet, at the same time, the most entertaining and agreeable.[29]

Tunbridge is the same distance from London that Fontainebleau is from Paris, and is, at the season, the general rendezvous of all the gay and handsome of both sexes. The company, though always numerous,

[29] The French Ambassador, Comminges, writes (July 1663): "The Queen with her numerous Court is still at Tunbridge, where the waters have done nothing of what was expected. Well may they be called *les eaux de scandale*, for they nearly ruined the good name of the maids and of the ladies (those, I mean who were there without their husbands). It took them a whole month, and for some more than that, to clear themselves and save their honour; and it is even reported that a few of them are not quite out of trouble yet. For which cause the Court will come back in a week; one of the ladies of the Queen stays behind and will pay for the others. A few days will be spent here to gather strength, and then a new journey will be undertaken towards the Baths, eight miles distant from here. Nothing will be left unattempted to give an heir to the British Crown (August 1663). The Queen after all this physic feeling very sick, her doctors go about whispering the great news, but to their shame it turns out that the symptoms are only due to the quality of

is always select: since those who repair thither for diversion, ever exceed the number of those who go thither for health. Everything there breathes mirth and pleasures: constraint is banished, familiarity is established upon the first acquaintance, and joy and pleasure are the sole sovereigns of the place.

The company are accommodated with lodgings in little, clean, and convenient habitations, that lie straggling and separated from each other, a mile and a half all round the Wells, where the company meet in the morning. This place consists of a long walk, shaded by spreading trees, under which they promenade while they are drinking the waters. On one side of this walk is a long row of shops, plentifully stocked with all manner of toys, lace, gloves, stockings, and where there is raffling, as at Paris, in the Foire de Saint Germain; on the other side of the walk is the market; and, as it is the custom here for every person to buy their own provisions, care is taken that nothing offensive appears on the stalls. Here young, fair, fresh-coloured country girls, with clean linen, small straw hats, and neat shoes and stockings, sell game, vegetables, flowers, and fruit: here one may live as one pleases: here is, likewise, deep play, and no want of amorous intrigues. As soon as the evening comes, every one quits his little palace to assemble at the bowling-green, where, in the open air, those who choose, dance upon a turf more soft and smooth than the finest carpet in the world.

Lord Muskerry[20] had, within two or three short

the waters that are vitriolées" (see Jusserand's *French Ambassador at the Court of Charles II.* pp. 89-90). *N.B.*—This visit to Tunbridge has been confounded with a later one in July 1666.

[30] Charles M'Carty, Viscount Muskerry, eldest son to the Earl of Clancarty; "a young man," says Lord Clarendon, "of extraordinary courage and expectation, who had been colonel of a regiment of foot in Flanders, under the Duke, and had the

miles of Tunbridge, a very handsome seat called
Summer-hill. Miss Hamilton, after having spent eight
or ten days at Peckham, could not excuse herself from
passing the remainder of the season at his house; and,
having obtained leave of Mr. Wetenhall, that his lady
should accompany her, they left the melancholy residence of Peckham, and its tiresome master, and fixed
their little court at Summer-hill.[81]

They went every day to Court, or the Court came to
them. The Queen even surpassed her usual attentions
in inventing and supporting entertainments: she endeavoured to increase the natural ease and freedom of
Tunbridge, by dispensing with, rather than requiring,
those ceremonies that were due to her presence; and,
confining in the bottom of her heart that grief and
uneasiness she could not overcome, she saw Miss
Stewart triumphantly possess the affections of the
King without manifesting the least uneasiness.

Never did love see his empire in a more flourishing
condition than on this spot: those who were smitten
before they came to it, felt a mighty augmentation of
their flame; and those who seemed the least susceptible
of love, laid aside their natural ferocity, to act in a new

general estimation of an excellent officer " (see also footnote,
p. 96).
[81] Somerhill or Summerhill, the old stone Jacobean mansion
(built 1611) near Tonbridge, was built by the Earl of Clanricard
(ob. 1636), who was created by James I. Baron Somerhill and
Viscount Tonbridge, and by Charles I. Earl of St. Albans.[1] At
the Commonwealth the estate was granted to President Brad-
shaw, who died possessed of it in 1659. His natural son succeeded to the property, but at the Restoration it was given back
to Margaret, the grand-daughter of the Earl of St. Albans, who
married Lord Muskerry. She died in very reduced circumstances
in 1698, having married, *secondly*, John Villiers, Viscount Purbeck (nephew of George, first Duke of Buckingham), and *thirdly*,
"Beau" Fielding, who married the Duchess of Cleveland in her
old age.

[1] He must not be confused with Jermyn, who was created Earl of St. Albans
at the Restoration.

character. For the truth of the latter, we shall only
relate the change which soon appeared in the conduct
of Prince Rupert.[82]

He was brave and courageous, even to rashness; but
cross-grained and incorrigibly obstinate: his genius
was fertile in mathematical experiments, and he possessed some knowledge of chemistry: he was polite
even to excess, unseasonably; but haughty, and even
brutal, when he ought to have been gentle and courteous: he was tall, and his manners were ungracious:
he had a dry, hard-favoured visage, and a stern look,

[82] Prince Rupert was third son of Frederick, Prince Palatine
of the Rhine, by Elizabeth, daughter of James I., nephew to
Charles I. and cousin to Charles II., born 1619. From a very
early age he was distinguished on the battlefield, where his daring
and valour were always conspicuous, though his successes were
marred to a great extent by his hot-headed rashness. At the
commencement of the Civil Wars he joined Charles I. at York
and fought with conspicuous gallantry at Edgehill, Marston
Moor, and Naseby. By the surrender of Bristol to the enemy
he lost his reputation as a soldier as well as the good opinion
of his uncle, who cancelled all his commissions for this fatal
step, which in a great measure helped to ruin the royalist cause.
After the Restoration he became distinguished in naval warfare
with the Dutch in 1665 and in 1673, and in later years passed
much of his time in the study of philosophy, chemistry, mechan-
ism, and the arts. Several inventions of much utility in warfare
were the result of his studies, and it is well known the origin
of mezzotint engraving was discovered by him, though the result
of an accident. Lord Clarendon briefly summarises the character of the valiant Prince as follows:—"He was rough and
passionate and loved not debate; liked what was proposed as
he liked the persons who proposed it." He died at his house in
Spring Gardens, 29th November 1682. "I think the Prince was
buried on Friday night," says John Verney, "but if he was it
was no hindrance of the Court going to see a play" (Verney
MS., *Hist. MS. Com. Rep.* 7, Appendix, p. 480). Doctor Plot
says Rupert was a remarkable shot, and with a horse pistol sent
two balls successively through the weathercock on the steeple
of Stafford Church. Mention of Prince Rupert's daughter by
Margaret Hughes will be found in the note of her on the next
page. He had also a son, Dudley Rupert, *alias* Bard, by Fran-
cesca, daughter of Henry Bard, Viscount Bellomont. He is mentioned in the Prince's will (see Wood's *Fasti*, vol. i. p. 268).

even when he wished to please; but, when he was out of humour, his countenance was forbidding.

The Queen had sent for the players, either that there might be no intermission in the diversions of the place, or, perhaps, to retort upon Miss Stewart, by the presence of Nell Gwyn,[33] part of the uneasiness she felt from hers. Prince Rupert found charms in the person of another player called Hughes,[34] who brought down and greatly subdued his natural fierceness. From this time, adieu alembics, crucibles, furnaces, and all the

---

[33] Hamilton has confused this visit to Tunbridge Wells with a later one in July 1666, for Nell Gwyn was unknown in 1663.

[34] Margaret, better known as "Peg" Hughes, one of the earliest English actresses, commenced her career at the Drury Lane Theatre in 1663. Here she was the first Desdemona—the original Theodosia in Dryden's *Evening's Love*. Shortly before January 1669, when she became Prince Rupert's mistress, she was playing "Panura" in Fletcher's *Island Princess*. Upon her return to the stage in 1676 she joined the Duke's company, and acted in several plays by Sedley, Behn, Ravenscraft, etc.

"Ruperta," her daughter by the Prince, was born in 1673, and at his death in 1682 received a handsome provision. John Verney, writing 29th November 1682, says: "The Prince died this morning at 6 o'clock. Some say he sent his garter a day or two ago to the King, desiring Lord Burford (Nell Gwyn's son) might have it with his daughter by Pegg Hughes, to which last two he had left all his jewels and personal estate and arrears due from his Majesty. His estate in Germany, which is but small, he has given to his son by Lady Francis Bellemont, an Irish lady" (Verney MS., *Hist. M.S. Com. Rep.* 7, Appendix, p. 480). See also footnote, p. 312.

By the Prince's will (dated 1st December 1682) he left all his goods, chattels, jewels, plate, furniture, etc., and all his estates, etc., to William, Earl of Craven, in trust for the use and behoof of Margaret Hughes and her daughter, and in a book of accounts at the old Warwickshire seat of the Earls of Craven may still be seen a document signed by the actress and Ruperta. The latter married Emanuel Scrope Howe, by whom she left a daughter, Sophia Howe, who was afterwards Maid of Honour to Caroline, Princess of Wales.

Peg Hughes died in 1719 and was buried (15th October) at Lee, having resided the last part of her life at Eltham (see Lee Parish Registers). Some years before she lived at Brandenburgh House, Hammersmith, originally the seat of Sir Nicholas Crisp,

black furniture of the forges: a complete farewell to
all mathematical instruments and chemical speculations: sweet powder and essences were now the only
ingredients that occupied any share of his attention.
The impertinent gipsy[35] chose to be attacked in form;
and proudly refusing money, that in the end she might
sell her favours at a dearer rate, she caused the poor
Prince to act a part so unnatural, that he no longer
appeared like the same person. The King was greatly
pleased with this event, for which great rejoicings were
made at Tunbridge; but nobody was bold enough to
make it the subject of satire, though the same constraint was not observed with other ridiculous per-
sonages.

There was dancing every day at the Queen's apartments, because the physicians recommended it, and no
person thought it amiss: for even those who cared
least for it, chose that exercise to digest the waters
rather than walking. Lord Muskerry thought himself
secure against his lady's rage for dancing. The dis-
consolate lady seeing Miss Hamilton and Mrs. Wetenhall set out every morning, sometimes on horseback
and sometimes in a coach, but ever attended by a gallant troop to conduct them to Court, and to convey
them back, she fancied a thousand times more delights
at Tunbridge than in reality there were, and she did
not cease in her imagination to dance over at Summer-hill all the country dances which she thought had

and purchased for her by Prince Rupert. The house was pulled
down some years ago.

The following from the Belvoir MSS. is worthy of note.
"One of the King's servants," says Lady Chaworth, writing to
her brother, Lord Roos, 20th June 1670, "hath killed Mr. Hues,
Peg Hues' brother, servant to P(rince) Robert [Rupert], upon
a dispute whether Mrs. Nelly (Gwyn) or she was the handsomer now at Windsor" (*Hist. MS. Com. Rep.* 12, Appendix 5,
pt. ii. See also *Dict. of Nat. Biography*, vol. xxviii. p. 185).

[35] Creature (Vizetelly).

been danced at Tunbridge. She could no longer support the racking torments which disturbed her mind, when relenting Heaven, out of pity for her pains and sufferings, caused Lord Muskerry to repair to London, and kept him there two whole days. As soon as ever he had turned his back, the Babylonian Princess declared her resolution to make a trip to Court.

She had a domestic chaplain who did not want sense, and Lord Muskerry, for fear of accidents, had recommended her to the wholesome counsels and good prayers of this prudent divine; but in vain were all his preachings and exhortations to stay at home; in vain did he set before her eyes her husband's commands, and the dangers to which she would expose herself in her present condition. These remonstrances were altogether ineffectual. Miss Hamilton and her cousin Wetenhall, having the complaisance to confirm her in her resolution, they assisted in dressing her the next morning, and set out along with her. All their skill and dexterity were requisite to reduce her shape into some kind of symmetry; but, having at last pinned a small cushion under her petticoat on the right side, to counteract the untoward appearance the little infant occasioned by throwing itself on the left, they almost split their sides with laughter, assuring her at the same time that she looked perfectly charming.

As soon as she appeared, it was generally believed that she had dressed herself in a farthingale, in order to make her court to the Queen; but every person was pleased at her arrival. Those who were unacquainted with the circumstances assured her in earnest that she was pregnant with twins; and the Queen, who envied her condition, notwithstanding the ridiculous appearance she then made, upon being told the motive of her journey, was determined to gratify her inclinations.

As soon as the hour for country dances arrived, her

cousin Hamilton was appointed her partner. She made some faint excuses at first on account of the inconvenient situation she was then in, but soon suffered them to be overcome, in order, as she said, to show her duty to the Queen; and never did a woman in this world enjoy such complete satisfaction.

We have already observed, that the greatest prosperity is liable to the greatest change. Lady Muskerry, trussed up as she was, seemed to feel no manner of uneasiness from the motion in dancing; on the contrary, being only apprehensive of the presence of her husband, which would have destroyed all her happiness, she danced with uncommon briskness, lest her ill stars should bring him back before she had fully satisfied herself with it. In the midst, therefore, of her capering in this indiscreet manner, her cushion came loose, without her perceiving it, and fell to the ground in the very middle of the first round. The Duke of Buckingham, who watched her,[36] took it up instantly, wrapped it up in his coat, and, mimicking the cries of a new-born infant, he went about inquiring for a nurse for the young Muskerry among the maids of honour.[37]

This buffoonery, joined to the strange figure of the poor lady, had almost thrown Miss Stewart into hysterics; for the Princess of Babylon, after this accident, was quite flat on one side, and immoderately protuberant on the other. All those who had before suppressed their inclinations to laugh, now gave themselves free scope, when they saw that Miss Stewart was ready to split her sides. The poor lady was greatly disconcerted: every person was officious to console her; but the Queen, who inwardly laughed

[36] Was following her (Vizetelly).
[37] Pepys records a somewhat similar incident at a Court ball in February 1663.

more heartily than any, pretended to disapprove of their taking such liberties.

Whilst Miss Hamilton and Mrs. Wetenhall endeavoured to refit Lady Muskerry in another room, the Duke of Buckingham told the King that, if the physicians would permit a little exercise immediately after a delivery, the best way to recover Lady Muskerry was to renew the dance as soon as ever her infant was replaced; this advice was approved, and accordingly put into execution. The Queen proposed, as soon as she appeared, a second round of country-dances; and Lady Muskerry accepting the offer, the remedy had its desired effect, and entirely removed every remembrance of her late mishap.

Whilst these things were passing at the King's Court, that of the Duke of York took a journey on the other side of London;[38] the pretence of this journey was to visit the county whose name he bore; but love was the real motive. The Duchess, since her elevation, had conducted herself with such prudence and circum-

[38] See Sir John Reresby's *Memoirs*, 1875, p. 64, 5th August 1665 : " His Royal Highness the Duke and his Duchess came down to York. They stayed till September the 23rd, when the Duke went for Oxford, where the King was to meet the Parliament. The Duchess went not till some time after—she was a very handsome woman and had a great deal of wit, therefore it was not without reason that Mr. Sidney, the handsomest youth of his time, of the Duke's bedchamber, was so much in love with her as appeared to us all, and the Duchess not unkind to him, but very innocently; he was afterwards banished the Court for another reason, as was reported." Burnet mentions this transaction, and insinuates that to this cause is to be ascribed the Duchess's conversion (see Burnet's *History of his Own Time*, vol. i. p. 318). The following extract is from Spence's *Anecdotes* (ed. Singer, p. 329) : " 'How could the Duke of York make my mother a papist,' said the Princess Mary to Dr. Burnet. 'The Duke caught a man in bed with her,' said the Doctor, ' and then had power to make her do anything.' " Pepys, referring to this amour, says, 17th November 1665 (by Lord Sandwich's account), " how the Duchess is fallen in love with her new Master of the Horse, one Harry Sidney." See also footnote, p. 328.

spection as could not be sufficiently admired. Such
were her manners, and such the general estimation in
which she was held, that she appeared to have found
out the secret of pleasing every one: a secret yet more
rare than the grandeur to which she had been raised;
but, after having gained universal esteem, she was
desirous of being more particularly beloved; or, more
properly speaking, malicious Cupid assaulted her heart,
in spite of the discretion, prudence, and reason, with
which she had fortified it.

In vain had she said to herself a hundred times,
that if the Duke had been so kind as to do her justice
by falling in love with her, he had done her too much
honour by making her his wife; that with respect to
his inconstant disposition, which estranged him from
her, she ought to bear it with patience, until it pleased
Heaven to produce a change in his conduct; that the
frailties on his part, which might to her appear injurious, would never justify in her the least deviation
from her duty; and, as resentment was still less allowable, she ought to endeavour to regain him by a conduct entirely opposite to his own. In vain was it, as
we have said before, that she had long resisted Love
and his emissaries by the help of these maxims: how
solid soever reason, and however obstinate wisdom and
virtue may be, there are yet certain attacks which tire
by their length, and, in the end, subdue both reason
and virtue itself.

The Duchess of York was one of the highest feeders
in England. As this was an unforbidden pleasure,
she indulged herself in it, as an indemnification for
other self-denials. It was really an edifying sight to
see her at table. The Duke, on the contrary, being
incessantly in the hurry of new fancies, exhausted
himself by his inconstancy, and was gradually wasting
away; whilst the poor Princess, gratifying her good

appetite, grew so fat and plump that it was a blessing to see her. It is not easy to determine how long things would have continued in this situation, if Love, who was resolved to have satisfaction for her late conduct, so opposite to the former, had not employed artifice as well as force to disturb her repose.

He at first let loose upon her resentment and jealousy, two mortal enemies to all tranquillity and happiness. A tall creature, pale-faced, and nothing but skin and bone, named Churchill,[39] whom she had taken for a maid of honour, became the object of her jealousy, because she was then the object of the Duke's affection.

The Court was not able to comprehend how, after having been in love with Lady Chesterfield, Miss Hamilton, and Miss Jennings, he could have any inclination for such a creature; but they soon perceived that something more than unaccountable variety had a great share in effecting this conquest.

The Duchess beheld with indignation a choice which seemed to debase her own merit in a much greater degree than any of the former. At the very instant that indignation and jealousy began to provoke her spleen, perfidious Cupid threw in the way of her pas-

[39] Arabella Churchill, daughter of Sir Winston Churchill of Wotton Basset, Wilts, and sister to the celebrated John, Duke of Marlborough. Born 1648. By the Duke of York she was mother of James, Duke of Berwick; Henry Fitz-James, commonly called the Grand Prior, born 1673, who was, after the Revolution, created by his father Duke of Albemarle, and died 1702; Arabella, a nun, who died at the age of ninety in 1762 (vide *Notes and Queries*, 2nd Series, vol. iv. p. 488) ; Henrietta, born 1670, married to Lord Waldegrave, and died 1730. Miss Churchill afterwards became the wife of Charles Godfrey, Esq. (*ob.* 1715, *æt.* sixty-seven), Clerk-Comptroller of the Green Cloth, and Master of the Jewel Office, by whom she had two daughters: one, Charlotte, Maid of Honour to Queen Mary, married to H. Boscawen, afterwards Viscount Falmouth, and the other, Elizabeth, to Edmund Dunch, Esq., of Wallingford. Mrs. Godfrey died at Whitehall in May 1730, at the age of eighty-two.

sions and resentments the amiable, handsome Sidney;[40] and, whilst he kept her eyes fixed upon his personal perfections, diverted her attention from perceiving the deficiency of his mental accomplishments. She was wounded before she was aware of her danger; but the good opinion Sidney had of his own merit did not suffer him long to be ignorant of such a glorious conquest; and, in order more effectually to secure it, his eyes rashly answered everything which those of her Royal Highness had the kindness to tell him, whilst his personal accomplishments[41] were carefully heightened by all the advantages of dress and show.

The Duchess, foreseeing the consequences of such an engagement, strongly combated the inclination that hurried her away; but Miss Hobart, siding with that inclination, argued the matter with her scruples, and, in the end, really vanquished them. This girl had insinuated herself into her Royal Highness's confidence by a fund of news with which she was provided the whole year round. The Court and the city supplied her; nor was it very material to her whether her stories were true or false, her chief care being that they should prove agreeable to her mistress. She knew, likewise, how to gratify her palate, and constantly provided a variety of those dishes and liquors which she liked best. These qualifications had rendered her necessary; but, desirous of being still more so, and having perceived both the airs that Sidney gave himself, and what was passing in the heart of her mistress, the cunning Hobart took the liberty of telling her Royal Highness that this unfortunate youth was pining away solely on her account; that it was a thousand pities a man of his figure should lose the respect for her which was most certainly her due, merely because she had reduced him to such a state that he could no

[40] Henry Sidney. See note, p. 98. [41] Attractions (Vizetelly).

longer preserve it; that he was gradually dying away
on her account, in the sight of the whole Court; that
his situation would soon be generally remarked, except she made use of the proper means to prevent it;
that, in her opinion, her Royal Highness ought to pity
the miserable situation into which her charms had reduced him, and to endeavour to alleviate his pain in
some way or other. The Duchess asked her what she
meant by "endeavouring to alleviate his pain in some
way or other." "I mean, madam," answered Miss
Hobart, "that, if either his person be disagreeable, or
his passion troublesome, you will give him his discharge; or, if you choose to retain him in your service,
as all the princesses in the world would do in your
place, you will permit me to give him directions from
you for his future conduct, mixed with a few grains
of hope to prevent his entirely losing his senses, until
you find a proper occasion yourself to acquaint him
with your wishes." "What!" said the Duchess, "would
you advise me, Hobart—you, who really love me—to
engage in an affair of this nature, at the expense of my
honour, and the hazard of a thousand inconveniences!
If such frailties are sometimes excusable, they certainly
are not so in the high station in which I am placed;
and it would be an ill-requital on my part for his
goodness who raised me to the rank I now fill, to——"

"All this is very fine," interrupted Miss Hobart;
"but is it not very well known that he only married
you because he was importuned to do so? Since that,
I leave you to decide whether he has ever restrained
his inclination a single moment, giving you the most
convincing proofs of the change that has taken place in
his heart, by a thousand provoking infidelities? Is it
still your intention to persevere in a state of indolence
and humility, whilst the Duke, after having received
the favours, or suffered the repulses, of all the co-

quettes in England, pays his addresses to the maids of honour, one after the other, and at present places his whole ambition and desires in the conquest of that ugly skeleton,[42] Churchill? What! madam, must then your prime of life be spent in a sort of widowhood in deploring your misfortunes, without ever being permitted to make use of any remedy that may offer? A woman must be endowed with insuperable patience, or with an inexhaustible degree of resignation, to bear this. Can a husband, who disregards you both night and day, really suppose, because his wife eats and drinks heartily, as, God be thanked, your Royal Highness does, that she wants nothing else than to sleep well too? Faith, such conduct is too bad: I therefore once more repeat that there is not a princess in the universe who would refuse the homage of a man like Sidney, when a husband pays his addresses elsewhere."

These reasons were certainly not morally good; but had they been still worse the Duchess would have yielded to them, so much did her heart act in concert with Miss Hobart, to overthrow her discretion and prudence.

This intrigue began at the very time that Miss Hobart advised Miss Temple not to give any encouragement to the addresses of the handsome Sidney. As for him, no sooner was he informed by the confidante Hobart that the Duchess accepted his adoration, than he immediately began to be particularly reserved and circumspect in his behaviour, in order to divert the attention of the public; but the public is not so easily deceived as some people imagine.

As there were too many spies, too many inquisitive people and critics, in a numerous Court, residing in the midst of a populous city, the Duchess, to avoid

[42] Jade (Vizetelly).

exposing the inclinations of her heart to the scrutiny of so many inquisitors, engaged the Duke of York to undertake the journey before mentioned; whilst the Queen and her Court were at Tunbridge.

This conduct was prudent; and, if agreeable to her, was far from displeasing to any of her Court, except Miss Jennings. Jermyn was not of the party; and, in her opinion, every party was insipid in which he was not one of the company. He had engaged himself in an enterprise above his strength, in laying a wager which the Chevalier de Gramont had laid before, and lost. He betted five hundred guineas that he would ride on the high road twenty miles in one hour upon the same horse. The day he had fixed upon for this race was the very same in which Miss Jennings went to the fortune-teller's.

Jermyn was more fortunate than her in this undertaking: he came off victorious; but as his courage had far exceeded the strength of his constitution in this exertion to win the wager, he got a violent fever into the bargain, which brought him very low. Miss Jennings inquired after his health; but that was all she dared to do. In modern romances, a princess need only pay a visit to some hero, abandoned by his physicians, and a perfect cure would be wrought in three days; but since Miss Jennings had not been the cause of Jermyn's fever, she was not certain of relieving him from it, although she had been sure that a charitable visit would not have been censured in a malicious Court. Without therefore paying any attention to the uneasiness she might feel upon the occasion, the Court set out without him. She had, however, the gratification to show her ill-humour throughout the whole journey, by appearing displeased with everything which seemed to afford satisfaction to all the rest of the company.

Talbot made one of the company; and flattering himself that the absence of a dangerous rival might produce some change in his favour, he was attentive to all the actions, motions, and even gestures, of his former mistress. There was certainly enough fully to employ his attention: it was contrary to her disposition to remain long in a serious humour. Her natural vivacity hurried her away from being seemingly lost in thought, into sallies of wit, which afforded him hopes that she would soon forget Jermyn, and remember that his own passion was the first she had encouraged. However, he kept his distance, notwithstanding his love and his hopes, being of opinion that it ill became an injured lover to betray either the least weakness, or the smallest return of affection, for an ungrateful mistress, who had deserted him.

Miss Jennings was so far from thinking of his resentments, that she did not even recollect he had ever paid his addresses to her; and her thoughts being wholly occupied upon the poor sick man, she conducted herself towards Talbot as if they never had had anything to say to each other. It was to him that she most usually gave her hand, either in getting into or out of the coach; she conversed more readily with him than any other person, and, without intending it, did everything to make the Court believe she was cured of her passion for Jermyn in favour of her former lover.

Of this he seemed likewise convinced, as well as the rest; and thinking it now proper to act another part, in order to let her know that his sentiments with respect to her were still the same, he had resolved to address her in the most tender and affectionate manner upon this subject. Fortune seemed to have favoured him, and to have smoothed the way for this intended harangue. He was alone with her in her chamber; and, what was still better, she was rallying him concerning Miss Boynton, saying, "that they were undoubtedly much obliged to him for attending them on their journey, whilst poor Miss Boynton had fainting fits at Tunbridge, at least twice a day, for love of him." Upon this discourse Talbot thought it right to begin the recital of his sufferings and fidelity, when Miss Temple, with a paper in her hand, entered the room. This was a letter in verse, which Lord Rochester had written some time before, upon the intrigues of the two Courts; wherein, upon the subject of Miss Jennings, he said, "that Talbot had struck terror among the people of God by his gigantic stature; but that Jermyn, like a little David, had vanquished the great Goliath." Jennings, delighted with this allusion, read it over two or three times, thought it more entertaining than Talbot's conversation, and at first heartily laughed at it; but soon after, in a tender air, she said, with a deep sigh, "Poor little David!" and turning her head on one side during this short reverie, shed a few tears, which assuredly did not flow for the defeat of the giant. This stung Talbot to the quick; and, seeing himself so ridiculously deceived in his hopes, he went abruptly out of the room, vowing never to think any more of a giddy girl, whose conduct was regulated neither by sense nor reason; but he did not keep his resolution.

The other votaries of love, who were numerous in this Court, were more successful, the journey being undertaken solely on that account. There were continual balls and entertainments upon the road; hunting, and all other diversions, wherever the Court halted in its progress. The tender lovers flattered themselves with the thought of being able to crown their happiness as they proeeded in their journey; and the beauties who governed their destiny did not forbid them to hope. Sidney paid his court with wonderful assi-

duity.   The Duchess made the Duke take notice of his
late perfect devotion to her service; his Royal Highness observed it, and agreed that he ought to be
remembered upon the first opportunity, which happened soon after.

Montagu, as before mentioned, was Master of the
Horse to the Duchess; he was possessed of a great
deal of wit, had much penetration, and loved mischief.
How could she bear such a man near her person, in
the present situation of her heart?   This greatly
embarrassed her; but Montagu's elder brother having,
very *àpropos,* got himself killed where he had no business,[43] the Duke obtained for Montagu the post of
Master of the Horse to the Queen, which the deceased
enjoyed; and the handsome Sidney was appointed to
succeed him in the same employment to the Duchess.
All this happened according to her wish, and the Duke
was highly pleased that he had found means to promote these two gentlemen at once, without being at the
least expense.

Miss Hobart greatly applauded these promotions.
She had frequent and long conversations with Sidney,
which, being remarked, some did her the honour to
believe it was upon her own account; and the com-

[43] Montagu's elder brother, Edward, eldest son of Edward,
second Lord Montagu of Boughton, was killed before Bergen,
2nd August 1665.   He was in disgrace at Court at the time.   Referring to this disgrace, Pepys says (20th May 1664) : " His fault
I perceive was his pride and most of all his affecting to be
great with the Queen; and it seems, indeed, he had more of her
care than everybody else, and would be with her talking alone
two or three hours together, insomuch that the lords about the
King, when he would be jesting with them about their wives,
would tell the King that he must have a care of his wife too, for
she hath now the gallant; and they say that the King himself
did once ask Montagu how his mistress (meaning the Queen)
did.   He grew so proud and despised everybody, besides suffering
nobody, he or she, to get or do anything about the Queen, that
they all laboured to do him a good turn.   So he is gone, nobody
pitying but laughing at him."

pliments that were made her upon the occasion she most willingly received. The Duke, who believed it at first, observed to the Duchess the unaccountable taste of certain persons, and how the handsomest young fellow in England was infatuated with such a frightful creature.

The Duchess confessed that taste was very arbitrary; the truth whereof he himself seemed to be convinced of, since he had fixed upon the beauteous Helen for his mistress.[44] I know not whether this raillery caused him to reflect for what reasons he had made his choice; but it is certain he began to cool in his affections for Miss Churchill; and perhaps he would entirely have abandoned this pursuit, had not an accident taken place, which raised in him an entirely new inclination for her.

The Court having halted for a few days in a fine open country, the Duchess was desirous of seeing a greyhound course. This diversion is practised in England upon large downs, where the turf, eaten by the sheep, is particularly green, and wonderfully even. She was in her coach, and all the ladies on horseback, every one of them being attended by her squire; it therefore was but reasonable that the mistress should likewise have her squire. He accordingly was at the side of her coach, and seemed to compensate for his deficiencies in conversation by the uncommon beauty of his mien and figure.

The Duke attended Miss Churchill, not for the sake of besieging her with soft flattering tales of love, but, on the contrary, to chide her for sitting so ill on horse-

[44] 9th January 1665-6. The Duke's surgeon, Pierce, tells Pepys: "How great a difference hath been between the Duke and Duchess, he suspecting her to be naught with Mr. Sidney. But some way or other, the matter is made up, but he was banished the Court, and the Duke for many days did not speak to the Duchess at all." See also Spence's *Anecdotes*, p. 329.

back. She was one the most indolent creatures in the world; and although the maids of honour are generally the worst mounted of the whole Court, yet, in order to distinguish her, on account of the favour she enjoyed, they had given her a very pretty, though rather a high-spirited horse: a distinction she would very willingly have excused them.

The embarrassment and fear she was under had added to her natural paleness. In this situation, her countenance had almost completed the Duke's disgust, when her horse, desirous of keeping pace with the others, set off at a gallop, notwithstanding her greatest efforts to prevent it; and her endeavours to hold him in, firing his mettle, he at length set off at full speed, as if he was running a race against the Duke's horse.

Miss Churchill lost her seat, screamed out, and fell from her horse. A fall at so quick a pace must have been violent; and yet it proved favourable to her in every respect; for, without receiving any hurt, she gave the lie to all the unfavourable suppositions that had been formed of her person, in judging from her face. The Duke alighted, in order to help her; she was so greatly stunned, that her thoughts were otherwise employed than about decency on the present occasion; and those who first crowded around her found her rather in a negligent posture. They could hardly believe that limbs of such exquisite beauty could belong to Miss Churchill's face. After this accident, it was remarked that the Duke's tenderness and affection for her increased every day; and towards the end of the winter, it appeared that she had not tyrannised over his passion, nor made him languish with impatience.

The two Courts returned to London much about the same time, equally satisfied with their respective excursions; though the Queen was disappointed in the hopes she had entertained of the good effects of the Tunbridge waters.

It was about this time that the Chevalier de Gramont received a letter from the Marchioness de Saint-Chaumont,[45] his sister, acquainting him that he might return when he thought proper, the King having given him leave. He would have received this news with joy at any other time, whatever had been the charms of the English Court; but, in the present situation of his heart, he could not resolve to quit it.

He had returned from Tunbridge a thousand times deeper in love than ever; for, during this agreeable excursion, he had every day seen Miss Hamilton, either in the marshes of melancholy Peckham, in the delicious walks of cheerful Summer-hill, or in the daily diversions and entertainments of the Queen's Court; and whether he saw her on horseback, heard her conversation, or observed her in the dance, still he was persuaded that Heaven had never formed an object in every respect more worthy of the love, and more deserving the affection, of a man of sense and delicacy. How then was it possible for him to bear the thoughts of leaving her? This appeared to him absolutely impracticable; however, as he was desirous of receiving the credit of the determination he had made to neglect his fortune, rather than to be separated from her charms, he showed her his sister's letter; but this confidence had not the success he expected.

Miss Hamilton, in the first place, congratulated him upon his recall. She returned him many thanks for the sacrifice he intended to make her; but as this testimony of affection greatly exceeded the bounds of mere gallantry, however sensibly she might feel this mark

[45] Susan Charlotte de Gramont, wife of Marquis de Saint-Chaumont, stepsister of the Chevalier (*vide* Vizetelly's edition, vol. ii. p. 172).

of his tenderness, she was determined not to abuse it. In vain did he protest that he would rather meet death than part from her irresistible charms; and her irresistible charms protested that he should never see them more unless he departed immediately. Thus was he forced to obey. However, he was allowed to flatter himself, that these positive orders, harsh as they might appear, did not flow from indifference; that she would always be more pleased with his return than with his departure, for which she was now so urgent; and having generously given him assurance that, so far as depended upon himself, he would find, upon his return, no variation in her sentiments during his absence, he took leave of his friends, thinking of nothing but his return, at the very time he was making preparations for his departure.[46]

[46] This was in the middle of December 1663. The French Ambassador, Comminges, wrote to King Louis that, on the point of starting, Charles II. detained him for a day, as he surmises, either to make him a present or to facilitate the payment of a debt of Lady Castlemaine amounting to 800 pieces. But at that time he had other sums owing to him, which he proposed to come and fetch when he declared himself on the subject of Miss Hamilton.

Strange to say, only a few days later (22nd December), the union took place. Comminges declared that the affair was so involved that those with the most penetration could not fathom it. By general repute the Chevalier was on his way to his native country, but was overtaken at Dover by Miss Hamilton's brothers George and Anthony, who asked him whether he had not forgotten anything in London. "I have forgotten to marry your sister," answered Gramont, whereupon he returned with them, probably under compulsion. That the Count's son was born under the usually allotted time can scarcely be brought forward as an argument that matters had gone farther than they should have done before Gramont's departure.

CHAPTER XI

THE nearer the Chevalier de Gramont approached the Court of France, the more did he regret his absence from that of England; not but that he expected a gracious reception at the feet of his master, whose anger no one provoked with impunity; but who likewise knew how to pardon, in such a manner as to make the favour he conferred in every respect to be felt.

A thousand different thoughts occupied his mind upon the journey. Sometimes he reflected upon the joy and satisfaction his friends and relations would experience upon his return; sometimes upon the congratulations and embraces of those who, being neither the one nor the other, would, nevertheless, overwhelm him with impertinent compliments. All these ideas passed quickly through his head; for a man deeply in love makes it a scruple of conscience not to suffer any other thoughts to dwell upon his mind than those of the object beloved. It was then the tender, endearing remembrance of what he had left in London that diverted his thoughts from Paris; and it was the torments of absence that prevented his feeling those of the bad roads and the bad horses. His heart protested to Miss Hamilton, between Montreuil and Abbeville, that he only tore himself from her with such haste to return the sooner; after which, by a short reflection, comparing the regret he had formerly felt upon the same road, in quitting France for England, with that which he now experienced, in quitting England for

France, he found the latter much more insupportable than the former.

It is thus that a man in love entertains himself upon the road; or rather, it is thus that a trifling writer abuses the patience of his reader, either to display his own sentiments, or to lengthen out a tedious story; but God forbid that this character should apply to ourselves, since we profess to insert nothing in these *Memoirs* but what we have heard from the mouth of him whose actions and sayings we transmit to posterity.

Who, except Squire Feraulas, has ever been able to keep a register of all the thoughts, sighs, and exclamations of his illustrious master? For my own part, I should never have thought that the attention of the Count de Gramont, which is at present so sensible to inconveniences and dangers, would have ever permitted him to entertain amorous thoughts upon the road, if he did not himself dictate to me what I am now writing.

But let us speak of him at Abbeville. The postmaster was his old acquaintance. His hotel was the best provided of any between Calais and Paris; and the Chevalier de Gramont, alighting, told Termes he would drink a glass of wine during the time they were changing horses. It was about noon; and, since the preceding night, when they had landed at Calais, until this instant, they had not eaten a single mouthful. Termes, praising the Lord, that natural feelings had for once prevailed over the inhumanity of his usual impatience, confirmed him as much as possible in such reasonable sentiments.

Upon their entering the kitchen, where the Chevalier generally paid his first visit, they were surprised to see half a dozen spits loaded with game at the fire, and every other preparation for a magnificent entertainment. The heart of Termes leaped for joy; he gave private orders to the hostler to pull the shoes off some of the horses, that he might not be forced away from this place before he had satisfied his craving appetite.

Soon after, a number of violins and hautboys, attended by all the mob of the town, entered the court. The landlord, being asked the reason of these great preparations, acquainted the Chevalier de Gramont that they were for the wedding of one of the most wealthy gentlemen in the neighborhood, with one of the handsomest girls in the whole province; that the entertainment was to be at his house; and that, if his lordship chose to stop, in a very short time he would see the new-married couple arrive from the church, since the music was already come. He was right in his conjectures; for these words were scarce out of his mouth, when three uncommonly large coaches, loaded with lackeys, as tall as Swiss,[1] with most gaudy liveries, all covered with lace, appeared in the court, and disembarked the whole wedding company. Never was country magnificence more naturally displayed. Rusty tinsel, tarnished lace, striped silk, little eyes, and full swelling breasts, appeared on every side.

If the first sight of the procession surprised the Chevalier de Gramont, faithful Termes was no less astonished at the second. The little that was to be seen of the bride's face appeared not without beauty; but no judgment could be formed of the remainder. Four dozen patches, at least, and ten ringlets of hair, on each side, most completely concealed her from all human eyes; but it was the bridegroom who most particularly attracted the Chevalier de Gramont's attention.

He was as ridiculously dressed as the rest of the company, except a coat of the greatest magnificence,

[1] Swiss Guards (Vizetelly).

and of the most exquisite taste. The Chevalier de Gramont, walking up to him to examine his dress, began to commend the embroidery of his coat. The bridegroom thought himself much honoured by this examination, and told him he bought it for one hundred and fifty louis, at the time he was paying his addresses to his wife. "Then you did not get it made here?" said the Chevalier de Gramont. "No," replied the other; "I bought it of a London merchant, who had ordered it for an English lord." The Chevalier de Gramont, who now began to perceive in what manner the adventure would end, asked him if he would recollect the merchant if he saw him again? "Recollect him!" replied the other, "I surely ought; for I was obliged to sit up drinking with him all night at Calais, while I was endeavouring to beat down the price." Termes had vanished out of sight as soon as ever this coat appeared, though he little supposed that the cursed bridegroom would have any conversation with his master concerning it.

The Chevalier's thoughts were some time wavering between his inclination to laugh, and a desire for hanging Master Termes; but the long habit of suffering himself to be robbed by his domestics, together with the vigilance of the criminal, whom his master could not reproach with having slept in his service, inclined him to clemency; and yielding to the importunities of the country gentleman, in order to confound his faithful servant, he sat down to table, to make the thirty-seventh of the company.

A short time after, he desired one of the waiters[2] to call for a gentleman whose name was Termes. He immediately appeared; and as soon as the master of the feast saw him, he rose from table, and offering him his hand: "Welcome, my friend," said he; "you

[2] Servants (Vizetelly).

see that I have taken good care of the coat which you sold me with so much reluctance, and that I have kept it for a good purpose."

Termes, having put on a face of brass, pretended not to know him, and pushed him back with some degree of rudeness. "No, no!" said the other; "since I was obliged to sit up with you the whole night, in order to strike the bargain, you shall pledge me in the bride's health." The Chevalier de Gramont, who saw that Termes was disconcerted, notwithstanding his impudence, said to him with a smile: "Come, come, my good London merchant, sit down, as you are so civilly invited: we are not so crowded at table but that there will be room enough for such an honest gentleman as yourself." At these words five-and-thirty of the guests were in motion to receive this new visitor: the bride alone, out of an idea of decorum, remained seated; and the audacious Termes, having swallowed the first shame of this adventure, began to lay about him at such a rate, as if it had been his intention to swallow all the wine provided for the wedding, if his master had not risen from the table as they were taking off four-and-twenty soups, to serve up as many other dishes* in their stead.

The company were not so unreasonable as to desire a man who was in such haste to remain to the end of a wedding dinner; but they all got up when he arose from table, and all that he could obtain from the bridegroom was that the company should not attend him to the gate of the inn. As for Termes, he wished they had not quitted him till the end of their journey, so much did he dread being left alone with his master.

They had advanced some distance from Abbeville, and were proceeding on in the most profound silence, when Termes, who expected an end to it in a short

* Entrées (Vizetelly).

time, was only solicitous in what manner it might happen, whether his master would attack him with a torrent of invectives, and certain epithets which were most justly his due, or whether, in an insulting, ironical manner, he might make use of such commendations as were most likely to confound him; but finding instead of either, that he remained in sullen silence, he thought it prudent rather to prevent the speech the Chevalier was meditating than to suffer him to think longer about it; and, accordingly, arming himself with all his effrontery: "You seem to be very angry, Sir," said he, "and I suppose you think you have reason for being so; but the devil take me, if you are not mistaken in reality."

"How! traitor! in reality!" said the Chevalier de Gramont. "It is then because I have not had thee well thrashed, as thou hast for a long time merited." "Look ye, Sir," replied Termes, "you always run into a passion, instead of listening to reason! Yes, Sir, I maintain that what I did was for your benefit." "And was not the quicksand likewise for my service?" said the Chevalier de Gramont. "Have patience, if you please," pursued the other. "I know not how that simpleton of a bridegroom happened to be at the custom-house when my portmanteau was examined at Calais; but these silly cuckolds thrust in their noses everywhere. As soon as ever he saw your coat, he fell in love with it. I immediately perceived he was a fool; for he fell down upon his knees, beseeching me to sell it him. Besides being greatly rumpled in the portmanteau, it was all stained in front by the sweat of the horses. I wonder how the devil he has managed to get it cleaned; but, faith, I am the greatest scoundrel in the world, if you would ever have put it on. In a word, it cost you one hundred and forty louis d'ors, and seeing he offered me one hundred and fifty for it:

'My master,' said I, 'has no occasion for this tinselled bauble to distinguish him at the ball; and, although he was pretty full of cash when I left him, how know I in what situation he may be upon my return? there is no certainty at play. To be brief, Sir, I got ten louis d'ors for it more than it cost you: this you see is all clear profit. I will be accountable to you for it, and you know that I am sufficiently substantial to make good such a sum. Confess now, do you think you would have appeared to greater advantage at the ball, if you had been dressed out in that damned coat, which would have made you look just like the village bridegroom to whom we sold it? and yet how you stormed at London when you thought it lost; what fine stories you told the King about the quicksand; and how churlish you looked, when you first began to suppose that this country looby wore it at his wedding!"

What could the Chevalier reply to such impudence? If he indulged his resentment, he must either have most severely bastinadoed* him, or he must have discarded him, as the easiest escape the rogue could expect; but he had occasion for him during the remainder of his journey; and, as soon as he was at Paris, he had occasion for him for his return.

The Maréchal de Gramont had no sooner notice of his arrival than he went to him at the hotel; and, the first embraces being over on both sides: "Chevalier," said the Maréchal, "how many days have you been in coming from London hither? for God knows at what a rate you travel on such occasions." The Chevalier told him he had been three days upon the road; and, to excuse himself for making no more haste, he related to him his Abbeville adventure. "It is a very entertaining one," said his brother; "but what is yet more entertaining is, that it will be your fault if you do not

* Thrashed (Vizetelly).

find your coat still at table; for the country gentry are not accustomed to rise very soon from a wedding dinner." And then, in a very serious tone, told him, "he knew not who had advised him to this unexpected return, which might probably ruin all his affairs; but he had orders from the King to bid him go back again without appearing at Court. He told him afterwards that he was very much astonished at his impatience, as, up to this time, he had conducted himself uncommonly well, and was sufficiently acquainted with the King's temper to know that the only way to merit his pardon was to wait until it freely came from his clemency."

The Chevalier, in justification of his conduct, produced Madame de Saint-Chaumont's letter, and told the Maréchal that he would very willingly have spared her the trouble of writing him such kind of news, to occasion him so useless a journey. "Still more indiscretion," replied his brother; "for, pray how long has our sister been either secretary of state or minister, that she should be employed by the King to make known his Majesty's order? Do you wish to know the real state of the case? Some time ago the King told Madame[5] how you had refused the pension the King

[5] Henrietta, youngest daughter of Charles I., born at Exeter 16th June 1644, from whence she was removed to Oatlands Palace in 1646, her governess, Lady Dalkeith,[1] soon afterwards conveying her secretly to France. She came over to England with her mother in September 1660, but returned to France the following January, and was married to Philip, Duke of Orleans, only brother of Louis XIV., on the 30th March 1661. In May 1670 she came again to Dover to transact the well-known Secret Treaty between Charles and Louis XIV. She died suddenly soon after her return to France in the following month, not without suspicion of having been poisoned by her husband. King James, in his Diary, says: "It was suspected that counter-poisons were given her; but when she was opened, in the presence of the English Ambassador, the Earl of Ailesbury, an English physician and surgeon, there appeared no grounds of suspicion of any

[1] Anne, daughter of Sir Edward Villiers, and wife of Robert Douglas, Lord Dalkeith.

of England offered you: he appeared pleased with the manner in which Comminges had related to him the circumstances attending it, and said he was pleased with you for it. Madame interpreted this as an order for your recall; and Madame de Saint-Chaumont being very far from possessing that wonderful discretion she imagines herself mistress of, she hastened to despatch to you this consequential order in her own hand. To conclude: Madame said yesterday, when the King was at dinner, that you would very soon be here; and the King, as soon as dinner was over, commanded me to send you back as soon as you arrived. Here you are; set off again immediately."

This order might have appeared severe to the Chevalier de Gramont at any other time; but, in the present state of his heart, he soon resolved upon obeying. Nothing gave him uneasiness but the officious advice which had obliged him to leave the English Court; and being entirely unconcerned that he was not allowed to see the French Court before his departure, he only desired the Maréchal to obtain leave for him to stay a few days to collect in some play debts which were owing to him. This request was granted, on condition that he should not remain in Paris.

He chose Vaugirard[6] for his retreat. It was there that he had several adventures which he so often re-

foul play. Yet Bucks talked openly that she was poisoned; and was so violent as to propose to foreign ministers to make war on France" (Macpherson's *Original Papers,* vol. i.). At the end of Lord Arlington's *Letters* are five very remarkable ones from a person of quality, who is said to have been actually on the spot, giving a particular relation of her death. Madame de Montespan, in her *Memoirs,* does not hesitate to express her opinion that the Princess was poisoned. There is however but little doubt that she died of peritonitis (*vide* Anatole France's edition of Madame de la Fayette's *Histoire d'Henriette d'Angleterre,* 1882; and *Madame,* by Julia Cartwright, 1894).

[6] At this time a small village beyond the limits of the city of Paris (see Vizetelly's edition, vol. ii. p. 168).

lated in so humorous and diverting a manner, that it
would be tedious to repeat them; there it was that the
administered the sacrament in so solemn a manner,
that, as there did not remain a sufficient number of
Swiss at Versailles to guard the chapel, Vardes[7] was
obliged to acquaint the King that they were all gone
to the Chevalier de Gramont, who was administering
the sacrament at Vaugirard; there likewise happened
that wonderful adventure which threw the first slur
upon the reputation of the great Saucourt, when, having a *tête-à-tête* with the gardener's daughter, the
horn, which was agreed upon as the signal to prevent
surprises, was sounded so often, that the frequent
alarms cooled the courage of the celebrated Saucourt,[8]
and rendered useless the assignation that was procured
for him with one of the prettiest girls in the neighbourhood. It was, likewise, during his stay at Vaugirard,
that he paid a visit to Mademoiselle de l'Hôpital at
Issy,[9] to inquire into the truth of a report of an amour
between her and a man of the long robe; and it was
there that, on his arriving unexpectedly, the President
de Maisons[10] was forced to take refuge in a closet, with
so much precipitation, that half of his robe remained
on the outside when he shut the door; while the Chevalier de Gramont, who observed it, made his visit excessively long, in order to keep the two lovers upon
the rack.

His business being settled, he set out for England on
the wings of love. Termes redoubled his vigilance
upon the road. The post horses were ready in an
instant at every stage; the winds and tides favoured

[7] Marquis de Vardes, Captain of the Swiss Guard.

[8] Marquis de Soyecourt.

[9] A fashionable locality in the seventeenth century, on the
road to Versailles (Vizetelly, ii. p. 188).

[10] René Longueil de Maisons, President of the Parliament,
whose daughter married Soyecourt (*ibid.*).

his impatience; and he reached London with the highest satisfaction. The Court was both surprised and charmed at his sudden return. No person condoled with him upon his late disappointment, which had occasioned him to come back, as he testified no manner of uneasiness concerning it himself; nor was Miss Hamilton in the least displeased at his readiness in obeying the orders of the King, his master.

Nothing new had happened in the English Court during his short absence; but it assumed a different aspect soon after his return: I mean with respect to love and pleasure, which were the most serious concerns of the Court during the greatest part of this gay reign.

The Duke of Monmouth,[11] natural son to Charles the Second, now made his first appearance in his father's

[11] James Crofts, who took the name of Scott (upon his marriage with the heiress to the Earldom of Buccleuch in 1663), generally acknowledged to be son of Charles II., though certain accounts give the paternity to Colonel Robert Sidney, brother to the "handsome Sidney" who figures in these *Memoirs*. Monmouth's mother, a beautiful Welsh woman, who passed by the name of Mrs. Barlow, though her real name was Lucy Walter, was far from faithful to her royal protector. She was therefore left to follow her own downward course, but not until her son had been forcibly taken from his mother's protection. He was then placed under the care of Lord Crofts (who also figures in the *Memoirs*) and the Queen Mother. Lucy Walter did not live to see the Restoration. Honours, titles, and riches were lavished upon her son by the King, who always had a sincere affection for him, and secretly protected him, while openly he had to defend his own brother's interests. Monmouth's rash acts threw him continually into disgrace at Court. His handsome appearance made him generally a favourite, but his weakness of character, an easy foil for the most dangerous political intriguers. Such crafty statesmen as Shaftesbury, and still more dangerous companions, as Lord Grey and James Ferguson, used the weak-minded Duke mainly for their own ends, which ultimately resulted in his ruin. But that Monmouth was guilty of any knowledge of the murder scheme in the Rye House Plot, except with a view to frustrate it, must not be entertained. For further particulars of his career, the insurrection, Sedgemoor fight, etc., vide *King Monmouth*.

Court. His entrance upon the stage of the world was so brilliant, his ambition had occasioned so many considerable events, and the particulars of his tragical end are so recent, that it were needless to produce any other traits to give a sketch of his character. By the whole tenor of his life, he appeared to be rash in his undertakings, irresolute in the execution, and dejected in his misfortunes, in which, at least, an undaunted resolution ought to equal the greatness of the attempt.

His figure and the exterior graces of his person were such, that nature perhaps never formed anything more complete. His face was extremely handsome; and yet it was a manly face, neither inanimate nor effeminate, each feature having its beauty and peculiar delicacy. He had a wonderful genius for every sort of exercise, an engaging aspect, and an air of grandeur: in a word, he possessed every personal advantage; but then he was greatly deficient in mental accomplishments. He had no sentiments but such as others inspired him with; and those who first insinuated themselves into his friendship took care to inspire him with none but such as were pernicious. The astonishing beauty of his outward form caused universal admiration: those who before were looked upon as handsome were now entirely forgotten at Court; and all the gay and beautiful of the fair sex were at his devotion.[12] He was particularly beloved by the King; but the universal terror of husbands and lovers. This, however, did not long continue; for nature not having endowed him with qualifications to secure the possession of the heart, the fair sex soon perceived the defect.

The Duchess of Cleveland was out of humour with the King, because the children she had by his Majesty were like so many little puppets compared to this new Adonis. She was the more particularly hurt, as she

[12] Service (Vizetelly).

might have boasted of being the queen of love, in comparison with the Duke's mother.[13] The King, however, laughed at her reproaches, as, for some time, she had certainly no right to make any; and, as this piece of jealousy appeared to be more ill founded than any she had formerly affected, no person approved of her ridiculous resentment. Not succeeding in this, she formed another scheme to give the King uneasiness. Instead of opposing his extreme tenderness for his son, she pretended to adopt him, in her affection, by a thousand commendations and caresses, which she was daily and continually increasing. As these endearments were public, she imagined they could not be suspected, but she was too well known for her real design to be mistaken. The King was no longer jealous of her; but, as the Duke of Monmouth was of an age not to be insensible to the attractions of a woman possessing so many charms, he thought it proper to withdraw him from this pretended mother-in-law,[14] to preserve his innocence, or at least his fame, uncontaminated: it was for this reason, therefore, that the King married him so young.[15]

An heiress of five thousand pound a-year in Scotland[16] offered very *àpropos;* her person was full of charms, and her mind possessed all those perfections in which the handsome Monmouth was deficient.

[13] Lucy Walter. For particulars of her career, vide *King Monmouth.*   [14] Step-mother (Vizetelly).

[15] There is no truth in this assertion, as Monmouth's marriage had been thought of a year before his appearance in England, viz. in 1661 (vide *King Monmouth,* p. 31).

[16] Lady Anne, daughter and sole heir of Francis Scott, second Earl of Buccleuch, was aged eleven in June 1662, when she was brought to London by her mother, the Countess of Wemyss. The marriage was solemnised in the following year, when Monmouth, in addition to Earl of Doncaster and Baron Tynedale, was created Duke of Buccleuch, Earl of Dalkeith, and Lord Scott, he being her senior by two years. A re-grant of the titles was made 16th January 1666, enjoining that either Monmouth or his wife

New festivals and entertainments celebrated this marriage.[17] The most effectual method to pay court to the King was to outshine the rest in brilliancy and grandeur; and whilst these rejoicings brought forward all manner of gallantry and magnificence, they either revived old, or established new amours.

The fair Stewart, then in the meridian of her glory, attracted all eyes, and commanded universal respect and admiration. The Duchess of Cleveland endeavoured to eclipse her at this *fête,* by a load of jewels, and by all the artificial ornaments of dress; but it was in vain: her face looked rather thin and pale, from the commencement of a third or fourth pregnancy, which the King was still pleased to place to his own account; and, as for the rest, her person could in no respect stand in competition with the grace and beauty of Miss Stewart.

It was during this last effort of her charms, that she[18] would have been queen of England, had the King been as free to give his hand as he was to surrender his heart; for it was at this time that the Duke of Richmond took it into his head either to marry her, or to die in the attempt.

should be independent in the event of the death of one of them; thus when Monmouth was executed in 1685, the title of Duke of Buccleuch could not be revived until 1732, when her death occurred. In that year the successor, Francis (grandson of Monmouth), also took the title of Earl of Doncaster and Baron Tynedale, which had become extinct in 1685. The title of Duke of Monmouth was not revived.

After the decease of her husband, the Duchess of Monmouth married (in 1688) Charles, third Lord Cornwallis (*ob.* 1693), by whom she had a son and two daughters. There were several children by the first marriage. According to Luttrell she was married for a third time in 1703 to the Earl of Selkirk, brother of the Duke of Hamilton.

In 1685 the private fortune of the Duchess of Monmouth was so far impoverished that an annuity from the Crown was settled upon her. For further particulars, vide *King Monmouth.*

[17] 20th April 1663.   [18] Frances Stewart.

A few months after the celebration of the Duke of Monmouth's nuptials, Killegrew,[19] having nothing better to do, fell in love with Lady Shrewsbury; and, as Lady Shrewsbury, by a very extraordinary chance, had no engagement at that time, their amour was soon established. No one thought of interrupting an intimacy which did not concern any one; but Killegrew thought proper to disturb it himself. Not that his happiness fell short of his expectation, nor did possession put him out of love with a situation so enviable; but he was amazed that he was not envied, and offended that his good fortune raised him no rivals.

He possessed a great deal of wit, and still more eloquence, which most particularly displayed itself when he was a little elevated with the juice of the grape: he then indulged himself in giving luxurious descriptions of Lady Shrewsbury's most secret charms and beauties, which above half the Court were as well acquainted with as himself.

The Duke of Buckingham was one of those who could only judge from outward appearances; and appearances, in his opinion, did not seem to promise anything so exquisite as the extravagant praises of Killegrew would infer. As this indiscreet lover was a frequent guest at the Duke of Buckingham's table, he was continually employing his rhetoric on this subject, and he had full opportunity for his harangues; for they generally sat down to dinner at four o'clock,[20] and only rose just in time for the play in the evening.

The Duke of Buckingham, whose ears were continually deafened[21] with descriptions of Lady Shrewsbury's merits, resolved at last to examine into the truth of the matter himself. As soon as he had made the experiment, he was satisfied; and, though he fancied that

[19] Henry Killigrew (see *ante,* footnote, p. 178).
[20] In the morning (Vizetelly).   [21] Dinned (Vizetelly).

fame did not exceed the truth, yet this intrigue began in such a manner, that it was generally believed its duration would be short, considering the fickleness of both parties, and the vivacity with which they had engaged in it; nevertheless, no amour in England ever continued so long.

The imprudent Killegrew, who could not be satisfied without rivals, was obliged, in the end, to be satisfied without a mistress. This he bore very impatiently; but so far was Lady Shrewsbury from listening to, or affording any redress for the grievances at first complained of, that she even pretended not to know him. His spirit could not brook such treatment; and, without ever considering that he was the author of his own disgrace, he let loose all his abusive eloquence against her ladyship. He attacked her with the most bitter invectives from head to foot; he drew a frightful picture of her conduct; and turned all her personal charms, which he used to extol, into defects. He was privately warned of the inconveniences to which these declamations might subject him, but despised the advice, and, persisting, he soon had reason to repent it.

As he was returning one evening from the Duke of York's apartments at St. James's, three passes with a sword were made at him through his chair, one of which went entirely through his arm. Upon this, he was sensible of the danger to which his intemperate tongue had exposed him, over and above the loss of his mistress. The assassins made their escape across the Park, not doubting but they had despatched him.[22]

[22] Pepys, alluding to this affair, says (19th May 1669): "Here the news was first talked of Harry Killigrew's being wounded in nine places last night by footmen in the highway going from the Park in a hackney-coach towards Hammersmith to his house in Turnham Green; they being supposed to be my Lady Shrewsbury's men, she being by in her coach with six horses; upon an

Killegrew thought that all complaints would be useless; for what redress from justice could he expect for an attempt of which his wounds were his only evidence? And, besides, he was convinced that if he began a prosecution founded upon appearances and conjectures, the parties concerned would take the shortest and most effectual means to put a stop to all inquiries upon the subject, and that their second attempt would not prove ineffectual. Being desirous, therefore, of deserving mercy from those who had endeavoured to assassinate him, he no longer continued his satires, and said not a word of the adventure.

The Duke of Buckingham and Lady Shrewsbury remained for a long period both happy and contented. Never before had her constancy been of so long a duration; nor had he ever been so submissive and respectful a lover.

old grudge of his saying openly that he had lain with her . . . his man is quite dead, and [Buckingham] there in discourse did say that he had spoke with someone that was by (which all the world must know that it must be his friend, my Lady Shrewsbury), who says that they did not mean to hurt, but beat him, and that he did run first at them with his sword; so that he do hereby clearly discover that he knows who did it and is of conspiracy with them, being of known conspiracy with her."

Some further particulars may be gathered from a letter from the French ambassador Colbert to the minister Lionne, on 20th May. "Infuriated against Killigrew," he says, "because he boasted she had denied him no favour, the Countess nursed her anger against him until she could wreak vengeance. She was able to do this yesterday. Killigrew had arranged to visit her at her house, which is six miles from London. He went alone in a coach, and on the way fell asleep. He was awoke by a thrust of a sword, which pierced his neck and came out at the shoulder. Before he could cry out he was flung from the vehicle and stabbed in three other places by the varlets of the Countess. The lady herself looked on from her coach and six, in which she was with her three daughters, and cried out to the assassins, 'Kill the villain.' Nor did she drive off until he was thought dead. He was but badly wounded and has sworn informations."

This continued until Lord Shrewsbury,[23] who never before had shown the least uneasiness at his lady's misconduct, thought proper to resent this. It was public enough, indeed, but less dishonourable to her than any of her former intrigues. Poor Lord Shrewsbury, too polite a man to make any reproaches to his wife, was resolved to have redress for his injured honour. He accordingly challenged the Duke of Buckingham; and the Duke of Buckingham, as a reparation for his honour, having killed him upon the spot, remained a peaceable possessor of this famous Helen. The public was at first shocked at the transaction; but the public grows familiar with everything by habit, and by degrees both decency, and even virtue itself, are rendered tame, and overcome.[24] The Queen

---

[23] Francis, eleventh Earl of Shrewsbury. Reresby, in his *Memoirs*, mentions (20th June 1666) how the intrigue between Buckingham and the Countess first became known to the Earl of Shrewsbury, at York, where Buckingham was entertaining a house party. The Countess's brother, Lord Brudenel, was sent for very late at night to act as mediator between them, there having been "a great quarrel of jealousy."

[24] Regarding the notorious duel Pepys says, 17th January 1667-8: "Much discourse of a duel yesterday between the Duke of Buckingham, Holmes, and one Jenkins, on one side, and my Lord of Shrewsbury, Sir John Talbot, and one Bernard Howard, on the other side, and all about my Lady Shrewsbury, who is at this time and hath for a great while been a mistress to the Duke of Buckingham. And so her husband challenged him, and they met yesterday in a close near Barne Elmes, and there fought; and my Lord Shrewsbury is run through the body, from the right breast through the shoulder; and Sir John Talbot all along, up one of his arms; and Jenkins killed upon the place, and the rest all in a little measure wounded. This will make the world think that the King hath good councillors about him, when the Duke of Buckingham, the greatest man about him, is a fellow of no more sobriety than to fight about a mistress. And this may prove a very bad accident to the Duke of Buckingham, but that my Lady Castlemaine do rule all at this time as much as ever she did, and she will, it is believed, keep all matters well with the Duke of Buckingham; though this is a time that the King will be very backward, I suppose, to appear in such a business. And it is pretty to hear how the King had some notice of

was at the head of those who exclaimed against so
public and scandalous a crime, and against the impunity

this challenge a week or two ago, and did give it to my Lord
General to confine the Duke, or take security that he should not
do any such thing as fight; and the General trusted to the King
that he, sending for him, would do it, and the King trusted
to the General. And it is said that my Lord Shrewsbury's case is
to be feared, that he may die too; and that may make it much
worse for the Duke of Buckingham; and I shall not be much
sorry for it, that we may have some sober man come in his
room to assist in the Government." Again, 15th May 1668: "I
am told that the Countess of Shrewsbury is brought home by the
Duke of Buckingham to his house, where his Duchess, saying
that it was not for her and the other to live together in a house,
he answered, 'Why, madame, I did think so, and therefore have
ordered your coach to be ready to carry you to your father's,'
which was a devilish speech, but they say true; and my Lady
Shrewsbury is there, it seems."

Walpole says that during the encounter the Countess, disguised
as a page, held Buckingham's horse (*Noble Authors*, ii. p. 82).
In August 1671, according to Andrew Marvell, still "Buckingham
runs out with the Lady Shrewsbury, whom he believes he had a
son (by), to whom the King stood godfather. It died young,
Earl of Coventry, and was buried in the sepulchre of his fathers."
(Marvell's *Works*, i. p. 406.) In the Burial Register of Westminster Abbey for 12th March 1670-1 is the following entry:
"A young male child was layd in the Duke of Buckingham's
vault, being related to that family."

Notwithstanding that the Duchess was alive at the time, James
II. says that Buckingham married the Countess of Shrewsbury
(Macpherson's *Original Papers,* i. p. 58), but her brother Francis,
Lord Brudenel, and others, nevertheless petitioned the House of
Lords to interfere, and the guilty pair had each to give security
for their future conduct in the amount of £10,000 a-piece (*Lords'
Journal,* xii. p. 628).

Pope's allusion to—

> "Cliefden's proud alcove
> The bow'r of Wanton Shrewsbury and Love "

cannot be accepted as true, as the Duke of Buckingham's beautiful riverside mansion was only in course of erection in 1680,
when the Countess had become the wife of George Rodney
Bridges. Still, with such an abandoned woman, it is possible
the liaison may have continued. Buckingham died in 1687 (*vide*
G. S. Steinman's *Althorp Memoirs*). A brief account of the
famous duel will also be found among the Verney MSS., 23d
January 1667-8, *Hist. MS. Com. Rep.* 7, App. p. 486.

of such a wicked act. As the Duchess of Buckingham[25] was a short fat body, like her Majesty, who never had had any children, and whom her husband had abandoned for another, this sort of parallel in their situations interested the Queen in her favour; but it was all in vain: no person paid any attention to them; the licentiousness of the age went on uncontrolled, though the Queen endeavoured to raise up the serious part of the nation, the politicians and devotees, as enemies against it.

The fate of this Princess was in many cases truly melancholy. The King, indeed, paid her every outward attention; but that was all. She easily perceived that the respect he entertained for her daily diminished, in proportion as the credit of her rivals increased. She saw that the King, her husband, was now totally indifferent about legitimate children, since his all-charming mistresses bore him others. As all the happiness of her life depended upon that blessing, and as she flattered herself that the King would prove kinder to her if Heaven would vouchsafe to grant her desires, she had recourse to all the celebrated secrets against sterility: pious vows, nine days' prayers, and offerings

[25] Mary, Duchess of Buckingham, only daughter of Thomas, Lord Fairfax, born 1639, married the profligate Duke of Buckingham in 1657. Bryan Fairfax, in his *Life* of the Duke, says she was a virtuous and pious lady in a vicious Court, and lived lovingly and decently with her husband, bearing submissively his constant infidelities. She appears, however, to have had spirit enough to resent the outrageous insult mentioned by Pepys (*Diary,* 15th May 1668), referred to above. By all accounts she had not many personal attractions. The Countess Dunois describes her in her *Memoirs* "as little, brown, and lean," and old Viscountess de Longueville, who died in 1763, aged nearly a hundred, spoke of her as "a little round crumpled woman, very fond of finery." Upon one occasion when she visited her, the Duchess was lying on a sofa, arrayed in a loose robe, "all edged or laced with gold." The Duchess died in 1705, aged sixty-six, and was buried in the Villiers vault, in Henry VII.'s Chapel at Westminster.

having been tried in all manners, but all to no purpose, she was at last obliged to return to natural means.

What would she have given on this occasion for the ring which Archbishop Turpin wore on his finger, and which made Charlemagne run after him, in the same manner as it had made him run after one of his concubines, from whose finger Turpin had taken it after her death! But it is now many years since the only talismans for creating love are the charms of the person beloved, and foreign enchantments have been looked upon as ineffectual. The Queen's physicians, men of great prudence, sagacity, and wisdom, as they always are, having duly weighed and considered that the cold waters of Tunbridge had not succeeded in the preceding year, concluded that it would be advisable for her to try the warm baths at Bristol.[26] This journey was therefore fixed for the next season; and in the confidence of its proving effectual, this excursion would have afforded her much pleasure, if the most dangerous of her rivals had not been one of the first that was appointed to attend the Court. The Duchess of Cleveland being then near her time, there was no uneasiness on her account: the common rules of decency required a little attention. The public, it

[26] The warm baths alluded to doubtless were those at Bath, where the Court removed to in August 1663. Pepys records the royal progress: "Started from Whitehall on 26th August. The first night was spent at Maidenhead, and the second near Newbury" (probably at Shaw House). On September the 5th the King and Queen, Duke and Duchess of York, etc., visited Bristol, where they were sumptuously entertained by the Mayor and Sheriffs (see Barrett's *History of Bristol*). According to Godolphin, on 22nd September the King and Queen left Bath for Badminton, Lord Herbert's seat, where they dined, being met by the county gentry (*State Papers, Dom.*, 28th September 1663); but Pepys records on the same date: "This day (22nd September) the King and Queen are come to Oxford," whither Lady Castlemaine repaired to meet them after the birth of her second son (in London), on 20th September 1663 (afterwards created Duke of Grafton).

is true, was not either more or less acquainted with the circumstances of her situation, by the care which she now took to conceal it; but her appearing at Court in her present condition would have been too great an insult to the Queen. Miss Stewart, more handsome than ever, was appointed for this excursion, and began to make magnificent preparations. The poor Queen durst say nothing against it; but all hopes of success immediately forsook her. What could the baths, or the feeble virtue of the waters, perform against charms that entirely counteracted their effects, either through the grief and uneasiness they occasioned her, or by their still more powerful consequences?

The Chevalier de Gramont, to whom all pleasures were insipid without the presence of Miss Hamilton, was yet unable to excuse himself from attending the Court: the King delighted too much in his sprightly conversation to leave him behind; and however pleasing his company might have been in the solitude occasioned by the absence of the Court, Miss Hamilton did not think it right to accept his offer of staying in town, because she was obliged to remain there. She, however, granted him the permission of writing her an account of any news that might occur upon the journey. He failed not to make use of this permission, in such a manner as one may imagine; and his own concerns took up so much space in his letters, that there was very little room left for other subjects during his stay at the baths. As absence from the object of his affections rendered this place insupportable, he engaged in everything that might dissipate his impatience, until the happy moment of return arrived.

He had a great esteem for the elder of the Hamiltons; no less esteem, and far more friendship for his brother, whom he made the confidant of his passion and attachment for his sister. The Chevalier was also

acquainted with his first engagements with his cousin
Wetenhall; but being ignorant of the coldness that had
interrupted a commerce so brisk in its commencement,
he was surprised at the eagerness he showed upon all
occasions to please Miss Stewart. His assiduity appeared to the Chevalier de Gramont to exceed those
civilities and attentions that are usually paid for the
purpose of making court to the favourites of princes.
He observed him more strictly, and soon perceived that
he was deeper in love with her than was consistent
either with his fortune or his repose. As soon as the
remarks he made had confirmed him in his suspicions,
he resolved to use his endeavours to prevent the consequences of an engagement pernicious in every respect; but he waited for a proper opportunity of
speaking to him upon the subject.

In the meantime, the Court enjoyed every kind of
diversion, in a place where amusement is sought with
avidity. The game of bowls, which in France is the
pastime of mechanics and servants only, is quite the
contrary in England, where it is the exercise of gentlemen, and requires both art and address. It is only in
use during the fair and dry part of the season, and
the places where it is practised are charming, delicious
walks,* called bowling-greens, which are little square
grass plots, where the turf is almost as smooth and
level as the cloth of a billiard-table. As soon as the
heat of the day is over, all the company assemble
there: they play deep; and spectators are at liberty to
make what bets they please.

The Chevalier de Gramont, long before initiated in
the English games and diversions, had been engaged
in a horse-race, in which he was indeed unsuccessful;
but he had the satisfaction of being convinced by experience that an English horse can go twenty miles

* Enclosures (Vizetelly).

upon the high road in less than an hour. He was
more fortunate at cock-fighting; and in the bets he
made at the bowling-green, the party he betted upon
never failed to win.

Near all these places of diversion there is usually a
sort of inn, or house of entertainment, with a bower
or arbour, in which are sold all sorts of English
liquors, such as cider, mead, bottled beer, and Spanish
wines. Here the rooks meet every evening to drink,
smoke, and to try their skill upon each other, or, in
other words, to endeavour to trick one another out of
the winnings of the day. These rooks are, properly
speaking, what we call *capons* or *piqueurs* in France:
men who always carry money about them, to enable
them to lend to losing gamesters, for which they receive a gratification, which is nothing for such as play
deep, as it is only two per cent, and the money to be
repaid the next day.

These gentlemen are so nice in their calculations,
and so particularly skilful in all manner of games,
that no person would dare to enter the lists with them,
were they even assured that no unfairness would be
practised. Besides, they make a vow to win four or
five guineas a day, and to be satisfied with that gain:
a vow which they seldom or never break.

It was in the midst of a company of these rooks
that Hamilton found the Chevalier de Gramont, when
he called in one evening to get a glass of cider. They
were playing at hazard; and as he who holds the dice
is supposed to have the advantage, the rooks did the
Chevalier de Gramont that honour out of compliment.
He had the dice in his hand when Hamilton came into
the room. The rooks, secure of their odds, were
betting against him at a high rate, and he took all.

Hamilton could hardly believe his eyes, to see a
man of his experience and knowledge engaged in so

unequal a contest; but it was to no purpose that he informed him of his danger, both aloud in French, and in private by signs; he still disregarded his warnings, and the dice, that bore Cæsar and his fortunes, performed a miracle in his favour. The rooks were defeated for the first time, but not without bestowing upon him all the encomiums and praises of being a very fair and honourable player, which they never fail to lavish upon those whom they wish to engage a second time; but all their commendations were lost, and their hopes deceived: the Chevalier was satisfied with the first experiment.

Hamilton, when the King was at supper, related to him how he found the Chevalier de Gramont rashly engaged with the rooks, and in what manner he had been providentially preserved. "Indeed, Sir," said the Chevalier de Gramont, "the rooks were discomfited for once," and thereupon related the adventure to his Majesty in his usual way, attracting the attention of all the company to a circumstance trifling in itself, but rendered interesting by his humour.

After supper, Miss Stewart, in whose apartment there was play, called Hamilton to her to tell the story. The Chevalier de Gramont, perceiving that she attended to him with pleasure, was fully confirmed in the truth of his first conjectures; and, having carried Hamilton home with him to supper, they began to discourse freely together as usual. "George," said the Chevalier de Gramont, "are you in any want of money? I know you love play; perhaps it may not be so favourable to you as it is to me. We are at a great distance from London. Here are two hundred guineas: take them, I beseech you; they will do to play with at Miss Stewart's." Hamilton, who little expected this conclusion, was rather disconcerted. "How! at Miss Stewart's!" "Yes, in her apartments.

Friend George," continued the Chevalier de Gramont, "I have not yet lost my eyes. You are in love with her, and, if I am not mistaken, she is not offended at it; but tell me how you could resolve to banish poor Wetenhall from your heart, and suffer yourself to be infatuated with a girl, who perhaps, after all, is not worth the other, and who, besides, whatever favourable dispositions she may have for you, will undoubtedly in the end prove your ruin. Faith, your brother and you are two pretty fellows in your choice. What! can you find no other beauties in all the Court to fall in love with except the King's two mistresses! As for the elder brother, I can pardon him: he only took Lady Castlemaine after his master had done with her, and after Lady Chesterfield had discarded him; but, as for you, what the devil do you intend to do with a creature on whom the King seems every day to dote with increasing fondness? Is it because that drunken sot Richmond has again come forward, and now declares himself one of her professed admirers? You will soon see what he will make by it. I have not forgotten what the King said to me upon the subject.

"Believe me, my dear friend, there is no playing tricks with our masters; I mean, there is no ogling their mistresses. I myself wanted to play the agreeable in France with a little coquette, whom the King did not care about, and you know how dearly I paid for it." I confess she gives you fair play, but do not trust to her. All the sex feel an unspeakable satisfaction at having men in their train whom they do not care for, and to use them as their slaves of state, merely to swell their equipage. Would it not be a great deal better to pass a week or ten days incognito at Peckham, with the philosopher Wetenhall's wife,

---

²⁸ Gramont here refers to his attentions to Mademoiselle de la Motte Houdancourt, before alluded to (see *ante*, p. 85).

than to have it inserted in the Dutch Gazette—We hear from Bristol that such a one is banished the Court on account of Miss Stewart, and that he is going to make a campaign in Guinea[20] on board the fleet that is fitting out for the expedition, under the command of Prince Rupert."

Hamilton, who was convinced of the truth of this discourse, the more he considered it, after musing some time, appeared to wake from a dream, and addressing himself with an air of gratitude to the Chevalier de Gramont: "Of all the men in the world, my dear friend," said he, "you have the most agreeable wit, and at the same time the clearest judgment with respect to your friends: what you have told me has opened my eyes. I began to suffer myself to be seduced by the most ridiculous illusion imaginable, and to be hurried away rather by frivolous appearances than any real inclination. To you I owe the obligation of having preserved me from destruction at the very brink of the precipice. This is not the only kindness you have done me: your favours have been innumerable; and, as a proof of my gratitude for this last, I will follow your advice, and go into retirement at my cousin Wetenhall's, to eradicate from my recollection every trace of those chimeras which lately possessed my brain; but so far from going there incognito, I will take you along with me, as soon as the Court returns to London. My sister shall likewise be of the party; for it is prudent to use all precautions with a man who, with a great deal of merit, on such occasions is not over-scrupulous, if we may credit your philosopher."

"Do not pay any attention to that pedant," replied the Chevalier de Gramont; "but tell me what put it into your head to form a design upon that inanimate statue,

[20] This expedition was intended to have taken place in 1664 (*vide* footnote, p. 380).

Miss Stewart?" "How the devil should I know?" said Hamilton. "You are acquainted with all her childish amusements. The old Lord Carlingford[30] was at her apartment one evening, showing her how to hold a lighted wax candle in her mouth, and the grand secret consisted in keeping the burning end there a long time without its being extinguished. I have, thank God, a pretty large mouth, and, in order to out-do her teacher, I took two candles into my mouth at the same time, and walked three times round the room without their going out. Every person present adjudged me the prize of this illustrious experiment, and Killegrew maintained that nothing but a lanthorn could stand in competition with me. Upon this she was like to die with laughing; and thus was I admitted into the familiarity of her amusements. It is impossible to deny her being one of the most charming creatures that ever was : since the Court has been in the country, I have had an hundred opportunities of seeing her, which I had not before. You know that the dishabille of the bath is a great convenience for those ladies who, strictly adhering to all the rules of decorum, are yet desirous to display all their charms and attractions. Miss Stewart is so fully acquainted with the advantages she possesses over all other women, that it is hardly possible to praise any lady at Court for a well-turned arm, and a fine leg, but she is ever ready to dispute the point by demonstration. After all, a man must be very insensible to remain unconcerned and unmoved on such happy occasions; and, besides, the good opinion we entertain of ourselves is apt to make us think a woman is smitten, as soon as she distinguishes us by habitual familiarity,

[30] Theobald Taafe, the second Viscount Taafe, created Earl of Carlingford, in the county of Louth, the father of the Lord Taafe who had the intrigue with Miss Warminster (see *ante*, pp. 239-245).

which most commonly signifies nothing. This is the truth of the matter with respect to myself: my own presumption, her beauty, the brilliant station that set it off, and a thousand kind things she had said to me, prevented me from making serious reflections; but then, as some excuse for my folly, I must likewise tell you, that the facility I found in making her the tenderest declarations by commending her, and her telling me in confidence a thousand things which she ought not to have entrusted me with, might have deceived or infatuated any other man as well as myself.

"I presented her with one of the prettiest horses in England. You know what peculiar grace and elegance distinguish her on horseback. The King—who, of all the diversions of the chase, likes none but hawking, because it is the most convenient for the ladies—went out the other day to take this amusement, attended by all the beauties of his Court. His Majesty having galloped after a falcon, and the whole bright squadron after him, the rustling of Miss Stewart's petticoats frightened her horse, which, at full speed, was endeavouring to come up with mine, that had been his[31] companion; so that I was the only witness of a disorder in her clothes, which displayed a thousand new beauties to my view. I had the good fortune to make such gallant and flattering exclamations upon that charming disorder as to prevent her being concerned or out of countenance upon it: on the contrary, this subject of my admiration has been frequently since the subject of our conversation, and did not seem to displease her.

"Old Lord Carlingford, and that mad fellow, Crofts[32] (for I must now make you my general con-

---

[31] Stable companion (Vizetelly).
[32] William, Lord Crofts, eldest son of Sir Henry Crofts of Little Saxham, Suffolk, Gentleman of the Bedchamber to the

fession), those insipid buffoons, were frequently telling
her some diverting stories, which passed pretty well
with the help of a few old threadbare jests, or some
apish tricks in the recital, which made her laugh
heartily. As for myself, who know no stories, and do
not possess the talent of improving them by telling, if
I did know any, I was often greatly embarrassed when
she desired me to tell her one. 'I do not know one,
indeed,' said I, one day, when she was teasing me on
the subject.

" 'Invent one, then,' said she. 'That would be still
more difficult,' replied I; 'but if you will give me
leave, madam, I will relate to you a very extraordinary dream, which has, however, less appearance of
truth in it than dreams generally have.' This excited
her curiosity, which would brook no denial. I therefore began to tell her that the most beautiful creature
in the world, whom I loved to distraction, paid me a
visit in my sleep. I then drew her own portrait, with
a rapturous description of all her beauties; adding,
that this goddess, who came to visit me with the most
favourable intentions, did not counteract them by any
unreasonable cruelty. This was not sufficient to satisfy
Miss Stewart's curiosity: I was obliged to relate every
particular circumstance of the kindness I experienced
from this delicate phantom; to which she was so very
attentive, that she never once appeared surprised or
disconcerted at the luscious tale. On the contrary, she
made me repeat the description of the beauty, which I
drew as near as possible after her own person, and

King and Duke of York. Groom of the Stole, and captain of
a regiment of Guards to the Queen Mother. He was appointed
to act as guardian to the young Duke of Monmouth, who adopted
his name until he took that of Scott in 1663. Pepys (23rd October 1668) mentions a drinking bout by the King, Buckhurst,
Sedley, and others at Saxham, which old Hall was pulled down
in 1771.

after such charms as I imagined of beauties that were unknown to me.

"This is, in fact, the very thing that had almost deprived me of my senses. She knew very well that she herself was the person I was describing. We were alone, as you may imagine, when I told her this story; and my eyes did their utmost to persuade her that it was herself whom I drew. I perceived that she was not in the least offended at knowing this; nor was her modesty in the least alarmed at the relation of a fiction, which I might have concluded in a manner still less discreet, if I had thought proper. This patient audience made me plunge headlong into the ocean of flattering ideas that presented themselves to my imagination. I then no longer thought of the King, nor how passionately fond he was of her, nor of the dangers attendant upon such an engagement: in short, I know not what the devil I was thinking of; but I am very certain that, if you had not been thinking for me, I might have found my ruin in the midst of these distracted visions."

Not long after, the Court returned to London; and from that time, some malevolent star having gained the ascendant, everything went cross in the empire of Love: vexation, suspicions, or jealousies, first entered the field, to set all hearts at variance; next, false reports, slander, and disputes completed the ruin of all.

The Duchess of Cleveland had been brought to bed while the Court was at Bristol; and never before had she recovered from her lying-in with such a profusion of charms. This made her believe that she was in a proper state to retrieve her ancient rights over the King's heart, if she had an opportunity of appearing before him with this increased splendour. Her friends being of the same opinion, her equipage was prepared for this expedition; but the very evening before the day she had fixed on to set out, she saw young Churchill[33] and was at once seized with a disease which had more than once opposed her projects, and which she could never completely get the better of.

A man who, from an ensign in the Guards, was raised to such a fortune, must certainly possess an uncommon share of prudence, not to be intoxicated with his happiness. Churchill boasted in all places of the new favour he had received. The Duchess of Cleveland, who neither recommended to him circumspection in his behaviour, nor in his conversation, did not seem to be in the least concerned at his indiscretion. Thus this intrigue had become a general topic in all companies, when the Court arrived in London,[34] and occasioned an immense number of speculations and reasonings. Some said she had already presented him with Jermyn's pension, and Jacob Hall's salary,[35] because the merits and qualifications of both were united

[33] John Churchill (then Page of Honour to the Duke of York and an ensign), afterwards the famous Duke of Marlborough (born 1650, *ob.* 1722). Lord Chesterfield, who knew the Duke well, says "he possessed the highest graces, and to these, in a great measure, he owed his subsequent greatness and riches." At the same time he was far from brilliant, though he was remarkably clear-headed, and had sound judgment. Like the Duke of Monmouth, he had a handsome face and figure, and had a particularly affable and gracious manner, which made him courted by both sexes. He could refuse more gracefully than others could grant, and those who left him disappointed were invariably charmed with his courteous manner. Of all historians Macaulay is perhaps the most severe upon Marlborough; on the other hand, Lord Wolseley handles him a little too leniently (see *Life of the Duke of Marlborough*). According to King's *Anecdotes,* when old and infirm the Duke always walked to save sixpence for a chair.

[34] 2nd October 1663 was the date of the return of the Court from Bristol. Hamilton has confused this with a later event. Young Churchill was about thirteen in 1663, and his intrigue with Lady Castlemaine was at the earliest in 1668, probably two or three years later.

[35] Lord Chesterfield relates in his *Letters* (No. 136) that when Churchill was an ensign of the Guards, the Duchess, struck by

in his person; others maintained that he had too indolent an air, and too delicate a shape, long to maintain himself in her favour; but all agreed that a man who was the favourite of the King's mistress, and brother to the Duke's favourite, was in a fair way of preferment, and could not fail to make his fortune. As a proof, the Duke of York soon after gave him a place in his household: this was naturally to be expected; but the King, who did not think that Lady Cleveland's kindness to him was a sufficient recommendation to his favour, thought proper to forbid him the Court.

This good-natured King began now to be rather peevish: nor was it altogether without reason. He disturbed no person in their amours, and yet others had often the presumption to encroach upon his. Lord Dorset, First Lord of the Bedchamber, had lately debauched from his service Nell Gwyn, the actress.[36]

his graces, gave him £5000, with which he bought an annuity of £500 from Halifax, Chesterfield's grandfather. Mrs. Manley, who, in after years, lived as a companion to the Duchess of Cleveland, says that though Churchill had received thousands from the Duchess, he refused the common civility of lending her twenty guineas at the basset table (vide *History of Rivella*, 1725).

According to the French Ambassador Courtin, Churchill received not only money, jewels, but even estates from some of the wealthy women at Court. Upon discovering the intrigue with his mistress, Charles said he would forgive him, as he had become a lover to save himself from starving.—MS. Affaires Estrangères Angleterre (Forneron's *Louise de Keroualle*).

"The Duchess of Cleveland," says Burnet, "finding that she had lost the King, abandoned herself to great disorders, one of which, by the artifice of the Duke of Buckingham, was discovered by the King in person, the party concerned leaping out of the window" (Burnet's *Own Time*, vol. i. p. 264).

[36] Boyer, the first translator of the *Memoirs*, says truly enough that Nell Gwyn was Lord Dorset's mistress before the King became enslaved to her, and adds that Dryden told him that, with the object of getting her into his possession, her protector was sent on a "sleeveless errand" into France. On 13th July 1667, Pepys records Nell's abduction from the stage by Lord Buck-

Lady Cleveland, whom he now no longer regarded, continued to disgrace him by repeated infidelities with unworthy rivals, and almost ruined him by the immense sums she lavished on her gallants; but that

hurst. "Poor girl!" he exclaims, "I pity her, but more the loss of her at the King's House." On 26th August following he says (on the authority of Sir W. Pen) how "Nell is already left by my Lord Buckhurst, and that he makes sport of her and swears she hath had all she could get of him." See also footnote, p. 211. On 11th January 1667-8, Knepp tells Pepys that "a good while ago"—"the King did send several times for Nelly, and she was with him."

Hereford claims to be Nelly's birthplace, and the house is said by tradition to have been in "Pipe Well Lane," recently rechristened Gwyn Street, where a tablet marking the site may be seen attached to a garden wall (see Wheatley's edition of Cunningham's Story of Nell Gwyn, p. xxi.); but Peter Cunningham thought there was no foundation for the story. Oldys says she was born in the Coal Yard, Drury Lane, now called Goldsmith Street, a turning on the east side towards St. Giles (vide Cunningham's London). The date of her birth, according to her horoscope in the Ashmolean MS., is 2nd February 1650-1.

Prior to being the mistress of Lord Buckhurst, she was kept by Charles Hart, the celebrated actor, who introduced her to the stage. The comedian, John Lacy, also is said to have kept her. This state of affairs can hardly be wondered at, when she herself admitted that she had been brought up in a brothel. From an orange girl she was promoted to actress in 1665, when she made her appearance at Drury Lane in Dryden's Indian Emperor. From this time there are several plays mentioned by Pepys in which she either pleased or displeased him, according to how the parts suited her. Charles Beauclerc, afterwards created Earl of Burford and Duke of St. Albans, Nelly's eldest son by the King, was born 8th May 1670. She died 14th November 1687 at her house on the south side of Pall Mall, now the Eagle Insurance office. The garden of this house adjoined the gardens of St. James's Palace (vide Evelyn's oft-quoted entry in his Diary of 1st March 1671). The site of a house on the north side of Pall Mall, where she also lived for a short time (described by Pennant), is now occupied by the Army and Navy Club, where her looking-glass may still be seen in the visitors' dining-room. One apartment was formed entirely of mirrors, including the ceiling. Nell Gwyn was buried in the old church of St. Martin's-in-the-Fields. For further particulars see Cunningham's Story of Nell Gwyn, Pepys's Diary, Wheatley's edition, and the same author's Introduction to his edition of Cunningham's Nell Gwyn, 1892.

which most sensibly affected him was the late coldness
and threats of Miss Stewart. He long since had
offered her all the settlements and all the titles she
could desire, until he had an opportunity more effectually to provide for her, which she had pretended only
to decline, for fear of the scandal they might occasion,
on her being raised to a rank which would attract the
public notice; but since the return of the Court, she
had given herself other airs: sometimes she was for
retiring from Court, to appease the continual uneasiness her presence gave the Queen; at other times it
was to avoid temptations, by which she wished to insinuate that her innocence was still preserved: in short,
the King's heart was continually distracted by alarms,
or oppressed by ill humour and caprice.

As he could not for his life imagine what Miss
Stewart wished him to do, or what she would be at, he
thought upon reforming his establishment of mistresses, to try whether jealousy was not the real occasion of her uneasiness. It was for this reason that,
after having solemnly declared he would have nothing
more to say to the Duchess of Cleveland, since her intrigue with Churchill, he discarded, without any excep-
tion,[37] all the other mistresses which he had in various
parts of the town. The Nell Gwyns, the Misses Davis,[38]

[37] Began to discard (Vizetelly).

[38] Moll Davis, the actress of the Duke's Theatre, who first appeared on the stage in 1664, was the illegitimate daughter of
Colonel Charles Howard, son of Thomas Howard, first Earl
of Berkshire, not, as Pepys heard from Mrs. Pearse, the daughter of the Earl himself, whom he succeeded in 1679 as second
Earl (vide Pepys's Diary, 14th January 1667-8; see also King
Monmouth, pp. 13-14 note). There is a tradition at the village
of Charlton, Wilts, near where stands the ancestral home of
the Howards, that Mary Davis was the daughter of the black-
smith there and at no time was a milkmaid[1] (see Lord Braybrooke's History of Audley End, also Cunningham's Story of
Nell Gwyn); but this is probably incorrect. By Pepys's account,
it was through the influence of the noble father that the actress

and the joyous train of singers and dancers in his
Majesty's theatre, were all dismissed. All these sacrifices were ineffectual: Miss Stewart continued to torment, and almost to drive the King to distraction; but
his Majesty soon after found out the real cause of this
coldness.

This discovery was owing to the officious Duchess
of Cleveland, who, ever since her disgrace, had railed
most bitterly against Miss Stewart as the cause of it,
and against the King's weakness, who, for an inanimate[39] idiot, had treated her with so much indignity.
As some of her Grace's creatures were still in the King's
confidence, by their means she was informed of the
King's uneasiness, and that Miss Stewart's behaviour
was the occasion of it; and as soon as she had found
the opportunity she had so long wished for, she went
directly into the King's cabinet, through the apartment
of one of his pages called Chiffinch. This way was not
new to her.

The King was just returned from visiting Miss
Stewart, in a very ill humour. The presence of the

became the King's mistress, though this is also not probable, as
her dancing and singing won Charles's heart prior to Nell Gwyn
becoming his mistress. It was the part of Celania in *The Rivals*,
a lovesick shepherdess, which won the actress her equivocal
position. From that time forward she lived sumptuously in
Suffolk Street, Haymarket, removing afterwards to a house in
St. James's Square (*vide* Dasent's *History of St. James's
Square*). There are several allusions to Moll Davis in Pepys's
Diary,—of her superior dancing (in boy's clothes) to Nell Gwyn,
—of Lady Castlemaine's jealousy—and of the Queen's resentment
at her being brought into favour.

In the *Lives of the Most Celebrated Beauties*, 1715, a scandalous anecdote is related how Nell Gwyn introduced a dose of
jalap into the new favourite's supper upon her first introduction
into royal favour. Mary Tudor, Moll's daughter, born in 1673,
was the mother of the Jacobite, James, Earl of Derwentwater,
beheaded in 1716.

[39] Gaily bedecked (Vizetelly).

[1] Lord Braybrooke says a family of the name of Davis was for many genera-
tions at Charlton, the last dying about 1830, aged ninety (*Hist. Audley End*).

Duchess of Cleveland surprised him, and did not in the least diminish it. She, perceiving this, accosted him in an ironical tone, and with a smile of indignation. "I hope," said she, "I may be allowed to pay you my homage, although the angelic Stewart has forbid you to see me at my own house. I will not make use of reproaches and expostulations, which would disgrace myself: still less will I endeavour to excuse frailties which nothing can justify, since your constancy for me deprives me of all defence, considering I am the only person you have honoured with your tenderness, who has made herself unworthy of it by ill conduct. I come now, therefore, with no other intent than to comfort and to condole with you upon the affliction and grief into which the coldness, or new-fashioned chastity of the inhuman Stewart have reduced your Majesty."

These words were attended by a fit of laughter, as unnatural and strained as it was insulting and immoderate, which completed the King's impatience. He had, indeed, expected that some bitter jest would follow this preamble; but he did not suppose she would have given herself such blustering airs, considering the terms they were then upon; and, as he was preparing to answer her: "Be not offended," said she, "that I take the liberty of laughing at the gross manner in which you are imposed upon. I cannot bear to see that such particular affectation should make you the jest of your own Court, and that you should be ridiculed with such impunity. I know that the affected Stewart has sent you away, under pretence of some indisposition, or perhaps some scruple of conscience; and I come to acquaint you that the Duke of Richmond will soon be with her, if he is not there already. I do not desire you to believe what I say, since it might be prompted either through resentment or envy: only follow me to her apartment, either that, no longer trusting calumny and malice, you may honour her with a just preference, if I accuse her falsely; or, if my information be true, you may no longer be the dupe of a pretended prude, who makes you act so unbecoming and ridiculous a part."

As she ended this speech, she took him by the hand, while he was yet undecided, and pulled him away towards her rival's apartments. Chiffinch[40] being in her interest, Miss Stewart could have no warning of

[40] William Chiffinch or Cheffing, Page of the Backstairs and Keeper of the King's Closet, brother and successor to Thomas Chiffinch, who held the confidential post under Charles I., and was caretaker of the jewels, pictures, etc., at Whitehall. William and his wife, Barbara Nunn, succeeded to the backstair duties in 1666, with a salary of £1200. In Fisher's plan of the Palace, Chiffinch's apartments may be seen adjoining those of the King, the stairs leading directly up to them from the river. Here it was that the most secret interviews were held by both Charles and his brother James.

In a letter from Charles to Sir John Shaw, he says: " I could not get time to speake with your man that is come over, but now if you will *send him to Will Chiffines at 7 this evening he will bring him privately into my closet.—C. R.*" The duties also of Mrs. Chiffinch are alluded to in Scott's *Peveril of the Peak*, an idea of which may be gathered from a contemporary satire which commences—

" It happened in the twilight of the day,
    As England's monarch in his closet lay,
    And Chiffinch stepped to fetch the female prey."

Chiffinch was the receiver of the pension from King Louis. The family came from Kent, but settled at Salisbury, to which town William was a benefactor. By the Verney Papers it appears he was knighted. "Last week," says John Verney, "the King being at Windsor did Mr. Chiffinch the favour to dine with him, and after dinner conferred the honor of knighthood on him" (*Hist. MS. Com. Rep.* 7, App. p. 467). Chiffinch lived not far from Windsor, at Bray, at a house still existing, called " Philberts." Tradition says the King made many of his private pleasure trips there (vide *History of Bray*). Here Chiffinch died in 1691 (?1688). He also owned property at Iden Green, near Staplehurst. His daughter Barbara married Edward Villiers, first Earl of Jersey.

the visit; and Babiani,[a] who owed all to the Duchess
of Cleveland, and who served her admirably well upon
this occasion, came and told her that the Duke of
Richmond had just gone into Miss Stewart's chamber.
It was in the middle of a little gallery, which, through
a private door, led from the King's apartments to those
of his mistresses. The Duchess of Cleveland wished
him good-night, as he entered her rival's chamber, and
retired, in order to wait the success of the adventure,
of which Babiani, who attended the King, was charged
to come and give her an account.

It was near midnight. The King, in his way, met
his mistress's chambermaid, who respectfully opposed
his entrance, and in a very low voice whispered his
Majesty that Miss Stewart had been very ill since
he left her; but that, being gone to bed, she was, God
be thanked, in a very fine sleep. "That I must see,"
said the King, pushing her back, who had posted herself in his way. He found Miss Stewart in bed, indeed,
but far from being asleep: the Duke of Richmond was
seated at her pillow, and in all probability was less
inclined to sleep than herself. The perplexity of the
one party, and the rage of the other, were such as may
easily be imagined upon such a surprise. The King,
who, of all men, was one of the most mild and gentle,
testified his resentment to the Duke of Richmond in
such terms as he had never before used. The Duke
was speechless, and almost petrified: he saw his master
and his King justly irritated. The first transports
which rage inspires on such occasions are dangerous.
Miss Stewart's window was very convenient for a
sudden revenge, the Thames flowing close beneath it.
He cast his eyes upon it; and, seeing those of the King

[a] Possibly "Bab" May, who, according to Pepys, was attached
to her interests. He was Page of the Bedchamber and confidant
of the King's amours. Born 1627, *ob.* 1693.

more incensed and fired with indignation than he thought his nature capable of, he made a profound bow, and retired, without replying a single word to the vast torrent of threats and menaces that were poured upon him.

Miss Stewart, having a little recovered from her first surprise, instead of justifying herself, began to talk in the most extravagant manner, and said everything that was most capable[42] to inflame the King's passion and resentment; that, if she were not allowed to receive visits from a man of the Duke of Richmond's rank, who came with honourable intentions, she was a slave in a free country; that she knew of no engagement that could prevent her from disposing of her hand as she thought proper; but, however, if this was not permitted her in his dominions, she did not believe that there was any power on earth that could hinder her from going over to France, and throwing herself into a convent, to enjoy there that tranquillity which was denied her in his Court. The King, sometimes furious with anger, sometimes relenting at her tears, and sometimes terrified at her menaces, was so greatly agitated, that he knew not how to answer, either the nicety of a creature who wanted to act the part of Lucretia under his own eye, or the assurance with which she had the effrontery to reproach him. In this suspense, love had almost entirely vanquished all his resentments, and had nearly induced him to throw himself upon his knees, and entreat pardon for the injury he had done her, when she desired him to retire, and leave her in repose, at least for the remainder of that night, without offending those who had either accompanied him, or conducted him to her apartments, by a longer visit. This impertinent request provoked and irritated him to the highest degree. He went out

[42] Calculated (Vizetelly).

abruptly, vowing never to see her more, and passed the most restless and uneasy night he had ever experienced since his restoration.

The next day the Duke of Richmond received orders to quit the Court, and never more to appear before the King; but it seems he had not waited for those orders, having set out early that morning for his country seat,[43]

Miss Stewart, in order to obviate all injurious constructions that might be put upon the adventure of the

[43] *20th March* 1666-7—Pepys says: "I hear that the Duke of Richmond and Mrs. Stewart were betrothed last night"; and on *3rd April* 1667: "I hear how the King is not so well pleased of this marriage between the Duke of Richmond and Mrs. Stewart as is talked, and that he [the Duke] by a wile did fetch her to the Beare, at the Bridge foot [a well-known hostelry at Southwark], where a Coach was ready and they are stole away into Kent without the King's leave and that the King hath said he will never see her more: but people do think that is only a trick." On *16th April*: "Pierce told us the story how in good earnest [the King] is offended with the Duke of Richmond's marrying, and Mrs. Stewart's sending the King his jewels again—it is the noblest romance and example of a brave lady that ever I read in my life." *26th April*: [Evelyn] "told me" (writes Pepys) "the whole story of Mrs. Stewart going away from Court, he knowing her well, and believes her, up to her leaving the Court, to be as virtuous as any woman in the world; and told me, from a Lord that she told it to but yesterday, with her own mouth, and a sober man, that when the Duke of Richmond did make love to her, she did ask the King, and he did the like also, and that the King did not deny it, and [she] told this Lord that she was come to that pass as to resolve to have married any gentleman of £1500 a year that would have had her in honour; for it was come to that pass, that she could not longer continue at Court without prostituting herself to the King, whom she had so long kept off, though he had liberty more than any other had, or he ought to have, as to dalliance. She told this Lord that she had reflected upon the occasion she had given the world to think her a bad woman and that she had no way but to marry and leave the Court, rather in this way of discontent than otherwise, that the world might see that she sought not anything but her honour; and that she will never come to live at Court more than when she comes to town to come to kiss the Queen her mistress's hand, and hopes, though she hath little reason to hope, she can please her Lord so as to reclaim him, that they may yet live comfortably in the country on his estate. . . . She

preceding night, went and threw herself at the Queen's feet, where, acting the new part of an innocent Magdalen, she entreated her Majesty's forgiveness for all the sorrow and uneasiness she might have already occasioned her. She told her Majesty that a constant and sincere repentance had induced her to contrive all possible means for retiring from Court: that this reason had inclined her to receive the Duke of Richmond's addresses, who had courted her a long time; but since this courtship had caused his disgrace, and had likewise raised a vast noise and disturbance, which perhaps might be turned to the prejudice of her reputation, she conjured her Majesty to take her under her protection, and endeavour to obtain the King's permission for her to retire into a convent, to remove at once all those vexations and troubles her presence had innocently occasioned at Court. All this was accompanied with a proper deluge of tears.

It is a very agreeable spectacle to see a rival prostrate at our feet, entreating pardon, and at the same time justifying her conduct. The Queen's heart not only relented, but she mingled her own tears with those

---

is gone yesterday with her Lord to Cobham." On 17th July (1667) : [Creed] "told me over the story of Mrs. Stewart much after the manner which I was told it long since, and have entered it in this book told me by Mr. Evelyn; only he says it is verily believed that the King did never intend to marry her to any but himself, and that the Duke of York and Lord Chancellor were jealous of it; and that Mrs. Stewart might be got with child by the King, or somebody else, and the King own a marriage before his contract, for it is but a contract, as he tells me, to this day, with the Queen, and so wipe their noses of the Crown; and that therefore the Duke of York and Chancellor did do all they could to forward the match with my Lord Duke of Richmond that she might be married out of the way; but, above all, it is a worthy part that this good lady hath acted." Frances Stewart was the third wife of the Duke of Richmond. His second wife had died only three months previously. It would be interesting to know if the Duchess reclaimed her husband from his intemperate habits.

of Miss Stewart. After having raised her up, and most tenderly embraced her, she promised her all manner of favour and protection, either in her marriage, or in any other course she thought fit to pursue, and parted from her with the firm resolution to exert all her interest in her support; but, being a person of great judgment, the reflections which she afterwards made induced her to change her opinion."

She knew that the King's disposition was not capable of an obstinate constancy. She therefore judged that absence would cure him, or that a new engagement would by degrees entirely efface the remembrance of Miss Stewart; and that, since she could not avoid having a rival, it was more desirable she should be one who had given such eminent proofs of her prudence and virtue. Besides, she flattered herself that the King would ever think himself eternally obliged to her, for having opposed the retreat and marriage of a girl,

" Rumours had been constantly afloat that the King contemplated a separation from the Queen on the plea of her barrenness. Buckingham and other of his unprincipled advisers and enemies of the Duke of York favoured the idea of a divorce, which they undertook to carry through the Parliament and had Frances Stewart not taken the step she did, there is no telling but that the report that was current both in this country as well as in Portugal, may have proved only too true. Whether Lord Clarendon brought about the match between the Duke of Richmond and the King's favourite is doubtful, though his enemies failed not to make the most of the opportunity; but the King certainly thought he was at the bottom of the secret marriage, and showed his resentment accordingly.

On the night that Frances Stewart fled from Whitehall, Clarendon's son, Lord Cornbury, unaware of her departure, was going towards her lodgings, when he met the King coming out " full of fury," who, suspecting him to be in the plot, " spoke to him as one in a rage that forgot all decency, and for some time would not hear Lord Cornbury speak in his own defence." As is well known, Clarendon's disgrace happened shortly afterwards. The Seal was delivered up on 30th August 1667. See Burnet's *History of his Own Time,* Clarendon's *Continuation of his Life, History of the Revolutions of Portugal,* 1740, Jesse's *Memoirs of the Stuarts,* etc.

whom at that time he loved to distraction. This fine reasoning determined her conduct. All her industry was employed in persuading Miss Stewart to abandon her schemes; and what is most extraordinary in this adventure is, that, after having prevailed upon her to think no more either of the Duke of Richmond, or of a nunnery, she charged herself with the office of reconciling these two lovers.

Indeed it would have been a thousand pities if her negotiation had miscarried; but she did not suffer this misfortune; for never were the King's addresses so eager and passionate as after this peace, nor ever better received by the fair Stewart.[45]

[45] *26th December* 1667—Pepys says: " I hear this day that Mrs. Stewart do at this day keep a great court at Somerset House with her husband, the Duke of Richmond, she being visited for her beauty sake by people, as the Queen is at nights; and they say also that she is likely to go to Court again and there put my Lady Castlemayne's nose out of joint." On the following day Sir Hugh Cholmely tells him "that the business of getting the Duchess of Richmond to Court is broke off, the Duke not suffering it, and thereby great trouble is brought among the people that endeavoured it, and thought they had compassed it." On 14th January 1667-8, Mrs. Pierce tells Pepys "that the Duchesse of Richmond do not yet come to Court, nor hath seen the King, nor will not, nor do he own his desire of seeing her, but hath used means to get her to Court, but they do not take." A little over two months afterwards a great calamity befalls the great beauty, she is seized with the smallpox. *26th March* 1668— Pepys writes: "This noon, from Mrs. Williams my Lord Brouncker sent to Somerset House to hear how the Duchess of Richmond do; and word was brought him that she is pretty well but mighty full of the smallpox, by which all do conclude she will be wholly spoiled, which is the greatest instance of the uncertainty of beauty that could be in this age; but then she hath had the benefit of it to be first married and to have kept it so long under the greatest temptations in the world, from a King, and yet without the least imputation." *8th May* 1668— Lord Sandwich tells Pepys the Duchess of Richmond has recovered from her illness. "The King hath made several public visits to her and [she is] like to come to Court." *19th May* 1668—Pierce tells Pepys the King is "mighty hot upon the Duchess of Richmond, insomuch that upon Sunday was se'nnight at night, after he had ordered his Guards and coach to be ready

His Majesty did not long enjoy the sweets of a reconciliation, which brought him into the best good-humour possible, as we shall see. All Europe was in a profound peace, since the treaty of the Pyrenees.

to carry him to the Park, he did on a sudden take a pair of oars or scullers, and all alone, or but one with him, go to Somerset House, and there, the garden door not being open, himself clamber over the walls to make a visit to her, which is a horrid shame." 6th July 1668—Pepys enters: "The Duchesse of Richmond sworn last week of the Queen's Bedchamber." On 18th August Pepys saw the Duchess of Richmond and Lady Castlemaine in the Park and they appeared strange to one another. 30th August—Pepys goes to the Park and in the King's garden saw the Duchess of Richmond, "who is of a noble person as ever I saw, but her face worse than it was considerably by the smallpox." On 9th September 1668 Pepys visits the Duke of Richmond "at his lodgings in the little building in the bowling-green at Whitehall," but to his disappointment his wife was in the country. This is the last we hear of La Belle Stewart in the famous *Diary*. Lord Dartmouth says: "After her marriage she had more complaisance than before, as King Charles could not forbear telling the Duke of Richmond, when he was drunk at Lord Townshend's in Norfolk [Raynham Hall]." After her husband's death in 1672, the Duchess sold her life interest in Cobham, probably about the year 1677, as among the Verney papers (*Hist. MS. Com. Rep.* 7, App. p. 468), in a letter from John to Sir Ralph Verney, 28th May 1677, is the following "The Duchess of Richmond hath lately sold her interest in Cobham to Lord O'Brien, so 'tis believed she will suddenly *own her marriage to Lord Mulgrave*." Whatever may have been the cause of this rumour, no such marriage ever took place.

In 1679, a young amorous gallant at Court named Jack How boasted of certain favours he had received from the widowed Duchess, whereupon she complained to the King, who appointed a committee (viz. Monmouth, Essex, Sunderland, and Halifax) to inquire into the matter, and How was forbidden again to come to Court, as upon examination the King decided that a certain letter of the Duchess had been forged [see *Sidney Correspondence*, vol. i. pp. 100, 122]. For some years the once famous beauty was in receipt of a pension from the Royal Purse of £150 a year.

The Duchess was present at the Coronation of Queen Anne, dressed in the robes which are to be seen upon her wax effigy at Westminster Abbey. (N.B.—The parrot by her side is said to have been a pet of the Duchess's for forty years, and only survived its mistress a few days.) She died 15th October 1702, and was buried in the Richmond vault in Henry VII. Chapel.

Spain flattered herself she should be able to recruit, by means of the new alliance she had contracted with the most formidable of her neighbours; but despaired of being able to support the shattered remains of a declining monarchy, when she considered the age and infirmities of her prince, or the weakness of his successor. France, on the contrary, governed by a king indefatigable in business, young, vigilant, and ambitious of glory, wanted nothing but inclination to aggrandise herself.

It was about this time that the King of France, not willing to disturb the tranquillity of Europe, was persuaded to alarm the coasts of Africa, by an attempt, which, if it had even been crowned with success, would have produced little good. But the King's fortune, ever faithful to his glory, has since made it appear, by the miscarriage of the expedition of Gigeri,[46] that such projects only as were planned by himself were worthy of his attention.

A short time after, the King of England, having resolved also to explore the African coasts, fitted out a squadron for an expedition to Guinea,[47] which was to be commanded by Prince Rupert. Those who, from their own experience, had some knowledge of the country, related strange and wonderful stories of the

[46] In October 1664. Gigeri is about forty leagues from Algiers. The French had a factory there; but attempting to build a fort on the seacoast, to be a check upon the Arabs, they came down from the mountains, beat the French out of Gigeri, and demolished their fort. Sir Richard Fanshaw, in a letter to the Deputy Governor of Tangier, dated 2nd December 1664, says, "We have certain intelligence that the French have lost *Gigheria,* with all they had there, and their fleet come back, with the loss of one considerable ship upon the rocks near Marseilles" (Fanshaw's *Letters,* vol. i. p. 347). The French expedition against Gigeri was despatched there early in the previous October. See also Pepys, 11th October 1664.

[47] This was in August 1664, a year before the Duke of York's visit to York (see *ante,* p. 357).

dangers attendant upon this expedition: that they would have to fight not only the inhabitants of Guinea, a hellish people, whose arrows were poisoned, and who never gave their prisoners better quarter than to devour them, but that they must likewise endure heats that were insupportable, and rains that were intolerable, every drop of which was changed into a serpent; that, if they penetrated farther into the country, they would be assaulted by monsters a thousand times more hideous and destructive than all the beasts mentioned in the Revelation.

But all these reports were vain and ineffectual; for so far from striking terror into those who were appointed to go upon this expedition, it rather acted as an incentive to glory upon those who had no manner of business in it. Jermyn appeared among the foremost of these; and, without reflecting that the pretence of his indisposition had delayed the conclusion of his marriage with Miss Jennings, he asked the Duke's permission, and the King's consent to serve in it as a volunteer.

Some time before this, the infatuation which had imposed upon the fair Jennings in his favour had begun to subside. All that now inclined her to this match was the advantages of a settlement. The careless indolence of a lover, who faintly paid his addresses to her, as it were from custom or habit, disgusted[48] her; and the resolution he had taken, without consulting her, appeared so ridiculous in him, and so injurious to herself, that, from that moment, she resolved to think no more of him. Her eyes being opened by degrees, she saw the fallacy of the splendour, which had at first deceived her; and the renowned Jermyn was received according to his real merit when he came to acquaint her with his heroical project. There appeared so much

[48] Disheartened (Vizetelly).

indifference and ease in the raillery with which she complimented him upon his voyage, that he was entirely disconcerted, and so much the more so, as he had prepared all the arguments he thought capable of consoling her, upon announcing to her the fatal news of his departure. She told him, "that nothing could be more glorious for him, who had triumphed over the liberty of so many persons[49] in Europe, than to go and extend his conquests in other parts of the world; and that she advised him to bring home with him all the female captives he might make in Africa, in order to replace those beauties whom his absence would bring to the grave."

Jermyn was highly displeased that she should be capable of raillery in the condition he supposed her reduced to; but he soon perceived she was in earnest. She told him that she considered this farewell visit as his last, and desired him not to think of making her any more before his departure.

Thus far everything went well on her side. Jermyn was not only confounded at having received his discharge in so cavalier a manner; but this very demonstration of her indifference had revived, and even redoubled, all the love and affection he had formerly felt for her. Thus she had both the pleasure of despising him, and of seeing him more entangled in the chains of love than he had ever been before. This was not sufficient: she wished still farther, and very unadvisedly, to strain her resentment.

Ovid's *Epistles,* translated into English verse by the greatest wits at Court, having lately been published,[50] she wrote a letter from a shepherdess in despair, addressed to the perfidious Jermyn. She took the

[49] Women (Vizetelly).
[50] Viz. *circulated.* The translation of Ovid's *Epistles* was not *printed* until 1680.

epistle of Ariadne to Theseus for her model. The beginning of this letter contained, word for word, the complaints and reproaches of that injured fair to the cruel man by whom she had been abandoned. All this was properly adapted to the present times and circumstances.

It was her design to have closed this piece with a description of the toils, perils, and monsters, that awaited him in Guinea, for which he quitted a tender mistress, who was plunged into the abyss of misery, and was overwhelmed with grief and despair; but not having had time to finish it, nor to get that which she had written transcribed, in order to send it to him under a feigned name, she inconsiderately put this fragment, written in her own hand, into her pocket, and, still more giddily,[61] dropped it in the middle of the Court. Those who took it up, knowing her writing, made several copies of it, which were circulated all over the town; but her former conduct had so well established the reputation of her virtue, that no person entertained the smallest doubt that the circumstances were exactly as we have related them. Some time after, the Guinea expedition[62] was laid aside for reasons that are universally known, and Miss Jen-

[61] Foolishly (Vizetelly).

[62] With the object of trading on the African coast, a company was formed under royal patronage in opposition to the Dutch settlers. A small fleet sailed to Guinea in 1664 and seized several strongholds, including Cape Corse Castle, the settlements of Cape Verde, and the Isle of Goree. The States of Holland naturally resented, and as the animosity increased, Prince Rupert was ordered out with a new fleet, which, however, never sailed.

De Ruyter, having received secret orders, appeared in time to expel the English from their recent acquisitions, excepting Cape Corse. This led to 150 Dutch merchant vessels being captured, after which war with Holland was declared. A full account of the Guinea expedition is given in Clarendon's *Continuation*, p. 225. See also Hume, Lingard, and Vizetelly's *Gramont*, ii. p. 232.

ning's subsequent proceedings fully justified her letter; for, notwithstanding all the efforts and attentions Jermyn practised to regain her affections, she would never more hear of him.

But he was not the only man who experienced the whimsical fatality, that seemed to delight in disuniting hearts, in order to engage them soon after to different objects. One would have imagined that the God of Love, actuated by some new caprice, had placed his empire under the dominion of Hymen, and had, at the same time, blindfolded that God, in order to cross-match most of the lovers of whom we have been speaking.

The fair Stewart married the Duke of Richmond; the invincible Jermyn, a silly[53] country girl;[54] Lord Rochester, a melancholy heiress;[55] the sprightly Temple, the serious Lyttelton; Talbot, without knowing why or wherefore, took to wife the languishing Boynton; George Hamilton, under more favourable auspices, married the lovely Jennings;[56] and the Chevalier de

[53] Conceited (Vizetelly).

[54] Miss Gibbs, daughter of a Cambridgeshire gentleman. There was no issue from this marriage. In 1685 Jermyn was created Baron Dover. He retired to Cheveley Cambs, where he died in 1708. See Saint Evremond's *Works*, vol. ii. p. 223.

[55] Elizabeth, daughter of John Mallet of Enmore, Somersetshire. Rochester's runaway match is thus referred to by Pepys, 28th May 1665: "To my Lady Sandwiche's, where to my shame I had not been a great while. Here upon my telling her a story of my Lord of Rochester's running away on Friday night last with Mrs. Mallett, the great beauty and fortune of the north, who had supped at Whitehall with Mrs. Stewart, and was going home to her lodgings with her grandfather, my Lord Hally, by coach; and was at Charing Cross seized on by both horse and footmen, and forcibly taken from him and put into a coach with six horses, and two women provided to receive her, and carried away. Upon immediate pursuit, my Lord of Rochester (for whom the King had spoke to the lady often, but with no success) was taken at Uxbridge; but the lady is not yet heard of, and the King mighty angry, and the lord sent to the Tower. Hereupon my lady did confess to me as a great secret her being

Gramont, as the reward of a constancy he had never before known, and which he never afterwards practised, found Hymen and Love united in his favour, and was at last blessed with the possession of Miss Hamilton.[57]

concerned in this story, for if this match breaks between my Lord Rochester and her, then by the consent of all her friends, my Lord Hinchingbroke stands fair, and is invited for her. She is worth, and will be at her mother's death (who keeps but little from her), 2500l. per annum." Pepys mentions seeing Rochester and his wife at the play on 4th February 1666-7.

[56]George was knighted by Charles II. He went abroad with his wife and entered the service of Louis XIV. Lady Hamilton as a widow is mentioned in Evelyn's *Diary,* 12th November 1675. She is described then as "a sprightly young lady—now turned Papist."

[57]He was married in December 1663. When a son was born the following year "as beautiful as the mother," Comminges tells us. "All the Court has rejoiced with him, and he looks much the younger for the event"—8th September 1664 (Comminges to Lionne), *A French Ambassador at the Court of Charles II.* p. 95.